The Globalization of Tourism and Hospitality

A Strategic Perspective

Second Edition

Tim Knowles, Dimitrios Diamantis and Joudallah Bey El-Mourhabi

SOUTH-WESTERN
CENGAGE Learning™

Australia • Brazil • Japan • Korea • Mexico • Singapore • Spain • United Kingdom • United States

SOUTH-WESTERN
CENGAGE Learning™

The Globalization of Tourism and Hospitality, Second Edition
Tim Knowles. Dimitrios Diamantis and Joudallah Bey El-Mourhabi

Publishing Director: John Yates

Publisher: Pat Bond

Manufacturing Manager: Helen Mason

Senior Production Controller: Maeve Healy

Marketing Manager: Jason Bennett

Typesetter: Laserscript, Mitcham, Surrey

Printed by Lightning Source, UK

For product information and technology assistance, contact **emea.info@cengage.com**.

For permission to use material from this text or product, and for permission queries, email **clsuk.permissions@cengage.com**

make no claim to these trademarks.
British Library Cataloguing-in-Publication Data
A catalogue record for this book is available from the British Library.

ISBN: 978-1-84480-046-9

Cengage Learning EMEA
High Holborn House, 50-51 Bedford Row
London WC1R 4LR

Cengage Learning products are represented in Canada by Nelson Education Ltd.

For your lifelong learning solutions, visit
www.cengage.co.uk

Purchase e-books or e-chapters at:

The Globalization of
Tourism and Hospitality

Tourism, Hospitality and Leisure Series

Contents

List of figures

List of tables

List of acronyms and abbreviations

ABTA	Association of British Travel Agents
ADR	average daily rate
ADS	Approved Destination Status
AIO	Activities-Interests-Options
AIT	air inclusive tour
ALADI	Latin American Integration Association
ASEAN	Association of South East Asian Nations
ASEANTA	Association of South East Asian Tourist Associations
BCD	Beirut Central District
BOT	build operate transfer
BS	balance statement
CACM	Central American Common Market
CARICOM	Caribbean Community and Common Market
CEBR	Centre for Economics and Business Research
CFS	cashflow statement
CPC	(Provisional) Central Product Classification
CR	corporate ranking
CRS	computer reservation system
CRT	corporate risk threshold
DCF	discounted cashflow analysis
DMS	Destination management system
DPB	discounted payback
DPBI	discounted payback index
EIU	Economist Intelligence Unit
EMEIA	Europe, the Middle East, India, Africa
EMU	European Monetary Union
ESF	European Social Fund
EU	European Union
EUREN	European Employment Network
FAP	financial appraisal profile
FASB	Financial Accounting Standards Board
FMCG	Fast moving consumer goods
FTAA	Free Trade Area of the Americas
GATS	General Agreement on Trade in Services
GATT	General Agreement on Tariffs and Trade
GCC	Gulf Cooperation Council
GDP	gross domestic product
GDS	global distribution system
GOP	gross operating profits

HIRO	Holiday Inn Revenue Optimization
HLC	household life cycle
HRD	human resource development
HRM	human resource management
IATA	International Air Transport Association
ICAO	International Civil Aviation Authority
ICDT	information, communication, distribution, transaction
ILO	International Labour Organization
IMC	integrated marketing communication
IRR	internal rate of return
JATA	Japan Association of Travel Agents
JEV	Joint European Venture
MERCOSUR	Southern Common Market
MFN	most-favoured nation
MGR	marginal growth rate
MICE	meetings, incentive, conference, exhibitions
MIS	management information system
MNHC	multinational hotel chain
NAFTA	North American Free Trade Agreement
NAP	National Action Plan
NPL	non-performing loan
NPV	net present value
NPVP	net present value profile
NTA	National Tourism Administration
NTO	national tourism organization
NTS	Net Traveler Survey
OECD	Organization for Economic Co-operation and Development
OPEC	Organization of Petroleum Exporting Countries
P&L	profit and loss
PATA	Pacific Asia Tourist Association
PDI	personal disposable income
PRC	People's Republic of China
PSSV	project strategic score value
PV	present value
RDA	Regional Development Agency
revPAR	revenue per available room
RI	risk index
ROI	return on investment
SAR	Special Administration Region
SI	strategic index
SME	small or medium-sized enterprise
SWOT	Strengths, Weaknesses, Opportunities and Threats
TALC	Tourist Area Life Cycle
TNC	transnational corporation
TSA	Tourism Satellite Account
TTRS	tourism and travel-related services
UAE	United Arab Emirates
UNCTAD	United Nations Conference on Trade and Development
VALS	values and lifestyles

WCED	World Commission on Environment and Development
WCS	World Conservation Strategy
WTO	World Tourism Organization
WTO	World Trade Organization
WTTC	World Travel and Tourism Council
WWW	World Wide Web

Introduction

The main aim of this book is to illustrate the global nature of tourism and hospitality, and its implications for strategic planning and development. Throughout the text, a world-wide perspective is adopted, and Chapter 12 uniquely applies many of the key principles to South America, Asia-Pacific and the Middle East.

Chapter 1 sets the context by investigating the concept of the Tourist Area Life Cycle (TALC), whereby resorts are viewed as 'products' that experience a series of evolutionary stages in consumer demand. It illustrates the important link with planning and sets it within the context of a sectoral industry. Equally, the chapter draws attention to the unhealthy dependency relationship that exists between resorts and the tour operator consolidators who continue to control the crucial marketing function. Practical implications of these issues are included in a case study of the Chinese hotel industry.

The relevance of Butler's model comes with its operationalization and the application of marketing principles, matters discussed in Chapter 2. In this chapter it is shown that independent travel should not be seen automatically as the antithesis of the package holiday. The central point explored here is that life-stage is the key determinant of holiday choice. While the tendency to regard the concept of 'independence' in travel as the antithesis of the package holiday is understandable, in practice, however, the holiday market is much more complicated than this approach implies. The widening choice being made available to consumers, and the reduction of traditional barriers, are themes that run throughout this chapter. Two key market drivers are highlighted – recession and security – with a special emphasis on the effects of the terrorist incidents in New York and Washington of 11 September 2001.

While many use the words tourism, travel and hospitality interchangeably, Chapter 3 shows that the holiday market is now comprised of a continuum of travel arrangements, stretching from the fully packaged, 'all-inclusive' AIT (air inclusive tour) through to the completely independent journey in which the traveller arranges separately for transport and accommodation, without even consulting a travel agent, and may not even book the return fare in advance. The interdependence of all these sectors is discussed, and this chapter is primarily concerned with holidays abroad, although limited coverage is given of the domestic holiday market, where independent holidays (mainly by car, using a variety of accommodation) dominate. It is shown how travellers taking holidays abroad can book either flights or accommodation from separate sources, possibly through a tour operator but usually through a travel agent or directly with an airline or hotel. This chapter also discusses the inclusive tour, or package holiday, which is defined as the simultaneous sale of at least two elements of a holiday to the traveller: fares on public transport (e.g., flights) and commercial accommodation (e.g., hotel or self-catering apartment). The role of governmental and non-governmental organizations is also central to these issues.

Chapter 4 builds on the comments of Chapter 2 by illustrating the dynamics of the tourism industry from a strategic marketing perspective and shows the susceptibility of operators to fluctuations in the general economic environment. From a strategic view, Chapter 4 discusses the importance of firms consolidating, vertically integrating both backwards and forwards in order to control the transport element and distribution channels of the business and to maintain competitive pricing. The chapter explores the requirement to make strategic forecasts of likely demand levels. Equally, within this forecasting process, an ageing and more sophisticated market is increasingly interested in new holiday experiences rather than the sun and beach product of the Mediterranean mass tourist resorts. However, when forecasts invariably do not prove accurate, the chapter discusses how firms revert to tactical price-based marketing in order to sell surplus supply. Other aspects of marketing cover the battle for market share that has led to endless marketing gimmicks (e.g. early booking discounts, free travel for children, three weeks for the price of two in the low season), almost always relying on market stimulation by price discounting. The need to use price as the most effective marketing tool reflects the price sensitivity of the mass market. In terms of promotion, as consumers from the mature northern European markets become more sophisticated and adventurous in their holiday habits and new technologies supersede traditional ways of distributing the holiday product (e.g., teletext, Internet, direct booking), these promotional and distribution elements of the marketing mix are considered. An additional aim of this chapter is to build on Chapter 2 by outlining aspects related to the topic of promotion, including advertising, which is a subject of great importance to organizations in today's competitive and changing market conditions. More specifically, the role of advertising as a strategic marketing tool in managing destination image is also introduced. Destination advertising is an increasingly complicated field, mainly due to lack of consistent and commonly accepted attitudes related to the magnitude of its impact regarding the favourable impression of a destination and how to significantly convert this interest into actual visits. Additionally, this chapter comments on the concept of the Internet as a prevailing new technology, by tracking the development of e-business through recent years from a promotional perspective. Thus, Chapter 4 aims to review the case of destination advertising and provide a theoretical framework for the proposed methods and techniques that are commonly used for assessing its effectiveness in destination marketing programmes while shedding some light on issues related to the use of the World Wide Web (WWW) within tourism and hospitality.

In Chapter 5 the issue of global branding is explored, and towards the end of the chapter the matter is applied to the international hotel industry. The main reason why brands have evolved is to do with the issue of globalization, which has brought forward a significant increase in competition and subsequently an increase in consumer choice of hotels. However, contrary to popular belief, consumers do not desire choice *per se*. Choice is mainly a mechanism that allows consumers to obtain the products and services that they want at the price they can afford. Branding within the hotel industry allows for the possibility of catering to this diversity.

The real value of a hotel brand lies in its ability to persuade and please consumers. This does not necessarily mean that technically the best products or services will always win consumers over; rather, the knowledge of what consumers need, how they behave, how they think, how they perceive value, and how they reason and decide defines such outcomes. As a consequence, in this world of competition and globalization, companies in tourism and hospitality need to create customer-oriented brands that cater for individual needs and experiences.

Chapter 6 develops the argument that the images, beliefs and perceptions that individuals in the market have about a destination may have as much to do with an area's tourist development success as more tangible recreation and tourist resources. The discussion goes on to note that this occurs because decision-makers, having very limited personal experience of the destination, act upon their own images, beliefs and perceptions of the destination rather than objective reality. What is important is the image that exists in the mind of the holidaymaker. The image of a destination is a critical factor when choosing a holiday and therefore an examination of the image formation process in this chapter helps understanding of how a tourism promotion organization can change an individual's perception of a destination. As such, this chapter looks at the issues surrounding destination image and examines the eco-tourism product.

Having considered both the supply and demand elements of the tourism industry at both a strategic and tactical level, Chapter 7 investigates the key difficulty of resorts remaining sustainable as they move through the TALC. The distinction drawn in this chapter is between sustainable tourism and the sustainable development of tourism. With this in mind, the purpose of this review is to examine the concept of sustainability both from the environmental and tourism perspectives, and to assess the different policies and structures enveloping the debate within this concept. The review begins with the issues surrounding sustainability, followed by the issues of sustainable tourism development, and it concludes with the practices of sustainable tourism.

Chapter 8 integrates generic strategic planning and life cycle analysis with the tourism and hospitality industry. While many resorts may intuitively know their position within the life cycle, an attempt is made to quantify and explore appropriate strategies at each stage. At each stage of the life cycle the mix of evolutionary and competitive forces differs and thus strategies to deliver a sustainable tourism industry at the destination should be distinctive at each life cycle stage. The nature of tourism and hospitality seems to reflect characteristics that fit well into what has been described as a fragmented industry. Specifically, an industry in which no firm has a significant market share can strongly influence the industry's outcome, and essentially involves undifferentiated products. Furthermore, the industry appears to represent what could be classified as a hostile environment. That is an environment where overall market growth is slow and erratic, there is a significant upward pressure on operating costs and there is intense competition resulting in high market concentration. Clearly, the tourism and hospitality industry possesses many of these characteristics that would classify it as fragmented with a low market share set within the context of a hostile environment. In the face of such conditions strategic positioning is shown to be of particularly crucial significance.

Chapter 9 explores the economic activities and effects of economies of scale in tourism development. It illustrates the pressure for larger facilities which are normally more economical to operate per unit than small ones, and thus as business increases most operators wish to expand profits. Of course, one way both to increase numbers and reduce relative costs per guest is to increase facility size. However, it will be shown in this chapter that large is not automatically better. It will be illustrated that development, however sensitive, will ultimately change the mix of tourists coming to a destination. Investment in travel and tourism is an important aspect of its development and planning, and is often made by international organizations such as the World Bank, the World Tourism Organization, as well as the government-funded bodies. Focusing on government, analysis of investment in travel and tourism services illustrates a considerable diversity from country to country, not only in terms of the level of revenue earned from tourism, but also in terms of government funding for tourism. During the 1980s many countries relied heavily on government funding to support the tourism sector. However, in the 1990s private sector contributions to national tourism budgets increased as governments withdrew from the sector and regulated with a 'lighter touch'.

These variations are a clear reflection of the policies and priorities governments held, and the relationship between the private and the public sectors on a country-by-country basis. Against this background, Chapter 9 provides an overview of the issues that influence investment decisions in general, as well as specifically, in travel and tourism. As such, two themes are discussed: first, the *institutional* aspects of investments that arise from the impact of certain agreements such as the General Agreement on Trade in Services (GATS) and the European Currency (Euro) which will influence the decision-making at the tourism destinations and country level; second, the *operational* aspects of investment decisions such as the risk management and detailing decision-making techniques, which will influence the tourism and hospitality enterprises. Overall, the chapter highlights the issues that should be considered as investment agendas for the tourism and hospitality sectors.

The theme of globalization is further expanded in Chapter 10 with its impact upon labour issues in the hotel, catering and tourism markets. Simply stated, to cope with the international intensity of competition brought about by globalization, a knowledge-based economy has emerged to replace the previously dominant 'Fordist' mode of production. This knowledge-based economy utilizes the skills of the workforce to the full, so creating a new way of thinking about human resources, and also new responses to the management of human resources by organizations.

Chapter 10 illustrates that this new paradigm for human resource management (HRM) and organizational behaviour is characterized by speed, flexibility, integration and innovation.

Chapter 11 notes that while discussion on tourism and hospitality inevitably centres on the major firms, it is the smaller family-owned or independently owned operations that dominate the market. In focusing on these smaller operations, policies must aim to:

1. Create a favourable business environment via the removal of unnecessary and costly administrative, physical and legal burdens (deregulation).
2. Encourage cross-border co-operation between enterprises.
3. Commit to providing business information and support.

At the heart of this discussion in Chapter 11 is the topic of partnerships. In an effort to contextualize this section of the chapter, prior research on partnerships has led to valuable insights on the behaviour of firms and the consequence for performance. Central to this critique is the need to explore two questions:

1. What factors influence the success of partnerships?
2. What is the effect of partnerships on the performance of firms/ organizations entering into them?

The consensus from the literature seems to be that 'partnerships' are the way forward, but what of the potential impacts of these partnerships? What are the real benefits, and what do they actually mean for resorts? What sort of problems are likely to be encountered? It is these and many more questions that are explored in this chapter.

A further matter explored in Chapter 11 is the key issue for the operation of transnational organizations of the means by which they transfer their corporate practice, philosophy and culture from headquarters to subsidiaries overseas. This is critical in the hotel, tourism and catering field where the essence of the product is international and the encounter with the consumer is intercultural. The rationale behind this comment is that global tourism organizations are dependent upon the delivery of the tourism product at individual destinations in culturally specific settings. In other words, while transnational corporations (TNCs) may appear to act as monolithic forces, their products depend upon delivery of the tourism service by personnel based at the destination, whether it be the hotel, restaurant or attraction.

From an HRM perspective, the global tourism company is a caricature, where the reality is locally derived: management structures, behaviour and labour practice.

However, a global economy must be increasingly culture- and context-sensitive, not only in terms of delivering the product, but also in terms of flexible labour practices and the increasing likelihood of employing foreign nationals. In part, it is through the medium of the informal labour markets that cultures and contexts will be preserved in the face of globalization. Globalization therefore poses key problems for the labour market.

Finally, in Chapter 12 a full review of tourism and hospitality within the regions of South America, Asia-Pacific and the Middle East is presented, along with authoritative projections for future trends.

This text is based on both the authors' wide experience of the international tourism and hospitality industry and lectureship experience at both under-graduate and postgraduate level. It will provide a good basis for students of the industry. Equally, managers already pursuing their careers will find this book a useful reminder of the industry's structure, globalization and consolidation trends at the beginning of the new millennium.

Dr Tim Knowles
Principal Lecturer in Hospitality Management
Manchester Metropolitan University, UK
Email: timknowles@msn.com

Dr Dimitrios Diamantis
Assistant Professor in Tourism and Hospitality
Swiss Hotel Association
Les Roches Management School, Switzerland
Email: dimitriosdiamantis@yahoo.co.uk

Dr Joudallah Bey El-Mourhabi
Lecturer in Business and Marketing
Hawaii University,
Hamra District
Beiruit, Lebanon
Email: beyjoud@inco.com.lb

Jan 2004

Tourist policy, resorts and life cycle theories

Background

In the era of the so-called 'global village' where many products have become standardized with individuality increasingly being squeezed out, there are, in terms of tourism, rapidly developing consumer markets, where holiday decisions are increasingly being made on the basis of quality, variety and environmental sustainability. The issue for tourism and its constituent supply sectors, such as hospitality, is whether the first wave of resorts such as Brighton and Bournemouth in the UK or, indeed, the second wave of Spanish and Greek resorts can effectively compete with these constantly evolving trends, as consumers seek evermore exotic experiences.

A number of attempts have been made to devise a model of resort evolution. Perhaps the most widely quoted model is Plog's continuum from emerging resort attracting the trendsetting 'allocentrics' to declining resort fed by low-income 'psychocentrics'. However, the Plog model (1974) relied solely on a demand-side perception of resort development and was superseded in 1980 by the Tourist Area Life Cycle (TALC).

One such approach to looking at these issues is to consider the patterns and processes of tourism development. Despite the fact that such a process is complex and multifaceted, one view developed by Richard Butler (1980) is to characterize resorts as 'products' which experience a series of evolutionary stages in consumer demand. This concept, known as the TALC, is generally well accepted by tourism development academics and practitioners (Agarwal, 1997).

The basic premise of the TALC is that a tourist resort should be viewed as a consumer product and thus exhibits a product life cycle, with numbers of visitors effectively representing product sales. Butler identified five separate stages to the evolutionary cycle which describes the resort's development over time from its initial discovery by tourists to a point of stagnation, at which point a sixth stage, of rejuvenation or decline, would take place, depending on the resort management/government response to stagnation. Briefly, the conditions present at each stage are as follows:

1. *Exploration*: small numbers of adventurous tourists are attracted by the natural beauty of the destination. Access may be difficult.
2. *Involvement*: as visitor numbers grow, interaction develops with the local community and basic services are provided.
3. *Development*: outsiders take greater control over the tourist trade as the resort is promoted and attracts considerable growth in business.

Additional facilities are provided. Numbers of tourists at the peak season far outweigh the number of residents.

4. *Consolidation*: tourism has by now become a major part of the local economy, but growth rates begin to level off. The destination is firmly established in the international market, with representation from major operators and an identifiable recreational business district.

5. *Stagnation*: capacity levels are reached in the resort and it begins to lose its fashionable status. Property turnover rates are high and there is an over-reliance on repeat visits. Environmental and social problems emerge.

The end of the cycle is characterized by the post-stagnation phase during which the resort may follow one of two directions, to varying degrees:

1. *Rejuvenation*: a major response is made to stagnation, repositioning the resort, seeking new markets and investing in major new facilities. The public and private sectors work together in close harmony.

2. *Decline*: visitor numbers decline as the resort becomes dependent on day rather than staying visitors and accommodation is converted into alternative uses.

While discussion of the TALC has tended to be diffused by its generic rather than specific application, this book will set Butler's approach within the context of strategic planning and will attempt to operationalize the development process.

Planning: the heart of the issue

Planning is essential to effective performance and success in every sector of today's tourism and hospitality industry, and should be regarded as a managerial process of developing and maintaining a viable fit between the organization's objectives, resources and its changing market opportunities. A number of aspects define the planning process. First, the tourism resort should be managed as a portfolio of connected firms, with the central issue being to decide which entities deserve to be built, maintained, stepped down or closed. As each element has a different profit potential it does not make sense to allocate management time and funds equally to all sectors. Therefore a reallocation of resources is required. The next key issue is to accurately assess the future profit potential of each sector. A number of analytical scenarios of future conditions in each market need to be determined. The third key idea underlying planning is that of strategy. For each of its businesses, the tourism or hospitality company must develop a *game plan* for achieving its long-term objectives, which requires the setting of such objectives. Furthermore, there is no one strategy that is optimal for all competitors in that tourism or hospitality sector. Each company must determine what makes the most sense in the light of its industry position, its mission, objectives, opportunities and resources.

Implicit in this discussion of strategic planning is the concept of an open system, one that considers the topic of environmental analysis and its effect on the organization or, indeed, the resort. It can be recognized that adapting to environmental change is the essence of the strategic management process and is central to strategic planning. More specifically, what is being considered is the management of change.

While there are a number of approaches to considering environmental analysis, in essence they all suggest that the environment (general and competitive) influences decision-making through both managerial perceptions and the objective dimensions of the tourism industry structure. To maintain a co-alignment between the tourism resort and its environment, so necessary for survival and growth, strategic managers must respond to that environment. Environmental scanning is the process by which senior executives become aware of events and trends outside their resort. This element of the planning process can be considered from both tactical (short-term) and strategic (long-term) perspectives, and the latter is initially considered here. Whereas many firms, and indeed tourism resorts, operate without such plans, their adoption does encourage systematic thinking, can improve performance and allow an effective response to a continually changing environment. As Kotler points out: 'a strategic plan involves taking advantage of opportunities in a constantly changing environment' (Kotler *et al.*, 1996: 70). This strategic planning process at a marketing level inevitably focuses on the four Ps of the traditional marketing mix: product, price, place and promotion; and if correctly applied, it attempts to relate them to the four Cs of: customer needs and wants, cost to the customer, convenience and communication. Such a strategy presents a plan to achieve clearly set objectives within the capabilities of the tourism resort and the myriad of stakeholders that make up that resort. The key matter being raised here is an approach described by Sasser (1976) as: 'the level capacity strategy'. Demand can be left to find its own level, or it can be managed in two ways. There can be an attempt to shape demand first through changing one or more of the four Ps. The second approach, explored by Armistead (1988), is to tailor capacity to follow demand or to chase variations in demand. Strategic planning at resort destinations is still not commonplace, and a short-term tactical approach is still the norm.

Implicit in the need for strategic planning at tourist resorts is the requirement for a positioning strategy that allows the resort to distinguish its offerings from those of its competitors in order to give it a competitive advantage within the market place. Such a view can be looked at from a regional, national and internal perspective. Thus, a resort that adopts a product position, based on high reliability/high cost will appeal to a sub-segment which has a desire for reliability and a willingness to pay for it. Positioning is more than merely promotion but involves considerations of pricing, distribution and the nature of the service offer itself, the core around which all positioning strategies revolve. Re-positioning is where the nature of customer demand has changed over time. An example relevant to this discussion is that UK customer attitudes changed towards packaged holidays during the 1980s away from an emphasis on low price and towards a position where consistent standards became of greater concern.

Developing the TALC framework

The framework of the TALC revolves around an explanation of the development process and from that point could be extended into, for instance, the forecasting of tourism numbers or more specific market segments. One way of looking at this development process is through classifying resorts by type or generation.

The first generation of UK mass tourist resorts, the early coastal resorts of the north, were largely products of the railway age. In the south, resorts such as Brighton, Bournemouth and Torquay were originally patronized by the aristocracy and developed in the wealthy Victorian era. The resorts began to attract the masses from Britain's industrial cities from the 1920s. In those days, each major city tended to have a favoured resort based on proximity. Thus, the aristocratic resorts of the south coast that were patronized by London's high society had a very different social tone than the resorts of the industrial, working-class north such as Blackpool and Skegness (Urry, 1990). The consolidation phase of these resorts extended from the 1920s to the 1950s, as access by car became more frequent and annual holiday leave was generally extended. Decline did not become apparent until the 1960s, when air transport and overseas holidays began to erode traditional markets. Thus, the British seaside resort (to adopt Butler's TALC) experienced a pre-stagnation life cycle of around 150 years, and has been coping with life in the post-stagnation phase for some 40 years.

British resorts generally responded slowly to market decline. In an era when only the fittest have survived, some smaller resorts have accepted their fate as retirement towns; others have become shadows of their former selves with decaying local economies. The more resilient resorts have accepted the shrinking of their accommodation bases as they re-orient themselves to the day visitor market where appropriate and invest in new facilities to attract family holidays (e.g. indoor 'wet weather' leisure facilities, new indoor attractions). In addition, efforts have been made to tap into growth markets, such as conferences and domestic short breaks, which help to extend the season through product development initiatives (e.g. conference centres, restoration of heritage). More enlightened resorts, such as Brighton and Bournemouth, have also sought, successfully, to diversify their economic base into areas such as financial services and education (Smith, 1992). Therefore to summarize, the British resorts have proved most resilient because:

1. Their development was over a sufficiently long period of time to the extent that tourism was not the only component of the economy.
2. They were not dependent on tour operators to provide visitors since the domestic UK market has traditionally by-passed the middle man.
3. They are, in most cases, within one hour's drive of vast metropolitan catchment areas, the source of day visitors.

Resort survival in Britain has been achieved by a diversification of the economic base; a contraction of the accommodation base; a re-orientation to new consumer markets, with a level of post-stagnation stabilization achieved by the UK survivors after 40 years.

A second generation of resorts evolved in the 1960s, typified by Spanish destinations, followed by Greek resorts, which at the same time saw the emergence of mass tourism. Poon (1993) regards mass tourism as: 'a phenomenon of large scale packaging of standardised leisure services at fixed prices for sale to a mass clientele'. Such a category of tourism requires the shifting of large volumes in order to work, with quality and differentiation being sacrificed for low prices; the commencement of perhaps a touristic 'global village'. The economic philosophy of mass consumption implies the production of goods and services on assembly line principles leading to homogeneity in production. Urry (1990) describes mass tourist consumption as producer, not consumer, driven with minimal differentiation between commodities and individual producers tending to dominate markets.

Mass tourism in Europe emerged in the 1960s as cheaper air travel brought warm Mediterranean destinations within holiday range of an increasingly affluent north European market. The domestically oriented holidaymakers of the UK, Germany and Benelux were enticed on their first foreign holidays by the promise of uninterrupted sunshine and by tour operators able to package the holiday product in an attractive format. The appeal was easy to understand with hindsight and is humorously encapsulated by Ritchie (Ritchie and Goeldner, 1994): 'As a child I greatly appreciated the replacement of fortnights in Llandudno by package tours to Mallorca as going for a swim no longer merited a Duke of Edinburgh award!' For the consumer, the package deal removed the uncertainty associated with foreign travel. For producers, conscious that demand would be price dependent, it was necessary to build high volume so as to maximize economies of scale in purchases from their sub-contractors. This relationship evolved over the next two decades, with tour operators becoming more efficient in consolidating the product and seeking market growth in volume rather than value. In order to achieve ambitious volume targets, tour operators relied heavily on price in developing the market. In Spain, where the cost of living was well below the European average until the 1980s, very economical packages were offered and visitors' purchasing power was high.

Through such competitive pricing, more latterly accentuated by early booking and late season discounts, price has always been the dominant feature of the tour operator commercial marketing mix. The increasingly competitive nature of tour operating has reinforced the role of price in driving volume in their economic equation.

The rapidity of demand growth and the volume ambitions of the leading tour operators were reflected in the emergence of a new type of holiday resort, based on high accommodation density and a remarkable pandering to the tastes of the northern European 'invaders'. The philosophy demanded that large numbers of visitors should be sought and all should be accommodated as closely as possible to the beach (hence the high rise). Spain, with its amenable summer climate, plethora of golden beaches and the encouragement of its national government, became the host to a succession of mass tourist resorts that subsequently attracted a degree of notoriety. Benidorm, Torremolinos, Lloret de Mar and Magaluf in Majorca were all transformed from fishing villages into high rise urban resorts in 15 years of intense development between 1960 and 1975.

These resorts were characterized by the speed of their development, uncontrolled land speculation, reliance on access by jet aircraft and the degree of foreign control exerted by northern European tour operators, such that their character was largely homogeneous – based on massification and imported rather than indigenous values. The standardization of packaging extended to food, entertainment, activities and even souvenirs.

From the resort perspective, mass tourism engendered an unhealthy dependency relationship. The original entrepreneurs who built hotels and developed attractions in the resorts were frequently financed in part by the foreign tour operators who were then guaranteed future volume or 'bed quotas' at preferential rates. The new breed of Mediterranean hotelier, though skilled at the delivery of hospitality services, was not required to develop selling and marketing skills. Bedrooms were pre-contracted in bulk to the tour operators who then took responsibility for marketing and sales to the consumer. The huge volume of beds required continued consolidation of the selling process in foreign markets.

By the mid-1980s, signs of fatigue in the physical fabric of these resorts were already apparent, barely two decades after the first package tourists had arrived. Weaknesses were revealed in the resort infrastructure while the evident disregard for the region's natural ecology was increasingly being questioned by a segment of the consumer base.

The market did show some resilience after the recessionary doldrums of 1990–1, but the high volumes of 1994, and particularly 1995, required a major stimulation of the market by the tour operators through price discounting. Indeed, the tour operators were left with considerable excess holiday capacity in the summer of 1995 that was eventually 'dumped' on the market at give-away prices. In these situations, it is predominantly the consolidator who suffers, though the contracted hoteliers also lose out by way of contracts designed to protect the operator. Profit margins were slim for these intermediaries in a year that was described as 'the industry's worst trading season on record' (Curtis and Knowles, 1999). In response, the industry cut capacity by around 12 per cent in the late 1990s and achieved a more realistic balance between demand and supply.

The dynamics of the tour operator industry are such that a 'boom and bust' cycle from year to year has become the norm (Middleton, 1994). The susceptibility of operators to fluctuations in the general economic environment is heightened by the long lead times required to assemble a holiday programme (around 18 months). Tour operators are required to make strategic forecasts of likely demand levels and hope that their judgement proves accurate. When it invariably does not, they revert to tactical price-based marketing in order to sell surplus supply.

Recent developments in the UK package holiday market have further demonstrated that low prices remain the backbone of mass tourism, or the mainstream holiday market. The major tour operators have continued to consolidate, vertically integrating both backwards and forwards in order to control the transport element and distribution channels of the business, and to maintain competitive pricing. The top five tour operators now control over 65 per cent of the total UK package tour market (Howitt, 1996). Vertical integration has enabled major tour operators to fully harness new developments in information technology and to extend efficiencies in aircraft load factors and distribution through tied agents. However, allegations of consumer manipulation and uncompetitive practice have arisen from the march of the multiples.

The battle for market share has led to endless initiatives (e.g. early booking discounts, free travel for children, three weeks for the price of two in the low season), almost always relying on market stimulation by price discounting. The need to use price as the most effective tool reflects the price sensitivity of the mass market.

The implication that cost is the major motivating factor in holiday selection by the mass tourism consumer seems to be confirmed. It can be demonstrated that, taking account of exchange rates and inflation, sharp rises and falls in package tourism to specific countries are closely related to the price of holidays there. In addition to the key issue of price, a number of other consumer pressures are affecting the competitiveness of these second generation resorts.

Relating these discussions back to the TALC, it is difficult, for example, to use the concept to contrast an inland resort such as Bath with a coastal resort such as Brighton, or indeed historic resorts such as Deauville with modern resorts such as Canet-Plage. Resorts may evolve by accident of geography or by specific planning; tourism may be a component of the local economy or its driving force; the source of a destination's attractiveness may be heritage- or climate-based; and it may rely on mass consolidators to provide visitors to a greater or lesser extent (Cooper, 1990; Pearce, 1995). Indeed, the international perspective of tourism and hospitality adds another complicating dimension to the TALC.

Looking to the two categories of resorts discussed so far, among the first generation that have stemmed decline, most have relied heavily on their nineteenth-century built heritage and on a re-orientation of product towards the day rather than overnight visitor. The second generation of mass tourist resort generally lacks an attractive built legacy and is frequently located in areas without a large regional catchment population. Most tellingly, these resorts are struggling to overcome the confinement caused by overly rapid and uncontrolled development. The argument could therefore be put forward that in order for such mass tourist destinations to be sustainable over the longer term, there is a need to take a strategic planning perspective.

Globalization

These comments on the TALC, tourism and hospitality, set within the context of the UK and Europe can also be placed alongside the potential impact of globalization. More specifically, the independence of thousands of small and medium-size enterprises (SMEs), including hotels and tour operators, is at risk when compared with the multinationals. While globalization of tourism and hospitality will certainly create jobs and boost investment, many developing countries are facing the prospects of a huge growth in leakage of foreign exchange earnings in a sector that has long prided itself on being the biggest foreign exchange generator. Countries, for instance, could be paying high prices in franchise, licensing, distribution, management and a variety of other fees as globalization takes hold in the world-wide tourism and hospitality industry.

While the pro-globalization voices have drowned those urging a cautious approach, a small warning light has been switched on as developing countries need to handle negotiations on the travel, tourism and hospitality component in a better manner. While globalization is irreversible, developing countries need to bolster their bargaining positions in the fields of tourism services supplied by global hotels, tour operators, travel agents and transport companies, air access and global distribution systems and electronic commerce. They also need to negotiate better terms in exchange for opening their markets and eliminating doing-business barriers under the multilateral free trade agreements.

However, most national tourism organizations and travel trade associations, which should theoretically be addressing these issues on behalf of their taxpayers and members, do not fully understand what is at stake.

The issues are extremely complicated and cut across the three components of getting a product to market:

1. contracts with tour operators;
2. airline access;
3. distribution.

How, for example, can hotels, tour operators, travel agencies and suppliers of transport services confront the globalizing tour operators and travel agency consortia, hampered as they are by their weak bargaining position and their lack of negotiating skills, which often result in unfavourable contract conditions? What policies can be adopted to take advantage of liberalizing air transport regulations even as many airlines face the prospect of becoming bit players in global alliances? How can small tourism service suppliers negotiate better terms to ensure lower costs in the global distribution systems? There are of course different options available – for example, the choices facing independent hotels in deciding whether to surrender total ownership, forge a joint venture, franchise or management agreement, become part of a consortia of independent hotels or retain their independence. The same choices apply to tour operators and travel agents. The critical issue that does emerge, however, is the impact of globalization on leakage of foreign exchange and on SMEs, essentially the family-owned companies facing the same pressures as in Europe and North America. While the total sell-out of a company leaves the owner with no further financial risk, the primary downside is the large outflow of income from tourism. The more companies that sell out, the higher the outflow. These days, with many Asia-Pacific companies, especially SMEs, facing a major cash-flow problem, their choice of options narrows and negotiating power decreases proportionately. Once they start fading, the radical restructuring of travel and tourism that could result could strike at the heart of national economies.

Over the next few years, billions of dollars will be required to upgrade airport infrastructure, air traffic control systems, back- and front-office systems, distribution technology, workforce quality, environmental standards and the product itself. Many more millions will be needed for marketing. Where will this money come from? And what conditions will be attached to making it available?

One approach is that SMEs look seriously at forming consortia to centralize common activities like market research and analysis, dealing with tour operators and travel agents, production of brochures, purchasing, technical assistance, management consultancy services and, very importantly, human resources development. In the field of airline access, while thinking global is critical, it might be better to act regionally rather than locally through the establishment of regional alliances or joint-venture agreements which can be promoted through regional liberalization mechanisms.

On the regulatory side, the relevant suggestion is the formulation of codes of conduct for global distribution systems. E-commerce offers, for instance, the Asia-Pacific travel industry a unique opportunity to 'cut out the costs of intermediaries' (Knowles and Egan, 2002) and can be developed if national tourism organizations take the lead. If there is a minimal critical mass of information infrastructure in a given country, the new technologies can offer substantial cost savings.

Meeting even part of this exercise will be a major undertaking. It will require national tourism organizations (NTOs), airlines and travel trade associations to understand fully the issues involved and analyse how they will be affected locally and regionally. Policy responses will then have to be prepared and communicated to all local stakeholders, especially those responsible for negotiating the global agreements. Eventually, it will require money, bringing into further focus the role of regional travel industry associations like Pacific Asia Travel Association (PATA) and Association of South East Asian Tourist Associations (ASEANTA). Whatever price has to be paid, it will pale in the face of that which will be paid if no preparatory work is undertaken, and soon.

Consumer pressures

As consumers from the mature northern European markets become more sophisticated and adventurous in their holiday habits, and new technologies supersede traditional ways of distributing the holiday product (e.g. teletext, Internet, direct booking), there is every reason for concern over the long-term future of the original breed of mass tourist resorts. The key consumer and facilitating trends of recent years have been as follows:

1. A growing preference for long-haul holidays, which are becoming more affordable and offer a higher degree of exoticism. The proportion of the UK air holiday market attributable to long haul has risen from 8 per cent to 16 per cent in the last decade.

2. In the UK, the late 1990s saw a fall in the sale of short-haul packages by 14 per cent and an increase in long-haul sales by 21 per cent.

3. An ageing and more sophisticated market increasingly interested in new holiday experiences rather than the traditional sun and beach product of the Mediterranean mass tourist resorts. A growing movement of 'beach boredom' is now taking hold.

4. A shift away from the traditional package holiday as technology allows tour operators to reach the consumer directly, thus saving the commission costs of travel agents. Travel agents' share of the UK package market has fallen from 87 per cent to 74 per cent in the last decade. Such a scenario will allow the operator to feed distribution savings into improving the quality of the holiday product.

5. A market shift towards independently arranged holidays as consumers become increasingly aware of booking techniques, seeking a higher

degree of control and flexibility over their holidays. An increase of 22 per cent in the UK independent market has been registered between 1996 and 2002 against 13 per cent growth in the air inclusive (package) market. The growth of tailor-made holidays is further testament to this trend.

6. Legislative changes are likely to reduce the price of independent holidays (e.g. the ongoing deregulation of the airline industry), which will increase the relative price of the traditional Mediterranean package holiday.

A third generation of resorts?

In considering the typology of resorts (first and second generation), a third category of mass-market resorts emerged in the mid- to late 1980s and is currently in the growth and consolidation stages of the life cycle. These resorts have emerged predominantly in the developing world and are characterized by a higher degree of planning, control and quality specification.

Poon (1993) is a leading advocate of a 'new tourism', the notion that mass production in tourism is rapidly being replaced by a more flexible form of production characterized by quality, innovation and market segmentation. Urry (1990) refers to the movement as 'post-Fordist consumption'. The move towards new tourism is stimulated by a more quality-conscious and independently minded consumer and by new technologies now being used to maximize yield rather than volume.

'New tourism' may represent the end of the mass tourism era of the twentieth century. The new model resorts are typified by: development restraint; environmental sensitivity; and direct marketing to a newly independent consumer.

The applicability of the TALC

It is perhaps surprising that to date very little research has been carried out on the post-stagnation phase of resort evolution. The second generation of mass tourist resorts is generally a good fit to the TALC but is showing signs of worryingly short life cycles. A period of discovery was typically followed by rapid development during which outside interests (foreign tour operators) took control. Consolidation was generally reached in the late 1970s and stagnation set in during the late 1980s as, first, environmental concerns and, then, prolonged recession in the northern European markets took effect. In the post-stagnation era of the 1990s, a limited number of resorts struggled to offset decline but most reacted quickly to implement rejuvenation measures.

The survival of these resorts is likely to depend upon their inherent strengths and on the strategic choices which they make regarding rejuvenation and, perhaps more specifically, repositioning. At present, many resorts claim to be investing heavily in their product, but are actually only tinkering, while others have concentrated resources into marketing at the peril of new product investment initiatives. Ultimately, as new competition emerges throughout the world, only the fittest and most enlightened will survive in the longer term.

Of most concern is the inherent vulnerability of resorts that continue to function at the whim of their 'masters', the foreign tour operators. Where supply is so concentrated and diversity of markets limited, vulnerability is most apparent.

The TALC is a valuable conceptual framework in which to place the evolution and current status of mass tourist resorts. While individual resorts will follow a different life cycle evolution, which may evolve over a century or just a few decades, they ultimately reach the critical stagnation phase. For decline to be offset, it would appear that the resort reaction should consist of the following:

1. the gradual usurping of control from outsiders and encouragement of greater local involvement and power;
2. the swift formulation of a rejuvenation strategy;
3. the implementation of radical rejuvenation measures aimed at re-structuring the resort rather than temporary and arbitrary face-lifts.

Agarwal (1994) has suggested that rejuvenation may be more appropriately described as 'reorientation' as continued efforts at re-structuring are characterized by market targeting, specialization and segmentation, as investment is simultaneously channelled into transforming the physical appearance of the resort and heightening the quality of its attractions. She argues that re-orientation can be repeated indefinitely to offset decline and that the life cycle may display a series of peaks and falls within the post-stagnation phase. Agarwal has suggested that there is a need for the theoretical reformulation of the final post-stagnation phase, viewing re-orientation as a continual process operating on a series of levels.

TALC and the practical implications for the Chinese hotel industry: an example

Background

The emerging economies of Southeast Asia, including the People's Republic of China, have attracted a great deal of foreign direct investment and trade with the industrialized countries of western Europe and North America over the past decade. This economic trend brings increased business travel to the region with the inevitability of demand for hotel accommodation (Knowles et al, 2002).

Owing to its economic growth, easing of political tensions and sheer size, China is regarded as a fertile land for hotel industry development. According to the 2001 annual report issued by the Chinese National Tourism Administration, from 1978 to 2001 the total number of hotels that were authorized to receive foreign travellers increased from 203 to 6029. By 2000, about 10 per cent of the top 300 corporate chains had entered China (Pine, Zhang and Qi, 2000). In 2001 the upscale hotel market, mainly four- or five-star hotels, had grown to 469 properties, 21.9 per cent of total accommodation capacity. A significant portion of these upscale hotels are operated by foreign hotel groups.

Distribution of properties

The distribution of upscale hotels is very uneven in China and largely a reflection of the unbalanced economic development of the region. They are mainly located in the northern, eastern and central southern regions where accommodation accounts for over 70 per cent of the country's upscale properties in total. Among China's 31 provinces, autonomous cities and regions, there are four capital cities without upscale hotels and eight without a hotel managed by a multinational hotel corporation (China National Tourism Administration, May 2002).

A review of the economic forces underlying price competition

A key issue for the TALC is the current growing price competition in many of the sub-markets in mainland China, which can be explained by the application of economic theory. The market for business hotels in China is a series of local oligopolistic markets with a small number of multinational hotel chains (MNHCs) becoming increasingly dominant in individual sub-markets. The classic model of oligopoly would suggest a stable market with limited price competition between the main players in each sub-market, with occasional price wars breaking out usually when one of the key players is losing market share. However, price wars usually mean that all players in the market lose because of lower prices unless there is a clear winner of the war. Thus, firms in oligopolistic markets tend to avoid direct price competition and compete via non-price methods, often with tacit agreements to avoid excessive, overt price competition. Such a model could probably be applied to most mature sub-markets for business hotels, where there are long periods of relative price stability and hotels compete via non-price mechanisms such as quality of service, location, air miles, loyalty schemes, etc. This stability may well break down as a result of extraneous shocks such as September 11 or the recent foot-and-mouth crisis in the UK. However, as stability returns to the market there will be a tendency to return to stable prices and non-price competition. The reasons why this is likely to happen are clear if we consider the damaging price war now being fought out in many of the sub-markets in China.

The hypothesis we are suggesting here is that the structure of the Chinese market is such that the current price wars are not a short-term phenomenon but are likely to continue in the medium term until the Chinese market reaches maturity. Such market conditions will obviously have implications for what are the most appropriate marketing strategies and the appropriateness of the TALC.

The current market situation in China and other sub-markets can be explained by reference to the more modern theories of market behaviour. The traditional structure-conduct-performance paradigm has been replaced by an increasing emphasis on the conduct of firms within a market, reflecting the dynamic nature of markets rather than an emphasis on static market structure based on concentration ratios. Three main schools of thought have developed: the 'contestable market', the 'Austrian School' and 'workable markets'. Although a detailed review of these schools of thought is inappropriate in this chapter, suffice it to say that underlying all of them is a belief that more important than the structure of a market at a given point in time are the dynamic conditions in which a market operates and, thus, how companies conduct themselves in competing with their rivals. One of the key features of all these models is the role of 'barriers of entry' in determining the level of competition in a particular market. The essential premise is that, unless there are significant 'barriers of entry', either price competition will result in downward pressure on prices as new entrants fight for market share or existing firms will price at a level which does not encourage new entrants.

A key feature of the Chinese markets is that in the current marketization of the Chinese economy the barriers of entry are low compared to more mature markets, leading to significant oversupply in many sub-markets as new firms enter the gateway cities. This trend is being further exacerbated by the desire of MNHCs to position themselves in major gateway cities ready for the continued growth of the Chinese market. Thus, compared to more mature markets we have a dynamic and unstable market where competition is primarily via prices. Although, obviously, other attributes are important, compared to more mature markets it is likely that the lack of barriers of entry, together with the desire of MNHCs to position themselves in the main gateway cities that oversupply, will be the norm for the medium-to-long term, resulting in fierce price competition.

Developing a marketing strategy in China

There is no consensus as to what a marketing strategy actually is, and instead there is a wide array of competing visions (Schnaars, 1998). Schnaars' (1998) view is that a marketing strategy can be applied to at least three types of marketing issues:

1. manipulation of marketing mix variables: product, price, place, and promotion;
2. application of individual elements of the marketing mix: skimming vs. penetration pricing strategies;
3. product market entry strategies, which aim to build, defend or harvest market share.

Porter (1985), expanded the discussion by offering differentiation (beside lower cost), as a generic strategic option to achieve business success. He suggested that higher quality and status products could allow a company to differentiate itself from competitors while selling at a higher price. He postulated that cost leadership and differentiation are not compatible.

However, the real business world seldom provides the conditions on which Porter's strategy can be executed. This strategy requires a clearly defined boundary between the firm and its competitors. This condition can be satisfied when there are only two major participants in the competition, or all competitors take a similar approach in attacking the market leader so that they can be classified into a group. Frequently in the hotel industry, there are many four- or five-star properties competing in the same market in a city. Often the competitors may take various approaches in order to attack the market share of the lead hotel all at the same time. Under this situation, the market leader may be confused by these numerous and disorderly competing strategies which cannot be clearly defined. They will also be in the dilemma that one strategy, which is considered effective to one competitor, may seem ineffective to another (Knowles and Egan, 2002).

The marketing mix and the centrality of price

In practice, in order to carry out an effective defensive strategy, a hotel business has to consider its marketing mix, within which price is of unique importance to marketers (Lewis and Chambers, 2000). It is the only direct revenue generating part of the marketing mix available to meet financial objectives. It is also a powerful force in attracting attention and increasing sales, as well as establishing the market positioning of the product. However, product and price are inseparable because of the importance that buyers place on price in relation to value.

Interestingly, Gabor (1988) classifies pricing practices into two basic categories: cost-based pricing and market-oriented pricing. Most firms claim to follow the former in determining their prices although they may take different starting points. Lewis and Chambers (2000) note that the cost-driven approach makes many hotels automatically raise rack rates quarterly or semi-annually, regardless of occupancy and business trends. What follows in the wake of this practice is a multiple discount process that is, at best, unsophisticated, naïve, confusing to the customer and, in the final analysis, self-defeating.

Market-oriented pricing takes the customer as its starting point. It bases price on the customer's perceived value of the product. Theoretically, it overcomes the shortcomings of cost-based pricing. However, since judgements on the customer's attitudes and behaviour are often arbitrary and subjective, market-oriented pricing can sometimes be misleading. Alternatively, Drucker (1993) lists five deadly business sins leading to downfall, including worship of premium pricing and charging whatever the market will bear. This view can have serious implications for the hotel industry.

First, in the overcrowded upscale hotel market in China, where the new entrants are usually equipped with updated facilities and new innovations, these advantages increase the gap between the new entrants and existing properties and frequently put the older properties in a disadvantageous position. However, due to lack of recognition, the new entrants also find it difficult to get customers to initially trial the product. This difficulty very often forces new entrants to employ a price-cutting strategy.

Second, a luxury hotel will offer a unique product when it is the first one in the upscale market, but as more and more new entrants enter the market, and more and more customers try the product, the perceived uniqueness will inevitably fade.

Third, in most market economies the hotel industry is a deregulated industry. In China it was among the first batch of industries untied by the government in the early stages of the country's 'open reform' policy in the 1980s. When there was no competitor in the upscale market, the existing hotels enjoyed a prosperous business based on a highly differentiated product. Once new entrants came with comparable products, they tended to compete on price in a deregulated market.

An important issue within this discussion is perception. The dependence on price as a proxy for quality is especially strong when two conditions exist: first, the consumer believes that differences between alternative product offerings exist; second, consumers have little information or experience with the products concerned. A survey by INSEAD's Euro-Asia Centre shows that the perception of higher price signalling higher quality is strong in China. The saying '*yi fen jia qian yi fen huo*' ('even a penny difference in price makes a difference in quality') shows how people perceive a quality difference between similar goods at different prices (Knowles, 1999).

Some cultural implications in hotel consumer behaviour

In a collectivist culture, product and brand preferences are more likely to express attitudes arising from social norms than from internal drives or motives (Schutte and Ciarlante, 1998). Thus, product or brand preferences represent expressions of what is considered socially acceptable rather than individual preferences. Loyalty is not individually established but is a reflection of conformity with group norms. Chinese consumers, extremely sensitive to social risk, will not deviate in their purchases from the brand or product recommended by their reference group. Thus, once a product is established as the normative standard of a group, loyalty is extremely strong, particularly for social-use products (Knowles, 1999).

However, since the open reform policy commenced in 1979, foreign products and brands have been introduced to Chinese consumers in many realms. More options are available, and sometimes consumers feel confused by too many options. On the other hand, curiosity drives Chinese consumers to sample many brands, if their purchasing power allows, and therefore leads to a high level of variety-seeking brand switching. If a product fails to deliver on important product attributes, or catch up with new products with desirable attributes, the pragmatism of the Chinese and their relative lack of emotional ties with specific products or brands allows them to try another brand without hesitation (Schutte and Ciarlante, 1998). To a great extent, the sudden flood of new brands into China has impeded the creation of brand loyalty. Thus, Chinese consumers become more complex to analyse and the market becomes an ever-changing field, which makes it more difficult for MNHCs to find an appropriate positioning for their business.

On one hand, launching a product early can provide valuable brand awareness in a country where brands are highly regarded and serve as reassurance of quality to risk-averse consumers. It can be illustrated by the saying '*xian ru wei zhu*' ('whosoever comes first, becomes the master'). On the other hand, since new products contain the latest desirable attributes, it is necessary for existing brands to constantly rejuvenate themselves and retain an image of providing the latest desirable attributes.

The areas that need to be explored in the Chinese hotel industry *vis-à-vis* the TALC are:

1. Is price cutting a major competitive strategy of new entrants in the overcrowded upscale market?
2. Is the value-added approach strategically viable for an established property to defend its long-term profitability?

3. What are the implications of a value-added strategy for established properties in defending themselves in an overcrowded upscale market?

Summary

Though conclusions are difficult to draw in the absence of detailed information and analysis, it would appear that second generation mass tourist resorts do share the same structural characteristics of dependency and an overly price-conscious clientele, and that the post-stagnation life cycle model is a valid one to apply generically, albeit within a different temporal framework.

Mass tourism will not disappear. Rather, it will be replaced by a more responsible, and more sustainable, variety of mass tourism where price is no longer the critical factor in consumer choice. This point has been explored with a discussion of the key trends affecting the tourism and hospitality industry in the early years of this new century. It remains to be seen whether any of the Spanish or Greek mass-market resorts will still be favoured destinations for such a re-fashioned market or, indeed, how a market like China will evolve.

References

Agarwal, S. (1994) 'The resort cycle revisited – implications for resorts', *Progress in Tourism, Recreation and Hospitality Management*, 5, 194–207.

Agarwal, S. (1997) 'The resort cycle and seaside tourism: an assessment of its applicability and validity', *Tourism Management*, 18, 2, 65–73.

Armistead C.G. (1988) *Operations Management in Service Industries in the Public Sector*, Chichester: John Wiley.

Butler, R. (1980) 'The concept of a tourist area cycle of evolution', *Canadian Geographer*, 24, 5–12.

China National Tourism Administration (2002) www.cnta.com

Cooper, C. (1990) 'Resorts in decline – the management response', *Tourism Management*, 11, 1, 63–7.

Drucker, P. (1993) *Innovation and entrepreneurship: practices and principles*, London, Penguin.

Gabor, A. (1988) *Pricing, Concepts and Methods for Effective Marketing*, 2nd edn, London Gower Publishing Company.

Howitt, S. (1996) *Travel Agents and Overseas Tour Operators*, 12th edn, London: Keynote.

Knowles, T. (1999) 'Strategic marketing in the hospitality sector', in: F. Vellas and L. Becherel, (eds) *The International Marketing of Travel and Tourism: A Strategic Approach*, London, Macmillan Press Ltd, 119–212.

Knowles, T., and Egan, D. (2002) 'The Asia Pacific hotel industry' *Travel and Tourism Analyst*, 4: 1–25.

Knowles, T., and Curtis, S. (1999) 'The market viability of European mass tourist resorts: a post stagnation life cycle analysis' *International Journal of Tourism Research*, 1(2): 87–96.

Kotler P., Armstrong G., Saunders J. and Wong V. (1996) *Principles of Marketing*, Englewood Cliffs, NJ: Prentice-Hall.

Lewis, R.C., and Chambers, R.E. (2000) *Marketing Leadership in Hospitality; Foundations and Practices*, New York, Van Nostrand Reinhold.

Middleton, V. (1994) *Marketing in Travel and Tourism*, 2nd edn, Oxford: Butterworth-Heinemann.

Pearce, D. (1995) *Tourism Today: A Geographical Analysis*. Harlow: Longman.

Pine, R., Zhang, H.Q. and Qi, P.Z. (2000) 'The challenges and opportunities of franchising in China's hotel industry', *International Journal of Contemporary Hospitality Management*, 12, 5.

Plog S.C. (1974) 'Why destination areas rise and fall in popularity', *Cornell Hotel and Restaurant Association Quarterly*, 14: 55–58.

Poon, A. (1993) *Tourism, Technology and Competitive Strategies*, Wallingford: CAB International.

Porter, M. (1985) *Competitive Advantage: Creating and Sustaining Superior Performance*, New York: The Free Press.

Ritchie, J.R.B. and Goeldner, C.R. (eds) (1994) *Travel, Tourism and Hospitality Research: A Handbook for Managers and Researchers*, 2nd edn, New York: John Wiley and Sons.

Sasser, W.E. (1976) 'Match supply and demand in service industries', *Harvard Business Review*, November–December, 133–40.

Schnaars, S. (1998) *Marketing Strategy, Customer and Competition*, 2nd edn, New York: The Free Press.

Schutte, H. and Ciarlante, D. (1998) *Consumer Behaviour in Asia*, London: Macmillan.

Smith, R. (1992) 'Beach resort evolution – implications for planning', *Annals of Tourism Research*, 19, 2, 304–22.

Urry, J. (1990) *The Tourist Gaze*, London: Sage.

Further reading

Bitran, G. and Mondschein, S. (1995) 'Application of yield management to hotel industry considering multiple day stays', *Operations Research*, 43, 3.

Bray, R. (1996) 'The package holiday market in Europe', *Travel and Tourism Analyst*, 4, 51–71.

Choi, T.Y. and Choi, V. (1997) 'A simplified approach to yield management using knowledge discovery technique for Hong Kong hotel industry', Second International Conference on Quality and Reliability, 1–3 September.

Cravens, D. (2000) *Strategic marketing*, 6th edn, London: Irwin/McGraw-Hill.

Drucker, P. (1985) *Innovation and Entrepreneurship: Practice and Principles*, Pan.

Dann, G. and Potter, R. (1997) 'Tourism in Barbados: rejuvenation or decline?', in D. Lockhart and D. Dukakis-Smith (eds) *Island Tourism: Trends and Prospects*, London: Pinter, 205–28).

Dunn, K. and Brooks, D. (1990) 'Profit analysis: beyond yield management', *Cornell HRA Quarterly*, 31, 3.

Far Eastern Economic Review (1990) 'Asian affluence Hong Kong, *Far Eastern Economic Review*, 82.

Global Market Information Database (2001) 'Travel and tourism in China, November 2001', last accessed 12 July 2002, available at: www.euromonitor.com/gmidv1/frame.asp.

Hawkins, D.E. (1993) 'Global assessment of tourism policy: a process model', in D. Pearce and R. Butler (eds) *Tourism Resources: Criticisms and Challenges*, London: Routledge, 175–200.

Haywood, K. (1985) 'Can the tourist area life cycle be made optional?', *Tourism Management*, 7, 154–67.

Haywood, K. (1992) 'Revisiting resort cycle', *Annals in Tourism Research*, 19, 351–54.

Inskeep, E. and Kallenberger, M. (1994) *An Integrated Approach to Resort Development*, Madrid: WTO.

Kimes, S. (1997) 'Yield management: an overview', In I. Yeoman and A. Ingold (eds) *Yield Management for Service Industries*, London: Cassell, Part 1, 3–11.

Lambert, C. and Lambert, J. (1988) 'Simple reservation policies can be harmful to profit margins', *International Journal of Hospitality Management*, 7, 3.

Laws, E. (1995) *Tourist Destination Management:- Issues, Analysis and Policies*, London: Routledge.

Li, J, and Feng, T. (1997) 'Economy hotel market awaits exploration', *Hotel China and Overseas*, 5.

Lovelock, H. (1984) 'Strategies for managing demand in capacity-constrained services organization', *Service Industry Journal*, 4, 3.

Luciani, P. (1999) 'Implementing yield management in small and medium sized hotels: an investigation of obstacles and success factors in Florence', *International Journal of Hospitality Management*, 18.

McDonald, M. and Dunbar, I. (1998) *Market Segmentation: How to Do It; How to Profit from It*, 2nd edn, London, Macmillan.

McIntosh, R. and Goldner, C. (1984) *Tourism: Principles, Practices, Philosophies*, Columbus, Ohio: Grid Publishing.

Rao, A., Bergen, M. and Davis, S. (2000) 'How to fight a price war', *Harvard Business Review*, March–April.

Reich, A. (1997) *Marketing Management for the Hospitality Industry: A Strategic Approach*, New York: John Wiley and Sons, Inc.

Salmon, K. (1995) *The Modern Spanish Economy:- Transformation and Integration into Europe*, 2nd edn, London: Pinter.

Sola, E. (1992) 'A strategic outlook for regional tourism policy', *Tourism Management*, 13, 1, 45–9.

Valenzuela, M. (1991) 'Spain: the phenomenon of mass tourism', in A. Williams and G. Shaw (eds), *Tourism and Economic Development*, 2nd edn, West Sussex: Belhaven Press.

Williams, A. (1996) 'Mass tourism and international tour companies', in M. Barke, J. Towner and M. Newton (eds) *Tourism in Spain: Critical Issues*, Wallingford: CAB International, 119–36.

Wind Y.J. (1982) *Product Policy: Concepts, Methods and Strategy*, Reading, MA: Addison-Wesley.

2 The globalization agenda of tourism

Trends for the tourism and hospitality industry

Affecting the development of tourism resorts and the applicability of the Tourist Area Life Cycle (TALC) is a range of key trends. In the last decade, the tourism and hospitality industry has flourished, even as it has struggled to cope with some difficult challenges. In the years ahead, the global population will continue to grow and change, science and technology will tighten their hold on business and society, and the world will knit itself ever more tightly into a single market.

As a result, both opportunities and trials will abound which will come to affect the relevance and appropriateness of the TALC. The following trends outline the probable context in which the world's tourism, hotel and restaurant industry will continue to flourish in the first few years of this new century.

Economic conditions

Though global stock markets did reel in the aftermath of the financial crises of the late 1990s in Asia and Russia, underlying economic conditions remained strong in Europe and North America. Interest rates still remain low in the USA and relatively low elsewhere, capital is readily available, and employment stronger than it has been in years. All these factors point to continuing prosperity in the years ahead. The establishment of a common currency among most EU member states has encouraged and will continue to stimulate trade within mainland Europe. Unlike the Mexican financial crisis of the 1990s, which eased when the cheap peso boosted exports, the Asian recession of the same decade did not respond to currency devaluation because 50 per cent of Asian exports stay in the Pacific Rim. As a final point, Japanese banks wrote off their bad debts during the past few years, setting the stage for that country's economic recovery between 2003 and 2005.

Putting this all in a tourism context, global travel is well placed to grow rapidly for at least the next 20 years. For instance, world-wide arrivals have grown from 613 million in 1997 to an estimated 700 million in 2003, with projections of 1 billion by 2010 and 1.6 billion by 2020. The emerging positive economic situation during the second half of 2003 means that an improving balance of trade will result in more business for European tourist destinations with the region remaining the strongest magnet for tourism and arrivals growth holding between 3 per cent and 4 per cent. By 2002, air travel for both business and pleasure reached twice the 1985 rate and the growing strength of the US economy in 2003 will stimulate demand for tourism and hospitality services among American business and leisure travellers.

Turning to Asia, the positive side of the recent economic problems in the region is that low currency values will continue to promote travel to the Far East, for so long as they last; however, at the same time, travel from the Far East has declined in proportion. Overall, during the initial stages of the Far East economic crisis, the number of foreign visitors to the United States fell by 2 per cent in the first three months of 1998; visitors from Asia were down 12 per cent; from South Korea 62 per cent. The Asian financial crisis has put many Asian-owned hotels and other hospitality facilities in the USA and Europe on the market, as Pacific Rim corporations scrambled to raise cash. If the recession in Japan lasts beyond 2003, even Asian locations may be available to outside buyers.

Monetary union and the removal of trade restrictions within the EU also promise rapid growth of travel within the continent. Additionally, growth of the new middle and wealthy classes in Russia and other former Eastern bloc countries has created a profitable new market for vacation and business travel to the West. Demand from this quarter should grow for many years to come.

In the face of these developments, hotels have had to adapt in order to succeed. Marriott, for instance, looking for locations in Korea, Thailand, Indonesia and Malaysia, has increased its supply of hotel rooms in the region from 3700 to 21,000 in little more than a year with its reflagging of the new hotels as Ritz-Carltons, Marriotts and Courtyards.

Turning to restaurants, growing prosperity in Europe and the USA promises steady growth in the percentage of meals eaten in restaurants. Greatest strength will be in fast-food and other economy restaurants, which offer convenience for increasingly hurried two-income families, and in expensive restaurants known for quality, which offer an affordable taste of luxury. Mid-priced restaurants will find it difficult to compete. Like hotels, restaurants and food companies also adapt. All McDonald's 4700 restaurants in the Pacific region use Asian currencies for their business transactions. Therefore, in Indonesia, it costs 80 per cent less to build each restaurant due to lower costs for labour, land and other expenses. Debt on restaurants is lower, so it is easier to pay down existing loans or to take out new ones. In Singapore, using local currencies, restaurants buy chicken patties from Thailand, rather than the USA, at much lower cost.

Technology

Discovery of new ideas grows exponentially, as each new finding today opens the way to many more tomorrow. Thus the single greatest force for change in the twentieth century, technology, can only grow more powerful in the twenty-first century. Related to this matter of discovery and technology are what can be referred to as the four 'Is' of the product cycle which are becoming compressed – namely, idea, invention, innovation and imitation. In the 1940s and 1950s, it took 30 years to go from a theoretical idea to the release of competing products in an established market; in computing it now takes 18 months or less. This means that competition among service providers is speeding up year by year, which would imply an ever shortening of the TALC.

The implication for hotels is that as technology knits the world into one electronic marketplace, business travel will not decline, but will grow rapidly. In a high-tech world, executives increasingly need the 'high-touch' reassurance of personal relationships with their colleagues. The Internet changes the way consumers purchase goods and services; rings at the cash register are being replaced with cashless credit/debit systems of payment. This proliferation will allow the use of 'smart cards' to provide detailed customer information for more efficient target marketing. From a marketing communication perspective, resorts, conference centres and other destinations are finding it increasingly easy to market themselves directly to consumers, rather than relying on intermediaries; the same applies to air charter services and other transportation providers.

Tourism and hospitality will benefit as video – and eventually Internet 'movies' – replace printed brochures in promoting vacation destinations. Programmes include current, detailed information on accommodation, climate, culture, currency, language, immunization, and passport requirements. For instance, Holiday Inn's website already offers photo-illustrated 'tours' of about 350 hotels around the world, plus an on-line reservation system covering all 2,600 of the company's locations. The Internet makes it possible for small businesses throughout the world to compete for market share on an even footing with industry leaders and several Net-based booking services also have been established to represent small destinations on-line. On the cost control side, access to suppliers' inventory/order computers will make it easier to buy supplies and to control the firm's inventory of supplies and to cut inventory costs.

Turning to restaurants, the implication is that even the finest restaurants will serve more foods partly prepared off-premises, to be completed in the restaurants' own kitchens, with particularly the greater use of 'cook-chill' technology in bringing quality food products from outside. Food preparation equipment will also link to inventory control computers for automatic ordering of supplies. Hotel and restaurant chains will use this technology to make up for the scarcity of skilled chefs and to ensure uniformity of product in all locations.

The key benefit in relating this discussion on technology to the TALC, is that it allows a focus on what has variously been called 'segmented marketing', 'target marketing' and 'one-to-one marketing'. What each of these approaches is highlighting is how to reach customers, preferably directly; how to talk to them in their own language; how to cater to their specific needs; and how to satisfy them in every possible way. As technology develops within the travel and tourism industry, hotel owners are finding themselves with clear opportunities. One challenge emerging from this will be to streamline and simplify the transactions and consumption of products. This will require looking at global shifts in consumer attitudes, tracking new motivations and opportunities in order to communicate and convince. Direct marketing campaigns can cut out wastage, improve response rates and increase conversions to new and loyal customers. Hotels pay the highest distribution costs of all travel sectors and are anxious to reduce them with the benefit of the Internet. With the Internet, hoteliers can list out their entire product range to whatever detail they wish. In 1999, about 2 million hotel bookings were made on-line in North America. One forecast predicts 15 million reservations world-wide by 2005. If that happens, it won't be long before hotels join airlines in cutting travel agents' commissions. However, hotels still need to ensure a fine degree of revenue management in order to generate the best possible yield. This means juggling rates and room categories with seasonality and types of customers. Critical to this concept of one-to-one marketing will be another two issues: data-mining and, its first cousin, data-warehousing which involves collecting 'gold data' on customer information and converting it into recognition, loyalty and repeat traffic. Customer profiles are fed into computers and organized in ways they can be 'queried'.

Executives can know who has stayed for how long and when, what she ordered for dinner, or whether she used her laptop and the laundry service. By knowing all this, marketers think they can generate loyalty partly by letting regular guests know how much they know about them. The downside, of course, is that customers may not want hotels to know that much about them at all. Equally, too much cost-cutting has focused on throwing technological solutions at problems, when the industry must refocus on guest requirements, employee expectations and satisfaction, personal contact and service, relying on technology only to remove the burden of mundane tasks in order to increase service and value.

Demographics

Another issue affecting the evolution of the TALC is the demographic profile. In developed countries, healthier diets, more exercise, the decline of smoking in the USA, and the trend towards preventive medicine, are extending later life. Life expectancies in Japan are entering the nineties, and those in parts of Europe are not far behind. Medical advances could well help today's middle-aged baby boomers to live far longer than can be predicted even today. The elderly population is growing fastest throughout the developed world. In Europe, the USA and Japan, the elderly also form the wealthiest segment of society. Barring enactment of strict immigration controls, rapid migration will continue from the southern hemisphere to the North, and especially from former colonies to Europe. Birth rates appear to be slowly declining in parts of Africa, Asia and South America where population growth has been difficult to control.

The implication for hotels in all this is that global demand for tourism and hospitality services can only grow more quickly in the coming decades. With above average wealth and relatively few demands on their time, the elderly will make up a larger part of the tourist and hospitality market. The industry will prosper by catering to their needs for special facilities and services. Hotels will offer easy-to-read shop signs and brighter public areas suited to the needs of older visitors. Resorts that combine extra comforts for the elderly, with an adventure-vacation theme, will be in especially high demand. More retirees will travel off-season, tending to equalize travel throughout the year and eliminate the cyclical peaks and troughs typical of the industry.

Lower birth rates mean greater prosperity in regions where poverty traditionally has been endemic. In the long run, this should stimulate demand for travel and hospitality services in lands where only a tiny elite can now afford to travel.

Changing times: an example of Spain

Chapter 1 applied the TALC to Spain, yet many of the comments on the general environment discussed in this chapter can equally be applied to that country.

The Spanish population (see Table 2.1) is ageing, just like in most other countries across Europe. Spain presently has the lowest birth rate in the world and stands among countries with the highest rate of ageing population. In 2001 the population aged under 14 is forecast to account for over 14.5 per cent of the total compared to over 16.5 per cent in 1995. By contrast, those over 64 will represent 17 per cent of the population in 2001 compared to just over 15.3 per cent in 1995.

During the period 1995–2001 the Spanish population rose marginally to 40.3 million, a rise of nearly 3 per cent over the period (see Table 2.1). The country is increasingly becoming urbanized with over three-quarters of the population living in towns and cities. With the population profile clearly ageing, family size on average is falling, albeit marginally over the review period.

Trends in the Spanish child population show that the number of children (0–14 years of age) within the country has fallen by 9.4 per cent. While this could look bad for tourism this is not necessarily the case. As mentioned above, the adult population has generally been ageing, the demographic profile is therefore changing and so there are fewer children to spend household income on. This could mean that Spanish consumers are more open to buying into more sophisticated (and expensive) tourism products.

The changing demographic profile of Spain is significant for the tourism market. With more and more people in work, both men and women, the implication is clear that Spanish people feel that their leisure time is under pressure. There is also a growing choice of available leisure activities.

Additionally, the Spanish economy has improved substantially over the period 1995–2001 with unemployment falling from a high of 22.9 per cent to 12.8 per cent. While the total workforce grew by 9 per cent over the period, the

Table 2.1 Trends in the Spanish population by age group, 1995–2001

	1995		1997		1999		2001 (est)		% change
	000	%	000	%	000	%	000	%	1995–2001
Male	19,199	48.9	19,254	48.9	19,384	48.9	19,709	48.9	+2.7
Female	20,024	51.1	20,094	51.1	20,242	51.1	20,556	51.1	+2.7
0–4	1,915	4.9	1,857	4.7	1,837	4.6	1,903	4.7	−0.6
5–14	4,585	11.7	4,295	10.9	4,103	10.4	3,984	9.9	−13.1
15–24	6,459	16.5	6,233	15.8	5,914	14.9	5,563	13.8	−13.9
25–34	6,318	16.1	6,444	16.4	6,592	16.6	6,825	16.9	+8.0
35–44	5,296	13.5	5,521	14.0	5,796	14.6	6,139	15.2	+15.9
45–54	4,513	11.5	4,675	11.9	4,803	12.1	4,957	12.3	+9.8
55–64	4,127	10.5	4,015	10.2	3,986	10.1	4,049	10.1	−1.9
65+	6,011	15.3	6,308	16.0	6,596	16.6	6,846	17.0	+13.9
Total	39,223	100.0	39,348	100.0	39,626	100.0	40,266	100.0	+2.7

Source: INE/Mintel
Figures for 2001 are estimates

total of those in employment grew by 23 per cent. These developments are a reflection of sustained economic growth, strong government fiscal policies and a demographic profile that peaks with those in work within the 25–54 age group, i.e., people with traditionally high earning capacity (see Table 2.2).

Most economic analysts of Spain forecast continued growth in the economy and in personal disposable income. Many consumers will feel confident enough about their financial position and prospects to buy added-value tourism products regularly.

Table 2.3 shows trends in personal disposable income (PDI) and consumer expenditure over the period 1995–2001 and identifies consumer expenditure rising at a faster rate than PDI: 20 per cent as opposed to 18 per cent. This implies greater expenditure on added-value tourism products as the saving ratio is falling. The Spanish economy's recent strong performance provides the ideal background for the tourism industry.

Key issues

Time

One element of lifestyle is the issue of leisure time. Forecasters once imagined that computers would make it possible to cut the working week and give everyone more leisure. Instead, the opposite has happened. Companies have cut employee rosters, often dramatically, leaving more work to be done by fewer people. At the same time, rising costs and stagnant wages have driven former 'stay-at-homes' into the labour force. Entrepreneurs, whose numbers are growing rapidly in the USA and expanding elsewhere, work even longer hours than the rest of the workforce. Time that once would have been spent shopping and taking care of the household is now spent in factories and offices, and leisure is becoming ever more scarce. There is no sign that this trend will slow in the near future. Computers, electronic communications, the Internet, and other technologies are making national and international economies much more competitive. In the USA, workers spend about 10 per cent more time on the job

Table 2.2		Total workforce m	Index	Total in employment m	Index	% of workforce unemployed
Trends in Spanish employment, 1995–2001	1995	15.69	100	12.09	100	22.9
	1996	15.99	102	12.45	103	22.1
	1997	16.18	103	12.82	106	20.8
	1998	16.32	104	13.23	109	18.8
	1999	16.42	105	13.82	114	15.9
	2000	16.84	107	14.47	120	14.1
	2001 (est)	17.07	109	14.89	123	12.8

Source: INE/Mintel
Figures for 2001 are estimates

than they did a decade ago. European executives and other non-unionized workers face the same trend. On average, two-thirds of European women, from age 25 to 59, work outside the home. This sharply reduces the time they have for leisure activities. In this high-pressure environment, single workers and two-income couples are increasingly desperate for any product that offers to simplify their lives or grant them a taste of luxury.

The implication of all this for the TALC is significant. It means that in terms of hotels, brand names associated with high quality come to seem even more desirable, especially far from home. Two-earner households in particular want and can afford the small satisfactions of buying what they perceive to be 'the best'. Multiple, shorter holidays spread throughout the year will continue to replace the traditional two-week holiday. Demand for luxurious 'weekend getaways' will grow rapidly, especially in cultural centres and at destinations near large cities.

Values and lifestyles

It has already been shown that technology brings new opportunities, but it can also exacerbate conflicts with tradition, particularly as it brings news of distant lands. Western ideas infiltrate conservative cultures in Asia and the Middle East, often triggering an 'Islamic fundamentalist' backlash. These and many other pressures are eroding the values and lifestyles of previous generations. In their place, a new, opportunistic, technology-oriented eclecticism is beginning to appear throughout the developed world, among the intellectual and economic

Table 2.3	PDI Ptas bn	Index	Consumer expenditure Ptas bn	Index
1995	49,945	100	43,035	100
1996	50,788	102	43,922	102
1997	51,845	104	45,194	105
1998	53,793	108	47,052	109
1999	55,985	112	49,155	114
2000	58,757	118	51,706	120
2001 (est)	59,166	119	52,007	121
	€bn	Index	€bn	Index
1995	302	100	261	100
1996	311	103	269	103
1997	313	104	273	105
1998	324	107	283	108
1999	336	111	295	113
2000	353	117	311	119
2001 (est)	356	118	313	120

Trends in Spanish personal disposable income (PDI) and consumer expenditure at 1995 prices, 1995–2001

Source: INE/Mintel
Figures for 2001 are estimates

elites of some developing nations, and especially among the under-40 generation. Consumer needs are changing under this pressure. For business and pleasure, international and intercontinental travel is becoming a normal part of life for most affluent workers and their families.

The trend evolving from all this is a move towards ultra-high quality, authenticity, and convenience-luxurious accommodation, fresh meals, and constant pampering of customers, all done at a price that will not make consumers feel guilty. Two-income couples increasingly take several short, relatively luxurious short-break holidays rather than a single longer holiday.

One American trend that may reach Europe is the growing concern with good nutrition. This will raise the demand for resort foods that are low in fats and cholesterol, but with the same sense of luxury offered by traditional cuisines. Consumers are increasingly willing to try new flavours and unfamiliar dishes when dining out. National cuisines are becoming internationalized, as restaurants specializing in foods from other cultures are spreading through Europe and other regions of the world. Most consumers have learned to appreciate a wide variety of cuisines, but have not yet learned to prepare them from scratch. This represents a fast-growing market for prepared foods. Single people are spending more of their food budgets out, rather than buying groceries to cook at home. In the USA, supermarkets are beginning to prepare food for customers to heat and eat at home. Some even are setting aside restaurant-like areas for in-store consumption. This trend will grow rapidly and is expected to affect restaurant patronage in the next decade. It can be expected to migrate quickly to the European market.

Service, service, service

A final key trend, which will influence the evolution of the TALC over the coming years, is the issue of service. Competitive pressures are making it ever more difficult to distinguish one hotel or restaurant from the rest, especially at the global chain level. As soon as one corporation offers a product or service that attracts customers, its competitors match it and try to improve upon it. The result is a generally high standard in basic products and services. Increasingly, what distinguishes one provider from another is attention to detail. This is the battleground on which hotels and restaurants will fight the competitive wars of the new millennium. Most products and services are becoming commodities. Banks offer cheque and savings accounts with much the same terms. Most personal computers are virtually interchangeable. Airlines offer transportation, with few amenities that influence customer choice. Hotels are seen as offering the same basic facilities – a clean place to sleep and freshen up between more important activities. Personal service and attention to detail set the best hotels, restaurants and resorts apart from the rest. Restaurants record customers' preferred tables, drinks and other personal data. Hotels provide 'instant' check-in and meals guaranteed on-time. The best-laid plans require attentive management to implement them.

Unique location or facilities are the major exceptions to 'commoditization' in the hotel industry. The only inn at a major ski resort has no effective competition. The alternative is for hotels to become destinations in themselves, known for luxurious surroundings, fine food, special amenities for repeat visitors, and the best possible service. In the luxury market, customers are increasingly brand-conscious, so building and maintaining a respected name is more important than ever.

The implication for restaurants is that they compete on much the same features: quality, luxury and service. As customers grow more open to new experiences, unique cuisines offer a growing opportunity for restaurants to distinguish themselves from the competition.

Two key market drivers: recession and security

Setting the scene

The performance of the international hotel industry over the past 30 years has remained cyclical, tending to correspond with domestic and international economic cycles, although other world events have had an impact. Equally, the sector cannot be divorced from the wider tourism and travel industry, specifically, in recent years, airline travel. In general, the dynamics of the hotel cycle are such that occupancy recovers first from a recession as hoteliers pursue a volume increase strategy. Once occupancy rises above 70 per cent, capacity constraints allow operators to start increasing rates and therefore yields.

Before the attacks of 11 September 2001, when commercial jetliners were crashed into the World Trade Center and the Pentagon, the US economy was showing signs of an anemic recovery in the manufacturing sector and suggestions of weakness in the consumer sector. Inventories of unsold goods of all categories fell in July 2001 for the sixth consecutive month. All these economic trends have had negative implications for the international hotel industry over the period 2001–3, particularly those hotels in gateway cities heavily dependent on the US and Middle Eastern markets.

Hotels: a historical perspective

The economic forces driving the international hotel industry can be analysed from an historical viewpoint. Starting from the 1980s, and taking London as an example, hotel occupancy recovered between 1982 and 1985, reaching 83 per cent in 1985. The Chernobyl disaster and the raid on Libya had a marked impact on room occupancy in 1986, which declined to 75.6 per cent. While occupancy recovered to 80.6 per cent in 1987, it then declined slowly to 75.7 per cent in 1990, before falling to 66.4 per cent in 1991. This was due to the combined influences of the recession and the Gulf War. Levels rose to above 80 per cent in 1994, suggesting a time lag of 18 months between fluctuations in the economy and growth in hotel occupancy. There is a clear correlation between occupancy and growth in gross domestic product (GDP), despite this time lag. There is also a similar link between international airline passenger arrivals and the hotel sector, specifically within hotels located in the major gateway cities.

The impact of the Gulf War of 1990–1 on the hotel sector may, in the minds of some people, be a relevant comparison to September 2001, but there are some important economic differences that must be taken into account. Inflation in the global economy in 2001 was much lower, giving room for interest rates to respond to the economic implications of the attacks on the USA in a way that they were unable to in the early 1990s because of high inflation. Of course, the US economy has also slowed in 2001–3 as it did in 1990–1, but with much lower rates of unemployment and with the public sector in financial surplus, it is better able to expand spending, for instance through tax cuts, to alleviate the impact of an economic slowdown.

The key issue for hotels, which is difficult to measure, is the impact on consumer confidence of 11 September 2001, compared to the Gulf War effect some ten years ago. Consumer confidence in Britain took a sharp knock as a result of the terrorist attacks in the USA. The feel-good factor switched from positive to negative and substantial numbers feared losing their jobs or the value of their investments. During early August 2001, before the terrorist attacks, the feel-good factor – the proportion of people believing their household's financial situation will improve over the coming 12 months minus the proportion thinking it will deteriorate – stood at plus-four. By October 2001 it stood at minus-eight. The proportion of pessimists increased by half from August 2001; from 21 per cent to 31 per cent in October 2001. Safety fears were, and still are, similarly widespread, even though there are few signs in Britain of American-style panic. Much of this reluctance and unwillingness to travel is probably purely theoretical and will not affect people's actual behaviour, but some portion of it seems likely to have real economic consequences for the hotel sector. An illustration of these issues in the UK hotel industry is portrayed in Figure 2.1.

Figure 2.1   Average hotel occupancy in London and UK regions, 1977–2001

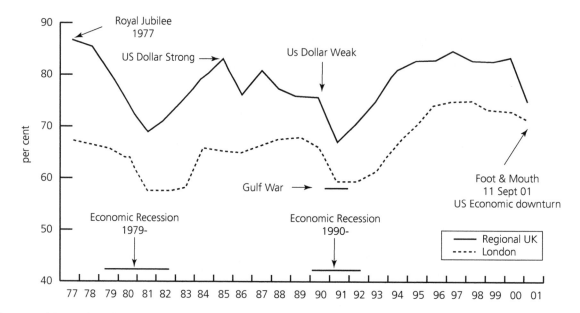

Source: Deloitte and Touche

The world economy: before and after

The shock of 11 September 2001 raised the degree of uncertainty about the short-to medium-term economic future, and resulted, for a time, in a pronounced disengagement from future commitments such as business and leisure travel, hotel investment and expansion. That, in the short run, implied a reduction from the current level of tourism and hotel activity. In the immediate aftermath, the attacks caused significant harm to parts of the economy, notably: airlines, tourism, hotels, and consumer behaviour and, particularly, confidence.

Prior to September 11 the USA was already on the brink of recession; the attack tipped it into recession in the last two quarters of 2001, moving into modest growth during 2002–3.

Because of the close trading relationship between the USA and UK – about 15 per cent of UK exports go to the USA – there was an unavoidable knock-on effect on British manufacturing. This sector had already been in severe difficulty, and an American downturn intensified the pressure. The US Federal Reserve cut interest rates by a half point to 3 per cent just before the US stock markets reopened for the first time after the attacks. The European Central Bank followed hours later with a half point cut to 3.75 per cent. In response to this sharp contraction, the Federal Reserve continued its series of interest rate reductions. Over the months following the attacks interest rates fell.

If the experience of the Iraqi invasion of Kuwait in August 1990 is any guide, consumer confidence and spending plunged. In the four months after the Iraqi attack consumer confidence dropped by 40 per cent. Consumer spending held up a bit longer, but it too hit its low in January 1991. The 1990 Iraqi invasion pushed down stock prices by 15 per cent. But after US tanks started to roll, markets rebounded sharply.

The long-term impact depends on whether the attack is a one-off event or the start of a new period of high uncertainty, which is a likely scenario. The danger is that further terrorist attacks and military retaliation could start a cycle of turmoil, forcing dramatically tightened security and new barriers to travel and trade.

Consequences for tourism

Any discussion of the international hotel industry is best placed within the context of travel and tourism. Mass tourism, although resilient to major world events in the past, is facing its greatest challenge. The events of September 11 have had economic consequences for the tourist industry. It could also lead to a fundamental shift in the way we behave as tourists, whether travelling to the south coast of England or the Far East.

Recent events that have affected tourism habits include the Gulf War in 1991, the terrorist attacks at Luxor in Egypt in 1997, and actions in both Afghanistan and Iraq during the period 2001–3. During the Gulf War, countries in the Middle East and eastern Mediterranean suffered heavy drop-offs in tourist visits. In Cyprus, for example, a popular destination close to the Middle East, numbers fell to 2.94 million in 1991 from 3.38 million in 1990. Mainland Europe also suffered – the number of tourists from the Americas visiting the continent in 1991 was, at 5 million, 23 per cent down on the year before.

While Britons are likely to respond to terrorist attacks with fewer visits to the USA, there could be serious repercussions for Middle Eastern economies, which have increasingly attempted to promote themselves as safe and idyllic destinations. Ironically, these conflicting choices for consumers could result in a boom in European tourism – and while some people fear that it will be a massive blow for UK tourism, others are more optimistic. It may end up being a positive thing for the UK market – as people focus more on travel nearer home.

Economic events in the USA often provide a taster of 'what's coming soon' to the UK. Together the two economies stand and, inevitably, together they fall. If peace is the best friend of travel and tourism, war is the worst enemy, as many global hotspots have shown.

Regardless of whether or not there is a wider conflict, security has already been stepped up world-wide at all points of transport. This will now become a permanent feature, meaning long delays at check-in counters, immigration and baggage inspection. Visas will almost certainly be reintroduced in many countries. Over the last few years, much effort has gone into improving technology specifically in order to move the travelling public more quickly through security checkpoints without compromising safety. That is clearly no longer going to be the case. Israeli-style checks at airports are going to irritate millions of innocent people, leading to the inevitable question: Why bother to travel at all?

This attitude to security could in turn impact on business world-wide. Travel to Islamic and Middle Eastern countries will probably fall off, especially by Americans. This could affect expansion of US hotel chains in many parts of the world. Investment by US travel companies will dry up as they weigh up very carefully where and how they expand. Also there will be major cutbacks in business travel, as well as travel for conventions, conferences and exhibitions.

One key tourism issue, which directly affects the hotel industry, is demand for air travel. European airlines feared the worst as panic after the September 11 attacks on the USA compounded the effects of an economic slowdown. Although US airlines have been affected harder by the attacks, European airlines also face falling passenger numbers, added security costs, falls in their share prices and increased insurance premiums. The economic slowdown left airlines suffering from excess capacity as passenger numbers, especially lucrative business travellers, fell. In particular, the US downturn has affected major airlines, such as British Airways, which generate much of their business and profits from the transatlantic route.

US and major European airlines that fly the transatlantic route all suffered losses of revenue from the four-day ban on flights to and from America immediately after 11 September. Looking forward, many leisure travellers will be more inclined to stay home or avoid taking long-haul flights, which will add to problems of over-capacity. The crisis also led to a significant fall in airline shares, halving the value of some companies in the USA, while others have gone into bankruptcy. In addition, the attacks led to an increase in insurance premiums paid by carriers. All airlines will also have to bear the added costs of extra security measures (see Table 2.4).

Prior to September 11 the airline industry was already suffering from a cyclical downturn. Airlines had been losing money in the previous few months and it now seems probable that these losses will increase dramatically. The financial pressures before the attacks, because of a slump in demand due to the economic downturn and high jet fuel prices, were only exacerbated by the September crisis.

US hotel comparisons with 1990–1

The pullback in travel in the first quarter of 1991, during the Gulf War, and the last quarter of the 1990–1 recession caused hotel demand to contract by 3.7 per cent compared to a year earlier. The resulting 6.1 per cent decline in occupancy combined with a 0.1 per cent decline in average daily rate (ADR) for the worst-ever quarterly revenue per available room (revPAR) performance prior to 2001. The first quarter of 1991 affected the total year 1991 revPAR, resulting in an annual decline of 2.4 per cent. That experience indicates that hotel demand took a full year to recover after the Gulf War. However, when the Gulf War broke out, the industry was already operating at a loss, and the loss was less in 1991 than it was the year before because the industry was already restructuring. Debt for all hotels, which includes public companies with lower leverage than others, was

---

Table 2.4

Crisis in the airline industry, September 2001

- American Airlines owner AMR Corporation, cut 20,000 jobs, shared between American and a number of smaller subsidiaries.
- United American Airlines cut 20,000 jobs.
- US Airways cut 11,000 jobs and slashed its schedule by 23 per cent.
- Continental cut 12,000 staff, reduced its schedule by 20 per cent and postponed the flotation of its ExpressJet unit.
- United Airlines, Delta, Air Canada, American Airlines and American Air Trans all cut schedules by 20 per cent.
- Northwest said they would announce cutbacks.
- Midwest Airways said it would abandon financial restructuring and proceed with bankruptcy immediately.
- British transatlantic carrier Virgin Atlantic shed 1,200 jobs.
- Dutch KLM and Spain's Iberia both warned the attacks could lead them to report losses.
- German Lufthansa cut three of its transatlantic routes and said it was freezing hiring.
- Belgium's Sabena predicted that it would not last beyond the end of the year so it restructured.
- Scandinavia's SAS said it would cut capacity in relation to the US crisis.
- Irish airline Aer Lingus announced that it was to cut its operations by 25 per cent and would let go more than 600 temporary staff.
- Air France said it was freezing hiring and retiring 17 planes from service.
- Swissair said the freezing of air travel in September 2001 cost it 65m Swiss francs ($41m, £28m). It expects its transatlantic passenger numbers to fall 10–15 per cent.

Source: Travel and Tourism Analyst, No 6, 2001

about 4 per cent of revenues in 2001 compared with 14.2 per cent in 1990 and 12.1 per cent in 1991.

US hotels: short-term effects 2002

US hotel revenues plunged 20 per cent on the day of the air attacks and continued in a downward spiral that saw business off by a full third by the weekend. Before the attacks, revPAR, the industry benchmark, was off by about 5.6 per cent compared with the same time in 2000, according to Smith Travel Research.

After the attacks, the number moved steadily downwards to 13.2 per cent on Tuesday, 24.1 per cent on Wednesday and 27.1 per cent on Thursday, according to Smith Travel Research, which provided the first day-to-day look at how badly business had deteriorated for one of the industries hardest hit by the disaster. By Friday revPAR was off by 28.1 per cent, and the week ended with the figure off by 33.2 per cent.

The business plunge was worst among the most expensive hotels, which were already being affected as the business travellers who formed a large part of their customer base traded down to cheaper brands in a cost-cutting move amid the economic slowdown.

Luxury chains' revenues were down a staggering 57.1 per cent by Saturday and 33.5 per cent for the week. Revenues for upscale chains, the next category down, were off by 33.9 per cent on Saturday and 19.5 per cent for the week. Even economy chains, which were holding up the best before the attacks, were hit, with business down 17.2 per cent on Saturday and off by 11.9 per cent for the week.

Despite the variation, shares for hotels across the spectrum were all down sharply.

Shares in Accor, the French hotels group, fell 7 per cent after it attempted to quantify the 'psychological impact' of the events of September 11. The company, which derives one-third of its hotel operating profits from the USA, lost nearly 30 per cent of its market value during the period September–December 2001. Accor said that 2001 pre-tax profits would be €700–50 million (US$644–90 million), instead of the €825 million expected, and that earnings per share would be €2.30 rather than €2.60. This implied little or no growth over 2000, against the 15 per cent anticipated. Amid the sometimes wild warnings during late 2001, Accor deserves credit for attempting a sober assessment of how it was affected by the terrorist attacks. It forecasted a strong immediate psychological effect, with consumers avoiding foreign travel. Accor's estimate of a 20 per cent sales fall over 100 days in its travel agencies and upmarket Sofitel business – 60 per cent of whose customers are international travellers – was reasonable. Those businesses account for 10 per cent of earnings before interest, tax, depreciation, amortization and rents. The other 90 per cent divides evenly between businesses, such as US economy hotels, where Accor saw sales falling 3–10 per cent, and those such as European economy hotels, with sales down less than 3 per cent. But, with Accor's high operational gearing, even relatively limited sales falls hit profits hard. Up to September 2001 Accor was maintaining its target of a 10 per cent full-year profits increase, but after September it recorded weak growth. This implied fourth-quarter profits down about 20 per cent. An illustration of these overall effects on the hotel industry is illustrated in Figure 2.2.

| **Figure 2.2** | Are Europe and the USA tracking each other? Monthly revPAR % change, 2001–2 |

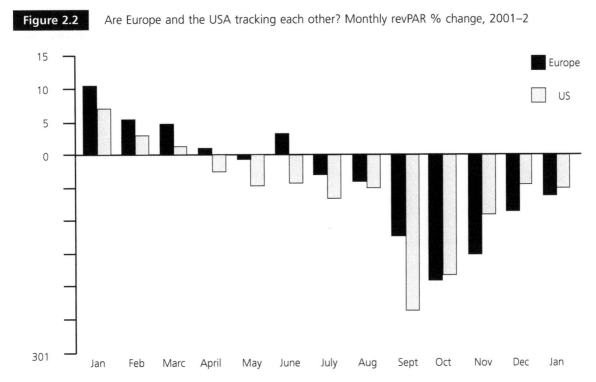

Source: Deloitte and Touche

Further reading

Cravens, D. (2000) *Strategic marketing*, 6th edn, London: Irwin/McGraw-Hill.

Deloitte and Touche www.hotelbenchmark.com accessed December 2001.

Drucker, P. (1985) *Innovation and Entrepreneurship: Practice and Principles*, London, Penguin.

Dunn, K. and Brooks, D. (1990) 'Profit analysis: beyond yield management', *Cornell HRA Quarterly*, 31, 3.

Gabor, A. (1988) *Pricing, Concepts and Methods for Effective Marketing*, 2nd edn, London, Gower Publishing Company.

INE/Mintel www.ine.es

Knowles, T. (1999) 'Strategic marketing in the hospitality sector', in F. Vellas and L. Becherel (eds) *The International Marketing of Travel and Tourism: A Strategic Approach*, London, Macmillan Press Ltd, 119–212.

Kotler P., Armstrong G., Saunders J. and Wong V. (1996) *Principles of Marketing*, Englewood Cliffs, NJ: Prentice-Hall.

Lambert, C. and Lambert, J. (1988) 'Simple reservation policies can be harmful to profit margins', *International Journal of Hospitality Management*, 7, 3.

Lovelock, H. (1984) 'Strategies for managing demand in capacity-constrained services organization', *Service Industry Journal*, 4, 3.

Luciani, P. (1999) 'Implementing yield management in small and medium-sized hotels: an investigation of obstacles and success factors in Florence', *International Journal of Hospitality Management*. 18.

McDonald, M. and Dunbar, I. (1998) *Market Segmentation: How to Do It; How to Profit from It*, 2nd edn, London, Macmillan.

Porter, M. (1985) *Competitive Advantage, Creating and Sustaining Superior Performance*, New York: The Free Press.

Reich, A. (1997) Marketing Management for the Hospitality Industry: A Strategic Approach', New York: John Wiley and Sons, Inc.

Schnaars, S. (1998) *Marketing Strategy: Customer and Competition*, 2nd edn, New York: The Free Press.

Smith Travel Research www.hotelbenchmark.com accessed dec 2001.

Wind, Y.J. (1982) *Product Policy: Concepts, Methods and Strategy*, Reading, MA: Addison-Wesley.

3 The influences of marketing on travel, tourism and hospitality

The market concept

The topic of marketing has been defined in various ways; however, the Institute of Marketing offers the following definition: 'Marketing is the management process responsible for identifying, anticipating and satisfying customer requirements profitably.'(Becherel and Vellers, 1999)

The marketing concept is a fairly new business philosophy that arose to challenge the previous concepts and was fully crystallized in the mid-1950s. It was a new idea in business that replaced a production-oriented way of thinking and can be described as: 'A philosophy of business which states that the customer's want and need for satisfaction is the economic and social justification of a company's existence.'

It is the marketing concept that proposes the best way to achieve organizational objectives and consists of determining the needs and wants of target markets and delivering products and services to satisfy those needs and wants more effectively and efficiently than competitors.

Market focus

No tourism or hospitality company can operate in every market and satisfy every need, nor can it even do a good job within one broad market. It is, in this respect, important to point out that such a firm must classify and target the markets it wishes to serve. Companies do best when they define their target markets and prepare a tailored marketing programme for each of them.

It is important that a tourism firm defines customer needs from the customer point of view, not from its own management perspective. Being customer-oriented, a company will not only retain its customers but it will also attract new customers. This market focus on customer satisfaction is the best indicator of the company's future profits. Thus it may be vital for a customer-oriented hotel or tourism company to regularly measure its customer satisfaction levels for each period and set, if necessary, improvement objectives.

Co-ordination is also important in marketing and means two things. First, it requires the various marketing functions, such as the sales force, advertising, product management, marketing research, and so on, to be well co-ordinated among themselves. These marketing functions also need to be co-ordinated from the customer point of view. Second, marketing needs to be well co-ordinated with the other departments within the firm. Marketing only works when all employees appreciate the effect they have on customer satisfaction. Therefore, a company managed under the marketing concept is required to organize, co-ordinate and control its entire operation as one system directed towards achieving a single set of objectives applicable to the operation. For this reason, the marketing concept requires the firm to carry out internal marketing as well as external marketing. Internal marketing involves applying the philosophies and practices of marketing to people who serve the external customers so that the best people can be employed and retained, and they will do the best possible work.

It is widely appreciated that the purpose of the marketing concept is to help organizations achieve their objectives, which are not only to satisfy customer needs but also to make profits. Hence, to achieve their objectives, they seek a profitable way to satisfy the target market's needs and wants. From an external perspective companies can make profits by satisfying customer needs better than competitors can. Therefore, companies are highly involved in analysing the profit potential of different marketing opportunities.

The process of market planning

The success of marketing planning is dependent to a large part on the strength of a competitive analysis, whatever the state of competition. The needs of such strategy and planning in relation to competition requires that, first, market share must be increased or maintained to improve profitability. Second, the competitor's products are launched head-on against existing products. Furthermore, the competition has advantages due to environmental considerations, such as new technology, government regulation, customer attitudes, etc. Finally, new opportunities develop when competition becomes vulnerable, e.g., in product shortages.

Strategic marketing planning can be seen as an advantageous tool, which provides a systematic framework guiding all the elements of an organization to the achievement of agreed objectives. Marketing, as one of the generational functions, plays a crucial role in the company's strategic planning by focusing exclusively on the formulation of the product.

Tourism or hotel marketing planning leads to the setting of long-term marketing objectives, which are consistent with the company's overall objectives, and the formulation of strategies and specific plans for achieving them. A strategic marketing plan represents the guidelines within which the short-term, detailed tactical or operational marketing plans must be developed concerning specific campaigns for target markets.

The precise steps in the process of strategic marketing planning are problematic due to various approaches by different writers. However, it is possible to envisage the marketing planning process as a staged sequence involving analysing marketing opportunities, researching and selecting target markets, designing marketing strategies, planning marketing programmes, and organizing, implementing and controlling marketing effects.

Hotel marketing strategies can be seen as broad issues that are central to the utilization of marketing planning. While a hotel marketing strategy can be defined as a basic statement about the desired impact to be achieved on demand in a given target market, the stress in the planning process is on the selection of target markets and the development of marketing resources so that marketing objectives are achieved.

The following principles can be suggested for consideration: the company profile, the prime prospects, the competitors and company objectives. The detailed approaches for implementing these strategies are determined through specific marketing programmes, such as advertising, sales promotion programmes, product development programmes, and sales and distribution programmes. It is evident that a strategy isolated from the competitive environment would be ineffective and unrealistic. Therefore, it requires marketers to be able to use competitive strategy effectively in order to achieve their goals.

One problem in drawing up a framework for marketing strategy is that some authors claim that the marketing of services is different from the marketing of goods while others disagree. Despite confusion over the approaches in services marketing, most of the themes may be related to the characteristics of the service industry, and by implication, tourism or hotel marketing.

The characteristics of services present both challenges and opportunities to tourism. To deal with these service characteristics, it is suggested that the right marketing mix should be developed and that objectives represent the ends that management seek in implementing a marketing programme. Therefore, marketing strategy can be seen as the composite of many decisions made in the programme's design. To some extent, a firm's marketing strategy may be described as a combination of two basic elements, namely:

- target marketing;
- the marketing mix.

Target marketing

The concept of target marketing is a refinement of the basic philosophy of marketing. It is an attempt by companies to relate the characteristics or attributes of the business that most closely matches the customer requirements. It may be the case that the total market is too large and consists of too many potential customers for the company to be able to deal with. The overall market may be geographically dispersed and the tourism company may lack the resources to serve it properly. It can often be seen that the overall market for a particular product or service is too heterogeneous, in terms of the purchasing requirements of individuals or organizations making up the market, for any one company to serve adequately.

By targeting specific groups of consumers or *market segments* instead of attempting to serve the demand requirements of an entire population for a particular product category, the hotel, for instance, is able to develop more effective programmes and gain a competitive advantage by developing a more satisfying marketing mix which should also be more profitable for the company.

Market segmentation is considered the first essential step in overall target marketing and is the act of dividing a market into distinct groups of buyers who might require separate product and marketing mixes. Market segmentation can be defined as: 'Pursuing a marketing strategy whereby the total potential market is divided into homogeneous subsets of customers, each of which responds differently to the marketing-mix of the organisation.'(Becherel and Vellers, 1999)

Marketing segmentation is used to identify those market segments that are likely to be heavy users of the product. At the same time, segments that hold little potential receive minimal or no attention, and scarce marketing resources are not wasted chasing after market segments with little sales potential. Therefore, after the segments have been identified, the company can design a marketing mix to meet the needs of consumers in the segments, that are attractive to the company. This can actually improve sales and profits as it allows the firm to target specific market segments that are much more likely to patronize the organization's facilities.

Traditionally, marketers have preferred to use demographic and geographic data for segmentation because it is easier to define and measure. However, nowadays, there is an increasing use of psychosocial criteria, such as social class, lifestyle and culture, for segmentation; these will be discussed later in this chapter.

Following on from this discussion, the related subject of product positioning can be seen as the act of designing the company's product and marketing mix to fit a given place in the consumer's mind. Product positioning can be defined as: 'A marketing strategy that chooses a package of benefits that is attractive to customers in the target market and distinguishes the product or company from its competitors.'(Becherel and Villers, 1999) Using marketing research, the tourism or hospitality firm should establish the position of competitors' products in any given market segment and then decide whether to offer a product very close to a competitor's offering or to attempt to fill a gap in the market. Once the firm has established its product positioning strategy it is then in a position to go on to plan the details of its marketing mix.

The marketing mix

As has already been discussed in Chapter 1, the nature of the service industry is different from that of the manufacturing industry. Therefore, while the traditional marketing mix of the four Ps of product, price, promotion and place, have been criticized as inappropriate in a service industry like tourism or hotels, others have proposed a modified framework – i.e. the seven Ps, with the addition of people, physical evidence and process.

In this sense, external marketing can be described as the normal work done by the company to prepare prices, distribute and promote the service of the firm. Internal marketing can be described as the work done by the company to train and motivate its internal customers, its customer contact employees and supporting service personnel, to work as a team in order to provide customer satisfaction. Interactive marketing can be described as the employees' skill in handling customer contact. The following four points comment on the traditionally viewed elements of the marketing mix as applied to hotels.

- *Product* is the most fundamental mix to satisfy the customer's needs, and in the hotel industry it includes both goods and services. The hotel product is judged on the basis of 'performance' rather than the tangible goods themselves. The manner and expertise factors, as well as the quality of the goods or services, are essential, but other experiential factors will enter into a guest's evaluation. The other guests are part of the service experience, as is every other factor that enters into the guest experience. Therefore, the 'total experience' during the stay at the hotel rather than just the room and its facilities and services is what the guest buys and remembers. Others have suggested that the product offered by the hotel comprises physical products such as food, beverages and accommodation services as well as 'emotional satisfaction'. 'Emotional satisfaction' has also been classified in two ways. First, there is the image – that is to say, the way in which the hotel represents itself. Second, there is atmosphere, which is to do with what people expect to take place in the hotel and what they think of these expectations. Neither image nor atmosphere can be separated from the physical aspects of the product or service, and changes in the physical or service environment will also lead to changes in the emotional environment.

- *Price* is regarded as a flexible and important variable in the marketing mix and can also be considered from a financial perspective. Too often hotel managers consider price from a financial perspective and ignore the marketing implications. Price is a powerful tool in increasing sales because it can be rapidly and frequently adjusted to bring supply and demand into balance at a relatively low cost, whereas other elements of the mix cannot be moved or easily changed. Price considerations include levels of prices, discounts, allowances and commissions, terms of payment and credit. Price may also have a different level of significance from one service to another and, therefore, the customer's perceptions of value obtained from a service and the interaction of purchase *vis-à-vis* quality are important considerations in many price mixes. In the hotel industry, perishability of services has a great impact on pricing considerations. The fluctuations in demand make it important to use the price mechanism to optimize and flatten out demand. Short-term price tactics, such as discount pricing, differential pricing and promotional pricing, are used to adjust to various market situations, where necessary. Pricing can also be strategic in marketing because business objectives such as profitability, sales volume, growth and elimination of rivals can be pursued. In a hotel marketing context, demand-oriented pricing based on the price sensitivities of customers and intensity of demand should generally be used. However, due to the rising cost and growing competition, more and more companies will use cost-base pricing and competitive pricing.

- *Place* or location of the service provider and their accessibility are important factors in services marketing. Accessibility relates not just to physical accessibility but to other means of communication and contact. Thus the types of distribution channels used and their coverage are linked to the crucial issue of service accessibility. For hotel marketers, location can be the strongest selling point if it is favourable. In contrast, price can be the main constraint as location cannot be moved to reach customers and may result in loss of business. Therefore, distribution channels play an important role in the delivery of services speedily and efficiently to the customers.

- *Promotion* is essential in order to communicate with targeted customers for effective selling through personal selling, advertising, sales promotion, packaging, merchandising and public relations. For long-term effect, advertising, personal selling, and packaging can be used while sales promotion generates a short-term effect. In strategic hotel marketing, promotion helps to smooth variations in customer demand, and to counter seasonality patterns as well as competitor pressures. Owing to the high degree of similarity among hotels, communication with target customers is essential. Personal selling is a two-way process while the remainders are one-way communications, going only from the marketer to the customer. This approach is believed to be the most powerful tool in a high customer contact industry because face-to-face communication can enhance deep personal relationships with customers and generate a quicker response. Personal selling generally refers to sales calls made by a company representative on prospects or existing customers. In the hotel industry, personal selling also includes the work of personnel who provide services such as waiters or waitresses or desk clerks in persuading guests to increase their level of expenditure. Advertising is on the increase as competition between hotels intensifies. Some advertising is aimed at building a company's image (generic advertising) while other advertisements are promotional and seek immediate patronage. Public relations uses newsworthy events related to an operation to gain news coverage. It includes speeches, charitable donations, and special events, which create publicity. Events are usually presented in a way that is of interest to readers. As a short-term marketing tactic, sales promotion is very useful to iron out the seasonality of demand. It is often supported by promotional advertising, offering an incentive for customers to induce purchase. It includes premiums, coupons and special packages. In facing rising sales, labour and media costs, it is obviously desirable that the expense should be kept down. Joint promotion may help to cut the cost. Hotels can get other organizations, such as tourist boards, a shopping centre or theme park, to contribute to their marketing effort, thus sharing the risk and cost as well as assisting in the implementation of the campaign.

Consumer behaviour: an introduction

The study of consumer behaviour is a complex topic, especially in the tourism sector, whereby the desire to buy of a consumer is of emotional importance. For instance, the purchase of a holiday will normally cost a considerable amount of money but will grant the purchaser an exciting and relaxing activity, away from everyday stresses and problems. Swarbrooke and Horner (1999: 6) define consumer behaviour in tourism as 'the study of why people buy the product they do, and how they make the decision'. Furthermore, the consumer can be viewed as a 'problem solver' with marketing managers defining a consumer as 'a decision making unit, individual, family, household or firm, that takes in information; processes that information, consciously and unconsciously, in light of the existing situation, and takes action to achieve satisfaction and enhance their lifestyle' (Hawkins *et al.*, 1992: 14). This chapter will explore the theory on consumer behaviour as used in the business sector and in particular service marketing. The analysis will proceed to focus on the tourism sector issues so as to adequately establish the ground for further analysis of the TALC in subsequent chapters of this book.

Overview of consumer behaviour

Consumers are affected in their decision-making by numerous internal and external motivators and determinants when they decide on products. This means that it is very difficult to separate out how these many motivators and determinants affect the individual when he or she is making the actual choice. The majority of problems and the following decisions revolve around contentment based on limited information processing. Equally, emotions and feelings play an important part in consumer behaviour together with the decision process. One definition by Engel *et al.* (1995) describes the procedure by which a customer decides to buy or use a product or service, and stresses the significance of the psychological process that the buyer runs through during the pre-purchase and post-purchase levels approach. These writers believe that consumer behaviour 'is those activities directly involved in obtaining, consuming and disposing of products and services including the decision processes that precede and follow these actions' (Engel *et al.*, quoted in Swarbrooke *et al.*, 1999: 46). Additionally, consumers may be influenced in disparate ways, according to the kind of product or service that they are acquiring. The overall feeling of buying a cruise holiday, for example, will differ from the feeling of buying an everyday article in the supermarket. Such a holiday purchase ordinarily takes much more time and includes more cautious deliberation and choice, particularly as the purchase of a cruise holiday generally entails a substantial amount of money.

A further complication with the discipline of consumer behaviour is that while numerous broad models of consumer behaviour have been advanced, there has been little empirical research undertaken in order to test these models against actual behavioural patterns. As Swarbrooke *et al.* (1999: 3) note: 'this is especially true in the tourism sector where research on consumer behaviour is very much in the early stages of development'. Nonetheless, some models of consumer behaviour will be later presented as a theoretical foundation for this analysis of the tourism and hospitality sectors.

Consumer behaviour: a successful marketing tool

This topic of consumer behaviour should be regarded as the lynchpin to supporting all marketing activity conducted in order to develop, promote and sell tourism and hospitality products. This view is supported and developed by Kotler *et al.* (1996: 12) who define marketing as 'a social and managerial process by which individuals and groups obtain what they need and want through creating and exchanging products and value with others'. Furthermore, Drucker (1973) (quoted in Kotler *et al.*, 1996: 1) observes that marketing is so basic that it cannot be examined as an independent function. He expands this view by noting that it is the entire business seen from the aspect of its ultimate outcome, the customer's point of view; success is not determined by the generator but by the end user.

In order to maximize both the effectiveness and efficiency of marketing activities, it is important to comprehend how consumers make their decisions to buy or consume tourism and hospitality products. Today's successful companies at all levels are heavily customer-centred and strongly committed to the marketing process. More specifically, the hospitality and travel industries have as an ultimate goal not only to create consumer value and satisfaction but also to retain those satisfied and profitable customers through their marketing activities. Additionally, the main focus is to provide a high level of perceived quality that begins with consumer needs and wants and ends with customer satisfaction.

On another matter, the duty of marketing is in no way to mislead the customer or endanger the company's image; it is to produce a product–service combination that renders real value to targeted buyers, motivates buying, and satisfies genuine consumer needs and wants. By understanding consumers' behavioural patterns one recognizes when it is necessary to intervene in the process so as to achieve the desired short- and long-term profitable results and who to target at a specific time with a specific tourism or hospitality product. In addition, by monitoring consumer behaviour, a company selling such products and services knows how to convince consumers to choose goods specially designed to meet their unique needs and wants. As Solomon and George (1977) (1977) (quoted in Swarbrooke and Horner, 1999: 6) notes: 'Consumer behaviour is the process involved when individuals or groups select, purchase, use, or dispose of products, services, ideas or experiences to satisfy needs and wants'. In short, a thorough investigation and comprehension of consumer behaviour will ultimately contribute to the success of the marketing activity undertaken by tourism and hospitality enterprises, proving beneficial to both companies and consumers. Finally, it should be mentioned that any marketing mix of a company must include: product; price; distribution; advertising; research. The information systems and planning process must be carefully and strategically designed for each targeted group and must always aim at the ultimate satisfaction of the existing and prospective customers' needs and wants.

A model of consumer behaviour

The basic notion regarding consumer behaviour can be summarized under five points:

- Consumer behaviour is purposeful and goal-directed: what appears like irrational behaviour to a manager is entirely reasonable to the customer.
- The customer has free choice: consumers are not obliged to observe marketing communications; messages are processed judiciously and in most events the consumer has various products or services from which to choose.
- Consumer behaviour is a process that requires to be understood by marketers.

- Consumer behaviour can be affected: by thinking about the buying decision process and the effects on this process, marketers can control how consumers behave.
- There is a need for consumer study: consumers may act against their selves because of a lack of knowledge and marketers have a social responsibility to educate consumers (Chambers *et al.*, in Kotler *et al.*, 1996).

In developing these five points, there is a connection between marketing stimuli and consumer response, and thus a model of buying behaviour can be proposed, as shown in Table 3.1.

The first column in Table 3.1 shows the marketing stimuli known traditionally as the four Ps (product, price, place, promotion) and the second column shows other stimuli including economic, technological, political and cultural events (sometimes referred to as the general environment), that exist in the buyer's surroundings. Both of these categories of stimuli go into the consumer's 'black box' and are converted into buyer's responses, shown in the final column of the table. What is of importance is that marketers comprehend how the stimuli are changed into responses inside the consumer's black box; the latter is made of both the buyer's characteristics, which influence how one understands and reacts to the stimuli, and the buyer's decision process, which affects the outcomes, namely purchase.

Furthermore, examination of consumer behaviour requires a consideration of internal and external processes affecting the traveller. Figure 3.1 shows the perplexing connection of various elements, ranging from arousal to decision and from purchase to post-purchase encounter, that are involved in consumer behaviour.

Personal characteristics affecting consumer behaviour

It has already been mentioned that managers need to understand consumer lifestyles and the issues that influence them. Two kinds of issues can be identified that have an effect on consumer lifestyle: external and internal influences (Hawkins *et al.* 1992 as cited by Swarbrooke and Horner (1999)).

External influences on marketing activities include: culture; values; demographics; social status; reference groups; households; whereas the internal influences are those of: personality; emotions; motives; perception; attitudes;

Table 3.1	Marketing stimuli responses	Other stimuli	Buyer's black box	Buyer's
The model of buying behaviour	Product	Economic	Buyer characteristics	Product choice
	Price	Technological $\Rightarrow$	& $\Rightarrow$	Brand choice
	Place	Political	Buyer decision	Dealer choice
	Promotion	Cultural	process	Purchase timing
				Purchase amount

Source: Kotler *et al.*, 1999: 180.

learning; memory. It is the processing of information that links these influences to consumers and enables them to determine their desired lifestyle. To further analyse these matters, a breakdown of the factors that influence behaviour, factors suggested by Kotler *et al.* (1996: 181) are as follows:

- *Cultural*: culture, subculture and social class;
- *Social*: groups, family, roles and status;
- *Personal*: age and life cycle stage, occupation, economic circumstances, lifestyle, personality and self-concept;
- *Psychological*: motivation, perception, learning, beliefs and attitudes.

For the purpose of this chapter, greater emphasis will be given to the personal and psychological factors, although each of these four categories will now be considered.

Cultural factors

Culture is a composite term that includes knowledge, beliefs, art, law, morals, customs and any other capabilities. The term refers to the habits acquired by an

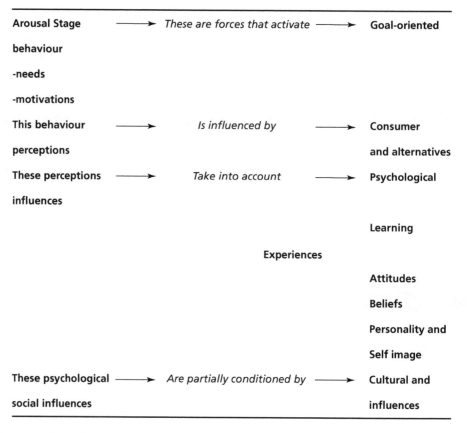

Figure 3.1

Interaction of elements in the psychological field of the consumer that influence behaviour

Arousal Stage	→	These are forces that activate	→	Goal-oriented
behaviour				
-needs				
-motivations				
This behaviour	→	Is influenced by	→	Consumer
perceptions				and alternatives
These perceptions	→	Take into account	→	Psychological
influences				
				Learning
		Experiences		
				Attitudes
				Beliefs
				Personality and
				Self image
These psychological	→	Are partially conditioned by	→	Cultural and
social influences				influences

Source: Kotler *et al.* (1996)

individual as a member of society and is the most fundamental determinant of a person's wants and behaviour. Furthermore, it includes the following four aspects:

- Culture is a comprehensive concept: it embodies almost everything that affects an individual's thought processes and behaviour. While culture does not establish the nature or frequency of biological drives, such as hunger or sex, it does influence if, when, and how these drives will be satisfied.
- Culture is acquired: it does not involve inherited responses and predispositions. Nonetheless, since most human behaviour is acquired rather than innate, culture does influence a wide array of behaviours.
- The complexity of prevalent societies is such that culture rarely provides explicit prescriptions for appropriate behaviour. Instead, in most industrial societies, culture provides boundaries within which most human beings think and act.
- The character of cultural influences is such that one is scarcely aware of them. One behaves, thinks and feels in a manner harmonious with other members of the same culture because it seems 'natural' or 'right' to do so.

A model of investigating the broad factor of culture is called cross-cultural analysis, and includes a systematic comparison of similarities and differences in both the tangible and behavioural aspects of culture. These analyses may be statistical, when dealing with factors explicating the structure of the culture, or functional, when dealing with factors stating behaviours and activities in diversified cultures. Furthermore, marketers are continually seeking to recognize cultural shifts in societies so as to invent new products and services that might find a receptive market. It should be mentioned that failure to comprehend cultural variances in customs from one country to another, can bring disaster for a company's international products and programmes; marketers must decide on the degree to which they will accustom their products and marketing programs to satisfy the unique needs of buyers in different markets. The question on whether to adapt or standardize the marketing mix across international markets has given birth to a constantly shifting debate.

In addition, *social classes* are the relatively permanent and ordered divisions in a society whose members share similar values, interests and behaviours and, hence, have a clear link with cultural issues.

Social factors

When planning, management must take into consideration the consumers' *reference groups, family, social roles* and *status*. Since people turn to specific groups for their basis of judgement, those reference groups exercise a key influence on one's beliefs, attitudes and choices. Furthermore, people tend to be influenced by other kinds of groups such as those aspirational, peer group, indirect, disclaimant and avoidance categories (Moutinho, 1987: 6). In expanding these points, family, opinion leaders and an individual's position in each group (family, club or organization) will influence the individual when making a decision to purchase a tourism or hospitality product.

Turning to the tourist, the individual's buying decision is expressed in a unique way: 'the vacation tourist will invest with no expectation of material and economic return on his or her purchase of an intangible satisfaction' (Moutinho, 1987: 3). Tourists are becoming more mature in their vacationing behaviour, so research must be ready to explain tourist behaviour and what influences it. This leads us to the view that in order to adopt adequate actions in the field of tourism marketing, management must comprehend:

- How people understand such concepts as destination regions, air travel, travel distances and travel advertising.
- How individuals consume and travel.
- How people take decisions to travel.
- How their personal characteristics and psychology affect those decisions.
- What motivations have an effect on one's travel decision.
- How attitudes are shaped.
- How numerous groups influence one's travel behaviour.

More specifically, travel decisions are influenced by drives outside the individual, incorporating the influences of other individuals. Those forces are called social influences, and include role and family issues, reference groups, social classes as well as culture and subculture. Figure 3.2 summarizes these social influences.

Personal factors

The decisions of consumers are also influenced by personal characteristics, such as *age*, in such a way that the kinds of goods and services people buy alters during one's life. Age has been found to affect the consumption of products and services and it influences the media individuals use; where they shop, how they use products and services, and how they think and feel about marketing activities, at different time periods. These age-related factors can be neglected by marketers, possibly due to the fact that there are vast differences in age

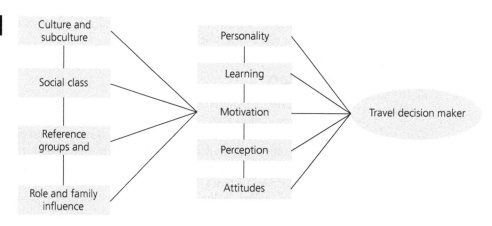

Figure 3.2

Major influences on individual travel behaviour

Culture and subculture

Social class

Reference groups and

Role and family influence

Personality

Learning

Motivation

Perception

Attitudes

Travel decision maker

Source: Moutinho (1985: 4)

between those who make the marketing strategies and those who actually buy the final product and/or service. For successful marketing in different age segments, distinct and targeted strategies are required, which will nearly always need segmented target publications, database marketing and a staff of varying ages and cultural backgrounds.

Furthermore, purchasing behaviour is also formed by the *family life cycle* as well as by the financial position and product interests of each group. In order for management to analyse their target group they must elaborate on its household consumption behaviour. For instance, the household life cycle (HLC) applies to both family and non-family households. It assumes that these entities act as individuals do, and move through a series of relatively distinct well-defined stages, with the passage of time. Each stage in the HLC poses a series of problems which household decision-makers must solve. The solution to these problems is bound intimately to the selection and maintenance of a lifestyle and, thus, to product consumption. Every single stage presents unique needs and wants as well as financial conditions and experiences. Thus, the HLC provides marketers with relatively homogeneous household-related problems and purchases. Also, marketers often label their target markets in life cycle terms and form applicable products and marketing plans. Table 3.2 shows the family life cycle stages as adapted and presented by Kotler (1994: 181).

Moreover, it is important to note that different *household life cycles* have different buying behaviours, as noted by Hawkins *et al.* (1992), as cited by Swarbrooke and Horner (1999). To illustrate, the young single, who are characterized by age (under 35) and by marital status (single), can be subdivided into those who live with their family and those who are independent. Each one of them has different patterns of behaviour relating to products and services according to their needs. Also, the middle-aged single are characterized by their age (35–45) and their marital status (single) and they normally have no worries about their financial and occupational situation, and the fact that they do not have any children to rear allows them a higher discretionary income. In addition, the young married is another stage of the HLC where the lifestyles of two young singles are generally altered as they develop a joint lifestyle. Joint decisions and shared roles in household responsibilities are in many instances a new experience. Also, within the full-nesters I category the addition of a child to the young married family creates different needs – of the children as well as the parents – in lifestyle. Finally, the full-nesters II group are couples that usually face bigger financial burdens due to their teenage children's higher needs.

Household decision-making involves consideration of some very important and complex questions. Who buys, who decides and who uses are only a few of the questions that marketers must ask when dealing with products purchased and used by and for households. They should analyse the household decision process separately for each product category within each target market. Household members' involvement in the decision process varies by involvement with the specific product as well as by stage in the decision process. Role specialization within the family also influences which household members are most likely to be directly involved in a purchase decision.

To analyse further, one's occupation also influences one's consumption pattern. Occupation is associated with education and income, although the association is not as strong as it once was. The kind of work one does and the different kinds of people the individual works with directly influence a preferred lifestyle and all aspects of the consumption process. Marketers are continually seeking to distinguish the occupational groups that hold above-average interest in their products and services, and a company can even specialize their products for specific occupational groups. Also, an individual's *economic condition* has an effect both on the selection of the product and on the decision to acquire a specific product. Kotler and Armstrong (1994) comment that an

Table 3.2	State in family life cycle	Buying or behavioural pattern
An overview of the family life cycle and buying behaviour	1. Bachelor stage: young, single people not living at home	Few financial burdens. Fashion opinion leaders. Recreation oriented. Buy: vacations, basic kitchen equipment, basic furniture, cars, equipment for the mating game.
	2. Newly married couples: young, no children	Better off financially that they will be in the near future. Highest purchase rate and highest average purchase of durables. Buy: vacations, cars, refrigerators, stoves, sensible and durable furniture.
	3. Full nest I: youngest child under six	Home purchasing at peak. Liquid assets low. Dissatisfied with financial position and amount of money saved. Interested in new products. Like advertised products. Buy: washers, dryers, TV, baby food, chest rubs and cough medicines, vitamins, dolls, wagons, sleds, skates.
	4. Full nest II: youngest child six or over	Financial position better. Some wives work. Less influenced by advertising. Buy larger-size packages, multiple-unit deals. Buy: many foods, cleaning materials, bicycles, music lessons, pianos.
	5. Full nest III: older married couples with dependent children	Financial position still better. More wives work. Some children get jobs. Hard to influence with advertising. High average purchase of durables. Buy: new, more tasteful furniture, auto travel, unnecessary appliances, boats, dental services, magazines.
	6. Empty nest I: older married couples, no children living with them, head in labour force	Home ownership at peak. Most satisfied with financial position and money saved. Interested in travel, recreation, self-education. Make gifts and contributions. Not interested in new products. Buy: vacations, luxuries, home improvements.
	7. Empty nest II: older married. No children living at home, head retired.	Drastic cut in income. Keep home. Buy: medical appliances, medical-care products that aid health, sleep and digestion.
	8. Solitary survivor, in labour force	Income still good but likely to sell home.
	9. Solitary survivor, retired	Same medical and product needs as other retired group; drastic cut in income. Special need for attention, affection and security.

Source: Kotler and Armstrong (1994: 181)

individual's financial circumstances are composed of their *spendable earnings* (their amount, stability and time pattern), *savings and assets* (in addition to the percentage that is liquid), *liabilities, borrowing power* and *viewpoint toward expenditure versus economy*. Marketers of bargain and lower-priced goods and services pay continual attention to tendencies in personal income, savings and interest rates. If financial indicators indicate a recession, marketers can try to reconstruct, reposition and reproduce their products so they keep on offering value to targeted consumers.

Moreover, individuals from similar subcultures, social classes and employment may lead quite different *lifestyles*. As Kotler and Armstrong (1994: 182) note: 'a person's lifestyle is the person's pattern of living in the world as expressed in the person's activities, interests and opinions'. The method of measuring lifestyles is known as 'psychographics'. The psychographic method of segmentation is used to describe the overall market based on variances that reflect the *interests, personalities, attitudes, opinions, perceptions* and *lifestyles* of consumers comprising that market. Psychographics sharpens the exploration for prospects beyond the demographic data. It has been said that lifestyle information gives the soul of the person; demographics alone gives only a skeleton.

Psychographic research attempts to position consumers on psychological – as opposed to purely demographic – dimensions. It initially focused on individuals' activities (behaviours), interests and opinions. The pioneer measuring instrument for this approach was an AIO (*Activities-Interests-Opinions*) inventory. These inventories contain a large number of statements about which large numbers of respondents express a degree of agreement or disagreement. Nowadays, psychographics or lifestyle studies typically involve the following, as analysed by Hawkins *et al.* 1992, as cited by Swarbrooke and Horner (1999):

- *Attitudes*: evaluative statements about other people, locations, ideas, commodities and so forth.
- *Values*: broadly held beliefs about what is agreeable and/or desirable.
- *Activities, interests and opinions*: non-occupational behaviours to which buyers devote time and effort, such as public service and religion. Table 3.3 shows the AIO framework and what it includes.

Table 3.3	Activities	Interests	Opinions	Demographics
The AIO framework	Work	Family	Themselves	Age
	Hobbies	Home	Social issues	Education
	Social events	Job	Politics	Income
	Vacation	Community	Business	Occupation
	Entertainment	Recreation	Economics	Family size
	Club membership	Fashion	Education	Dwelling
	Community	Food	Products	Geography
	Shopping	Media	Future	City size
	Sports	Achievements	Culture	Stage in life-cycle

Source: Kotler *et al.* (1996: 189)

- *Media Patterns*: which particular media, consumers use.
- *Usage Rates*: estimations of consumption within a specified product category.

More specifically, *demographics* are being adopted to characterize a population in terms of its size, distribution and structure. Size explains the number of human beings in a population, while structure illustrates the population in terms of age, education, income and occupation. Explicitly, as *education* levels grow, one can anticipate that many changes in preference will occur in the demand for specific products and services, particularly tourism and hospitality. It is therefore imperative, from a marketing point of view, to identify the educational level of target markets, in order to properly reach and communicate with them. In addition, the household's *income* level, linked with accumulated wealth, establishes purchasing power. Since income provides the means for consumers to satisfy their needs by purchasing products and services, it is not a surprise that marketers regard income to be a critical demographic variable. Income has conventionally been used as a measurement of both purchasing power and status, and historically the association between income and status has been high.

Finally, the *geographic method* in the AIO framework helps segment the market by dividing and allocating customers by geographic area, and is considered to be the oldest form of segmentation. This method is important particularly to media planners in deciding on national, regional and local advertising campaigns.

To conclude, *distribution* of the population illustrates the location of people in terms of geographic region and rural, urban or suburban location. Each of these factors influences the behaviour of consumers and contributes to the total demand for goods and services.

An additional framework of the psychographic method of measuring lifestyles and segmenting the market is *VALS* (*Values and Lifestyles*). VALS gives a systematic classification of people into nine distinct value and lifestyle patterns. More specifically, the newest version, VALS 2, groups individuals according to their consumption tendencies by how they spend their time and money. Martha Farnsworth Richie (1989) (quoted in Kotler *et al.* (1996: 190) has divided the American population, according to their lifestyles, into eight distinct groups: fulfilleds; believers; achievers; strivers; experiencers; makers; actualizers; strugglers. Table 3.4 contains some of these groups, which are the target market of the Patras-Brindisi network and thus relevant to tourism and hospitality.

Holidaymaker classifications

A tourist lifestyle assessment should be regarded as a study of market segments with reference to general holidaying behaviours. Specifically, Yiannakis and Gibson (1992) were able to identify 14 types of tourist based on responses to motivational factors such as tourist environments, high to low structure, stimulating–tranquil environments and strange–familiar environments. Table 3.5 shows these classifications.

Finally, one's *personality* and *self-concept* control an individuals' purchasing behaviour. Personality can be regarded as 'the distinguishing psychological characteristics that disclose a person's relatively individualized, consistent, and enduring responses to the environment (Weiss in Kotler *et al.*, 1996: 191). Personality can be helpful in studying consumer behaviour for particular products, services or brand choices. In addition, marketers utilize the terms self-concept or self-image to describe consumer behaviour that is a reflection of one's personality. Individuals tend to behave according to their perception of themselves; in other words, their self-image.

Table 3.4 VALS framework

Self orientation		
Principle	Fulfillers	Mature, satisfied, comfortable, reflective people who value order, knowledge and responsibility. Most are well educated, well informed about current events and alert to opportunities to broaden their knowledge. They are open-minded about new ideas and social change. They look for functionality, value and durability in the products they buy.
Status	Achievers	Successful, work-oriented people who get their satisfaction from their jobs and their families. They feel in control of their lives. Image is important to them, They are politically conservative and respect authority and the status quo. They favour established products and services that show off their success to their peers.
Action	Experiencers	People who like to affect their environment in tangible ways. They are the youngest of all groups. They are young, vital, enthusiastic and rebellious. They seek variety and excitement, savouring the new, the offbeat and the risky. They have a lot of energy, which they pour into physical exercise and social activities. They are avid consumers, spending heavily on clothing, fast food, music and other youthful favourites. They especially like new things. Still in the process of formulating life values and patterns of behaviour, they quickly become enthusiastic about new possibilities.
	Makers	People who like to affect their environment, but in more practical ways. They value self-sufficiency. They are focused on the family, work, and physical recreation and have little interest in the broader world. As consumers, they are unimpressed by material possessions other than those with a practical or functional purpose.
Resources	Actualizers	People with the highest incomes and so many resources that they can indulge in any or all self-orientations. They are successful, sophisticated, active, 'take-charge' people with high self-esteem and abundant resources. They are interested in growth and seek to develop, explore and express themselves in a variety of ways. Image is important to them but as an expression of their taste, independence and character. They have a wide range of interests, are open to change and their possessions and recreation reflect a cultivated taste for the finer things in life.

Source: Kotler *et al.* (1996: 191) and Hawkins *et al.* (1992: 332–3)

Psychological factors

An individual's purchase behaviour and selection of tourism or hospitality products are affected by four major psychological factors:

- motivation
- perception

- learning
- beliefs and attitudes.

Motivation

'Motivation refers to a state of need, a condition that exerts a "push" on the individual toward certain types of action that are seen as likely to bring satisfaction' (Moutinho, 1987: 14). Three theories are widely used for consumer analysis and marketing: Freud's, Maslow's and Herzberg's theories of motivation.

Sigmund Freud assumes that the genuine physiological forces forming people's behaviour are largely unconscious, due to the fact that he views people as repressing many urges in the process of growing up and receiving social rules.

Table 3.5		
Holidaymaker classifications	Sun Lover	Interested in relaxing and sunbathing in warm places with lots of sun, sand and ocean
	Action seeker	Mostly interested in partying, going to night clubs and meeting the opposite sex for uncomplicated romantic experiences.
	Anthropologist	Mostly interested in meeting local people, trying the food and speaking the language.
	Archaeologist	Mostly interested in archaeological sites and ruins; enjoys studying history of ancient civilizations.
	Organised Mass Tourist	Mostly interested in organized vacations, packaged tours, taking pictures and buying lots of souvenirs.
	Thrill Seeker	Interested in risky, exhilarating activities that provide emotional highs, such as skydiving.
	Explorers	Prefers adventure travel, exploring out-of-the-way places and enjoys challenges in getting there.
	Jetsetter	Vacations in elite world-class resorts, goes to exclusive night clubs, and socializes with celebrities.
	Seeker	Seeker of spiritual and/or personal knowledge to better understand self and meaning of life.
	Independent Mass Tourist	Visits regular tourist attractions but makes own travel arrangements and often 'plays it by ear'.
	High Class Tourist	Travels first class, stays in the best hotels, goes to shows, and dines at the best restaurants.
	Drifter	Drifts from place to place living a hippy-style existence.
	Escapist	Enjoys taking it easy and getting away from it all in quiet and peaceful places.
	Sport lover	Primary emphasis while on vacation is to remain active engaging in favourite sports.

Source: Yiannakis and Gibson in Ryan (1995: 70–1)

Later, Ernest Dichter (Kotler *et al.*, 1996) formed his motivational research through in-depth interviews by explaining buying situations and product selections in terms of underlying unconscious motives.

Abraham Maslow wanted to define why people are guided by specific needs at certain times. His answer is that human needs are classified in a hierarchy, from the most imperative to the least imperative. In order of significance, they are the physiological, safety, social esteem, and self-actualization. For a person to reach a higher level, for example to belong to a club, they must first be satisfied in their basic and safety needs. This theory helps marketers understand how various products fit into the plans, goals and lives of prospective customers.

Finally, *Frederick Herzberg* formed a 'two-factor theory' (Kotler *et al.*, 1996: 186) of motivation, which differentiates dissatisfiers – elements that cause dissatisfaction – and satisfiers – elements that cause satisfaction – in the choice of a product or service by a consumer. In essence, a potential customer should eliminate the dissatisfiers and promote the satisfiers for the product or service that is desirable.

Turning to tourism, Wahab has stated that the entire area of travel motivation is so fundamental and vital in tourism studies that overlooking it, or passing lightly over it, would overthrow the whole purpose of following any tourism development process (Wahab in Gilbert, 1991). Travel may be perceived as a satisfier of needs and wants; however, it is only when a need is identified that it changes into a want. At the moment a person tries to gratify a want it then becomes motivated action. An understanding of motivation is hence of basic significance since it forms a major influence on tourism demand patterns. Motivational models in tourism have a tendency to be theoretical in nature and based on the disciplines of sociology, anthropology and psychology. Empirical evidence, while quite rare, has been utilized to add some understanding to these theories. Figure 3.3 exhibits one of the major categorizations of the main motivating factors in tourism.

It should be noted that a study of this motivational stage can communicate the way in which people set goals for their destination choice and how these

Figure 3.3

A typology of motivators in tourism

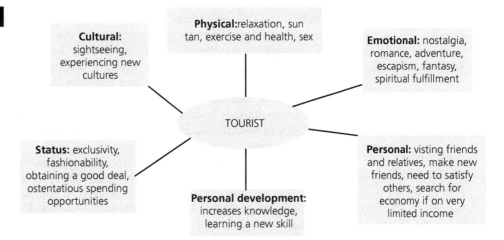

Source: Swarbrooke and Homer S (1999: 54)

goals are then embodied in both their choice and travel behaviour. Furthermore, it can provide tour operators, tourism planners, and other tourist-related institutions with a more valuable perception of the real expectations, needs and goals of tourists (Goodall and Jefferson in Mansfield, 1992). However, Dann, Nash and Pearce point out that 'few case studies have empirically tried to come to grips with the problem of travel motivation' (Dann, Nash and Pearce in Mansfield, 1992: 402). Furthermore, Mill and Morrison state that the numerous lists of travel motives that previous case studies have supplied do not reflect a uniform picture of the main determinants of travel behaviour and that the perplexity and level of subjectivity entailed in such studies account, in part, for the inadequate treatment (Mill and Morrison in Mansfield, 1992). However, Moutinho (1987: 15) has adapted a model created from J.A. Thomas and gives a list of examples of general travel motivators, which are presented in Table 3.6.

Finally, one should note that there is a correlation between motivators and determinants, meaning: between one's aspirations and the elements that form one's actual behaviour. It appears that the issue of motivation is extremely perplexing and relies on a number of factors, including:

- the nature and lifestyle of the prospective tourist;
- their former experiences;
- who they are considering taking holidays with;
- their demographic attributes;
- how far in advance they book their journey.

Perception and learning

Marketers can better predict tourist behaviour by understanding the processes of both knowledge acquisition and incorporation of experiences and by realizing that *perception* and *learning* heavily affect consumers' evaluation and judgement processes. As Moutinho (1987: 9) states: 'Perception is the process by which an individual selects, organizes and interprets stimuli in a meaningful and coherent way'; and Hawkins *et al.* (1992: 221) add, 'perception is the critical activity that links the individual consumer to group, situation, and marketer influences'. A motivated individual is ready to act via actions that are influenced by one's perception of the situation. It should be mentioned that people apprehend a stimulus object through the five senses of sight, hearing, smell, touch and taste, and take in, organize and translate this sensory information in an individual and unique way. In addition, what an individual perceives in numerous circumstances is determined not only by the intrinsic nature of the stimulus object or sensations, but also by one's own combination of values set by the social context.

The initial stage of perception and information processing is the *attention filter* in which a person, instead of perceiving all the incoming stimuli, grasps information in a selective way through a process of comparison of inputs with previous information. This process is called *selective exposure* and it is the point where marketers have to work hard and identify a unique selling point in their products or services so as to attract consumers' attention. Furthermore, the majority of stimuli to which one is exposed are screened out if they are

Table 3.6

Examples of general travel motivations

Educational and Cultural
1. To see how people in other countries live and work
2. To see particular sights, monuments or works of art
3. To gain a better understanding of current events
4. To attend special culture or artistic events

Relaxation, Adventure and Pleasure
1. To get away from everyday routine and obligations
2. To see new places, people, or seek new experiences
3. To have a good time and fun
4. To have some sort of romantic sexual experience

Health and Recreation
1. To rest and recover from work and strain
2. To practice sports and exercise

Ethnic and Family
1. To visit places your family came from
2. To visit relatives and friends
3. To spend time with the family and children

Social and 'Competitive'
1. To be able to talk about places visited
2. Because it is fashionable
3. To show that one can afford it

Source: Moutinho (1987: 15)

unexciting and irrelevant. The second stage is the *interpretation process*, in which the content of the stimulus is organized into one's own model of actuality, called *selective distortion*, ending in awareness and interpretation of the stimulus – that is, *cognition*. The final stage is *selective retention*, or memory, in which consumers recollect information that sustains their attitudes and beliefs and which, in advertising, is supported by drama and repetition techniques.

Also, *learning* 'describes changes in an individual's behaviour arising from experience' (Kotler *et al.*, 1996: 196) and arises through the interplay of drives, stimuli, cues, responses and reinforcement. It is important to note that *generalization* is a significant aspect of the learning process to be taken into consideration in the study of tourist behaviour. Stimulus generalization is the process by which the same response is created to similar but different stimuli, as when an individual responds to a given travel situation in the same way he or she has responded to different but similar situations in the past. Conversely, stimulus discrimination entails the learning of different responses to different but similar situations. The processes of generalization, stressing stimulus similarity, and of discrimination, stressing stimulus difference, are basic in consumer behaviour assessment. Tourists can discriminate between two similar products and show desire for one of them and they can generalize about distinct, not yet experienced, aspects of a destination on the basis of known stimuli.

Consequently, careful attention has to be given to the stimuli associated with travelling and the way they influence tourist behaviour; travel stimuli designate the different kinds of information given to the tourist which may have a significant or symbolic character linked to the product's characteristics such as quality, price, distinctiveness, prestige, and availability.

Attitudes

Consumer attitudes are made up by three components: cognitive; affective; and behavioural. The cognitive component consists of a consumer's beliefs and knowledge about an object. For most attitude objects, a total of beliefs exist. For example, consumers may believe that a specific ferry company offers passenger convenience, is competitively priced and guarantees safety. The complete configuration of beliefs about this ferry company denotes the cognitive component of an attitude towards travelling on a specific ferry from a specific company. It should be mentioned, however, that beliefs do not have to be correct or true; they only have to exist. Furthermore, marketing strategies aim to preserve, modify or create attitudes. In the field of tourism, attitudes are predispositions or emotions towards a holiday destination or service, based on various perceived product attributes. Also, intentions suggest the probability of buying a tourist product or service. They are a function of evaluative beliefs in relation to a tourist product, and include social elements that lean towards providing tourists with a group of normative beliefs and situational elements that can be expected at the time of the vacation plan or commitment. Figure 3.4 shows the connections between attitudes, intentions and the travel decision-making process.

Figure 3.4

Attitudes and the travel decision-making process

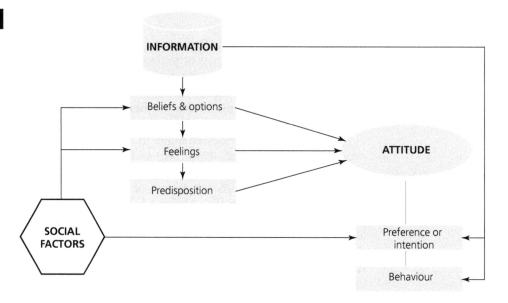

Source: Moutinho (1987)

Moreover, as Hawkins *et al.* (1992: 349–350, as cited by Scarbrooke and Horner 1999) state:

> [M]any beliefs about product and/or service attributes are evaluative in nature. The more positive beliefs there are associated with a brand and the more positive each belief is, the more favourable the overall cognitive component is presumed to be. And, since all of the components of an attitude are generally consistent, the more favourable the overall attitude is. This logic underlies what is known as the *multiattribute attitude model.*

This represents a non-conscious process that is much less accurate than suggested by the actual model and in its simplest form is:

$$A_b = \sum X_{ib}$$

where $\sum$ goes from i = 1 to n attributes;
A_b is the consumer's attitude toward a particular brand b;
X_{ib} is the consumer's belief about brand b's performance on attribute i; and
n are the number of attributes considered.

Another version which considers the importance of some attributes such as price, quality or style over the others and adds an importance weight for each attribute is the following:

$$A_b = \sum W_i X_{ib}$$

where $\sum$ goes from i = 1 to n attributes; and
W_i is the importance the consumer attaches to attribute i.

Furthermore, the affective component of an attitude is denoted by one's feelings or reactions to an object, and these affective reactions may differ in different situations. Finally, the behavioural component of an attitude is an individual's tendency to respond in a specific way towards an object or activity.

As mentioned above, through acting and learning, one obtains beliefs and attitudes, which, in turn, affect one's buying behaviour. It is important to note that attitudes are different from values in the way that they are more articulated and guided towards specific objects. They are also distinct from opinions, which include explanations or justifications of attitudes and not of the tendency to act *per se.* Marketers pay attention to the beliefs that consumers have about particular products and services since they strengthen product and brand images. Also, individuals tend to act on their beliefs; so if undiscovered consumer beliefs hinder purchases, marketers will need to launch a campaign to change them. It should be mentioned that it is very hard to change consumer attitudes, since one's attitude is part of a pattern, and changing it demands making very arduous adjustments. Thus, it is simpler for an enterprise to produce products and services that are consistent with existing attitudes than to attempt to modify the attitudes towards their products. Finally, in the case where negative attitudes are developed towards a product or even a destination, changing them requires a lot of effort from the marketers.

As Kotler (in Moutinho, 1987: 17) indicates, in order to change attitudes, marketers can:

- Modify the characteristics of the tourist product (real positioning).
- Alter beliefs about the product (psychological positioning).
- Alter beliefs about competitive products (competitive depositioning).
- Change the relevant weights of the product attributes.
- Induce attention to certain attributes.
- Modify the tourist's ideal levels for certain attributes.

Tourist behaviour modelling

In order to sum up the consumer behaviour process, a model by Luiz Moutinho (1987: 37–41) outlines the major behavioural processes that a tourist goes through in deciding, evaluating and buying a tourism product or service. This model consists of three parts: Part I Pre-decision; Part II Post-purchase evaluation; and Part III Future decision-making.

Pre-decision and decision processes

This part deals with the flow of events, from the tourist stimuli to the actual buying decision. The fields involved are:

Field 1: Preference structure that is a major process in the pre-decision phase.
Field 2: Decision.
Field 3: Purchase.

Since the last two points are results of pre-decision, the model is more specific in respect to that process and its study involves the sub-fields of stimulus filtration and attention, as well as learning processes and choice criteria.

Part I – pre-decision

The tourist's preference structure (Field 1) for a specific destination is set on a group of factors; information modifies that group, so affective judgements for the destination can be anticipated to change over time. Among those factors are:

- internalized environmental influences which include cultural norms and values;
- family and reference groups;
- financial status and;
- social class.

These are determinants of preference structure and, therefore, will influence the tourist product evaluation. Also, individual determinants of preference structure consist of concepts such as:

- personality
- lifestyle
- perceived role set
- learning
- motives.

Intention to buy is based on confidence generation – that is, trust and assurance towards the vacation destination or tourist service. Confidence generation is a 'summary' notion denoting feelings of uncertainty, caution, anxiety and indecisiveness. These feelings are no less present in travel than in other fields, and are no less consequential. They are tourist inhibitors which make one respond in a different manner from what one's attitude towards the destination or service dictates.

> Subfield A – Stimulus filtration
> Subfield B – Attention and Learning Processes
> Subfield C – Choice Criteria

The decision process (Field 2) may be studied as a continuity of conflicts; the conflict situations forming a decision process are those that come before the choice and are necessary to explain what is chosen. This decision ends in a psychological predisposition in terms of intention in relation to the buying act. A tourist's decisions may be grounded on:

- perceived images
- information from tourism destination promotion
- previous experience
- image of potential destinations
- travel intermediaries
- advice
- social interaction.

Finally, the decision process is set by the tourist's background awareness, which embodies the creation of beliefs and images (terms of reference), evaluation of vacation ideas and the travel decision.

Purchases (Field 3) can appear out of necessity; they can be received from culturally mandated lifestyles or from connected purchases; they can arise from simple conformity to group norms or from mimicking others. A purchase can be characterized as the result of psychic processes happening more or less consciously. The total tourist product is usually purchased in a sequence (transportation, accommodation, tours) and not regularly in a tour package.

Part II – post-purchase evaluation

Post-choice appraisal feedback has a vital impact on the decision-maker's attitude set and/or later behaviour. One of the key elements recorded as affecting a tourist's expectations is the satisfaction with post-purchase. Post-purchase has three significant aims:

1. It augments the tourist's experiences, and it is through post-purchase that experience is taken into one's frame of reference. Hence, it widens personal needs, ambitions, drives, perceptions and understanding.
2. It provides a review on market-related decisions.
3. It provides data to serve as a basis for settling future purchase behaviour.

Subfield D – Adequacy Evaluation

Part III – future decision-making

This part is mainly related to the study of the subsequent behaviour of the tourist by analysing different probabilities for repeat buying a particular vacation destination or tourist service. The fields involved are:

Field 4: Satisfaction/dissatisfaction Field 5: Repeat buying probabilities

Subsequent behaviour relies on levels of return expectation and may result in:

- straight re-buy;
- re-buy in different time criteria;
- modified re-buy behaviour.

Summary

To conclude, one must note that in the future a number of factors will guide changes in who tourists are, what they buy and how they buy it. Nevertheless, it has been noted by Swarbrooke and Horner (1999), that the behaviour of some individual tourists will not alter considerably. At the same time, even with the global tourism market as a whole, shifts in behaviour will be 'evolutionary' rather than 'revolutionary', and as noted by the Swarbrooke and Horner, variations and distinctions will be noted between countries, market segments and sectors of the tourism industry. However, consumer behaviour will remain the same in some basic parts, thus making researchers continue to research new and emerging tourist trends.

References

Becherel, L. and Vellas, E. (1999) *The international book of travel and marketing*, Ch 2, (eds) Becherel, L. and Vellas, E., London, Macmillan.
Drucker, P.F. (1973) *Management: Tasks, Responsibilities, Practices*, New York: Harper and Row.
Engel, J.F., Blackwell, R.D. and Miniard, P.W. (1995) *Consumer Behaviour*, Fort Worth, TX: Dryden Press.
Farnsworth Richie, M. (1989) 'Psychographics for the 1990s', *American Demographics*, July, 25–31.
Kotler, P. and Armstrong, g. (1994) *Marketing Management: Analysis, Planning Implementation and Control*, 8th edn, Englewood Cliff, NJ: Prentice-Hall.
Moutinho, L. (1987) 'Consumer behaviour in tourism', *European Journal of Marketing*, 21, 10, 3–44.
Mansfield, Y. (1992) 'From motivation to actual travel', *Annals of Tourism Research*, 19, 3, 399–419
Soloman, P.J. and George, W.R. (1977) 'The bicentennial traveller: a lifestyle analysis of the historian segment', *Journal of Travel Research*, 15, 3, 14–17.

Swarbrooke, J. and Horner, S. (1999) *Consumer Behaviour in Tourism*, Oxford: Butterworth-Heinemann.

Further reading

Arthur Andersen (1997) 'Hospitality and leisure', *Executive Report*, Fall, 4, 2, 1–6.

Bamford, R. (1998) 'New government, new expectations', *The Hospitality Yearbook 1998*, Guildford: University of Surrey.

Baum, T. (1993) *Human Resources Issues in International Tourism*, Oxford: Butterworth-Heinemann.

Bradley, F. (1991) *International Marketing Strategy,* Hemel Hempstead: Prentice-Hall.

Bradley, S.P., Hausmann, J.A. and Nolan, R.L. (1993) *Globalization, Technology and Competition*, Boston: Harvard Business School Press.

Brown, F. (1998) *Tourism Reassessed, Blight or Blessing?*, Oxford: Butterworth- Heinemann.

Buhalis, D. (1998) 'Information technology', in C. Cooper C *et al.* (eds) *Tourism Principles and Practice*, Harlow: Addison-Wesley Longman, 423–46.

Cooper, C. (1997) 'Strategic perspectives on the planning and evolution of sestinations: lessons for the Mediterranean', paper presented to the seminar: Tourism in the Mediterranean; University of Westminster, December.

Crotts, J.C. and Wilson, D.T. (1995) 'An integrated model of buyer–seller relationships in the international travel trade', *Progress in Tourism and Hospitality Research*, 1, 2, 125–40.

European Commission (1999) *Enhancing Tourism's Potential for Employment – Follow-up to the Conclusions and Recommendations of the High Level Group on Tourism and Employment*, Brussels, 28.04.1999 COM (1999) 205 final.

Gee, C. (1994) *International Hotel Development and Management*, Michigan: Educational Institute of the American Hotel and Motel Association.

Geller, L. (1998) 'The demands of globalization on the lodging industry', *Florida International University Hospitality Review*, 16, 1, 1–6.

Ghoshal, S. and Bartlett, C.A. (1990) 'The multinational corporation as an inter-organizational network', *Academy of Management Review*, 15, 4, 603–25.

Heung, V. (1993) 'Hong Kong' in T. Baum (ed) *Human Resources Issues in International Tourism*, Oxford: Butterworth-Heinemann.

IH&RA Human Resources Think-Tank (1999) *Organizational and Workforce Challenges for the 21st Century*, Paris: IH&RA, August.

ILO Hotel, Catering and Tourism Committee (1989) *Productivity and Training in the Hotel, Catering and Tourism Sector*, Geneva: International Labour Office.

Joyce, P. and Woods, A. (1996) *Essential Strategic Management: From Modernism to Pragmatism*, Oxford: Butterworth-Heinemann.

Juyaux, C. (1999) 'Quality of Service and Working Conditions in the European Tourist and hospitality industry', *Cahiers Espaces*, 61, 25–9.

Kappor, T. (1999) 'The New Hospitality', *Workplace Lodging*, November, 105–8.

Keller, P. (1996) 'Globalization and tourism', *Tourist Review*, 4, 6–7.

Kinsey, J. (1988) *Marketing in Developing Countries*, London: Macmillan.

Kotler, P., Bowen, J. and Makens, J. (1996) *Marketing for Hospitality and Tourism*, Englewood Cliffs: NJ: Prentice-Hall International.

Melin, L. (1992) 'Internationalisation as a strategy process', *Strategic Management Journal*, 13, 2, 99–118.

Morrison, A. (1989) *Hospitality and Travel Marketing*, New York: Delmar.

Morrison, A. (1998) 'Small firm statistics: a hotel sector focus', *Service Industries Journal*, 18, 1, 132–42.

Office for National Statistics (1997*) Business Monitor*, PA 1003, London: Stationery Office.

Paliwoda, S.J. and Thomas, M.J. (1998) *International Marketing*, 3rd edn, Oxford: Butterworth-Heinemann.

Poon, A. (1993) *Tourism, Technology and Competitive Strategies*, Wallingford: CAB.

Porter, M. (1990) *The Competitive Advantage of Nations*, New York: The Free Press.

Riley, M. (1993) 'Labour market and vocational education in human resources', in T. Baum (ed) *Issues in International Tourism*, Oxford: Butterworth-Heinemann.

Seaton, A.V. and Bennett, M.M. (1996) *The Marketing of Tourism Products: Concepts, Issues and Cases*, London: International Thomson Business Press.

Shaw, G. and Williams, A. (1994) *Critical Issues in Tourism: A Geographical Perspective*, Oxford: Blackwell, 143.

Shulze, G. (1999) 'Globalization and the economy', *World Economy*, 22, 3, 295–352.

Smeral, E. (1998) 'The impact of globalization on small and medium enterprises: new challenges for tourism policies in European countries', *Tourism Management*, 19, 4, 371–80.

Szivas, E. (1999) 'The influence of human resources on tourism marketing', in F. Vellas and L. Becherel (eds) *The International Marketing of Travel and Tourism*, Hampshire: MacMillan Press.

Teare, R. *et al.* (1997) *Global Directions: New Strategies for Hospitality and Tourism*, London: Cassell.

Thomas, R. (1996) 'Assessing and influencing the policies of the european union', in Kotas, R., Teare, R., Logie, J., Jayawardena, C. and Bowen, J. (eds) *The International Hospitality Business*, London: Cassell.

Thomas, R. (ed) (1998) *The Management of Small Tourism and Hospitality Firms*, London: Cassell.

Terpstra, V. and Sarathy, R. (1991) *International Marketing*, Florida: The Dryden Press.

UNCTAD (1998) 'Expert meeting on strengthening the capacity for expanding the tourism sector in developing countries, June, Geneva.

Vernon, R. (1966) 'The product cycle hypothesis in a new international environment', *Quarterly Journal of Economics*, May, 190–207.

World Tourism Organization (1999) *Marketing Tourism Destinations On-Line*, Madrid: WTO.

Yiannakis, A., and Gibson, H. (1992) 'Role tourists play', *Annals of tourism research*, 19, (2), 287–303.

4 Marketing communications

Introduction

The aim of this chapter is to build on Chapter 2 by outlining aspects related to the topic of promotion, including advertising which is a subject of great significance to organizations in today's competitive and changing market conditions. More specifically, the role and function of advertising as a strategic marketing tool in managing destination image will be introduced. Destination advertising is an increasingly complicated field, mainly due to lack of consistent and commonly accepted attitudes related to the magnitude of its impact on the favourable impression of a destination and the conversion of this interest into actual visits. Additionally, this chapter will comment on the concept of the Internet as a prevailing new technology by tracking the development of e-business through recent years from a promotional perspective. Thus, this chapter aims to review the case of destination advertising and provide a theoretical framework for the proposed methods and techniques that are commonly used for assessing its effectiveness in destination marketing programmes while shedding some light on issues related to the use of the World Wide Web (WWW) within tourism and hospitality.

The evolution of tourism and hospitality marketing

Despite the remarkable changes taking place in the international economy during the last two decades, tourism's growth has been constant compared with other major industries. The importance of tourism's social and economic activities in today's world is underlined by the steadily increasing numbers of both domestic and international travellers (Inskeep, 1991). Yet tourism is still a relatively new industry for many countries who do not have experience in developing this important economic sector (WTO, 1998). It is only in the last 30 or 40 years that tourism has become the established industry that we know today.

Throughout this period, practitioners and academics in the field have placed great emphasis on the importance of adopting flexible structures in order to become more competitive in this global industry. This in turn has resulted in certain suggestions for restructuring and remodelling businesses, most of which are based on the discipline of marketing. The development of such a perspective is the result of the discontinuities taking place in the tourism marketplace in recent years and the simultaneous need for a change in business functions to keep in touch with a rapidly evolving industry (Cooper *et al.*, 1998; Evans and Berman, 1997).

While many tourism and hospitality companies appear to be market-driven, marketing still remains under-utilized in these sectors, as the emphasis seems to be more on rhetoric rather than action (McDonald and Payne, 1998). However, evidence is growing that the principles of marketing have a powerful influence in supporting and implementing the competitive strategy of an organization. Similarly, as Cooper *et al.* (1998: 342) contend: 'the realities of increasingly intense competition are encouraging a new emphasis on marketing management and a greater marketing orientation within the industry'. Having recognized the importance of marketing in both the tourism and hospitality sectors, the discussion now focuses on the marketing concept itself.

The marketing concept

The new business trends emerging in the first decade of the twenty-first century are increasingly leading to the perception of marketing as a legitimate activity. Nevertheless, in spite of perceived legitimacy, marketing is still considered to be in its infancy within tourism and hospitality (Kitchen, 1999). In this respect, the need to be more precise in identifying the attributes of marketing has led many academics and practitioners to offer a spectrum of definitions. However, despite this movement towards the development of such definitions, a review of the relevant literature reveals that no widely acceptable theory of marketing exists (Sheth *et al.*, 1988). Nonetheless, as Kitchen (1999: 20) notes: 'If such a theory were to emerge it would rest on two pillars: a thorough understanding of consumer needs and behaviour and a critical analysis of opportunities of competitive advantage'.

This view has been thoroughly commented on by several academics (see, for example, Day, 1984; Bagozzi, 1986; McDonald and Payne, 1998). Furthermore, according to Cooper *et al.* (1998) the marketing function relies on a series of management tasks carried out to provide for a 'business-to-customer interface'. Contributing to the debate, McDonald (1995) believes the fundamental concept of marketing to be the matching process between a company's capabilities and the wants of customers by way of achieving the objectives of both parties. Figure 4.1 represents diagrammatically a summary of McDonald's beliefs.

It can be seen from the above description that a marketing orientation is based upon a 'three-pronged' interfacing act by organizations including: customer wants; organizational capabilities; and environmental factors (Kitchen, 1999). Considering the dynamic nature of tourism and hospitality, Figure 4.1 also ties in well with marketing research as a vital process in supplying organizations with up-to-date information in a changeable market (Crimp and Wright, 1995; Fredrickson and Mitchell, 1988). The process of market research is of great significance because of its contribution to creating the conditions necessary for the adoption of an appropriate strategic orientation. In this light, the concept of marketing from a strategic perspective will now be explored.

Strategic marketing in the tourism industry

The term 'marketing management' is probably one of the most extensively used terms in business, thus resulting in an inescapable misuse, both in terms of meaning and application (Witt and Moutinho, 1994). The fundamental problem appears to be that the terms 'strategic marketing' and 'marketing management' have become interchangeable in their scope and context. However, strategic marketing involves non-identical perspectives from those of marketing management in many aspects. In Jain's words: 'The strategic role of marketing is quite different from marketing management which deals with developing, implementing and directing programs to achieve designated intentions' (1997: 21). Table 4.1 summarizes the differences between the two terms.

Over the last decade, several approaches on strategic planning applied to the tourism industry have been developed (Cooper, 1998). According to Kotler *et al* (1986), strategic planning is the managerial process of matching the diversified elements of an organization while taking advantage of the arising opportunities in a changing marketplace. Furthermore, McDonald and Payne (1998) deem the strategic role of planning to be imperative for the settlement of today's organizational problems. The view of Jain (1997) is that strategic planning deals essentially with the interaction of the 'strategic three Cs: customer; competition; corporation.

Despite the development of these approaches and the amount of attention devoted to the topic, tourism and hospitality has been substantially under-represented in the strategic marketing literature (Athiyaman, 1995; Gilbert and Kapur, 1990). This is perhaps because recent research (see Cooper, 1995) suggests that the adoption of strategic planning in the tourism industry faces great difficulties mainly due to the vague boundaries of the sector within it. However, a variety of factors point to an increasingly important role for strategic marketing in the near future (Webster, 1986). As Kotler *et al.* (1998: 70) indicate: 'Marketing and strategic planning should be viewed as partnerships contributing to the long-run success of a hospitality firm'. Indeed, for marketing to fulfil any of its strategic objectives the use of certain marketing techniques are

Figure 4.1

Marketing: a
matching process

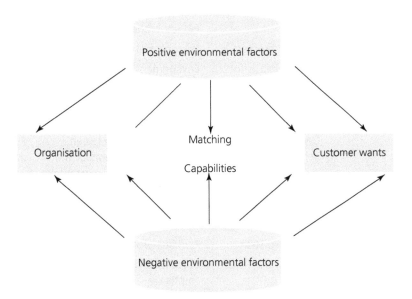

Source: McDonald and Payne (1998: 5)

necessary. These techniques, generally coming under the heading of the 'marketing mix', are commented upon in the following section.

The marketing mix

Earlier in this chapter marketing was portrayed as a matching process between the organizations' capabilities and the customers' wants. In effect, the marketing mix is the flexible pairing between the customer and organization that expedites the aforementioned process (McDonald and Payne, 1998). As Kotler and Armstrong (1994) state, the marketing mix consists of all the marketing tools and techniques that interact in order to influence the marketplace.

Generally speaking, it is customary to accept that the marketing mix consists of four elements defined by McCarthy (1978) as the four Ps and illustrated in Table 4.2.

However, in recent years the application of the four Ps in the service sector has been extensively questioned. As a result, alternative approaches where authors have attempted to extend the original concept have been developed. Probably, the most widely quoted of these approaches is the one introduced by Booms and Bitner (1981). In their view, the traditional four Ps of product, price, place and promotion remain, but they add three extra Ps (people, processes, and physical evidence). This expanded marketing mix is considered to be thorough enough to cover most service marketing situations (Payne, 1993; McDonald and

Table 4.1	Point of difference	Strategic marketing	Marketing management
Major differences between strategic marketing and marketing management	Time frame	Long range; i.e., decisions have long-term implications	Day-to-day; i.e., decisions have relevance in a given financial year
	Orientation	Inductive and intuitive	Deductive and analytical
	Decision process	Primarily bottom-up	Mainly top-down
	Relationship with environment	Environment considered ever-changing and dynamic	Environment considered constant with occasional disturbances
	Opportunity sensitivity	Ongoing to seek new opportunities	Ad hoc search for a new opportunity
	Organizational behaviour	Achieve synergy between different components of the organization, both horizontally and vertically	Pursue interests of the decentralized unit
	Nature of job	Requires high degree of creativity and originality	Requires maturity, experience, and control orientation
	Leadership style	Requires proactive perspective	Requires reactive perspective
	Mission	Deals with what business to emphasize	Deals with running a delineated business

Source: Jain (1997: 32)

Payne, 1998). In contrast, a sceptical viewpoint on this argument has been expressed by Cooper *et al.* (1998: 410): 'We believe that there is a need for more research into the industry and its marketing before the four Ps require revision. For the present it is believed the four Ps offer an adequate framework into which the differences can be incorporated'.

In comparing these two approaches, it can be seen that there is a need for research into the effectiveness of the current marketing mix elements and their strategies, especially from a tourism or hospitality perspective. This research reorientation should also take into account other dimensions of the marketing concept, in particular those who refer to the emergence of the information technology (IT) revolution and its potential impacts on this field of study.

Information technologies in tourism

In order to elaborate on the incorporation of the Internet as a marketing tool in tourism and hospitality and explain its role in modern organizations, it is necessary to comment on the development of IT by introducing its evolution over four main eras, as discussed by Robson (1994).

In the first era, beginning in the 1960s, 'data processing' aimed to ameliorate operational management through the automation of information-based processes. In tourism this era introduced the first computer reservation systems, which had a great impact on the reservation and accounting functions of tourism organizations, particularly airlines.

The second era, between the early 1970s and 1980s, brought 'management information systems' (MIS) aimed to improve organizational results by placing emphasis on the issue of meeting internal management requirements. At this stage the majority of large and international tourism organizations introduced the use of computers as an integral part of their administrative functions.

During the third 'strategic information systems' era, taking place from the early 1980s and through the 1990s, the principal objective was to improve competitiveness by transforming the patterns of existing business functions. As an outcome, tourism organizations became increasingly competitive by utilizing IT as an influential tool for decision-making.

The fourth and more innovative 'network era' commenced in the early 1990s. This era aimed to contribute to the development of 'seamless' tourist products

Table 4.2		
The marketing mix	*Product*	The product or service being offered.
	Price	The price or fees charged and the terms associated with marketing the product or service.
	Promotion	The communications program associated with marketing the product or service.
	Place	The distribution and logistics involved in making the product/service available.

Source: McDonald and Payne (1998: 18)

by empowering organizational networking and forceful communication. From a tourism perspective, this era introduced an expansion of tourism organizations' operational capabilities, which are now able to attract customers from all over the world.

Within this framework of fundamental changes, effective use of IT is considered to be a requisite for tourism and hospitality in the new millennium (Sheldon, 1994). As a consequence of this rapid development of IT, the Internet has emerged as an important partner of the tourism industry and an essential tool for marketing, distribution, promotion and co-ordination (Buhalis *et al.*, 1998).

Shifting from marketplace to market space

The constantly growing rates of Internet use within the last few years have placed great attention on the implications of its evolution in tourism and hospitality. As Smith and Jenner note (1998: 62), the Internet as a phenomenon has 'dramatically changed the way companies do business with one another, the way people research information of all kinds, the way people communicate, the way people make decisions, and the way people buy goods and services'. As Wardell (1998) illustrates, no other form of new technology has ever attracted the same kind of industry attention as the Internet or e-business. Nevertheless, whereas the Internet is becoming established as an integral part of a 'global information infrastructure', it is still in its infancy (Schonland and Williams, 1996; Branback, 1997; Smith and Jenner, 1998).

Before proceeding to further analysis, it would be wise to provide a definition of the 'I-word', as Kimber (1997) characterizes the Internet. According to Pfaffenberger (1993): 'The Internet is an electronic system of linked computer networks, worldwide in scope, that facilitates data communication services, such as e-mail, the World Wide Web (WWW) and newsgroups'.

Wardell (1998) draws attention to the strong emotions derived from the term 'electronic' and concludes by highlighting an ongoing debate related with the significance of the Internet for the tourism and hospitality sectors. Furthermore, he regards the opinions aroused by this debate as rather extreme as they regard e-business either as the cause of certain negative situations or as the 'industry saviour'. In addition, he focuses on the complexity of the real impact of the Internet which deals with aspects of both personal and work life. Welch (1996) believes the aforementioned complexity to be the main reason for the general lack of awareness about the importance of the Internet, which he considers as not being used to its full potential.

Despite these limitations, it would appear that the Internet and its use are spreading rapidly, affecting every type of business (Hoffman, 1994). Since this wave of technological novelty has expanded into every single industry, tourism is likely to be similarly affected.

Tourism and the Internet

As indicated previously, the Internet and its uses are growing in an unprecedented way. The services it offers are evolving at a considerable rate, providing excellent potential for both the public and private sectors. As the number of Internet 'hosts' increases, tourism organizations respond to the challenge by introducing the use of new technologies into their operational and strategic functions (Jung and Baker, 1998; Buhalis *et al.*, 1998).

At the same time, the wave of enthusiasm derived from the use of the Internet within the tourism and hospitality sector is reflected in the body of relevant literature on the topic. Burger (1997), for example, has commented on the Internet as being ideally designed to match the characteristics of the tourism industry. Similarly, Frew and Dorren (1996) highlight the significance of electronic communications for tourism service providers. To Schucan (1998), the information concept of the Internet enhances the destination management approach of tourism in a perfect way.

While, in the world of the Web, observers tend to accentuate stories of its effectiveness (Wardell, 1998), the extent to which the Internet will change business practices remains unclear. However, the establishment of a WWW presence by a number of tourist organizations highlights an increased level of commitment to the business potential of the Internet, which is perceived as an ideal mode for distributing products and services in a direct way by cutting down the role and number of intermediaries.

Eliminating intermediaries

Several authors have commented on the issue of disintermediation in both tourism and hospitality (see, for example, Karcher, 1996; Schulz, 1996). According to Wardell (1998), the rapid discontinuities that have affected the financial structures of businesses all over the world have encouraged the viewpoint that intermediaries add costs, which can be reduced or even eliminated. Additionally, Hoffman (1994) agrees that tourism and travel arrangements with intermediaries by way of meeting the 'peaks and valleys' of customer demand are very costly. In this respect, new technologies are increasingly regarded as the most efficient way for distributing products and services and thus getting close to the customers. The use of the Internet provides both the means and the reason to eliminate intermediaries (Hoffman, 1994; Wardell 1998).

On the other side of the argument, there is still opportunity for criticism. Wardell (1998) asserts that the elimination of intermediaries is just another business fad and there is no guarantee, that this approach it is not going to fail. Similarly, Shaw (1997) and Kimber (1997) underline the issue of the potentially immense costs required for large websites and ISDN lines able to handle the amount of data available on the Internet.

In contrasting the aforementioned approaches, it becomes evident that much is said and made of the possible savings in terms of disintermediation via the spread of Internet use. While cutting down on intermediaries appears to be an inevitable trend, only time will tell if the ongoing changes will really bring forth favourable financial outcomes for the sector. However, since the distribution process is no longer necessarily a physical process, comprehending the true meaning of market orientation in respect to technology appears to be a key factor for success (Branback, 1997). For this understanding to be realized, the way that the marketing concept itself is perceived needs to be revised.

Revising the dominant logic of marketing

Several authors argue that the Internet phenomenon has assisted an evolution in the 'marketing concept' (McKenna, 1995; Hoffman and Novak, 1996. Brannback (1997) believes that as we move into electronic markets there is a devolvement from 'marketplace' to 'market space'. The rule in marketing has been the principle of managing the marketing mix better than competitors (Kotler, 1997). However, though the marketing mix has in the past been easily defined, it is not today (Brannback, 1997).

Hoffman and Novak (1996), for instance, highlight the necessity of an evolution in terms of integrating the marketing concept with aspects of the Internet. A number of different models have been developed by authors (see Armstrong and Hagel III, 1996; McBride, 1997; Hoffman and Novak 1997) in order to serve this purpose. One of the most remarkable models is the ICDT model, generated by Angehrn (1997). The model stands as a means of interpreting the Internet in which the market space lies as an information space (IS), a communication space (CS), a distribution space (DS) and a transaction space (TS). Brannback (1997: 702) believes that the major advantage of the ICDT model is that: 'it puts the traditional marketing mix in a new light'.

Hence, a metamorphosis in the context and content of marketing is taking place (Brannback, 1997). Nevertheless, few tourism or hospitality organizations seem to have a thorough understanding of these ongoing changes. As Rayport and Sviokla (1994) point out, the ability of adapting to the new dynamic shifts of technology is a crucial factor for success, while inability to understand the differences between the marketplace and the market space can result in unfavourable outcomes. Considering the fact that the Internet is increasingly becoming an effective marketing tool, it is evident that a clear understanding of the emerging opportunities in the market space will have a impact on the process of integrating the elements of the promotion mix in an optimal way.

The promotion mix

Promotion is the term used for the description of the set of the communication activities designed and undertaken by tourism or hospitality organizations so as to affect the target markets on whom their sales depend (Cooper *et al.*, 1998; Witt and Moutinho, 1995). Every single element of the marketing mix has a communication function (Rossiter and Percy, 1998), but promotion is the only element charged with the responsibility to 'move products forward' (Shimp, 1997). Accordingly, 'the promotion mix' is the descriptive term for the total marketing communications programme of an organization consisting of four influential tools. Bennett (1998) defines these as:

1. *Advertising*: any paid form of non-personal presentation and promotion of ideas, goods and services by an identified sponsor.
2. *Sales promotion*: short-term incentives to encourage purchase of a product or service.

3. *Personal selling*: oral presentation in a conversational form with one or more prospective purchasers for the purpose of making sales.

4. *Public relations*: a variety of programmes to improve, maintain, build or protect a company or product image.

Each of the aforementioned promotional forms is characterized by its own advantages and disadvantages and, therefore, its diversified capacity in achieving different promotional objectives (Cooper *et al.*, 1998). They can be judged in terms of their relative strengths and weaknesses in terms of communication, awareness, comprehension, conviction and success in undertaking action. Having introduced the elements of the promotion mix, the discussion now focuses on the concept of advertising.

The advertising concept

Advertising and sales promotion are the most utilized elements of the promotion mix (Cooper *et al.*, 1998). However, advertising has always been unique mainly because of its presence in everyday life. As an outcome of this commonality, several definitions on the subject have been developed by authors in recent years. Although the myriad aspects embracing the field of advertising render the existence of a universally accepted theory rather unlikely, today most definitions converge with advertising being described as any paid form of non-personal communication through the media which details an idea, product or service that has an identified sponsor.

Currently, advertising is going through a rapid metamorphosis. As Rossiter and Percy (1998: xiii) point out: 'The whole field of advertising has changed radically and irrevocably, being conceived much more broadly than before'. This radical change is the result of the 'integrated marketing communications' (IMC) revolution that has occurred during the last decade. The concept of IMC is best reflected in the following basic principles (Rossiter and Percy, 1998: 7):

1. Selective combination of appropriate types of advertising and promotion.
2. Meeting a common set of communication objectives.
3. Integration over time with regard to customers.

The new emphasis put on the concept of IMC has had a great impact on advertising, which, according to Gopalakrishna and Chaterjee (1991), has evolved in at least four ways:

1. Detecting the accountability for overall advertising and promotion co-ordination.
2. Deciding the point of entry of advertising in the campaign.
3. Wider co-ordination between the existing media choices.
4. Achieving consistency of positioning in campaigns reaching multiple target groups.

Having identified what the new integrated orientation of advertising is about, we now look at how it fits into the elements of the marketing mix.

The marketing mix: an IMC approach

According to Van Waterschoot and Van de Bulte (1992) the new emphasis on IMC has produced a new marketing mix. The three traditional Ps (product, price and place) remain unchanged, while the fourth traditional P (promotion) has been renamed 'Personal selling'. Promotion now has a much broader meaning, becoming not only adaptive to new terms but also synonymous with a new marketing concept, expressed with an 'integrated marketing communications' perspective.

However, with regard to the indeterminacy that characterizes communication terminology, this situation becomes more confusing when traditional terms are changed and expressed in a way that complicates rather than clarifies the matters. In turn, attention needs to be paid both to the terminology used and to the applicability of such terms in the study and practice of marketing communications under the new framework brought forth by the introduction of technological changes in the field. In this respect, since the Internet is increasingly conceptualized as an effective marketing tool, the identification of the key marketing management issues involved in implementing effective Internet-based promotional strategies appears to be key for the tourism and hospitality industry in the twenty-first century.

The Internet: an emerging advertising medium

While in 1994 the WWW did not manage to attract any advertising dollars, in 1997 about US$200 million were spent on advertising in the medium (Yovovich, 1998). Although this is not much when compared to other media (e.g., US$32.4 billion spent on television advertising in 1995), the leap from zero spending to US$200 million in a period of only three years is characteristic of the revolutionary impact of the medium on the field of advertising. In the same respect, another recent survey undertaken by the Internet Advertising Bureau (see Table 4.3) indicates the growth in this area.

Because the WWW is fundamentally different from the traditional media, it is often difficult to implement conventional marketing activities in their existing form. Therefore, marketers have to reconsider the traditional principles of marketing and reconstruct them in a way that fits well into the characteristics of the new information-intensive environments (Glazer, 1991). However, from an advertising perspective the interactivity of the new medium is clearly far more

Table 4.3	Period of time	$ million
Advertising on the Internet, 1996–7	Jan–Jun 1996	81.8
	Jul–Dec 1996	185.1
	Full year 1996	266.9
	Jan–Jun 1997	343.9

Source: Internet Advertising Bureau (1999)

important (Hammil and Kitchen, 1999). Since the underlying assumption of all mass media advertising models is interaction, a new model that will allow consumers to interact with the medium needs to be developed (Hammil and Kitchen, 1999). These shifts in existing advertising patterns hold important implications for recognition of the Internet as a legitimate medium in the communication process for all economic sectors, including tourism and hospitality.

Advertising on the web: some issues for the tourism sector

The Internet is a generator of opportunities and new markets for all organizations (McBride, 1997). In this respect, with the continuing growth of the Internet, and in particular the WWW, a new marketing potential for tourist organizations has emerged. Therefore, the Internet can be thought of as a promotional tool, with the dimensions of the advertising concept expanded and the tourism experience enhanced. As such, the Internet has the potential to become an effective medium of advertising in destination marketing programmes.

While the communication concept appears to build upon the developments ocurring in IT, at present a lack of appreciation of the WWW is apparent in the tourism field. According to Cano and Prentice (1998: 67): 'The remedying of this under-development in hospitality and tourism may be hindered by the experiences of those tourism businesses using the WWW to meet the immediate demands of visitors but failing to "capture" business in this medium'. With the exception of the tourism industry, other sectors are taking the lead in offering full services through the Internet. This growing trend appears to be the outcome of the dominant notion that if an organization is not fully committed to doing business on the Internet, it will experience unfavourable consequences (Widdifield and Grover, 1995; Abraham, 1996). McBride (1997) believes that such rhetoric is leading companies to jump onto the Internet without considering the implications for their business. This contention does not imply that tourist organizations have adopted a more cautious approach towards the use of the Internet. Their under-utilization of the Web as a promotional tool in the tourism field is more the result of not fully realizing the potential that the new technology can offer than the consideration of costs and benefits of its use within the sector. Whatever the case may be, the need for a cautious approach involving the match of the business's structure with the elements of the Internet is important. This matching process should also take into account the characteristics of Internet respondents in order to identify the probability of their qualifying as potential travellers.

User characteristics: an eye on data

Before attempting to draw linkages between the Internet and the tourism industry, surveys identifying the characteristics of Web respondents have to be undertaken (Schonland and Williams, 1996). As Hoffman *et al.* (1995) note, a considerable number of surveys of this kind have been conducted in recent years. However, few studies make reference of the potential advantages and limitations of the methodologies applied in collecting and interpreting this information. As a result, the connotations derived from these surveys often generate a wide range of viewpoints that imply mistrust regarding the Internet (see, for example, Hoffman, 1996).

Nevertheless, some of the general conclusions emerging from these studies indicate that the average age of users is about 35 years old, that males as opposed to females predominate and that an increasing number of non-academics and non-professionals are accessing the Web. A Net Traveler Survey (NTS), based on 45 questionnaires conducted by CIC Research in 1995–6 and on data provided by Survey.Net, corroborated the aforementioned trends. From a respondent age-mix perspective almost 50 per cent of NTS participants were between 25 and 35, and over 20 per cent were between 18 and 24. The average age of respondents, as mentioned, was 35. The results of a similar survey conducted by Survey.Net (www.survey.net.inet2r.) confirm these outcomes. Therefore, as Cano and Prentice (1998) suggest: 'WWW homepages have the potential to become powerful advertising and marketing tools, as the demographics of Web users indicate a market of well educated and affluent groups of consumers'.

Establishing advertising objectives

The establishment of objectives is the prime decision to be taken in developing an advertising campaign. Similarly, Crossier (1999) believes that the development of specific advertising programmes requires the setting of certain objectives to serve as a 'prelude' to the stage of planning and implementation. According to Kotler *et al.* (1996), an advertising objective is an assessed communication task addressed to a specific audience during a stated period of time.

One of the most important aspects of this setting process is the need to recognize the relationship between advertising and marketing objectives. An early approach to this issue was taken by Boyd *et al.* (1972). According to their 'attitudinal approach', advertising objectives have to be correlated to the organization's marketing objectives by identifying both the advertising functions and the results that they will achieve. The need to distinguish between marketing and advertising objectives is also underlined by Crimp and Wright (1995: 206): 'In order to create effective advertising it is necessary to consider how advertising can work to further the marketing objective and, so, to arrive at a definition of a specific advertising objective'.

Another issue related to the function of establishing objectives for advertising plans is the concept of the product life cycle. In contrast to the common belief that the creative content of advertising is all that changes over time, today it is generally accepted that the role of advertising is being modified throughout the different stages of a product's life cycle (McDonald and Payne, 1998). This latter assumption seems to be in accordance with the classification of advertising objectives discussed by Kotler *et al.* (1996), according to which objectives can be classified as informative, persuasive or reminding, depending on the purpose they serve.

As clearly demonstrated in the figure, *informative* objectives are usually the most important ones during the early stages of the life cycle when awareness has not been created. Then the setting of *persuasive* objectives takes place by way of developing and establishing an attitude towards the advertised product, service or idea. Ultimately, *reminding* objectives are established later in the product life cycle when there is a need to reinforce the existing attitudes.

Finally, a common approach to the establishment of advertising objectives is to consider their impact on the selected target markets as a 'hierarchy of effects' (Aaker and Meyers, 1987). As Johnson and Messmer (1991: 18) explain, the notion of the 'hierarchy of effects' is that: 'Advertising may directly influence the sales of a product or service and also have an indirect effect on sales through its influence on intervening mental constructs'.

Having commented on the issues related to the process of establishing advertising objectives, the role of advertising in the destination marketplace is now introduced.

The role of advertising in managing destination image

As mentioned previously, tourism is a major world industry, and several countries rely on tourism revenues in their balance of payments (WTO, 1994). With tourism emerging as an influential growth sector in the world economy in recent years, national governments and local authorities have become increasingly aware of the influence this industry can exert in improving the trade balances of a country (Faulkner, 1997). Many have sought to improve their competitive position through the implementation of National Tourism Administration (NTA) activities, with an emphasis on deploying a co-ordinated approach to promoting their country's image abroad.

Country image can be defined as the sensations that an individual or a group of people have about a country in which they do not live (Hunt, 1975). As Bojanic (1991) states, perceptions and notions about country image are formed through advertising and promotion, travel agents, and previous experiences. Due to the inability of destinations to dramatically change their physical features (e.g., landscape), the necessity of basing their images on simplistic attributes that offer the conditions required for developing and sustaining some kind of competitive advantage is evident. For this purpose, an increased commitment of several national governments and authoritative bodies to the principles of tourism marketing, and particularly in the use of advertising as a strategic marketing tool, has been in evidence in recent years (WTO, 1994).

A number of studies have discussed the significance of promotional strategies in managing destination image via advertising (Goodrich, 1978; Reilly, 1990; Bojanic, 1991). According to Bojanic (1991), advertising is an essential part of promotional strategy as it provides one of the most effective means by which a country can promote its image to potential tourists and travellers. Additionally, Reynolds and Gutman (1984) believe advertising to be valuable in creating and regulating the image of a product. Furthermore, according to Gunn (1993), the impression people have of a place that they have never visited can be improved through advertising.

Before tackling these matters in this area it is first necessary to examine the different aspects involved in the evaluation research process of the tourism and hospitality sectors.

Advertising evaluation research

As the importance of the role of advertising in tourism has increased, the need for, and interest in, methods which evaluate its effectiveness with respect to an organization's ongoing planning and management processes has engendered great attention among practitioners and academic circles (see, for example, Pizam, 1990; Woodside, 1990). Meanwhile, the increasing external pressures on national tourism organizations (NTOs) to conduct more rigorous activities for the assessment of their advertising campaign outcomes, combined with the development of awareness of the concept of strategic marketing, have been conducive to the growing interest in evaluation research within the tourism sector (WTO, 1994; Cook and Azucenas, 1994). Additionally, as Siegel and Ziff-Levine (1990) state, calls for the implementation of more systematic evaluation procedures for the justification of marketing budgets are reasonable and are thereby likely to increase.

While evaluation research has been recognized as a function of great significance in the last few years, the fact that in the tourism context evaluation is a multidimensional procedure places destination marketing organizations in a rather uncomfortable position (Burke and Resnik, 1991). According to McWilliams and Crompton (1997), destination advertising evaluation efforts have become more complicated because of the lack of direct sales figures. However, it appears that although destinations have extensively used evaluation research as a tool for assessing the performance of their different promotional efforts, there have been very few studies that have actually recognized the aforementioned complexity.

Despite these problems, today most authoritative bodies related to tourism promotion campaigns undertake some kind of evaluation research, thus indicating a growing recognition that tourism advertisers have to take responsibility for assessing the impacts of advertising in the field (Burke and Resnik, 1989). This growing trend towards the adoption of advertising evaluation procedures was developed in the spring of 1988, when the US Department of Commerce formed a task force consisting of interested professionals to investigate the issues related to accountability in travel marketing (Wynegar, 1989).

In one sense, a well-structured evaluation programme plays an influential internal role by contributing to the organization's ongoing management processes while providing the means for assessing its performance with respect to its operating environment (Faulkner, 1997). Therefore, evaluation can be characterized as a multidimensional approach providing information both for rational decision-making and for assessing the results of those decisions on the basis of the set evaluation objectives (Stufflebeam and Shinkfield, 1985).

The dimensions of advertising evaluation research

According to the declaration of the New South Wales Office of Public Management (NSWOPM, 1991), evaluation can be defined as a systematically conducted process aimed at assessing a programme's performance in an unbiased way. However, no single approach that unambiguously draws linkages between the immediate impacts of advertising and the market's response exists.

In fact, this research task is central to the setting of appropriate objectives for the evaluation of the advertising programmes.

The issue of developing and establishing evaluation objectives has been a topic of heated debate both in the commercial and tourism sectors for many years. Despite the ongoing debate, recent research evidence indicated that, as a rule, the prime objective in any evaluation process is to quantify the net benefits of the questioned programme (Witt and Moutinho, 1995; Faulkner, 1997). Among the range of objectives that have a bearing on evaluation research, economic objectives have been arguably the most systematically examined and, therefore, their context is better understood. However, such a preoccupation with economic benefits and costs appears to be less understandable when evaluating promotional campaigns that have been developed in order to create awareness or generate enquiries and bookings (Burke and Resnik, 1990). In the same context, Hunt (1971) questions the application of economic objectives in destination advertising. In particular he believes that: 'Measuring return on investment (ROI) for tourism organizations is complicated because most are unable to be particularly product-specific or narrow in their marketing efforts'.

An alternative approach to the continuing issue of establishing evaluation advertising objectives is to assess destination advertising performance on the basis of converted visitor numbers. The validity of this statement has been a matter of heavy critique during recent decades (see, for example, Paraskevo-poulos, 1977; O'Hagan and Harrison, 1984). Indeed, as Faulkner (1997: 24) puts it: 'There is a strong case for using indicators other than this as a basis for evaluating results'. However, the unavailability of comparable data other than visitor numbers across many markets inevitably leads to discussing tourism advertising evaluation patterns in terms of actual visits (Barry and O'Hagan, 1972). Over and above these matters, the continued reliance on ROI objectives does not contribute to the improvement of either advertising quality or validity in accountability measures. The assessment of promotional performance in terms of visits is, only in part, justifiable from a research perspective (Schoenbachler et al., 1995; Burke and Resnik, 1991).

In order to meet its set objectives, the evaluation process involves four overlapping procedures. The effectiveness question, which is the central issue of interest in this section, is addressed mainly in the causal analysis and performance stages. In other words, effectiveness as a key criterion used to measure an organization's performance in this process, is assessed on the basis of examining outputs and outcomes, two of the most challenging tasks of the evaluation process where the establishment of links between advertising and market response is the major issue (Faulkner, 1992).

Assessing destination advertising effectiveness

What constitutes advertising effectiveness is most often viewed as a complicated topic as some in the field claim that advertising is effective only in the case of causing sales, while communication proponents contend that a sequence of stages interposes between the stage of unawareness and the final sale of a product or service (Barry, 1987). This contradiction has engendered a fierce debate, clearly reflected in the main body of the relevant literature. While empirical studies aimed at assessing the impact of advertising on sales date back to the 1930s (Butterfield *et al.*, 1998), the first attempt to consider advertising as an influential element of tourism demand took place almost 40 years later (Mok, 1990). Since the pioneering work of Diamond (1969), many changes have occurred in the techniques and methods utilized for measuring the effectiveness of destination advertising. The most important of these methods and techniques are commented on in the following sections.

Conversion studies

Today, destination advertising campaigns are, as a rule, evaluated by conversion studies (McWilliams and Crompton, 1997; Butterfield *et al.*, 1998). Tourism conversion studies are used as a tool for measuring the number of enquiries responding to travel advertisements converted to visitor numbers (Ellebrock, 1981; Gray, 1970; Woodside and Ronkainen, 1984). In addition, Schoenbachler *et al.* (1995: 3) point out that: 'Typically the conversion study involves drawing a sample from a database of inquirers who responded to advertising messages during the past year'.

According to Siegel and Ziff-Levine (1990), the conversion study model ensures a flow over time that leads from production of an advert to motivation and conversion. Although a considerable number of conversion studies have been reported since the pioneering work of Woodside and Ronkainen, little evolution or innovation in their approach has occurred (Woodside and Ronkainen, 1984). Nevertheless, despite the growing number of conversion studies being currently conducted, a review of recent articles focusing on issues emerging from the use of conversion methods for the measurement of the effectiveness of tourism destination advertising reveals that by 1990 the appraisal of this research had become resolutely unfavourable (see, for example, Mok, 1990; Woodside, 1990; Siegel and Ziff-Levine, 1990). As Messmer and Johnson (1993: 14) observe: 'The general conclusion, is that traditional conversion studies suffer from methodological and design problems which limit their usefulness.' With these limitations in mind, Burke and Resnik (1991) brought into the discussion a number of underlying assumptions on which this kind of research is based and which appear to have been substantially disregarded in the vast majority of relevant studies. As an outcome of this, most conducted studies based on the conversion approach do not meet rigorous research standards (Burke and Resnik, 1990).

It would seem that conversion studies have been extensively misused, affecting negatively the credibility of evaluation research in the tourism sector. However, the adoption of the extreme position that this approach should be disregarded as a factor in any advertising evaluation research should not be supported. Therefore, if conversion studies are to be utilized as an efficient technique for measuring advertising effectiveness: 'Strategies and procedures must be developed which assure that the results will be as accurate and useful as possible' (Burke and Resnik, 1991: 50).

Advertising tracking studies

An alternative method for measuring the effectiveness of destination advertising is the advertising tracking method. This model: 'Describes changes in levels of a destination's awareness and its image in target markets, before and after those markets have been exposed to the destination's advertising campaign' (McWilliams and Crompton, 1997: 129).

On the importance of tracking studies, Davidson (1994) draws attention to the relationship between an advertisement and its potential impact on a person's mind. This relationship is far more direct and easy to be studied than any other approach to the issue of advertising evaluation and should therefore be the focal point of any evaluation research. However, the fact that the advertising tracking approach hypothesizes that potential visitors may be convinced to purchase a tourism service solely on the basis of awareness and image-creation impacts seems to be a major drawback. Further, the fact that no definite conclusions can be drawn about the influence of advertising on travel behaviour renders tracking studies more valuable from a diagnostic perspective (Siegel and Ziff-Levine, 1990). Conclusively, as Faulkner (1997) claims, tracking studies are requisite if the early link in the causal chain is to be confirmed, but an alteration in the pre-adaptation of the market towards a specific destination is not necessarily translated into actual travel. This appears to be the main reason why tracking studies have not been as frequently used as the conversion approach.

True-field experiments

According to Faulkner (1997), the myriad of aspects that impinge on the market's response require great internal validity, which can only be achieved by adopting an experimental approach. Similarly, Woodside (1990) has advocated the use of true experiments to provide valid answers to the question of whether destination advertising causes visits. More specifically, he argues for the use of split-run tests to establish causal linkages between destination advertising and visitors. Split-run tests involve exposing distinct markets to a number of different adverts (Russell and Lane, 1992; Belch and Belch, 1993). In a split-run research project, two groups of subjects need to be appointed: a control group and a treatment group. Advertising effectiveness is then assessed by a questionnaire-based postal test in both groups and by contrasting the differences between them (Woodside, 1990; Haley and Baldinger, 1991).

According to the limited literature on this subject, the use of the split-run method in tourism research offers several advantages. First, by using this method tourism authorities can demonstrate causality between advertising and sales (Schoenbachler et al., 1995). Second, the findings of such methods have strong external validity (Stewart, 1989). Finally, the split-run technique is accordant with the setting and use of communications objectives in tourism research (Schoenbachler et al., 1995).

Taking the converse view, the major problem with true experiments is that: 'The targeting of areas for promotion is itself influenced by an assessment of the likely responsiveness of populations in these areas, which in turn compounds comparisons with control groups in non-targeted areas' (Faulkner, 1997: 28).

Furthermore, as Schoenbachler et al. (1995) observe, although split-run techniques have been suggested as efficient applicable methods for testing the significance of advertising effectiveness, because of their proper nature no published results from the implementation of this method in the tourism field exist up to date. Therefore, it appears that the major issue is not whether or not true experiments can be used as viable methods for assessing the impact of tourism advertising on sales, but whether the research conditions permit the interpretation of such studies to the tourism marketplace. In considering these limitations, it can be seen that there is a growing need for further research efforts on the topic, especially from the tourism standpoint.

Assessing the effectiveness of the WWW

As tourism organizations intensify their promotional efforts on the Web, questions related to the assessment of website advertising effectiveness arise. Despite the importance of the topic, up-to-date Internet evaluation research is heavily under-represented in the relevant literature. In one of the few studies conducted on the issue of measuring the effectiveness of the Internet, Hoffman and Novak (1996) suggest a three-tiered evaluation process. According to their belief, promotion on the Web should be measured in terms of the vehicle, page and advertisement level. In a study of similar context, Nielsen Media Research (1996) put forward a number of measurements such as number of respondents and time spent on the website in question.

In the absence of pertinent studies, further research efforts need to be undertaken so that tourism promotion on the Internet will not just turn out to be another unrealized potential opportunity for the sector.

Summary

This chapter has attempted to describe some of the main elements related to the concept of advertising as a strategic marketing tool. It began by attempting to illustrate the development of marketing, marketing communications and the various aspects contained in the promotion mix. In doing so, the aim was to mention some of the issues affecting them rather than to describe each element thoroughly. Furthermore, the role of the Internet in destination marketing programmes was introduced. Finally, the chapter has framed this discussion in the context of tourism advertising while providing a theoretical background to the techniques and methods used to evaluate destination advertising sales effectiveness. In conclusion, the main purpose of this chapter has been to provide a critical account of previous work in the area of marketing communications and particularly in the field of advertising evaluation research in the tourism context.

References

Aaker, D.A and Meyers, J.G (1987) *Advertising Management*, 3rd edn, Englewood Cliffs, NJ: Prentice-Hall.

Abraham, J. (1996) 'The Internet: the ultimate shopping worldwide mall', *Tourism*, Spring, 21.

Angehrn, A.A. (1997) 'The strategic implications of the Internet', in M. Branback 'Is the Internet changing the dominant logic of marketing?', *European Management Journal*, 15, 6, 698–707.

Armstrong, A. and Hagel III, J. (1996) 'The real value of online communities', *Harvard Business Review*, May–June, 134–41.

Athiyaman, A. (1995) 'The interface of tourism and strategy research: an analysis', *Tourism Management*, 16, 6, 447–53.

Bagozzi, R.P. (1986) *Principles of Marketing Management*, Chicago: Science Research Associates.

Barry, K. and O'Hagan, J. (1972) 'An economic study of tourism expenditure in Ireland', *Economic and Social Review*, 3, 2, 143–61.

Belch, G.E. and Belch, M.A. (1993) *Introduction to Advertising and Promotion management*, New York: Irwin.

Bennett, R. (1998) 'The booking process: the developers' perspective', presentation at Euro-Hotec, Nice, International Hotel and Restaurant Association, Paris.

Bojanic, D.C. (1991) 'The use of advertising in managing destination image', *Tourism Management*, 12, 4, 352–5.

Booms, B.H. and Bitner, M.J. (1981) 'Marketing strategies and organisation structures for service firms', in J. Donnelly and W.R. George (eds), *Marketing for Services*, Chicago: American Marketing Association, 47–51.

Boyd, H.W. Ray, M.L. and Strong, E.C. (1972) 'An attitudinal framework for advertising strategy', *Journal of Marketing*, Spring, 27–33.

Branback, M. (1997) 'Is the Internet changing the dominant logic of marketing?', *European Management Journal*, 15, 6, 698–707.

Buhalis, D., Tjoa, A.M. and Jafari, J. (1998) *Information and Communication Technologies in Tourism*, Vienna and New York: Springer-Verlag.

Burger, F. (1997) 'TIS and Web-Database supported tourist information on the web', in *Information and Communication Technologies in Tourism*, Proceedings of the International Conference in Edinburgh, Scotland, New York: Springer-Verlag, 39–46.

Burke, J.F. and Resnik, B.P. (1991) *Marketing and selling the travel product*, Cincinnati, South West Publishing.

Butterfield, D.W., Kenneth, R.D. and Kubursi, A.A. (1998) 'Measuring the returns to tourism advertising', *Journal of Travel Research*, 37, August, 12–20.

Cano, V. and Prentice, R. (1998) 'Opportunities for endearment to place through electronic visiting: WWW homepages and the tourism promotion of Scotland', *Tourism Management*, 19, 1, 67–73.

Cook, S.D. and Azucenas, V. (1994) 'Research in state and provincial travel offices', *Journal of Travel Research*, 35, Winter, 23–32.

Cooper, C. (1995) 'Strategic planning for sustainable tourism: the case of the offshore islands in the UK', *Journal of Sustainable Tourism*, 3, 4, 191–209.

Cooper, C., Fletcher, J., Gilbert, D., Shepherd, R. and Wanhill, S. (1998) *Tourism Principles and Practice*, Harlow: Addison-Wesley Longman.

Crimp, M. and Wright, L.T. (1995) *The Marketing Research Process*, 4th edn, Hemel Hempstead: Prentice-Hall.

Day, G. (1986) *Strategic Marketing Decisions*, New York: West Publisher.

Ellebrock, M. (1981) 'Improving coupon conversion studies', *Journal of Travel Research*, 19, Spring, 37–8.

Faulkner, B. (1997) 'A model for the evaluation of national tourism destination marketing programs', *Journal of Travel Research*, 35, Winter, 23–32.

Faulkner, H. W. (1992) 'The anatomy of the evaluation process', *Journal of Travel Research*, 35, Winter, 23–32.

Frew, A.J. and Dorren, C. (1997) 'Intelligent agents and the UK hotel sector', Proceedings of the Hospitality Information Technology Association World-Wide Conference, Edinburgh, 18–20 May.

Gilbert, D.C. and Kapur, R. (1990) 'Strategic marketing planning and the hotel industry', *Hospitality Management*, 9, 1, 27–43.

Glazer, R. (1991) 'Marketing in an information-intensive environment: strategic implications of knowledge as an asset', *Journal of Marketing*, 55, October, 1–19.

Goodrich, J.N. (1978) 'The relationship between preferences for and perceptions of vacation destination: application of a choice mail', *Journal of Travel Research*, Fall, 8–13.

Gopalakrishna, S. and Chaterjee, R. (1991) *A Communication Response Model for a Mature Industrial Product: Applications and Implications*, Working paper, College of Business Administration, Penn State University.

Gunn, C.A. (1993) *Tourism planning*, 3rd edition, Washington, D.C., Taylor and Francis.

Haley, R.I. and Baldinger, A.L. (1991) 'The ARF copy research validity project', *Journal of Advertising Research*, April–May, 11–32.

Hammil, J. and Kitchen, P. (1999) 'The Internet (international context)', in P. Kitchen (ed.) *Marketing Communications: Principles and Practice*, London: International Thomson Business Press, 381–402.

Hoffman, D.L. and Novak, T.P. (1997) 'Marketing in hypermedia computer-mediated environments: conceptual foundations', *Journal of Marketing*, 60, 3, 50–68.

Hoffman, J.D. (1994) 'Emerging technologies and their impact on travel distribution', *Journal of Vacational Marketing*, 1, 1, 95–103.

Hunt, J.D. (1991) *Image a factor in tourism*, unpublished doctoral thesis, Fort Collind CO, Colarado State University.

Inskeep, E. (1991) *Tourism Planning: An Integrated Planning and Development Approach*, New York: Van Nostrand Reinhold.

Jain, S.C. (1997) *Marketing Planning and Strategy*, 5th edition, Cincinnati, OH: South Western.

Johnson, R.R. and Messmer, D.J. (1991) 'The effect of advertising on hierarchical stages in vacation destination choice', *Journal of Advertising Research*, 31, 6, 18–24.

Jung, H.S. and Baker, M. (1998) 'Assessing the market effectiveness of the world wide web in national tourism offices', in D. Buhalis, A.M. Tjoa, and J. Jafarids (eds), *Information and Communication Technologies in Tourism*, Vienna and New York: Springer-Verlag, 94–102.

Karcher, K. (1996) 'The four global distribution systems in the travel and tourism industry', *EM-Electronic Markets*, 6, 2, 20–4.

Kimber, L. (1997) 'Net working for business', *Caterer and Hotelkeeper* 27 March, 77–8.

Kitchen, P.J. (1999) *Marketing Communications: Principles and Practice*, London: International Thomson Business Press.

Kotler, P. (1997) *Marketing Management Analysis, Planning and Control*, 9th edition, Englewood Cliffs, NJ: Prentice-Hall.

Kotler, P. and Armstrong, G. (1994) *Principles of Marketing*, 6th edn, Englewood Cliffs, NJ: Prentice-Hall International.

McBride, N. (1997) 'Business use of the Internet: strategic decision or another bandwagon?', *European Management Journal*, 215, 1, 58–67.

McCarthy, E.J. (1978) *Basic Marketing: A Managerial Approach*, 6th edn, Homewood, IL: Irwin.

McDonald, M. (1995) *Marketing plans – how to prepare them – how to use them*, Oxford, Butterworth Heinemann.

McDonald, M. and Payne, A. (1998) *Marketing Planning for Services*, Oxford: Butterworth-Heinemann.

McKenna, R. (1995) 'Real time marketing', *Harvard Business Review*, July–August, 87–95.

McWilliams, E.G. and Crompton, J.L. (1997) 'An expanded framework for measuring the effectiveness of destination advertising', *Tourism Management*, 18, 3, 127–37.

Mok, H. (1990) 'A quasi-experimental measure of the effectiveness of destination advertising: some evidence from Hawaii', *Journal of Travel Research*, 29, Summer, 30–4.

New South Wales Office of Public Management (1991) *New Requirements and Guidelines for Program Management*, Sydney: NSWOPM.

Nielsen Media Research (1996) *Web Audience Measurement: Issues, Challenges and Solutions*, http//www.nielsenmedia.com

O'Hagan, J.W. and Harrison, M.J. (1984) 'Market shares of US tourism expenditure in Europe: an economic analysis', *Applied Economics*, 16, 6, 919–31.

Paraskevopoulos, G.N. (1977) *An Economic Analysis of International Tourism*, Lecture Series 31, Athens: Centre for Planning and Economic Research.

Payne, R. (1993) *The Essence of Service Marketing*, Englewood Cliffs, NJ: Prentice-Hall International.

Pfaffenberger, B. (1993) *Que's Computer User Dictionary*, Que's University of Virginia.

Pizam, A. (1990) 'Evaluating the effectiveness of travel trade shows and other tourism sales-promotion techniques', *Journal of Travel Research*, 29, Summer, 3–8.

Rayport, J.F. and Sviokla, J.J. (1994) 'Managing in the marketplace', *Harvard Business Review*, November–December, 141–50.

Reilly, M.D. (1990) 'Free elicitation of descriptive objectives for tourism image assessment', *Journal of Travel Research*, 29, Spring, 21–6.

Reynolds, D.J. and Gutman, J. (1984) 'Advertising is image management', *Journal of Advertising Research*, 24, 1, 27–38.

Robson, W. (1994) *Strategic Management and Information Systems*, London: Pitman.

Rossiter, J.R. and Percy, L. (1998) *Advertising Communications and Innovation Management*, New York: McGraw-Hill.

Russell, J.T. and Lane, R.W. (1992) *Kleppner's Advertising Procedure*, Englewood Cliffs, NJ: Prentice-Hall International.

Schoenblacher, D., Di Benedetto, A., Gordon, G. and Kaminski, P. (1995) 'Destination advertising: assessing effectiveness with the split-run technique', *Journal of Travel and Tourism Marketing*, 4, 2, 1–22.

Schonland, A. and Williams, P. (1996) 'Using the Internet for travel and tourism research: experience from the net traveller survey', *Journal of Travel Research*, Autumn, 81–7.

Schulz, A. (1996) 'The role of global computer reservation systems in the travel industry today and in the future', *EM-Electronic Markets*, 6, 2, 17–20.

Shaw, R. (1997) 'Cost can influence internet decisions', *Hotel and Motel Management*, 15 September, 19 and 86.

Sheldon, P. (1994) 'Information technologies and computer systems', in S.F. Witt and L. Moutinho (eds) *Tourism Marketing and Management Handbook*, 2nd edn, Hemel Hempstead: Prentice-Hall, 126–30.

Sheth, J.N., Gardner, D.M. and Garrett, D.E. (1988) *Marketing Theory: Evolution and Evaluation*, New York: John Wiley and Sons.

Shimp, T.A. (1997) *Advertising, Promotion and Supplemental Aspects of Integrated Marketing Communications*, Fort Worth, TX: The Dryden Press.

Siegel, W. and Ziff-Levine, W. (1990) 'Evaluating tourism advertising campaigns: conversion vs advertising tracking studies', *Journal of Travel Research*, 28, 3, 51–5.

Smith, C. and Jenner, P. (1998) 'Tourism and the Internet', *Travel and Tourism Analyst*, 1, 62–81.

Stufflebeam, D.L. and Shinkfield, A.J. (1985) *Systemic Evaluation*, Boston: Kluwer Nijhoff.

Van Waterschoot, W. and Van de Bulte, C. (1992) 'The 4P classification of the marketing mix revised', *Journal of Marketing*, 56, 4, 83–93.

Wardell, D. (1998) 'The impact of electronic distribution on travel agents', *Travel and Tourism Analyst*, 2, 5–6.

Webster, F.E. (1986) 'Marketing strategy in a slow growing economy', *California Management Review*, Spring, 93–105.

Welch, S.J. (1996) 'The Internet: still not enough known about IT says conference', *Hospitality*, August–September, 31.

Widdifield, R. and Grover, V. (1995) 'Internet and the implications of the information systems for business', *Journal of Systems Management*, 65, 16–21.

Wigand, R.T. (1997) 'Electronic commerce: definitions, theory and context', *The Information Society*, 13, 1, 1–16.

Witt, S.F. and Moutinho, L. (1994) Tourism marketing and management handbook, 2nd edition, London Prentice Hall.

Woodside, A.G. (1990) 'Measuring advertising effectiveness in destination marketing strategies', *Journal of Travel Research*, 29, Autumn, 3–8.

Woodside, A.G. and Ronkainen, I.A. (1984) 'How serious in non-response bias in advertising conversion research', *Journal of Travel Research*, 26, Spring, 34–7.

WTO (1994) *National and Regional Tourism Planning: Methodologies and Case Studies*, London: Routledge.

WTO (1998) Tourism 2020 Vision, WTO, Madrid.

Wynegar, D. (1989) 'US Department of Commerce: Task Force on accountability research', *Journal of Travel Research*, 27, Spring, 41–2.

Yovovich, B.G. (1998) 'Webbed feat', *Marketing News*, January, 19.

Further reading

Arthur Andersen (1997) 'Hospitality and leisure', *Executive Report*, Fall, 4, 2.

Bradley, F. (1991) *International Marketing Strategy*, Hemel Hempstead: Prentice-Hall.

Bradley, S.P., Hausmann, J.A. and Nolan, R.L. (1993) *Globalization, Technology and Competition*, Boston: Harvard Business School Press.

Brown, F. (1998) *Tourism Reassessed, Blight or Blessing?*, Oxford: Butterworth- Heinemann.

Buhalis, D. (1998) 'Information technology', in C. Cooper C *et al.* (eds) *Tourism Principles and Practice*, Harlow: Addison-Wesley Longman, 423–46.

Cooper, C. (1997) 'Strategic perspectives on the planning and evolution of sestinations: lessons for the Mediterranean', paper presented to the seminar: Tourism in the Mediterranean; University of Westminster, December.

Gee, C. (1994) *International Hotel Development and Management*, Michigan: Educational Institute of the American Hotel and Motel Association.

Geller, L. (1998) 'The demands of globalization on the lodging industry', *Florida International University Hospitality Review*, 16, 1, 1–6.

Joyce, P. and Woods, A. (1996) *Essential Strategic Management: From Modernism to Pragmatism*, Oxford: Butterworth-Heinemann.

Kinsey J. (1988) *Marketing in Developing Countries*, London: Macmillan.

Kotler P., Bowen, J. and Makens, J. (1996) *Marketing for Hospitality and Tourism*, Englewood Cliffs: NJ: Prentice-Hall International.

Morrison, A. (1989) *Hospitality and Travel Marketing*, New York: Delmar.

Poon, A. (1993) *Tourism, Technology and Competitive Strategies*, Wallingford: CAB.

Porter, M. (1990) *The Competitive Advantage of Nations*, New York: The Free Press.

Seaton A.V. and Bennett M.M. (1996) *The Marketing of Tourism Products: Concepts, Issues and Cases*, London: International Thomson Business Press.

Szivas, E. (1999) 'The influence of human resources on tourism marketing', in F. Vellas and L. Becherel (eds) *The International Marketing of Travel and Tourism*, Hampshire: MacMillan Press.

Teare, R. *et al.* (1997) *Global Directions: New Strategies for Hospitality and Tourism*, London: Cassell.

Thomas, R. (1996) 'Assessing and influencing the policies of the European Union', in Kotas, R., Teare, R., Logie, J., Jayawardena, C. and Bowen, J. (eds) *The International Hospitality Business*, London: Cassell.

Thomas, R. (ed) (1998) *The Management of Small Tourism and Hospitality Firms*, London: Cassell.

Terpstra, V. and Sarathy, R. (1991) *International Marketing*, Florida: The Dryden Press.

Vernon, R. (1966) 'The product cycle hypothesis in a new international environment', *Quarterly Journal of Economics*, May, 190–207.

World Tourism Organization (1999) *Marketing Tourism Destinations On-Line*, Madrid: WTO.

5 Global branding

Branding definitions

Kotler and Armstrong (1999: 260) provide the following definition of a brand: 'A brand is a name, term, sign, symbol or design, or a combination of these, intended to identify the goods or services of one seller or group of sellers and to differentiate them from those of competitors.' In her article 'Brands and brand equity: definition and management' Wood (2000) criticized this definition for being too product-oriented. She presented a more customer-oriented definition of a brand developed by Ambler (1992), who characterizes a brand as: 'the promise of the bundles of attributes that someone buys and provide satisfaction... The attributes that make up a brand may be real or illusory, rational or emotional, tangible or invisible' (Wood, 2000: 664). Wood combines these two approaches to create her own definition, which gives a more holistic picture and illustrates how a brand benefits both customers and owners: 'A brand is a mechanism for achieving competitive advantage for firms, through differentiation (purpose). The attributes that differentiate a brand provide the customer with satisfaction and benefits for which they are willing to pay (mechanism)' (Wood, 2000: 666).

The definition offered by Kotler and Armstrong (1999) was based on the brand definition that The American Marketing Association first published in 1960 (Wood, 2000). However, due to increased globalization and a greater choice in products and services, organizations need to view their brands as more than a list of features, a logo or a slogan. A brand has to be thought of as a relationship with the customer (Khermouch, 2001). It is not the brand name or logo itself that differentiates a product or service as the associations people have to a brand are often more important.

A brand association is anything that is directly or indirectly linked in memory to a brand (Aaker, 1992: 211). These associations can be linked to the product/service class, the application or user of the product/service, a celebrity, or lifestyle and feelings. Specific brand associations can create a key competitive advantage. Colgate toothpaste, for example, is associated with clean white teeth, whereas Crest toothpaste is associated with cavity prevention (Aaker, 1992). Another example is Omega, which uses Pierce Brosnan, Anna Kournikova and Cindy Crawford to advertise their watches and therefore creates an image for their brand that is difficult to copy. An further example is the non-profit organization Save the Children, which in its adverts portrays young, hungry, abandoned children. These advertisements are meant to appeal to emotions in order to convince people to support their cause.

Brand equity

The term 'brand equity' has been developed to describe the relationship between brands and customers. Marketers employ this term to describe both the associations and beliefs consumers hold concerning a specific brand (image), and the strength of consumer attachment to a brand (loyalty). The accounting profession has a different approach to the term brand equity. The total value of the brand is viewed as an asset on the balance sheet, and an aid to increased profits. These various aspects of brand equity are believed to be related in a manner in which a successful brand image provides brand loyalty and therefore generates profit, or increased market share in the case of a non-profit organization (Wood, 2000).

Brand image

The associations and the beliefs that consumers have about a product or service make up the brand image (Kotler and Armstrong, 1999). David Ogilvy, who was one of the forefathers of advertising, developed the brand image philosophy based on the idea that a product or service could not be everything to all people. A product or service needed a personality or an image that consumers can identify with (Wilson and Gilligan, 1997), in order to obtain sustainable competitive advantage through differentiation (Kim and Lavack, 1996). Meenaghan states in his article 'The role of advertising in brand image development': 'the development of brand image involves the marketer in breathing life into an innate product' (Meenaghan, 1995: 25). This can appropriately be illustrated by Figure 5.1.

The image or symbols of a brand are developed to offer added value to the customer, yet only brands that proficiently create images and symbols that exploit the lifestyle and the adopted values and needs of customers will be successful. In addition, the brand name chosen should support the product and the symbolism in fulfilling customer expectations (Meenaghan, 1995).

Figure 5.1

The elements of branding

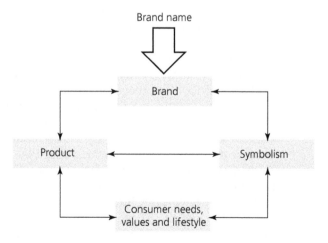

Source: Meenaghan (1995: 26)

Advertising is one of the primary elements in establishing brand image. According to Meenaghan 'It has two major functions, namely to present and thereby position brand attributes against consumer expectations and to imbue the brand with values symbolically attractive to the target market' (1995: 31). The first issue refers to informative communication of functional benefits, whereas the latter refers to creating a brand personality or symbolic values that appeal to the customer's values and lifestyle (see Figure 5.2).

In today's intensified competitive environment, and with the trend towards more homogeneous products as a result of technical advancement, a focus on symbolic values or image is becoming increasingly important. However, a successful brand image is dependent on both functional and symbolic components (Meenaghan, 1995). A brand can be communicated through both verbal (brand name) and non-verbal (design, logo, typeface or symbol) elements. However, in international marketing great emphasis is put on the non-verbal elements, since language can create barriers to effective communication of the brand (O'Sullivan, 1993).

Brand loyalty

'The main objective of the brand is gradually to establish brand goodwill through consumer brand awareness and recognition' (Usunier, 2000: 339). Building a brand image that is associated with specific values is a long-term process, and should therefore be regarded as an investment in the future, since a strong brand generates customer loyalty, which is one of the most important assets of an organization (Aaker, 1992; Meenaghan, 1995).

The majority of brands are launched nationally, and only a few achieve an international status. Those that do become world famous share a common feature of long-term orientation (Usunier, 2000). International brands have been built by persistent promotion, because brand goodwill is not achieved in a day; it is necessary to develop consumer trust over a substantial time frame (Davies, 1995; Godin, 1999). The goal of achieving customer loyalty will therefore only be

Figure 5.2

Practical and symbolic attitudes to buying brands

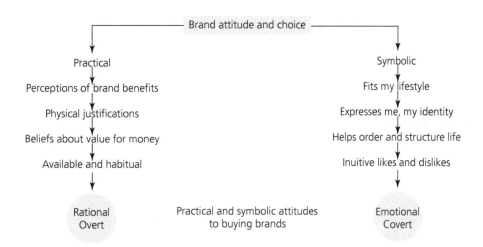

Source: Meenaghan (1995: 31)

achieved through a consistently maintained relationship with the firm's customers (Khermouch, 2001).

Competitive positioning

In today's global market there are numerous brands available to satisfy a specific need of a customer. However, which brand the customer ultimately chooses to purchase depends upon several factors (see Figure 5.3). First, the customer will only be able to choose from those brands he or she is aware of. Second, the customer will only consider those brands that meet the initial buying criteria. Third, several more brands will be excluded on the basis of the customer's perceptions of the brand attributes (Kotler, 1997). Finally, the brand that best fits the customer's values and lifestyle will be chosen (Meenaghan, 1995).

In her article 'Are your members loyal to your brand' Varela (1998) defines branding as 'positioning a company effectively in consumers' minds' (Varela, 1998: 1). The various elements in the marketing mix (price, place, product and promotion) are exploited and combined to create a specific brand image (Meenaghan, 1995). A successful brand image is, therefore, often the most effective method of defending an organizations' competitive position. It is not, however, necessary to use all the elements of the marketing mix to develop a brand – the potential alternatives are numerous (White, 1993).

Branding strategies

Several branding strategies exist to create brand equity and position a brand in the mind of the customer. An organization must therefore choose the strategy most likely to generate success for their products or services. Possible branding strategies include traditional strategies (which are discussed in most academic books), emerging strategies that are becoming increasingly accepted due to globalization and new technological developments to name but a few factors, and strategies that have existed for some time without receiving the same acknowledgement as more traditional ones. Traditional branding strategies consist of brand expansion, brand leveraging, multibrands and co-branding.

Figure 5.3	Total set	Awareness set	Consideration set	Choice set	Decision
Successive sets involved in consumer decision-making	IBM Apple Dell Hewlett Packard Toshiba Compaq NEC Tandy	IBM Apple Dell Hewlett Packard Toshiba Compaq	IBM Apple Dell Toshiba	IBM Apple Dell	?

Source: Kotler (1997: 194)

Brand expansion

A brand expansion (or brand extension) strategy aims at introducing a new product or service utilizing the established image of a core brand to gain acceptance for the new product or service in the marketplace (Kim and Lavack, 1996).

There are two principal approaches to brand extension; horizontal and vertical. Horizontal brand extension relates to situations where an organization takes on either additional related products/services to the existing brand portfolio or completely different products/services. The vertical approach refers to the introduction of products/services in the same category as the core brand, but in a different quality and price class (Kim and Lavack, 1996).

The brand extension strategy has several advantages. A recognized core brand will ease the acknowledgement of the new product or service, thus saving extensive promotional costs that normally are necessary when launching a new brand. However, there is a potential risk of diluting the image of the core brand if the new product or service does not conform to customers' expectations (Kotler and Armstrong 1999; Godin, 1999).

Brand leveraging

Brand leveraging (or umbrella marketing) is in reality a form of brand extension, but it has been allocated the status of a separate strategy by certain marketers (Kim and Lavack, 1996). This strategy comprises two methods, which are corporate umbrella branding and family umbrella marketing. The former refers to the decision to match the name of the products/services with the name of the organization. The latter method allows an organization to create several named product/service groups under a common name (Wilson and Gilligan, 1997). Brand leveraging is meant to bring to mind associations of common

Figure 5.4

How a brand fits together

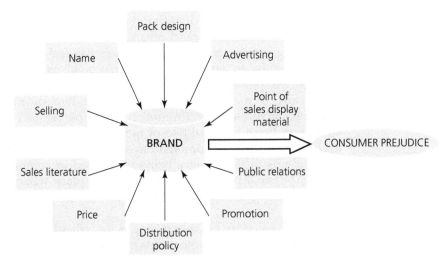

Source: White (1993: 5)

attributes, benefits and values of the products/services under the corporate or family umbrella (Keller, 1998).

There is a trend towards international companies placing their brand portfolios under house (corporate) or sub-house (family) brands. It has been argued that the brand leveraging strategy is necessary to achieve recognition in the global pool of products and services (Laverick, 1998). However, there is a certain risk that products/services that do not perform to customers' expectations will dilute the image of the brands under the family/corporate umbrella (Kim and Lavack, 1996).

Multibrands

Multibrands can also be said to be a sub-category of brand extension and the opposite of brand leveraging. They are formed when organizations launch several products/services in the same category but with different names and images. A multibrand strategy is adopted by organizations that aim to reach various market segments, with various values and/or lifestyles, with their products/services (Kotler, 1997; Meenaghan, 1995).

There are several reasons for an organization to decide to develop a multibrand strategy, including creation of flanker brands to protect and support the core brand (Kotler, 1997), ensuring more shelf space, and developing healthy competition between the various internal brands (Kotler and Armstrong, 1994). However, there is a fundamental risk that this strategy will be less effective, since resources will have to be distributed among the various brands instead of being concentrated on developing one (or a few) brand image(s) (Kotler, 1997). Furthermore, there is a potential risk of cannibalism if the market is not successfully segmented (Meenaghan, 1995).

Co-branding

Co-branding (dual branding, or brand alliances) takes place when the promotion of two or more brands is consolidated in order to strengthen the preference for the individual brands (Rao and Ruekert, 1994, in Keller, 1998).

Several varieties of brand alliances exist, including joint promotions, joint advertising, promotion of complementary use and physical product integration. The former is an attempt of the brands in the alliance to improve their competitive position by being associated with the other brand(s). Joint advertising is a specific technique where two or more brands create one combined advertisement. Promotion of complementary use is applied to create an illusory bond between two or more brands of products/services, which are likely to be utilized in combination, with the intention of enhancing the chance of all brands in the alliance being purchased in combination with each other. Finally, physical product integration takes place when two products/services are brought together to create an inseparable product/service (Washburn *et al.*, 2000).

One sub-category of co-branding is ingredient branding, which refers to the branding of materials, components and parts that are naturally enclosed in other branded products/services. This form of co-branding has increased in recent years as mature brands have been seeking cost-effective ways of establishing differentiation, and the ingredient products need opportunities for expansion (Keller, 1998).

It is expected that co-branding will enable the brands to reach a broader audience, since the associations related to the individual brands will differ (Kotler, 1997). However, there is a potential danger that a customer's negative experience with one of the brands will negatively affect the brand equity of the other brand(s) in the alliance (Washburn *et al*, 2000).

The key factor in the success of co-branding is that both brands have strong separate brand equity and that these are compatible, in order to maximize the positive and minimize the negative impacts. Co-branding decisions therefore require substantial research and consideration. In his book *Strategic Brand Management: Building, Measuring and Managing Brand Equity* Keller quotes an executive at Nabisco: 'Giving away your brand is a lot like giving away your child – want to make sure everything is perfect' (Keller, 1998: 286).

The financial arrangement between the two parties often takes the form of licensing fees and royalties from the brand that is dominant in the production process. Licensing refers to contractual agreements that allow a company to utilize another brand's identity to enhance the image of their own brand (Keller, 1998).

Alternative branding strategies

There are numerous alternative branding strategies, some that have been present for decades without attaining academic acknowledgement, and some that are emerging with the increasing speed of technological development, including branding for non-profit organizations, celebrity endorsement and building brands on the basis of celebrity image, generic branding, brand pirating, and branding on the Internet.

Branding of non-profit organizations

Non-profit organizations mainly offer intangible services and comprise several entities, i.e., education, health care, social causes, geographical areas, people, ideas, and religious principles (Zikmund and D'Amico, 1989). Previously, marketing of non-profit organizations was seen as unnecessary because it wasted valuable resources that could be spent in other areas (Kotler and Andreasen, 1996). Most non-profit organizations are financially weak and are therefore unable to achieve all their set objectives, which also has had an effect on their ability to apply expensive marketing tools (Zikmund and D'Amico, 1989). However, today it is becoming increasingly acknowledged that non-profit organizations need to develop a brand image to create differentiation from competitors, and attract potential donors, volunteers and supporters (Anonymous, 2002b). If a non-profit organization did not adopt a branding strategy and strive to manifest a clear vision, the organization would soon get an identity crisis in today's pool of global competition within this sector (Ydstie, 2001).

'Social marketing', which emerged in the 1990s, relates to one aspect of the non-profit sector (Kotler and Andreasen, 1996) and refers to marketing activities that aim to increase the acceptability of social causes, ideas or desirable behaviour (Zikmund and D'Amico, 1989). 'Social marketing seeks to influence social behaviour not to benefit the marketer but to benefit the target audience and the general society' (Kotler and Andreasen, 1996: 389).

In the branding of non-profit organizations it is important that the image created is appealing and strong enough to trigger attention (Anonymous, 2002b). Therefore, the success of a non-profit organization depends on the extent to which their brand(s) create(s) emotional associations for their volunteers and fundraisers, and on clear differentiation from their competitors who are competing for the same time, funding and attention (Anonymous, 2000). The price that people pay to maintain these organizations is represented by the money, time and effort they provide to support them. People, governments and businesses do not have resources to support all causes, and it is therefore extremely important to create a clear image in their minds of what values and beliefs the organization represents (Zikmund and D'Amico, 1989).

Celebrity endorsements and celebrities as brands

Branding can reach further than just products and services, because organizations, people and geographical places can also be branded. Organizations and people usually have established images that people associate them with (Keller, 1998). Celebrity endorsement, which became common several decades ago, was simply an attempt by marketers to achieve brand recognition by associating their products/services with a celebrity (Brewster, 2001). The justification for using celebrity endorsers was that the associations people have about the celebrity would have a positive effect on the associations people have about a brand (Keller, 1998). The use of a celebrity endorsement can therefore aid the development of brand image, efficiently assist the development of brand equity, and strengthen the brand's competitive position (Till, 1998).

The associations that customers have of the celebrity will be transferred to the brand, and it is therefore important to choose a celebrity that has a common image with what is desirable about the brand. Furthermore, extensive repetition of the pairing of the brand and the celebrity increases the chances of connected associations. The effect will therefore be greater if the celebrity endorser is used over a substantial length of time (Till, 1998). In addition, it is important that the celebrity endorser has a high level of visibility and an extended list of potential associations, and is regarded as trustworthy and amiable by the target audience (Keller, 1998).

There are several possible problems with associating a brand with a celebrity endorser. First, over-exposure of the celebrity will result in reduced effect. Second, if the brand and the celebrity are mismatched, the associations brought to the brand from the celebrity might be unfavourable. Third, the chosen endorser might lose popularity by, for example conducting unfavourable behaviour, and thus diluting the image of the brand. Fourth, customers might feel that the celebrity is only involved in the endorsement for personal gain and, thus, might not believe in the brand. Finally, the celebrity might take attention away from the brand, thus leaving customers to remember the star in an advertisement instead of the brand (Keller, 1998).

Nowadays, the marketplace is moving beyond celebrity endorsers, to the idea of developing new products/services based on a celebrity's image

(Brewster, 2001). There is a move away from celebrity endorsers and towards celebrity branding, since merely using celebrity endorsers means paying a famous person to pretend he/she uses a particular brand. By giving the celebrity ownership, including them in the design and production phase and making them personally involved in the process, credibility will increase, thus giving a greater return on investment (Fortin, 2002). Oprah Winfrey, for example, has expanded her brand portfolio well beyond her popular talk show by extending her life brand to include a magazine and a book club (Brewster, 2001).

Generic branding

Generic brands universally feature plain packaging and use names that are commonly accepted to describe the product. These 'no-name' products (Zikmund and D'Amico, 1989) use a cost-leader strategy in order to gain competitive advantage, (Wilson and Gilligan, 1997) by producing and distributing at low cost and offering no promise of high quality. These cost savings are transferred to the consumer, (Zikmund and D'Amico, 1989) which therefore can make a good deal if the purchase does not resemble a necessity for superior quality – i.e., the purchase of FMCGs (Fast Moving Consumer Goods) like flour, sugar, cooking oil and plain pasta (Schlitt, 2002).

There is a danger that some brand names will become commonly accepted as generics if the company does not take the necessary measures to protect their identity. This indicates situations where a brand becomes the name for all products/services of that type, for example Aspirin, which before the Second World War was a protected brand name for the German pharmaceutical company Bayer, and today is a commonly used name for headache tablets (Paliwoda and Thomas, 1998).

Brand pirating

D'Astous and Gargouri provided the following definition of brand pirating in their article 'Consumer evaluations of brand imitations': 'Brand imitation is a profitable marketing strategy based on the utilization of similarity (package, design, brand name, advertising, etc) in order to facilitate the acceptance of a brand by consumers' (D'Astous and Gargouri, 2001). Some perceive this definition to be somewhat limited and have therefore constructed a somewhat more complete definition. Brand pirating is an illegal activity (Biron, 2000) that seeks to copy established brands' logos, packaging, images and/or personalities, in order to take advantage of their recognition, to create economic gains and competitive advantage for a copycat product/service (Dobson, 1998).

Brand pirating is becoming an increasing problem in today's global market place (Anonymous, 2002a). There are two forms of pirating: first, there are those who imitate certain aspects of an established brand; second, there are the counterfeit products, which copy all the physical features of a recognized brand (D'Astous and Gargouri, 2001). It is not uncommon to see vendors on the street selling copies of acknowledged brands of clothes, watches, perfumes, etc, for a fraction of the price of the original brand. Another increasing problem involves retailers launching copycat products of established brands (Davies, 1998) based on a pure profit motive or in combination with a competitive motive. In other words, the brand imitation is created to make the customers 'think of' the original brand, whereas the counterfeit product is meant to 'be like' the original brand, just in a cheaper version (D'Astous and Gargouri, 2001).

Theft of and illegal use of identity is, as stated previously, becoming an increasing international problem, and the Internet is intensifying the problem. The Internet eliminates many of the physical barriers that originally made theft of identity difficult. Today, anyone with fundamental computer skills could with great ease copy an organization's logo, product and/or image (Anonymous, 2002a).

Protecting an organization's brands from brand pirating might seem difficult enough in the physical world, and might appear impossible on the Internet. However, there are measures that can be taken to lessen brand pirating and protect the reputation of an established brand (Anonymous, 2002a). First and foremost, it is important to take preventive measures in the form of various legal protections, i.e., copyright, patent trademark and/or register of designs (Davies, 1998). It is extremely important to protect every aspect of the brand's identity in all countries where the product/service is sold (Anonymous, 2002a). However, it is impossible to totally exclude pirating, and it might be necessary to take legal action against pirates that try to take advantage of any part of an established brand image (Biron, 2000). On the Internet several more measures can be applied to decrease the risk of others copying your logo, image etc. First, one could make logos and other graphics part of the wallpaper as opposed to a separate image, which would make it more difficult to copy. Second, one could, although at considerable cost, purchase software that makes it possible to track graphics that have been copied. Finally, one could make spot checks on the Internet to check where the brand name turns up when conducting a search on one of the major search engines (Anonymous, 2002a). In the UK, the Digital Millennium Copyright Act has been established to protect brand identities on the Internet. This act entitles companies to receive information about users from the Internet service providers regarding pirating activities (Biron, 1998).

Branding on the Internet

In his book *Permission Marketing, Turning Strangers into Friends, and Friends into Customers* Seth Godin (1999), the vice-president of direct marketing for Yahoo, states that many marketers make the mistake of treating the Internet as another broadcasting medium to communicate their brands, and that this causes losses of billions of dollars on-line. In turn this also leads to doubt about the usefulness of branding on the Internet. He further explains that the reason for this loss is that 'every time a new medium comes along, everyone wishes it were TV' (Godin, 1999: 144). Therefore, it is important to create a totally unique strategy, constructed around the Internet as a distinctive medium, in order to succeed with building brand equity on the Web (Godin, 1999).

According to Martin Lindstrom (2001a), in his article 'Where's the real risk', the use of the Internet has increased considerably faster than forecasted. However, brand builders are increasingly viewing on-line media as unfashionable and risky. Utilizing the Internet to build or assist building brand equity could therefore be extremely beneficial. First, the numbers of on-line brands have decreased distinctively, resulting in increased visibility. Second, this has resulted in decreased costs of on-line advertising. Finally, as stated above, the use of the Internet is increasing, not decreasing (Lindstrom, 2001a).

What is certain is that when migrating to the Web it is important that every aspect of the existing brand image is transferred. Web aesthetics has an important role, since it can deliver instant brand associations before the user reads a single word. However, this can cause problems. For example, blue colours have been proved to have a soothing effect, thus making users spend more time on a website, whereas bright colours have the opposite effect. This causes problems for well-established brands like Coca-Cola and McDonalds in migrating on-line (Anonymous, 2002d).

Interactivity on-line is a powerful tool in enhancing the brand experience, because the organization will be able to adapt future communications and interaction with consumers according to their previous behaviour on the website. Examples of interactive features include keyword searches, chat rooms, polls, competitions, rewards for completing surveys, games (Anonymous, 2002e) and email marketing. In email marketing the key is to encourage customers to give information about relevant values and preferences in addition to their contact information, in order to reach them quickly and efficiently with special promotions and offers (Phipps and Simmons, 2001)

Brand games are becoming a successful new marketing tool, and are anticipated to become one of the top five electronic channels along with the mobile phone, interactive TV, Internet advertising and email marketing. This can be illustrated by Red Bull's impressive success after being featured in the original Play Station. After each game an advertisement for the energy drink would appear, tempting the player to find out more about the new drink (Lindstrom, 2001b). Companies are also increasingly using SMS (Special Messaging Service) to enforce brand equity – for example, Coca-Cola is using individual passwords on bottles to enable customers to use SMS to see if they have won promotional prizes (Lindstrom, 2001c).

Globalization, branding and the hospitality industry

Having achieved a wider understanding of the complex world of branding, and of the ever-increasing globalization phenomenon (see Chapters 1 and 2) and how it is greatly affecting companies and consumer consumption, a parallel pathway can be drawn on the effects that globalization can have on branding. Powerful and influential firms have been around for a long time, but today it is the sheer scale and scope of globalization that changes the scene. As was demonstrated previously in this chapter, the world of the twenty-first century is dominated by brands; yet, while branding is not a new phenomenon, it seems that the inevitable trend towards globalization is forcing companies to modify their branding strategies and alter their brands to become more 'modernized' and universal – examples being, the Four Seasons Group and the Accor Group. The Accor Group originally adopted a multibrand strategy, whereas the Four Seasons Group adopted a brand leveraging strategy and has transferred its corporate image effectively to the Internet (see Case Studies 1 and 2 at the end of this chapter).

In the development of such companies, many find themselves forced to seek further opportunities to continue the process of brand expansion. In many cases, these opportunities exist by expanding into new countries. The benefits, which can be derived from the economies of production and the apparent similarity of the markets in other countries, have attracted some brands to expand beyond their original marketplaces. The process of developing global brands is very similar to that adopted for national brands, although inevitably the former is both more complex and time consuming. The functional areas of a product may be different from country to country. The fact that many consumers in many countries all drink instant coffee, for example, should not suggest that their expectations of product performance are the same.

Understanding the brand personality is, arguably, even more important in the international context. The dimensions of brand personality are largely perpetual; they relate to the images that have been created over time by the various aspects of marketing. Equally important, however, they relate to elements of consumer behaviour in the different markets.

In some markets the use or possession of a particular product may have no meaning beyond its functional purposes. In others, it may be regarded as a symbol of success or affluence. Setting what, for some, is an aspirational product in a mundane environment (a wholly appropriate setting for others) for advertising purposes is likely to undermine the values associated with the brand (Yeshin, 2000). It is important to ensure there is an adequate fit between the positioning of the brand and the perceptions of the consumers in all of the markets where the brand is to be sold. Ultimately, of course, it may be possible to alter the underlying perceptions and reach a point at which all markets share a common view of the brand.

Global brand names

In the past, most companies established new brand names that made sense in their country. When they later attempted to introduce their brand into foreign markets, some companies discovered that the existing brand name was not appropriate. The name was difficult to pronounce, offensive, funny, meaningless, or already co-opted by someone else. Many companies were then forced to launch new brand names for the same product. This issue resulted in very high costs for many companies. Today, with the globalization phenomenon on the rise, the trend is towards a 'borderless world'. In Europe, custom duties, border delays, and other impediments to inter-European trade are rapidly disappearing. Companies are now eager to launch new brands as 'eurobrands'; Proctor & Gamble, for example, launched its detergent Ariel as a Eurobrand. Clearly, some brand names have gained world-wide acceptance. Companies such as Kodak, McDonalds and Coca-Cola would not think of using different brand names as they enter additional countries. In the international marketing context, great emphasis is usually given to non-verbal elements, given the potential barriers to effective communication of the brand that language can create.

One main advantage of using a global brand name is economy of scale in preparing packaging, labels, promotions and advertising. Advertising economies result from using standard adverts and the fact that media coverage increasingly overlaps between countries. Another advantage is that sales may increase because travellers will see their favourite brands advertised and distributed in other markets. Finally, a world-wide brand name is a power in itself, especially when the country-of-origin associations are highly respected.

There are also costs and risks to global branding. A single brand name may not be as appealing as locally chosen names. If the company replaces a well-regarded local name with a global name, the change-over cost can be substantial. The company would have to inform millions of people that their brand still exists but under a different name. The over-centralization of branding may dissolve local creativity that might have produced even better ideas for marketing the product (Kotler, 1997). Even when a company has promoted its global brand name world-wide, it is difficult to standardize its brand associations in all countries. Heineken beer, for example, is viewed as a high-quality beer in the USA and France, as a grocery beer in the UK, and as a cheap beer in Belgium. A company should adopt a 'think global, act local' strategy that will allow them to globalize those elements that make or save substantial sums of money, and localize those that competitive positioning and success require.

Summary

The traditional perception of branding has been shortsighted and has cast brands as being cynically manipulative. This is due to the overly skewed attention given to one group of stakeholders, namely shareholders. It is time for brands to prove their worth to consumers, their guidance to employees and business partners and, as a result of these activities, their value to shareholders (Van Gelder, 2002).

The arguments that support the importance and value of brands have been provided previously in this chapter. This section aims to expose some anti-branding points of view, as well as to present some thoughts on the future of brands and branding strategies.

The main reason why brands have evolved is to do with the issue of globalization, which has brought forward a significant increase in competition and, subsequently, an increase in consumer choice. However, contrary to popular belief, consumers do not desire choice *per se*. Choice is mainly a mechanism that allows consumers to obtain the products and services that they want at the price they can afford (Van Gelder, 2002). Branding allows for the possibility of catering to this diversity.

Branding appears to be aimed at short-term enrichment of corporations and their shareholders. Consumers are cynically duped into believing that they are purchasing goods and services that have qualities over and above those offered by the competition, while in reality they are paying for fluff and hype (Van Gelder, 2002). Some brands may indeed be manipulative and intended to grasp as much money as possible while the outcome is positive. Such brands, however, do not offer lasting value to customers or manufacturers. The ever-increasing ambition for power and shares has evolved into a business principle where nothing matters except for pension funds, financial institutions and people with surplus cash who wish to wager on the future value of a listed company. As a result, and in many instances, healthy companies have been underestimated and undervalued, while esteemed brands and overvalued companies, with pretty brands yet lacking decent business models, have been the choice. This unfortunate situation has even led some of the healthiest companies to develop brands without substance in the pursuit of higher share prices (Van Gelder, 2002).

The real value of a brand lies in its ability to persuade and please consumers. This does not necessarily mean that technically the best products or services will always win consumers over; rather it means that the knowledge of what consumers need, how they behave, how they think, how they perceive value, and how they reason and decide, defines such outcomes (Van Gelder, 2002). Although none of this is new, the management of many companies is so involved in meeting short-term shareholder demands that they are unable to implement policies aimed at improving the consumer experience.

Progressive globalization, which entails increasing economic, regulatory and political interaction between societies across large parts of the globe, is an issue that brands are facing more and more these days. Conversely, the ever-quickening pace of globalization leads to the revival of local identity and pride among those affected (Van Gelder, 2002). In many countries this occurs in the form of historic awareness and national pride, and in a search for roots and authenticity. Societies are happy to acquire the benefits of modernization, but unwilling to commit to world citizenship. People cling to what binds them locally, emphasizing their differences with other societies, and thus rejecting cultural homogenization.

As a consequence, in this world of competition and globalization, companies in tourism and hospitality need to create customer-oriented brands that cater for individual needs and experiences. Brands will increasingly need to prove themselves to sophisticated customers. Not only will brand claims need increasing substantiation to consumers, but so too will the ethics and behaviour of the company behind the brand.

Case Study 1: Four Seasons

Four Seasons could rightly be described as the world's leading hospitality company within the luxury segment. However, the risk of catering exclusively to the luxury sector includes a possible downturn as a result of changes in the economic environment, changes in travel patterns, political instability and the threat of terrorism. However, the chain has a good reputation, and many of the company's properties have achieved excellent recognition soon after opening – for example, the Four Seasons Las Vegas and Four Seasons V Paris. The first offers an intimate, non-gambling atmosphere in a saturated gambling market. The property almost immediately achieved the American Automobile Association's Five Diamonds, and the average rate for the first year of operation was well above the market average. The latter property received two Michelin stars for its restaurant Le Cinq Rets, and became a field leader for luxury hotels around Paris (Four Seasons, 2002).

Brand extension

Currently, the company manages 51 hotels and resorts, and two residence clubs in 23 countries throughout North America, Europe, Asia, the Middle East, Australia, the Caribbean and South America. In addition, Four Seasons has several private residences, e.g., in San Francisco and Whistler, Canada. In 1999 Four Seasons opened more properties than ever before, e.g., Canary Wharf in London and a resort in Punta Mita, Mexico, and within the next ten years the company wishes to double its number of establishments. The company concentrates on internal expansion, and wishes to focus on the development of their services to the leisure market and of residence clubs and other residential projects (Four Seasons, 2002).

Brand leveraging

Four Seasons has clearly adopted a brand leveraging strategy, placing most hotels, resorts, residence clubs and other residential projects under the corporate umbrella of the Four Seasons name. Other residential projects encompass private residences, which can be rented on a short-term or temporary basis. Four Seasons has vacation villas, city apartments and freestanding estate homes in destinations such as Whistler, Canada, and San Francisco. However, the company also manages nine Regent properties through an agreement with Carlton Hospitality Group, which can be viewed as a family umbrella (Four Seasons, 2002).

Brand pirating

When searching under 'Four Seasons' on the search engine Yahoo, one can access several sites that presumably have tried to benefit from the high recognition of the Four Seasons name. One can, for example, access the website of the Four Seasons Golf and Ski Center, located in the USA. By viewing this company's website and even the logo one can draw the conclusion that the target audience is completely different from what Four Seasons wishes to attract (Four Seasons Golf and Ski Center, 2002). However, what is even more disturbing is the Four Seasons Family Nudist Resort, which appears on the same page as the website for the Four Seasons on the same search engine (accessed 15 April 2002). This company boasts of being the leading nudist facility in Canada, and is a member of the American Association for Nude Recreation (AANR) (Four Seasons Family Nudist Resort, 2002).

Internet

The company's website gives a refined and exclusive impression with the aid of a sophisticated font and style, which resembles the Four Seasons'. The homepage is structured under 'Vacation/Getaways', 'Business Travel', 'About Four Seasons', 'Residential Properties', 'Wedding/Events' and 'Meeting Planning'. This page has also a joint email communication request option, although there is no option for the visitor to contact the company with specific enquiries via email (Four Seasons, 2002).

Customers and employees

Four Seasons regards employees as the key to company's success, and has realized that it requires teamwork and joint effort to satisfy customers. Respecting each other's contribution towards the common goal of guest satisfaction and appreciating the importance of all employees within the company are therefore highly valued. Four Seasons is a customer-focused company, and quality standards emphasize personalized service and do not rely solely on product features such as architecture and décor (Four Seasons, 2002).

Bottom line

In 2000 Four Seasons Inc. achieved record earnings, which increased by 19.2 per cent from the previous year. This growth was due to both to the opening of new hotels and the improvement of earnings within existing properties. Four Seasons has for several years experienced revPAR and operation profits well above the average for luxury hotels. In Europe 1999, the revPAR for Four Seasons hotels was US$221, or 109 per cent above average. Similarly, in 2000 revPAR from core establishments in the North American market was US$242, or 126 per cent higher than average (Four Seasons, 2002).

Case Study 2: The Accor Group

Accor is the principal European group within travel, tourism and corporate services, and one of the world's largest groups within the same categories (see Table 4.4).

The Accor Group has approximately 3600 hotels in 90 countries, as well as travel agencies, restaurants and casinos. In addition, the group provides services to corporate clients and public relations to 12 million people in 31 countries each day. However, for the sake of this case study the focus will be mainly the group's hotel brands, and to a lesser extent the travel agencies, tour operators, onboard train services, restaurants and casinos (Accor, 2002).

Brand expansion

Accor has establishments to cover a wide range of segments around the world (with establishments ranging from zero stars to five stars (Accor, 2002) (see Figures 5.5 and 5.6).

Brand leveraging

The Accor Group has several hotel brands that they grouped together in 1997 under a corporate umbrella, with the goal of achieving a more comprehensive international reputation. Promoting one brand demands much less effort and fewer resources than promoting several different brands. The creation of a corporate umbrella brand has created an influential common identity, which has substantially increased awareness of the group (Accor, 2002).

Multibrands

Even though the Accor Group has grouped their brands under a corporate umbrella with the aim of creating a common image, the various hotel brands have distinctive and separate identities.

Table 5.1   Breakdown of consolidated revenues by geographical area and activity, € million

In € million	France	Europe (ex. France)	North America	Latin America	Other countries	World-wide structures	2001	2000
Hotels	1,677	1,371	1,518	81	304	101	5,052	4,739
Business & Leisure	1,130	926	189	69	289	101	2,704	2,525
Economy hotels	547	445	3	12	15		1,022	922
Economy hotels U.S.A	N/a	N/a	N/a 1,326	N/a	N/a	N/a	N/a 1,326	N/a 1,292
Services	73	166	20	234	5		498	437
Other Activities								
Travel Agencies	67	196	176	33	15	13	500	531
Casinos	302						302	243
Restaurants	83	203		176	10		472	542
On-Board Train Services	153	120				4	277	333
Holdings and others	65	99		13		9	189	187
Dec 31, 2001 total	2,420	2,155	1,714	537	337	127	7,290	
Dec 31, 2000 total	2,360	2,035	1,731	517	258	104		7,007

Source: Accor, *Annual Report*, (2001: 18)
Note: World-wide structure represents activities that are not tied down to a specific region

Figure 5.5   Accor Hotels: world-wide coverage, February 2002

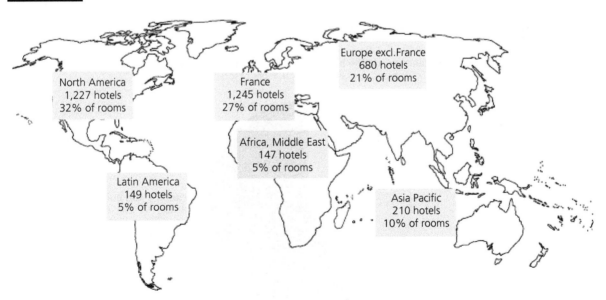

Source: www.accor.com, 2002

Sofitel has 120 hotels in 45 different countries, and operates as a strong competitor in the luxury market. The core characteristics of Sofitel are: refined, personal, efficient, generous, state-of-the-art facilities and advanced technological development.

Novotel is a modern hotel brand, which emphasizes comfortable accommodation among its 336 hotels in 56 countries. The hotels embrace functionality and 'easy-to-live-with' lodging.

Mercure has properties in the middle range of the hotel market. The Mercure network has several sub-brands, including Libertel in France and Belgium, Parthenon in Brazil, All Seasons in Australia and Orbis in Poland. The brand's establishments match the local market and culture, and make up a traditional hotel network.

Artira, which is a specialist in conferences and conventions, has operations connected to both the Novotel brand and the Mercure brand, in 14 different locations. However, the brands for the conference and convention centres are represented with their own identity.

Suitehotel has only three locations, in Lille and Paris, France. All Suitehotels have a functional and modern design, which can be easily rearranged throughout the day for work, holding meetings, relaxing or dining. The aim of this brand is to open establishments in modern buildings in major cultural, political and economic centres across Europe.

Coralia is the holiday expert from Accor with clubs and leisure hotels in 35 exotic destinations in Polynesia, the Caribbean, the Mediterranean, Egypt, the Indian Ocean, Africa, Asia and the Pacific. The 200 clubs and hotels range from three-star to five-star deluxe.

Thalassa has most of its establishments situated in France, but has also expanded and opened single properties in Portugal, Morocco and Sardinia. The

---

Figure 5.6   Accor presence across the hotel range: budget to luxury, February 2002

Presence across the hotel range, from budget to luxury
Hotel portfolio by brand, broken down by number of rooms (February 2002)

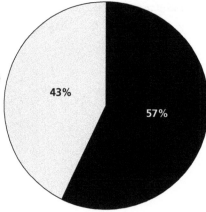

Upscale and midscale
149 Sofitel (29,325 rooms)
342 Novotel (58,224 rooms)
651 Mercure (72,041 rooms)
112 Other brands (19,939 rooms)

43%

57%

Economy and Budget
586 Ibis (61, 254 rooms)
241 Etap Hotel (18,204 rooms)
365 Formula 1 (27,152 rooms)
360 Red Roof Inns (39,592 rooms)
852 Motel 6 (90,130 rooms)

Source: www.accor.com, 2002

focus is on health and fitness in combination with relaxation and leisure, and the brand's specialty is seawater and spring spas for increased well-being.

Ibis boasts of having 586 establishments in 31 countries, with a strong presence in Europe. The majority of properties are situated in city centres, and easy access is emphasized. The brand is known for service and quality at affordable prices, and was the first international hotel chain to achieve the ISO 9002 certification in 1997.

ETAP consists of 241 establishments throughout France, Germany, Great Britain, Hungary, Switzerland and Israel. The brand is situated in the economy-lodging category and all rooms in ETAP hotels can accommodate up to three people.

Formule 1 claim to have the best-value accommodation in the economy class, with a basic though guaranteed level of comfort. All rooms have a TV, and reception and rooms service is open 24 hours a day. There are 365 Formule 1 hotels in 12 countries, and in Counterpaille, France, an affordable grill restaurant reserved solely for Formule 1 guests is to be found near each location.

Red Roof Inns, which have the distinctive and recognizable red roofs, are to be found in 360 locations throughout the USA. In addition to the feature of a red roof, the brand has its own mascot, which can be found on billboards and other promotional material. The Red Roof brand represents the economy-lodging sector and combines simplicity with reasonable prices, value, consistency and excellent service.

Motel 6 has 360 budget motels in the USA and Canada, and is the leader of this sector in the USA. The brand prides itself on offering guests free local phone calls and free coffee in the morning.

In addition, it would be worth mentioning, in brief, the Accor Group's complementary activities to the hotel industry, which include the following brands: Accor Tour (tour operator), Frantour (tour operator and travel agency), Couleurs Locales (tour operator specializing in Tunisia), Lênotre (restaurants), Compagnie des Wagons-Lits (restaurants), Gemeaz Cusin (restaurants), Accor Casinos and Accor Brazil (corporate services and catering) (Accor, 2002).

Co-branding/celebrity endorsement

With the aim of creating an international image, the Accor Group entered into an agreement with the French Olympic Committee in 1999 to sponsor the French team. In this regard a banner with a picture of the French Olympic team was placed on the Sofitel Paris Porte de Sèvre during the Winter Olympic games in Salt Lake City in February 2002 (Accor, 2002).

Internet

The Accor Group strives to make the Internet their number-one distribution vehicle. By grouping the hotel brands together under a corporate umbrella the company wishes to increase awareness of their various brands. Most of the brands are well known in specific regions, for example Formule 1 in France, Red Roof and Motel 6 in the USA and Ibis, Mercure and Novotel in Europe. Therefore, by grouping the brands under a corporate umbrella on the website, the company hopes to raise awareness among customers of the brands that they might not have been previously aware belonged to the group (Accor, 2002).

'Accor 2000' was an initiative to take advantage of the opportunities that the company had identified. One of the opportunities was creating a world-wide image and joint brand associations through the Internet. In 2000, 1 per cent of total bookings were made through the Internet; the figure is expected to increase to 20–5 per cent within the next few years (Accor, 2002). However, as of April 2002, two different websites exist for Accor: www.accorhotels.com and www.accor.com. The latter is without doubt the website that offers the greatest integration between the brands; however, there is a danger of potential guests viewing the first site and ignoring the second, since that is the site which comes up first if one types in Accor on the Yahoo search engine. The information varies somewhat according to which of the two sites the viewer visits – i.e., in relation to the number of establishments that exist under each brand and how many countries the various brands are represented in. The most surprising discovery was that in visiting the Coralia website, through www.accorhotels.com, the logo differed from that found on www.accor.com (Accor, 2002).

Customers and employees

Interlinked with 'Accor 2000', the company has launched the campaign 'Succeeding Together' with the common goal of guaranteeing customer satisfaction across all brands. 'Succeeding Together' further aims at ensuring professional realization of staff across the brands. 'L'esprit Accor' allows training, incentives and commitment to development of staff and fast-track career programmes for staff throughout the group. Accor regards staff to be the number-one asset and place heavy emphasis on training and development, as well as on international recruitment. Furthermore, the company puts great effort into the development of services and products that will enhance employee satisfaction as well as the productivity of the organization, such as employee care and social services (Accor, 2002).

Bottom line

Increased bookings through the Internet will have a positive effect on the bottom line since it is about three times cheaper to operate than more traditional reservation methods. The breakdown of consolidated revenue by geographical area and by activity will help to explain the reasons for the increase of €283 million (4 per cent) in consolidated revenue from 2000 to 2001.

References

Aaker, D.A. (1992) *Strategic Market Management*, New York: John Wiley and Sons, Inc.

Accor (2202) www.accor.com

Anonymous (2000) 'According to Interbrand, it's not enough to just do good, now you need to have a brand to make it as a nonprofit', available at www.elibrary.com

Anonymous (2002a) 'Protecting your logos and brands online', available at www.e-commercebc.ne

Anonymous (2002b) 'Creating a marketing image for your nonprofit organization', available at www.org.sg/news

Anonymous (2002d) 'Designing your site to be on-brand', available at www.connectedinmarketing.com

Anonymous (2002e) 'Quick guide. Using interactivity to enhance the brand experience', available at www.connectedinmarketing.com

Biron, J. (2000) 'The ethics of piracy', available at www.cs.rpi.edu/courses/fall00

Brewster, M. (2001) 'Celebrities – walking, talking brands', available at www.m1.mny.co.za

D'Astous, A. and Gargouri, E. (2001) 'Consumer evaluations of brand imitations', *European Journal of Marketing*, 35, 1/2, 153–67

Davies, A. (1995) *The Strategic Role of marketing*, London: McGraw-Hill.

Davis, G. (1998) 'Retail brands and the theft of identity', *International Journal of Retail and Distribution Management*, 26, 4, 140–6.

Dobson, P.W. (1998) 'The competition effects of look-alike products', available at www.nottingham.ac.uk

Fortin, L. (2002) 'Claudia's palm: reconsidering celebrity endorsement', available at www.brandera.com

Four Seasons Official Website (2002) available at www.fourseasons.com

Godin, S. (1999) *Permission Marketing: Turning Strangers into Friends, and Friends into Customers*, New York: Simon & Schuster.

Keller, K.L. (1998) *Strategic Brand Management: Building, Measuring and Managing Brand Equity*, Englewood Cliffs, NJ: Prentice-Hall.

Khermouch, G. (2001) 'Why advertising matters more than ever', *Business Week*, 6 August, 50–1.

Kim, C.K. and Lavack, A.M. (1996) 'Vertical brand extensions: current research and managerial implications', *Journal of Product and Brand Management*, 5, 6, 24–37

Kotler, P. (1997) *Marketing Management: Analysis, Planning, Implementation and Control*, Englewood Cliffs, NJ: Prentice-Hall, Inc.

Kotler, P. and Andreasen, A.R. (1996) *Strategic Marketing for Nonprofit Organizations*, Englewood Cliffs, NJ: Prentice-Hall, Inc.

Kotler, P. and Armstrong, G. (1999) *Principles of Marketing*, Englewood Cliffs, NJ: Prentice-Hall, Inc.

Laverick, S. (1998) 'Case study – the leveraging of brand equities to create a category champion: Nestlé's management of Cross & Blackwell', *British Food Journal*, 100, 9, 405–12.

Lindstrom, M. (2001a) 'Where's the real risk?', available at www.clickz.com

Lindstrom, M. (2001b) 'Brand games: are you ready to play?', available at www.clickz.com

Lindstrom, M. (2001c) 'Wireless power', available at www.clickz.com

Meenaghan, T. (1995) 'The role of advertising in brand image development', *Journal of Product and Brand Management*, 4, 4, 23–34.

Paliwoda, S.J. and Thomas, M.J. (1998) *International Marketing*, Oxford: Butterworth-Heinemann.

Phipps, R. and Simmons, C. (2001) *The Marketing Customer Interface*, Oxford: Butterworth-Heinemann.

O'Sullivan, T. (1993) 'International marketing', in Preston, A. (ed) *International Business, Text and Cases*, London: Pitman Publishing, 130–40.

Rao A., and Ruekert M. (1994) in K.L. Keller (1998) *Strategic Brand Management: Building, Measuring and Managing Brand Equity*, Englewood Cliffs, NJ: Prentice-Hall.

Schlitt, C. (2002) 'Are generic foods a better buy?', available at: www.urbanext.uiuc.edu

Till, B.D. (1998) 'Using celebrity endorsers effectively: lessons from associative learning', *Journal of Product and Brand Management*, 7, 5, 400–9.

Usunier, J.-C. (2000) *Marketing Across Cultures*, Harlow: Prentice-Hall.

Van Gelder, S. (2002) 'A view on the future of branding', available at www.brand-meta.com.

Varela, P. (1998) 'Are your members loyal to your brand?', available at www.elibrary.com

Washburn, J.H., Till, B.D. and Priluck, R. (2000) 'Co-branding: brand equity and trial effects', *Journal of Consumer Marketing*, 17, 7, 591–604.

White, R. (1993) *Advertising: What It Is and How to Do It*, London: McGraw-Hill.

Wilson, R.M.S. and Gilligan, C. (1997) *Strategic Marketing Management: Planning, Implementation and Control*, Oxford: Butterworth-Heinemann.

Wood, L. (2000) 'Brands and brand equity: definition and management', *Management Decision*, 38, 9, 662–9.

Ydstie, J. (2001) 'Commentary: many non-profit groups suffering from identity crisis', available at www.elibrary.com

Yeshin, T. (2000) *Integrated Marketing Communications*, Oxford: Butterworth-Heinemann.

Zikmund, W. and D'Amico, M. (1989) *Marketing*, New York: John Wiley & Sons.

Further reading

Anonymous (2001) 'Engaging employees through your brand', available at www.conference-board.org

Anonymous (2002c) 'Celebrity advertising: literature review', available at www.home.netvigator.com

Anonymous (2002f) 'The vast global brands', *Business Week European Edition*, 6 August, 44–53.

Anonymous (2002g) 'Rolex advertising through the years', available at www.tcjj.com

Anonymous (2002h) 'Fake and counterfeit watches', available at www.chronocentric.com

Anonymous (2002i) 'Gray market watches ', available at www.chronocentric.com

Buchinger, E.T. (1999) 'Time in motion today: a man's watch often reflects his personality', available at www.elibrary.com

Dautresme, B. (2000) 'A group that looks to the future', available at www.loreal.com

Disney Official Website (2002) available at: www.disney.go.com

Dowling, J. (1998) 'Why it's OK to hate Rolex', available at: http://turfers.com

Kim, H. (2002) 'Branding of nonprofit organizations', available at: www.ciadvertising.org

Klein, B. (1993) 'Brand names', in D.R. Henderson (ed) *The Fortune Encyclopedia of Economics*', New York: Warner Books.

L'Oréal Official Website (2002) available at www.loreal.com

Plan International Official Website (2002) available at: www.plan-international.org

Rolex Official Website (2002) available at: www.rolex.com

6 Destination image and eco-tourism

Introduction

Hunt (1975) argues that the images, beliefs and perceptions that individuals in the market have about a destination may have as much to do with an area's tourist development success as the more tangible recreation and tourist resources. He rationalizes that this occurs because decision-makers, having very limited personal experience of the destination, act upon their images, beliefs and perceptions of the destination rather than objective reality. Mayo and Jarvis (1981) also suggest that what is important is the image that exists in the mind of the vacationer.

Image of a destination is a critical factor when choosing a holiday (Britton, 1979; Mayo and Jarvis, 1981; Mathieson and Wall, 1982). Therefore, an examination of the image formation process may help understand how a tourism promotion organization can change an individual's perception of a destination (Chon, 1990). As such, this chapter looks at the issues surrounding destination image and examines the eco-tourism product.

Eco-tourism has been seen to represent the search for alternative travel, and an image of the product has been created to attract travellers with educational interests in environmental, ethical and cultural issues. However, when it comes to the projection of such an image, this approach has not always been successful.

Image formation process

'Destination images are formed by three distinctly different, but hierarchically interrelated components: cognitive, affective and conative. The interrelationships between these components will determine product predisposition' (Gartner, 1993: 193).

- The *cognitive image* may be viewed as the sum of beliefs and attitudes about an object leading to some internally accepted picture of its attributes. The amount of external stimuli received about an object is instrumental in forming a cognitive image.
- The *affective component of image* is related to the motives one has for destination selection. It becomes operational when the evaluation stage of destination selection begins. Using Goodall's model (1991), this takes place when the choice set of destinations is considered.

- *Conative image* is analogous to behaviour because it is the action component. After all internal and external information is processed a decision is reached – one destination from the decision set is selected. The relationship between the three components is direct and depends on the images developed during the cognitive stage and evaluated during the affective stage (Gartner, 1993: 193).

Gunn (1993) was one of the first to identify the different ways in which cognitive images are formed. He argued that they are formed through induced and organic agents (Gunn, 1988).

- *Organic images* are formed from sources not directly associated with a destination area, from a long history of non-tourist directed communication, unsolicited mass media communications appearing in magazines, newspapers, books, radio and TV programmes, geography books, fiction and non-fiction literature.
- *Induced images* emanate from the destination area and are a function of the marketing efforts of destination promoters; they are a conscious effort to develop and strategically promote a country's tourist attractions by its destination promotion bodies.

The key difference between organic and induced image formation agents is the control the destination area has over what is presented (Gartner, 1993).

From another point of view, Echtner and Ritchie (1993) suggest that destination image can be framed as consisting of three continuums:

- *Attribute–holistic*: destination image should be composed of perceptions of individual attributes (such as climate, accommodation facilities, friendliness of the people), as well as more holistic impressions (mental pictures or imagery) of the place.
- *Functional–psychological*: functional images are directly observable or measurable. On the other hand, psychological images are more intangible or difficult to observe and measure. Both components may be perceived as individual attributes or as more holistic impressions.
- *Common–unique*: this continuum highlights the idea that images of destinations can range from those perceptions based on 'common' characteristics to those based on more 'unique' features or auras.

In order to measure destination image, Echtner and Ritchie (1993) used a final list of 35 destination attributes for developing scale items. The attributes were arranged along the functional (directly observable)–psychological (difficult to observe) continuum (see Table 6.1).

The image formation process can be viewed as 'a continuum of separate agents that act independently or in some combination to form a destination image unique to the individual' (Gartner, 1993: 197). The different types of image formation agents are compared against credibility, market penetration and cost in Table 6.2).

The selection of the right image formation agents to build a desired tourist image depends on many factors, such as:

1. The amount of money budgeted for image development.
2. The characteristics of the target market (i.e., if the decision-making body comprises a family unit, traditional forms of advertising and information from tour operators may be a top priority).
3. Demographic characteristics (i.e., age can influence the credibility of information agents).

Destination attributes

Functional (physical, measurable)

Tourist Sites / Activities
National Parks / Wilderness Activities
Historic Sites / Museums
Beaches
Fairs, Exhibits, Festival
Scenery / Natural Attractions
Night-life and Entertainment
Shopping Facilities
Facilities for Information and Tours
Sports Facilities/ Activities
Local Infrastructure / Transportation
Cities
Accommodation / Restaurants
Architecture / Buildings
Costs / Price Levels
Climate
Crowdedness
Cleanliness
Degree of Urbanization
Economic Development / Affluence
Extent of Commercialization
Political Stability
Accessibility
Personal Safety
Ease of Communication
Customs / Culture
Different Cuisine / Food and Drink
Hospitality/Friendliness/Receptiveness
Restful/Relaxing
Atmosphere (familiar versus exotic)
Opportunity for Adventure
Opportunity to increase knowledge
Family or Adult Oriented
Quality of Service
Fame/Reputation

Psychological (abstract)

Source: Adapted from Echtner and Ritchie (1993)

4. The timing or planning horizon.
5. The product itself, which determines the type of image formation agents that are most useful.

Moutinho (1987) suggests that given the information possessed about a vacation destination, the tourist will form an image related to the destination attributes. The destination image tends to be an oversimplification in the mind of the tourist and, at the same time, a consistent configuration constructed according to the available information. There are three components in image formation:

1. *Level of awareness* in relation to the destination (information the tourist believes a tourist destination possesses).
2. *Beliefs and attitudes* developed about the product. This attitude is based partially on feelings, not solely on knowledge.
3. *Expectations* created about the product.

Concept of projected and perceived image

The OED (1993) defines 'projected image' as a transferred image to external individuals, and 'perceived image' as the understood image of a thing (i.e., a holiday destination) by individuals. In line with these definitions, projected images ultimately derive from the structure of tourism supply, while perceived images, though not directly stemming from it, have an intimate relationship with actual or anticipated tourism behaviour. Figure 6.1 shows the two approaches to place/product images.

Table 6.2 Image formation agents

Image change agent	Credibility	Market penetration	Destination cost
Traditional forms of advertising (i.e. brochures, TV, radio, print, billboards, etc.)	Low	High	High
Information received from tour operators, wholesalers	Medium	Medium	Indirect
Second party endorsement of products via traditional forms of advertising (i.e. celebrity spokesperson)	Low/Medium	High	High
Second party endorsement through apparently unbiased reports (i.e. newspaper, travel section articles)	Medium	Medium	Medium
News and popular culture: documentaries, reports, news stories, movies, television programmes	High	Medium-High	Indirect
Unsolicited information received from friends and relatives	Medium	Low	Indirect
Solicited information received from friends and relatives	High	Low	Indirect
Actual visitation	High	–	Indirect

Source: Gartner (1993: 210)

Messages received by the tourist are sometimes seen as ambiguous when confronted with previous experience. The filtration process serves to protect the tourist since it permits discrimination between facts and exaggerations in advertising. Advertisers and mass communicators attempt to attract attention to the tourist product. The basic assumption of the persuasion paradigm is that creation of a favourable attitude will lead to positive action towards the product (Moutinho, 1987).

In addition, decision-makers use only a few criteria when making a choice. From a marketing point of view it is imperative and highly useful to identify the select few factors which play a crucial role in the final purchase decision, since consumer awareness can be created only if these chosen factors are included in the advertising message. Similarly, including unimportant factors in the message may cause the decision-maker to ignore the entire message (Sirakaya *et al.*, 1996).

A problem with comparing projected and perceived images is that the methods of measurement and description are likely to be quite different. Projected images are nearly always investigated through some form of content analysis of publicity material, while perceived images are obtained through attitude questionnaires or tests of the visitors themselves.

It can be argued that promotional or supply images and tourists' naïve (or demand) images of destination areas may not coincide. The consequences of mismatch between demand and supply images are critical at two stages in the tourist's holiday cycle – the 'decision stage of holiday choice' and the 'reflective stage on return from holiday'. A better understanding is required of how the naïve images of potential tourists can be changed to increase the likelihood of them visiting particular destinations. Producers examine the reactions of consumers, specifically which holiday types and which destinations generated most complaints (Ashworth and Goodall, 1988).

Figure 6.1

Tourism place images in a simple system

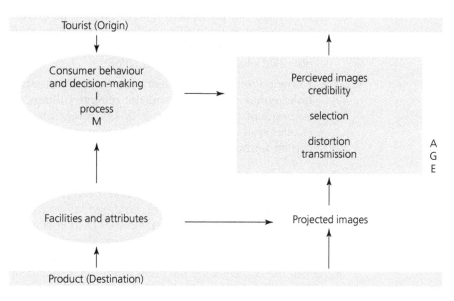

Source: Adapted from Ashworth (1991)

The projected, or marketed, image of a destination is a pull factor (Ashworth, 1991; Baloglu and Uysal, 1996). It is transmitted through various channels of communication, which themselves influence or distort the nature of the message, the strength, effectiveness or credibility of its transmission and the accuracy of the targeting of its reception.

Image, as perceived by customers, is identified as one of five components in the overall tourism product and as a vital element within the augmented product. Accordingly, the image or identity chosen for the purposes of promoting tourism destinations is a matter of the greatest importance to marketing managers, tourism agents and tour operators (Middleton, 1994). Much activity in the tourism industry is aimed not only at informing would-be tourists of the opportunities, but also at being persuasive and creating a favourable image of a particular destination. A positive, high-profile image is essential to keep the tourists coming (Goodall, 1988).

National and regional tourist boards seek to promote a favourable image of their particular destination area by various means. For example, familiarization tours for travel writers or special interest media groups are the vehicle used by many destination area promoters to project a particular image through the publications of those hosted (Gartner, 1993). However, generally, destination area promoters have no control over what appears in a news story and the projected image is based on someone else's interpretation of what is happening in the area.

Ashworth and Goodall (1988) point out that the images projected by destination agencies – the 'official image' – are not the most important source of ideas about a tourist destination held by the potential visitor. The images shaped by the news media, by the personal experience of the visitor on previous holidays and by the second-hand experiences of personal contacts of potential visitors, have emerged in many studies as far more important than the publicity emanating from the tourist destination itself. From this point of view, two main issues emerge:

1. This need not be a disadvantage as long as there is no serious conflict between sources; but in practice much official tourism promotion is 'defensive', that is, endeavouring to correct or counterbalance images obtained elsewhere (Goodall, 1988).

2. Knowledge about the major sources of information that the holidaymaker consults, and the relative influence each has on the subsequent place decision, is of key interest to the destination marketer (Kotler *et al.*, 1993). A classification of the main sources of information can be found in Table 6.3).

The relative influence of these information sources varies according to the destination and the tourist's personal preferences. Typically, the consumer receives most information from commercial sources, but the most trusted information comes from personal sources (Kotler *et al.*, 1993). Each source plays a different role in influencing the buying decision.

Images form part of a consumer's decision-making processes in that they will influence the choices they make (Stabler, 1988). According to Chon (1990, 1991) the role of a destination image in tourism has a greater significance in marketing when viewed through the framework of the traveller's buying behaviour.

Ahmed (1996) argues that tourists perceive many images of their destinations and that these images in turn influence their behaviour, attitudes and predispositions as consumers. The more positive a consumer's attitude, the more positive perception; and the more favourable an image of a product, the more likely it is that those perceptions and that image will influence subsequent behaviour. Quoted by Ahmed (1996), Fishbein's (1967) model states that a consumer's attitude towards an object (in our case, relative preference for one tourist destination over another) is a function of the number of valued attributes that a consumer perceives the object (destination) to have in relation to the significance of those attributes to the consumer (tourist). Thus, a tourist's choice of a destination is largely dependent on how favourable his or her attitude is.

Attitude is 'a predisposition, created by learning and experience, to respond in a consistent way toward an object, such as a product. This predisposition can be favourable or unfavourable' (Moutinho, 1987: 19). In the context of tourism, attitudes are predispositions or feelings towards a vacation destination or service, based on multiple perceived product attributes.

Tourists form 'selected impressions' in that they attend to the information that is most closely tied to their own personal interests. It is not what tourists as consumers know as objective fact, but what they 'think' or 'feel' subjectively about a country as a vacation destination, its tourism resources, its tourist services, the hospitality of its hosts, its sociocultural norms, and its rules and regulations, that affects their consumer behaviour. Thus a country's tourist image is a tourist's mental picture of that particular country. A given image is what tourists, as buyers, 'see' and 'feel' when the country or its attractions come to mind as a place suited to the pursuit of leisure (Ahmed, 1991).

Wherever there is no real change in the service/product itself, advertising naturally plays a vital role in communicating an image that strengthens an existing attitude or encourages a changed attitude towards the service or product (Mayo and Jarvis, 1981).

Table 6.3 The consumer information matrix

	Personal	*Impersonal (mass media)*
Commercial	Travel agents Tour operator reps	Advertising Brochures Tourist board leaflets Videos and displays Teletext
Non-commercial	Word of mouth: Friends, neighbours, relatives School teachers Peer groups (e.g. business, students). Visiting the places	Media output: travel programmes, newspaper travel pages, guide books, news programmes, novels, films, etc.

Source: Seaton (1996: 176a)

Factors influencing projected and perceived image

Some researchers, in particular Hunt (1975) and Mayo (1973, as cited in Chan 1990) indicate that images are both positive and negative, but that the overall view of a region might be favourable or unfavourable. Moreover, because of certain events, images can change radically. According to Stabler (1988), for UK residents the image of Spain has been of an inexpensive, sunny, friendly country with an attractive coastline. Publicity concerning muggings and the activities of the ETA terrorist group has tarnished this image somewhat, though a recent survey indicated visitors' lack of concern about possible violence, and the general image appears to be still favourable.

Gunn (1988) suggests that an individual's travel behaviour can be explained through seven phases, which involve a constant building and modification of images:

1. Accumulation of mental images about vacation experiences;
2. Modification of those images by further information;
3. Decision to take a vacation trip;
4. Travel to the destination;
5. Participation at the destination;
6. Return travel;
7. New accumulation of images based on the experience.

Gunn (1988) points out that the first three phases of his model, which encompass the processes of image accumulation and image modification, and which further influence the individual traveller's decision to take a trip, are the most important in the travel purchasing process. This is because potential tourists, when making a travel purchase decision, rely on their mental images about the destination, which are a sum of their previously accumulated images and modified images obtained through further information research (Mayo, 1973, as quoted by Chon, 1990).

In the same context, Gunn argues that, in most cases, a destination can do little about changing its organic image, but can influence a change of induced image to a greater extent through promotional and publicity efforts. Therefore, Gunn suggests that the end goal of 'image building' should be promoting the modification of an induced image. This view of destination image change has been supported by subsequent empirical studies (Ahmed, 1991; Gartner and Hunt, 1987; Phelps, 1986).

Consumers tend to form images of brands, stores and companies based on the inferences they draw from marketing and environmental stimuli. An image is a total perception of the object that is formed by processing information from various sources over time. Gestalt psychology suggests that forming an image is a natural process of developing a total perception of the object. An important objective of marketing strategy is to influence the perception of a brand, store or company. Thus, marketers are constantly trying to influence consumers' images (Assael, 1992). Personal images are not only influenced by forces external to the individual, but can also be manipulated and even created by them. This, therefore, represents an opportunity for the tourism industry. In practice, it must be admitted that these personal images are more often created as a result of the tourist's general media exposure than the promotional activities of tourism organizations (Goodall, 1988).

Gartner (1993: 205) points out that 'the larger the entity, the more slowly images change', as the speed of change is inversely related to the complexity of the system. The key element in image change is the amount and extent of new information that contrasts with the image currently held.

Tourist destinations spend billions of dollars annually on image building and image correction promotion programmes, such as familiarization tours, travel newsletters, advertising, etc. (Ahmed, 1996). Images change as holidaymakers accumulate experiences and as a result of their acquiring more information, much of which is provided by the tourism industry (Ashworth and Goodall, 1988).

What is needed – if holiday behaviour is to be predicted more accurately, and holiday choice assisted more effectively by the industry – is a thorough understanding of the social and external determinants of holiday choice. The industry needs to know how holidaymakers perceive destinations, air travel, travel distance, self-catering, etc. and to understand the attitudinal dimensions of their products in terms of how these relate to the ego involvement of the holiday-makers. Such an understanding is critical to the improvement of marketing strategies to maintain, change or create attitudes towards holiday products (Goodall, 1991).

Destination image model

Based on an interrelationship between destination image, the traveller buying process, traveller satisfaction and dissatisfaction, and the evaluative congruity approach to understanding consumer behaviour, Chon (1990) presents an integrated model of destination image and the traveller. The essence of evaluative congruity theory is a comparison between performance expectancy (perceived image of a destination) and performance outcome (perceived reality of the destination), as can be seen in Figure 6.2.

Travel motivation is subject to push/pull factors and, when both co-exist, a primary image of the destination is constructed. The individual traveller modifies his/her images of the destination through an information search process. The flow of new information can come from reading books and articles about the travel destination, advertising, news media items dealing with the destination area, or from a discussion of travel experiences with friends and relatives. A positive or negative modified image of a destination will help determine perceived image of a destination (i.e., performance expectancy of the destination).

In the choice process, the various images formed about different destinations or services are considered in relation to the travel motivation, in a conscious or unconscious way, until some alternatives are eliminated and only those whose image fits in with the basic motivations are left. According to Baloglu and Uysal (1996), although motivation is only one variable explaining tourist behaviour, it is regarded as one of the most important variables because it is an impelling and compelling force behind all behaviour.

Hu and Ritchie (1993) argue that familiarity with a destination, which is influenced by such factors as geographic distance, previous personal visitation experience, and the level of overall knowledge about a destination, play an important role in influencing an individual's perceptions of a particular destination. Thus, Hunt (1975) suggested that people who had visited the USA generally had a more favourable opinion than those who had not. Phelps (1986) conducted a survey on the primary and secondary images of Menorca held by returning visitors and first-time visitors. This study revealed that the visitation experiences positively altered respondents' impressions of that island.

When the tourist travels to a destination, has his/her holiday and returns, he/she will have accumulated new images about the destination and the general environment surrounding the entire trip. Therefore, the traveller's previous image of the destination will be reconditioned at the 'recollection stage' through the process of evaluating what he/she has actually experienced at the destination against his/her previous image, with the end result being congruity or incongruity. Chon's hypothesized relationships between previous destination image and what the visitor actually experiences at the destination (perceived reality of destination) are presented in Table 6.4.

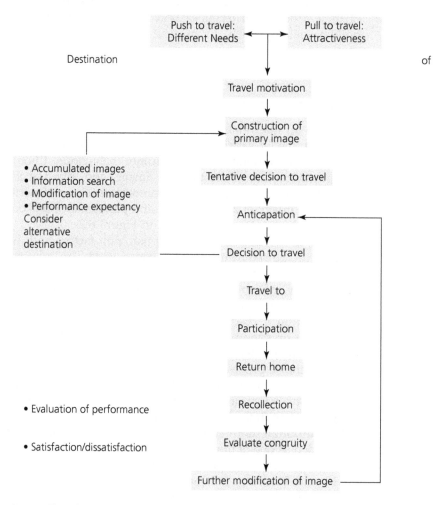

Figure 6.2

Traveller satisfaction and dissatisfaction model

Destination   of

Push to travel: Different Needs   Pull to travel: Attractiveness

Travel motivation

Construction of primary image

- Accumulated images
- Information search
- Modification of image
- Performance expectancy
Consider alternative destination

Tentative decision to travel

Anticapation

Decision to travel

Travel to

Participation

Return home

- Evaluation of performance

Recollection

- Satisfaction/dissatisfaction

Evaluate congruity

Further modification of image

Source: Chon (1990)

According to Chon (1990) and Ryan (1994) the degree of satisfaction and dissatisfaction resulting from the evaluation process may further reinforce the traveller's general images about the destination. Bigné and Zorío (1989) highlight the effects of satisfaction as a basic element of 'feedback' which makes up the future decisions. Thus, if the traveller experienced a high degree of dissatisfaction with the destination, arising from a positive incongruity between his/her perceived image and perceived reality of the experience, he may even consider not revisiting in the future and consider alternatives in future travel purchases.

As such, one of the tourism products receiving alternative preferences is that of eco-tourism. In this respect, eco-tourism has been associated with the changing preferences in consumer attitudes, from mass tourism to something alternative. That said, though this was initially thought to be alternative, unfortunately some eco-tourism practitioners have created false images of their products claiming that they provide eco-tourism services just to increase their demand.

The concept of eco-tourism

Introduction

Eco-tourism has become a concept that appeals to the various parties involved in tourism, although it seems to have been adopted more as a marketing tool than a sensitive planning mechanism. Suggested industry strategies on how to alleviate the problem of numbers include promoting tourism out of season. This can be interpreted as a growth strategy as it will not reduce numbers in peak season but will encourage tourists to visit in the off-season as well. Instead of promoting environmentally responsible behaviour, eco-tourism has provided the tourism industry with a perfect marketing strategy to survive in the modern Green era.

Rejecting mass tourism for eco-tourism development raises questions as to the loss of economic benefits generated by mass tourism. In order to justify the replacement of mass tourism with this alternative form, the assumption that eco-tourism will have fewer and less severe negative effects on destination areas and their populations without diminishing the positive economic effects must be made.

Table 6.4 Evaluative congruity theory

Perceived image of destination	Perceived reality of destination	Evaluative congruity	Degree of satisfaction/ dissatisfaction
Negative	Positive	Positive Incongruity	High Satisfaction
Positive	Positive	Positive Congruity	Moderate Satisfaction
Negative	Negative	Negative Congruity	Moderate Dissatisfaction
Positive	Negative	Negative Incongruity	High Dissatisfaction

Source: Chon (1990)

Looking at the definitions of eco-tourism, there have been a number of attempts at defining the concept. In particular, it has been claimed that the definitional structure of eco-tourism is divided into two schools of thought (Steward and Sekartjakrarini, 1994):

- activity-based perspective;
- eco-tourism as an industry perspective.

Here, the former school is divided into definitions which attest to the role of eco-tourists or what eco-tourists actually do – the value-based component of eco-tourism with a focus on minimum impact and local cultural elements, or what eco-tourists should do (Steward and Sekartjakrarini, 1994: 840). The latter school attests to the supply characteristics of eco-tourism as a tool of conservation and development based on the interrelationship between the local community and the tourism industry (Steward and Sekartjakrarini, 1994: 841).

Generally speaking, eco-tourism is treated both as a sub-component of alternative tourism and as a form of natural-based tourism, being a part of the concept of sustainability (Orams, 2001). In addition, other sustainable products (e.g. agro-tourism, wine tourism, rural tourism) have claimed to have similarities with eco-tourism, as well as being part of both nature-based and alternative tourism (Diamantis, 2003).

At the other end of the spectrum, both mass tourism and other forms of tourism – such as cruise tourism and business tourism – are searching for a sustainable ethos in their practices and, as such, are placed outside the sustainability borders. Eco-tourism's characteristics are opposite to those of mass tourism – especially the experiential aspects. For instance, eco-tourism activities depend on the natural and cultural environment whereas mass tourism activities mostly depend on built environments (see Figure 6.3).

More specifically, eco-tourism was first defined as 'travelling to relatively undisturbed or uncontaminated natural areas with the specific objective of study, admiring, and enjoying the scenery and its wild plants and animals, as well as any existing cultural manifestations (both past and present) found in these areas' (Ceballos-Lascurain, 1987: 14).

Ceballos-Lascurain's definition views eco-tourism in *the light of experimental and educational factors of the protected natural areas* (1987, 1991a, b). He claims that eco-tourism is a multidimensional, philosophical concept in which there is a component of eco-development (1993a: 13, b: 220) and that it requires planning based on strict guidelines and regulations that will enhance the sustainable operation (1993a, b, 1996).

Since the first definitions, myriad other definitions have emerged, all of which highlighted that eco-tourism has three common components (Lindberg and McKercher, 1997):

1. Practiced in a natural-based setting;
2. Sustainable management practices;
3. Environmentally educational programmes.

Although these components are more or less clear, limitations do arise from the fact that there is not an established and accepted definition, which inevitably raises questions over the credibility of the concept. As such, it can be seen that it is better to start to operationalize the issue based on conceptual and technical grounds.

From a conceptual perspective, eco-tourism can be seen occurring in natural settings (protected and non-protected) with an attempt to increase the benefits to the economy, society and environment through sustainable, educational practices from locals to tourists and vice versa (Diamantis, 2003). In measuring eco-tourism at the destination level this definition is still restrictive. It seems that it is better to operationalize the *technical* aspects, based on scenarios and themes.

Technical definitions of eco-tourism

Turning to the technical trade-off definitions of eco-tourism, four different approaches can be devised ranging from very weak to very strong (see Table 6.5).

- In the **very weak definition**, the core emphasis could be given to the natural-based component. For example, *a definition could be formed from measuring the basis of eco-tourism practices in both protected and non-protected areas*.
- In the **weak definition**, the core emphasis could be given mainly to the natural-based component and, to a lesser degree, to the educational and sustainability components. Here, *a definition could stress measuring the basis of eco-tourism practices in both protected and non-protected areas which generate a low level of educational/conservation/economic/social/cultural benefits for the destination*.

Figure 6.3

The position of sustainable tourism and eco-tourism products

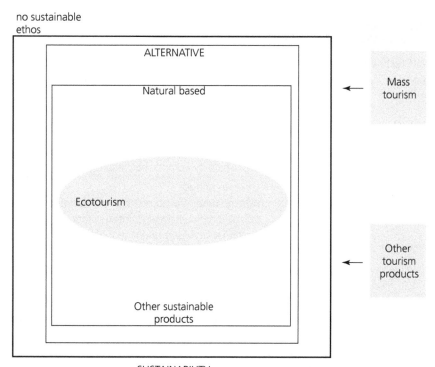

- In the **strong definition**, all three elements should be considered equally. For instance, *a definition could stress measuring the basis of eco-tourism practices in both protected and non-protected areas which generate a high level of educational/conservation/economic/social/cultural benefits for the destination.*

- In the **very strong definition**, all three elements should be equally considered but with less emphasis on the economic aspects of eco-tourism. In this case, *a definition could stress measuring the basis of eco-tourism practices in both protected and non-protected areas which generate a high level of educational/conservation/social/cultural benefits and a low level of economic reward to the destination.*

For the trade-off technical definitions to be operated, an understanding of the different costs and benefits embodied within the components of eco-tourism is also required.

The costs and benefits of eco-tourism: implications for destination image

Eco-tourism carries similar direct and indirect costs and benefits as those attributable to the mass tourism movement (see Table 6.6). Tourism, however, is an extremely dynamic, multidimensional agent of development and change, with social and economic linkages and political significance.

Table 6.5	Definition	Elements
Trade-off technical definitions of eco-tourism	Very weak	Core emphasis: *Natural-based component*: protected and non protected areas
	Weak	Core emphasis: *Natural-based component*: protected and non-protected areas
		Less emphasis: *Educational component*: interpretation and training programmes *Sustainability component*: economic and/or social-cultural elements
	Strong	Core emphasis: *Natural-based component*: protected and non-protected areas *Educational component*: interpretation and training programmes *Sustainability component*: equal emphasis on economic and social-cultural elements
	Very strong	Core emphasis: *Natural-based component*: protected and non-protected areas *Educational component*: interpretation and training programmes *Sustainability component*: emphasis on social-cultural elements rather than on economic elements

Source: Diamantis (2003)

Table 6.6 Hypothetical costs and benefits of eco-tourism

Environmental impacts

Direct benefits
- provides incentive to protect environment, both formally (protected areas) and informally
- provides incentive for restoration and conversion of modified habitats
- ecotourists actively assisting in habitat enhancement (donations, policing, maintenance, etc.)

Direct costs

danger that environmental carrying capacities will be unintentionally exceeded, due to:
- rapid growth rates
- difficulties in identifying, measuring and monitoring impacts over a long period
- idea that all tourism induces stress

Indirect benefits
- exposure to eco-tourism fosters broader commitment to environmental well-being
- space protected because of eco-tourism provide various environmental benefits

Indirect costs
- fragile areas may be exposed to less benign forms of tourism (pioneer function)
- may foster tendencies to put financial value on nature, depending upon attractiveness

Economic impacts

Direct benefits
- revenues obtained directly from ecotourists
- creation of direct employment opportunities
- strong potential for linkages with other sectors of the local economy
- stimulation of peripheral rural economies

Direct costs
- start-up expenses (acquisition of land, establishment of protected areas, superstructure, infrastructure)
- ongoing expenses (maintenance of infrastructure, promotion, wages)

Indirect benefits
- indirect revenues from ecotourists (high multiplier effect)
- proclivity of ecotourists to patronize cultural and heritage attractions as 'add-ons'
- economic benefits from sustainable use of protected areas (pharmaceuticals, research) and inherent existence (e.g. flood control)

Indirect costs
- revenue uncertainties to in situ nature if consumption
- revenue leakages due to imports, expatriate or non-local participation, etc.
- opportunity costs
- damage to crops by wildlife

Sociocultural impacts

Direct benefits
- eco-tourism accessible to a broad spectrum of the population
- aesthetic/spiritual element of experiences
- fosters environmental awareness among ecotourists and local population

Direct costs
- intrusions upon local and possibly isolated cultures
- imposition of elite lien value system
- displacement of local cultures by parks
- erosion of local control (foreign experts, in-migration of job seekers)

Indirect benefits
- option and existence benefits

Indirect costs
- potential resentment and antagonism of locals
- tourist opposition to aspects of local culture (e.g. hunting, slash-burn agriculture)

Source: Weaver (1998)

At present, there is little evidence of any real ability to manage and control the tourism industry at an international level, and even less ability to identify, accept and maintain appropriate levels of eco-tourism. Furthermore, by the very definition of eco-tourism, class prejudice is promoted. This niche market is constituted by affluent, well-educated and well-behaved tourists that take their holidays in small groups. It would seem that evaluating eco-tourism, and its implications for the destination and its image, needs to be examined more closely. Briefly, relevant issues include the reduction in numbers of tourists, the policy implications of eco-tourism, the education of all parties involved, and the application of sustainability within eco-tourism (Butler, 1992, Knowles and Felzensztein, 2003).

Reducing numbers of tourists has two aspects: reducing numbers in areas where they are currently too great, and limiting potential visitors to levels compatible with capacity parameters. It is extremely difficult to reduce numbers in a free market situation without prejudicing the viability of the industry. Revenues can be expected to decline (unless massive market replacement occurs at the same time), which can result in loss of employment and reduction in local standards of living. Local support is doubtful and certainly not likely to be unanimous. Limiting numbers before they become a problem is more attractive but assumes that capacity levels can be identified and agreed upon. Even if local preferences are accepted, there is no guarantee that these will match the goals of alternative tourism proponents with certain implications to the image of the eco-tourism product.

The policy implications of eco-tourism are less clear. Local control and initiative may be stimulated at first but eventually lost to external institutions, creating dissatisfaction. Preservation of resources and culture for eco-tourism may run counter to individual desires, and planning may be resented at the local level.

The education of people in eco-tourism is a hard and a long-term process with much-needed employment and income not necessarily coming from alternative tourism. It is debatable whether a tourism destination can avoid following the tourism area life cycle, and, however environmentally sympathetic, every tourist can be damaging to the environment, and few forms of alternative tourism are really viable to a no-change scenario over time.

In terms of the sustainability of eco-tourism products, the application of sustainability within tourism takes the form of either a tool used for its long-term survival in an attempt to enhance the profitable performance of its operations, or a tool used to maintain the resource base of tourism enterprises in order to generate more tourism demand. How sustainability is applied and what image is projected needs to be clarified.

Summary

Many definitions have been offered to describe the word 'image' in different academic fields. An image is 'the consumer perception of a product, institution, brand, business, or person that may or may not correspond with "reality" or "actuality". For marketing purposes the "image of what is" may be more important than "what actually is"' (Bennett, 1995).

In the words of Gunn (1988: 23):

> All of us have images of destinations, whether or not we have travelled to them. These images may be sharp or vague, fact or whimsical, but in all cases they are indicative of likes and dislikes. By means of many communication inputs throughout our lifetime – advertising, radio, television, magazines, books, comments from friends and relatives – we accumulate such images and assign values to them, good or bad. And although they arise from general information about the designed environment, these images are always highly personal.

As such, this chapter reviewed the process of projected and perceived image for tourism destinations and products. In this respect, different issues have emerged, one of which highlighted the issues associated with developing a false image. Taking that one step further, the chapter also viewed the concept of eco-tourism, its definition, position and costs and benefits. Here, the concern that exists is that eco-tourism products and services often project a false image to travellers, with practitioners claiming that they are delivering eco-tourism services simply in an attempt to increase their demand. As such, the chapter opens up an agenda of discussion of the considerations that need to be taken into account for delivering an eco-tourism image that is close to its values. Last, but not least, in doing so successfully, a better understanding of the concept of sustainability, with its advantages and disadvantages, could be beneficial to destination managers.

References

Ahmed, Z.U. (1991) 'The influence of the components of a state's tourist image on product positioning strategy', *Tourism Management*, 12, 4, 331–40.

Ahmed, Z.U. (1996) 'The need for the identification of the constituents of a destination's tourist image: a promotional segmentation perspective', *The Tourist Review*, 51, 2, 44–57.

Ashworth, G.J. and Goodall, B. (1988) 'Tourist images: marketing considerations', in B. Goodall and G. Ashworth (eds) *Marketing in the Tourism Industry: The Promotion of Destinations Regions*, London: Routledge, 213–38.

Ashworth, G.J. (1991) 'Products, places and promotion: destination images in the analysis of the tourism industry', in M.T. Sinclair and M.J. Stabler (eds.) *The Tourism Industry: An International Analysis*, Oxford: CAB International, 121–40.

Assael, H. (1992) *Consumer Behavior and Marketing Action*, Boston: PWS-KENT.

Baloglu, S. and Uysal, M. (1996) 'Market segments of push and pull motivations: a canonical correlation approach', *International Journal of Contemporary Hospitality Management*, 8, 3, 32–8.

Bennett, P.D. (1995) *Dictionary of Marketing Terms*, Chicago: American Marketing Association, NTC Business Books.

Bigné, J.E. and Zorío, M. (1989) 'Marketing turístico: el proceso de toma de decisiones vacacionales', *Revista de Economía y Empresa*, 9, 23, 91–112.

Britton, R.A. (1979) 'The image of the Third World in tourism marketing', *Annals of Tourism Research*, 6, 3, 318–29.

Butler, R. (1992) 'Alternative tourism: the thin end of the wedge', in V.L. Smith and W. R. Eadington (eds) *Tourism Alternatives*, Philadelphia: University of Pennsylvania Press, 31–46.

Ceballos-Lascurain, H. (1987) 'The future of ecotourism', *Mexico Journal*, January, 13–14.

Ceballos-Lascurain, H. (1991a) 'Tourism, ecotourism, and protected areas', in J.A. Kusler (compiler) *Ecotourism and Resource Conservation: A Collection of Papers*, Volume 1, Madison: Omnipress, 24–30.

Ceballos-Lascurain, H. (1991b) 'Tourism, ecotourism and protected areas', *Parks*, 2, 3, 31–5.

Ceballos-Lascurain, H. (1993a) 'Ecotourism as a worldwide phenomenon', in K. Lindberg and D.E. Hawkins (eds) *Ecotourism: Guide for Planners and Managers*, North Bennington: The Ecotourism Society, 12–14.

Ceballos-Lascurain, H. (1993b) 'Overview on ecotourism around the world: IUCN's ecotourism program', in *Proceedings of 1993 World Congress on Adventure Travel and Eco-tourism, Brazil*, Englewood: The Adventure Travel Society, 219–22.

Ceballos-Lascurain, H. (1996) *Tourism, Ecotourism, and Protected areas*, IUCN, Gland.

Chon, K.-S. (1990) 'The role of destination image in tourism: a review and discussion', *The Tourist Review*, 45, 2, 2–9.

Chon, K.-S. (1991) 'Tourism destination image modification process: marketing implications', *Tourism Management*, 12, 1, 68–72.

Diamantis, D. (2003) 'Ecotourism management', in D. Diamantis and S. Geldenhuys (eds) *Ecotourism: Management and Assessment*, London: Continuum.

Echtner, C.M. and Ritchie, J.R.B. (1993) 'The measurement of destination image: an empirical assessment', *Journal of Travel Research*, 31, 4, 3–13.

Gartner, W.C. and Hunt, J.D. (1987) 'An analysis of state image change over a twelve year period', *Journal of Travel Research*, 26, 2, 15–19.

Gartner, W.C. (1993) 'Image formation process', *Journal of Travel and Tourism Marketing*, 2, 2/3, 191–215.

Goodall, B. (1988) 'How tourists choose their holidays: an analytical framework', in B. Goodall and G. Ashworth (eds) *Marketing in the Tourism Industry: The Promotion of Destinations Regions*, London: Routledge, 1–17.

Goodall, B. (1991) 'Understanding holiday choice', in C. Cooper and A. Lockwood (eds) *Progress in Tourism, Recreation and Hospitality Management*, Volume 3, London: Belhaven Press, 58–77.

Gunn, C.A. (1988) *Vacationscape: Designing Tourist Regions*, New York: Van Nostran Reinhold.

Gunn, C.A. (1993) *Tourism planning*, 3rd edition, Washington D.C., Taylor and Francis.

Hu, Y. and Ritchie, J.R.B. (1993) 'Measuring destination attractiveness: a contextual approach', *Journal of Travel Research*, 32, 2, 25–34.

Hunt, J.D. (1975) 'Image: a factor in tourism development', *Journal of Travel Research*, 13, 3, 1–7.

Kotler, P., Haider, D.H. and Rein, I. (1993) *Marketing Places: Attracting Investment, Industry, and Tourism to Cities, States, and Nations*, New York: The Free Press.

Knowles, T. and Felzensztein, C. (2003) 'The marketing of ecotourism: a focus on Chile', in D. Diamantis and S. Geldenhuys (eds) *Ecotourism: Management and Assessment*, London: Continuum.

Lindberg, K. and McKercher, B. (1997) 'Ecotourism: a critical overview', *Pacific Tourism Review*, 1, 1, 65–79.

Mathieson, A. and Wall, G. (1982) *Tourism: Economic, Physical and Social Impacts*, London: Longman.

Mayo, E. and Jarvis, L. (1981) *The Psychology of Leisure Travel*, Boston: CBI Publishing.

Middleton, V.T.C. (1994) *Marketing in Travel and Tourism*, Oxford: Butterworth-Heinemann.

Moutinho, L. (1987) 'Consumer behaviour in tourism', *European Journal of Marketing*, 21, 10, 1–44.

Orams, M.B. (2001) 'Types of ecotourism', in D. Weaver (ed) *The Encyclopedia of Ecotourism*, Oxford: CABI, 23–36.

Phelps, A. (1986) 'Holiday destination image. The problem of assessment: an example developed in Menorca', *Tourism Management*, 7, 3, 168–180.

Ryan, C. (1994) 'Leisure and tourism – the application of leisure concepts to tourist behaviour – a proposed model', in A.V. Seaton (ed) *Tourism: The State of the Art*, Chichester: Wiley, 294–307.

Seaton, A.V. (1996a) 'The analysis of tourism demand: tourism behaviour', in A.V. Seaton and M.M. Bennett (eds) *Marketing Tourism Products*, London: International Business Press, 28–54.

Seaton, A.V. (1996b) 'The marketing mix: tourism promotion', in A.V. Seaton and M.M. Bennett (eds) *Marketing Tourism Products*, London: International Business Press, 175–205.

Sirakaya, E., McLellan, R.W. and Uysal, M. (1996) 'Modeling vacation destination decisions: a behavioral approach', *Journal of Travel and Tourism Marketing*, 5, 1/2, 57–75.

Stabler, M.J. (1988) 'The image of destination regions: theoretical and empirical aspects', in B. Goodall and G. Ashworth (eds) *Marketing in the Tourism Industry: The Promotion of Destinations Regions*, London: Routledge, 133–161.

Steward, W.P. and Sekartjakrarini, S. (1994) 'Disentangling ecotourism', *Annals of Tourism Research*, 21, 4, 840–1.

Further reading

Aaker, D.A. (1971) *Multivariate Analysis in Marketing: Theory and Application*, California: Wadsworth.

Ankomah, P.K., Crompton, J.L. and Baker, D. (1996) 'Influence of cognitive distance in vacation choice', *Annals of Tourism Research*, 23, 1, 138–150.

Ashworth, G.J. and Voogd, H. (1994) 'Marketing of tourism places: what are we doing?', in M. Uysal (ed) *Global Tourist Behaviour*, New York: International Business Press, 5–19.

Baloglu, S. (1997) 'The relationship between destination images and sociodemographic and trip characteristics of international travellers', *Journal of Vacation Marketing*, 3, 3, 221–33.

Baloglu, S. and Brinberg, D. (1997) 'Affective images of tourism destinations', *Journal of Travel Research*, 35, 4, 11–15.

Baum, T. (1996) 'Images of tourism past and present', *International Journal of Contemporary Hospitality Management*, 8, 4, 25–30.

Blythe, J. (1997) *The Essence of Consumer Behaviour*, Hemel Hempstead: Prentice-Hall.

Bramwell, B. and Rawding, L. (1996) 'Tourism marketing images of industrial cities', *Annals of Tourism Research*, 23, 1, 201–21.

Breakwell, G.M., Hammond, S. and Fife-Schaw, C. (1995) *Research Methods in Psychology*, London: Sage Publications.

Brucks, M. (1985) 'The effects of product class knowledge on information search behavior', *Journal of Consumer Research*, 12, June, 1–16.

Chisnall, P.M. (1985) *Marketing: A Behavioural Analysis*, Berkshire: McGraw-Hill.

Chisnall, P.M. (1995) *Consumer Behaviour*, Berkshire: McGraw-Hill.

Churchill, G.A. (1991) *Marketing Research: Methodological Foundations*, Orlando: The Dryden Press.

Cooper, C.P. (1981) 'Spatial and temporal patterns of tourist behaviour', *Regional Studies*, 15, 5, 359–71.

Cooper, C., Fletcher, J., Gilbert, D. and Wanhill, S. (1993) *Tourism: Principles and Practice*, London: Longman.

Crompton, J.L. (1979) 'Motivations for pleasure vacation', *Annals of Tourism Research*, 6, 408–24.

Crompton, J.L. (1992) 'Structure of vacation destination choice sets', *Annals of Tourism Research*, 19, 420–34.

Crompton, J.L. and Ankomah, P.K. (1993) 'Choice set propositions in destination decisions', *Annals of Tourism Research*, 20, 461–76.

Dabholkar, P.A. (1994) 'Incorporating choice into an attitudinal framework: analysing models of mental comparison processes', *Journal of Consumer Research*, 21, 100–17.

Dann, G.M.S. (1996) 'Tourists' images of a destination: an alternative analysis', *Journal of Travel and Tourism Marketing*, 5, 1/2, 4–55.

Davidson, R. and Maitland, R. (1997) *Tourism Destinations*, London: Hodder & Stoughton.

Dhar, R. and Sherman, S.J. (1996) 'The effect of a consumer's unique features on consumer choice', *Journal of Consumer Research*, 23, 193–203.

Dimanche, F. and Havitz, M.E. (1994) 'Consumer behavior and tourism: review and extension of four study areas', *Journal of Travel and Tourism Marketing*, 3, 3, 37–57.

Draper, D. and Minca, C. (1997) 'Image and destination: a geographical approach applied to Banff National Park, Canada', *The Tourist Review*, 2, 14–24.

East, R. (1990) *Changing Consumer Behaviour*, London: Cassell.

Ehrenberg, A.S.C. (1996) 'Towards an integrated theory of consumer behaviour', *The Journal of Market Research Society*, 38, 4, 397–427.

Engel, J.F., Blackwell, R.D. and Miniard, P.W. (1995) *Consumer Behaviour*. Orlando: The Dryden Press.

Enis, B.M. and Roering, K.J. (1980) 'Product classification taxonomies: synthesis and consumer implications', in C.W. Lamb and P.M. Dunne (eds) *Theoretical Developments in marketing*, Chicago: American Marketing Association, 186–9.

Evans, M.J., Moutinho, L. and Van Raaij, W.F. (1996) *Applied Consumer Behaviour*, Kent: Addison-Wesley.

Faulkner, B. (1997) 'A model for the evaluation of national tourism destination marketing programs', *Journal of Travel Research*, 35, Winter, 23–32.

Font, X. (1997) 'Managing the tourist destination's image', *Journal of Vacation Marketing*, 3, 2, 123–31.

Foxall, G.R. and Goldsmith, R.E. (1994) *Consumer Psychology for Marketing*, London: Routledge.

Gilbert, D.C. (1989) 'Tourism marketing – its emergence and establishment', in C. Cooper and A. Lockwood (eds) *Progress in Tourism, Recreation and Hospitality Management*, Volume 1, London: Belhaven Press, 77–90.

Gilbert, D.C. (1991) 'An examination of the consumer behaviour process related to tourism', in C. Cooper and A. Lockwood (eds) *Progress in Tourism, Recreation and Hospitality Management*, Volume 3, London: Belhaven Press, pp 78–105.

Gitelson, R.J. and Crompton, J.L. (1983) 'The planning horizons and sources of information used by pleasure vacationers', *Journal of Travel Research*, 23, 3, 2–7.

Gitelson, R. and Kerstetter, D. (1994) 'The influence of friends and relatives in travel decision-making', *Journal of Travel and Tourism Marketing*, 3, 3, 59–68.

Gnoth, J. (1997) 'Tourism motivation and expectation formation', *Annals of Tourism Research*, 24, 2, 283–304.

Goodrich, J.N. (1978) 'The relationship between preferences for and perceptions of vacation destinations: application of a choice model', *Journal of Travel Research*, 16, Fall, 8–13.

Goossens, C.F. (1994) 'External information search: effects of tour brochures with experiential information', *Journal of Travel and Tourism Marketing*, 3, 3, 89–107.

Gordon, W. and Langmaid, R. (1988) *Qualitative Market Research*. Aldershot: Gower.

Haahti, A.J. (1986) 'Finlands competitive position as a destination', *Annals of Tourism Research*, 13, 11–35.

Haywood, K.M. (1990) 'Revising and implementing the marketing concept as it applies to tourism', *Tourism Management*, 11, 3, 195–205.

Heath, E. and Wall, G. (1992) *Marketing Tourism Destinations: A Strategic Planning Approach*. Montreal Canada, Wiley.

Heylen, J.P., Dawson, B. and Sampson, P. (1995) 'An implicit model of consumer behaviour', *The Journal of the Market Research Society*, 37, 1, 51–67.

Hooley, G.J. and Hussey, M.K. (1994) *Quantitative Methods in Marketing*. London: The Dryden Press.

Howard, J.A. (1977) *Consumer Behaviour: Application of Theory'*, New York: McGraw-Hill.

Howard, J.A. (1989) Consumer Behaviour in Marketing Strategy. Englewood Cliffs, NJ: Prentice-Hall.

Howard, J. A., and Sheth, J.N. (1969) *The Theory of Buyer Behaviour'*, New York: Wiley.

Hsieh, S., O'Leary, J.T. and Morrison, A.M. (1994) 'A comparison of package and non-package travelers from the United Kingdom', in M. Uysal (ed) *Global Tourist Behaviour*, New York: International Business Press, 79–99.

Jefferson, A. and Lickorish, L. (1988) *Marketing Tourism. A Practical Guide*, London: Longman.

Kent, P. (1991) 'Understanding holiday choices', in M.T. Sinclair and M.J. Stabler (eds) *The Tourism Industry: An International Analysis*, Oxford: CAB International, 165–83.

Krippendorf, J. (1987) *The Holiday Makers: Understanding the Impact of Leisure and Travel*, Oxford: Butterworth-Heinemann.

Kotler, P. (1984) *Marketing Management: Analysis, Planning and Control*, New York: Prentice-Hall.

Kotler, P. (1986) *Principles of marketing*, Englewood Cliffs, NJ: Prentice-Hall.

Kotler, P., Bowen, J. and Makens, J. (1996) *Marketing for Hospitality and Tourism*, Englewood Cliffs, NJ: Prentice-Hall.

Laws, E. (1991) *Tourism Marketing. Service and Quality Management Perspectives*, Cheltenham: Stanley Thornes Ltd.

Laws, E. (1995) Tourist Destination Management. Issues, Analysis and Policies, London: Routledge.

Laws, E. (1996) 'Marketing strategies for traditional tourist resorts', *Second International Forum on Tourism*, Benidorm, Spain.

Laws, E. (1997) *Managing Packaged Tourism. Relationships, Responsibilities and Service Quality in the Inclusive Holiday industry*, London: International Thomson Business Press.

Le Blanc, R. (1989) 'An exploratory investigation into the relationship between evoked set decisions and final purchase choice', *Developments in Marketing Science*, 12, 7–11.

Lefkoff-Hagious, R. and Mason, C.H. (1993) 'Characteristic, beneficial, and image attributes in consumer judgments of similarity and preference', *Journal of Consumer Research*, 20, 100–10.

Leiper, N. (1990) 'Tourist attractions systems', *Annals of Tourism Research*, 17, 367–84.

Lewis, B.R. (1993) 'Service quality measurement', *Marketing Intelligence and Planning*, 11, 4, 4–12.

Loudon, D. and Della Bitta, A.J. (1988) *Consumer Behavior: Concepts and Applications*, Singapore: McGraw-Hill.

MacKay, K.J. and Fesenmaier, D.R. (1997) 'Pictorial element of destination in image formation', *Annals of Tourism Research*, 24, 3, 537–65.

McWilliams, E.G. and Crompton, J.L. (1997) 'An expanded framework for measuring the effectiveness of destination advertising', *Tourism Management*, 18, 3, 127–37.

Malhotra, N.K. (1993) *Marketing Research: An Applied Orientation*, Englewood Cliffs, NJ: Prentice-Hall.

Mansfeld, Y. (1992) 'From motivation to actual travel', *Annals of Tourism Research*, 19, 399–419

March, R. (1994) 'Tourism marketing myopia', *Tourism Management*, 15, 6, 411–15.

Medlik, S. (1996) *Dictionary of Travel, Tourism and Hospitality*, Oxford: Butterworth-Heinemann.

Menon, S. and Kahn, B.E. (1995) 'The impact of context on variety seeking in product choices', *Journal of Consumer Research*, 22, 285–95.

Moscardo, G., Morrison, A.M., Pearce, P.L., Lang, C.-T. and O'Leary, J.T. (1996) 'Understanding vacation destination choice through travel motivation and activities', *Journal of Vacation Marketing*, 2, 2, 109–22.

Mullen, B. and Johnson, C. (1990) *The Psychology of Consumer Behaviour*, New Jersey: Lawrence Erlbaum Associates.

Nicosia, F.M. (1966) *Consumer Decision Processes: Marketing and Advertising Implications*, Englewood Cliffs, NJ: Prentice-Hall.

Oliver, G. (1990) *Marketing Today*, Hemel Hempstead, Prentice Hall.

O'Shaughnessy, J. (1987) *Why People Buy*, Oxford: Oxford University Press.

Owen, F. and Jones, R. (1994) *Statistics*, London: Pitman Publishing.

Papadopoulos, S.I. (1989) 'A conceptual tourism marketing planning model: Part 1', *European Journal of Marketing*, 23, 1, 31–40.

Pearce, P.L. (1982) 'Perceived changes in holiday destinations', *Annals of Tourism Research*, 9, 2, 145–64.

Pearce, P.L. (1982) 'The social psychology of tourist behaviour', *International Series in Experimental Social psychology*, Volume 3, Oxford: Pergamon Press.

Pitts, R.E. and Woodside, A.G. (1986) 'Personal values and travel decisions', *Journal of Travel Research*, 25, 1, 20–5.

Poiesz, T.B.C. (1989) 'The image concept: its place in consumer psychology', *Journal of Economic Psychology*, 10, 457–72.

Poon, A. (1993) *Tourism, Technology and Competitive Strategies*, Oxford: CAB International.

Pritchard, A. and Morgan, N. (1995) 'Evaluating vacation destination brochure images: the case of local authorities in Wales', *Journal of Vacation Marketing*, 2, 1, 23–38.

Rita, P. and Moutinho, L. (1994) 'An expert system for promotion budget allocation to international markets', in M. Uysal (ed) *Global Tourist Behaviour*, New York: International Business Press, 101–21.

Ryan, C. (1991) 'Tourism and marketing: a symbiotic relationship', *Tourism Management*, 12, 101–11.

Ryan, C. (1995) Researching Tourist Satisfaction: Issues, Concepts, problems, London: Routledge.

Santos, J.L. (1992) 'Las nuevas tendencias de los consumidores turistas', *Estudios sobre Consumo*, 23, 29–36.

Schiffman, L.G. and Kanuk, L.L. (1994) *Consumer Behavior*, Englewood Cliffs, NJ: Prentice-Hall.

Selwyn, T. (1996) *The Tourist Image: Myths and Myth Making in Tourism*, Chichester: John Wiley and Sons.

Solomon, M. R. (1992) *Consumer Behavior*, Boston: Allyn & Bacon.

Spiggle, S. and Sewall, M.A. (1987) 'A choice sets model of retail selection', *Journal of Marketing*, 51, 97–111.

Spotts, D.M. (1997) 'Regional analysis of tourism resources for marketing purposes', *Journal of Travel Research*, 35, Winter, 3–15.

Stabler, M.J. (1991) 'Modelling the tourism industry: a new approach', in M.T. Sinclair and M.J. Stabler (eds) *The Tourism Industry: An International Analysis*, Oxford: CAB International, 15–43.

Teare, R., Mazanec, J.A., Crawford-Welch, S. and Calver, S. (1994) *Marketing in Hospitality and Tourism: A Consumer Focus*, London: Cassell.

Thrane, C. (1997) 'Vacation motives and personal value systems', *Journal of Vacation Marketing*, 3, 3, 234–44.

Um, S. and Crompton, J.L. (1990) 'Attitude determinants in tourism destination choice', *Annals of Tourism Research*, 17, 432–48.

Van Raaij, W.F. (1986) 'Consumer research on tourism: mental and behavioural constructs', *Annals of Tourism Research*, 13, 1–9.

Veal, A.J. (1992) *Research Methods for Leisure and Tourism: A Practical Guide*, London: Pitman Publishing.

Walle, A.H. (1997) 'Quantitative versus qualitative tourism research', *Annals of Tourism Research*, 24, 3, 524–36.

Weaver, D. (1998) *Ecotourism in the Less Developed World*, Oxford: CAB International.

Webb, J.R. (1992) *Understanding and Designing Marketing Research*, London: Academic Press.

Wilson, C.E. (1981) 'A procedure for the analysis of consumer decision making', *Journal of Advertising Research*, 21, March–April, 31–8.

Witt, S. and Moutinho, L. (1995) *Tourism Marketing and Management Handbook*, Hemel Hempstead, Prentice-Hall.

Woodside, A.G. and Lysonski, S. (1989) 'A general model of traveler destination choice', *Journal of Travel Research*, 27, 4, 8–14.

Woodside, A.G. (1990) 'Measuring advertising effectiveness in destination marketing strategies', *Journal of Travel Research*, 29, 2, 3–8.

Yale, P. (1995) *The Business of Tour Operations*, London: Longman.

Zeithaml, V.A. (1998) 'Consumer perceptions of price, quality, and value: a means-end model and synthesis of evidence', *Journal of Marketing*, 52, 2–22.

7

Implications for sustainability

Introduction

The theme of sustainable development has one strong agreement among all established researchers examining this concept. This refers to its initial treatment, that of the Brundtland Report by the World Commission on Environment and Development (WCED). Prior to this report the role of the environment shifted from a state of idealism to a realism stage (Dowling, 1992). Initially, during the 1950s and early 1970s a handful of studies were conducted regarding the effects of negative practices of development (*ibid*.).

During these years, tourism was seeing a surge towards the concept of 'mass development' throughout the world, with its environmental practices bringing suggestions for an inventory of natural resources, zoning and development guidelines (Farrell and Runyan, 1991; Dowling, 1992). In the late 1970s studies on the impacts of tourism were introduced concentrating on the nature of the relationship between tourism and the environment. These were documented studies which enhanced the symbiosis between tourism and the environment (Budowski, 1976; Bosselman, 1978; Dowling, 1992: 35), followed by attempts to assess the environmental impacts of tourism (Cohen, 1978; Dowling, 1992: 35).

During the first half of the 1980s environmental concerns started to enjoy wider attention throughout the world from both environmental agencies and tourism-led bodies. Initially, the *World Conservation Strategy* was published by the International Union for the Conservation of Nature and Natural Resources (IUCN, 1980), then the Worldwatch Institute published a report entitled *Sustainable Society* in 1981 (Kidd, 1992), followed by the establishment of the World Resources Institute in 1982, and the creation of the Environmental Department in the World Bank.

In terms of tourism, the co-operation between environmental and tourism issues was highlighted by the Manila Declaration (Edgell, 1990) as well as by the study by the Organization for Economic Co-operation and Development (OECD, 1980). Next, two non-governmental organizations stated the view that resources include the biosphere, the ecosystem which is used, as well as the human-created environment and socio-economic aspects, and these were also underlined in a variety of research studies (Dowling, 1992: 38–9).

During the second half of the 1980s, the transformation occurred from *idealism* to *realism* (Dowling, 1992), where the environment agenda attracted wider attention in Europe through its inclusion in the Single European Act, and world-wide acknowledgement came through the much published report *Our Common Future* by the World Commission on Environment and Development (WCED, 1987). The end of this decade brought the first studies on sustainable development, sustainable tourism development, and alternative forms of tourism all reflecting three states of the tourism–environment relationship – those of co-existence, conflict and symbiosis (Dowling, 1992: 40). It was during these years that sustainable tourism products emerged such as eco-tourism, placing this concept at the centre of the re-orientation of tourism. In the 1990s, environmental issues became a much researched area throughout the globe, reflecting the integration of tourism and the environment (Dowling, 1992), with the terms sustainability, sustainable tourism development and eco-tourism being included as key concepts in a vast array of research studies.

With this in mind, the purpose of this review is to examine the concept of sustainability both from the environmental and tourism perspectives, and to assess the different policies and structures surrounding the debate within this concept. The review begins with the issues surrounding sustainability, followed by the issues of sustainable tourism development and it concludes with the practices of sustainable tourism.

Sustainability: overview and events

The roots of sustainable development branched out into six different perspectives which assisted with the transformation from the early idealism view to the current realism stance of the importance of sustainability (Kidd, 1992; Mitlin, 1992; Pezzey, 1992):

1. *Ecological/carrying capacity view*: deals with the physical phenomena and sociocultural resources and issues.
2. *Resources/environmental view:* concerns the research instruments of the adequacy of resources and environmental quality.
3. *Biosphere view*: focuses on the concerns over human activity and its impacts on the biosphere.
4. *Technological view*: assesses the effects of the technological movement.
5. *No-growth, slow-growth view*: concerns the era of growth theories, especially in terms of economics, and 'no-growth' philosophies in terms of resources used.
6. *Eco-development view:* refers to the research in the late 1970s, especially in terms of harmonizing social and economic objectives in line with ecological management principles.

These views primarily outlined the socio-environmental effects of the non-sustainable development era since the Industrial Revolution, and assessed the unsustainable practices that stemmed from the two-tier world system (rich versus poor countries) (Strong, 1997). Their effects were captured in the early 1980s by the World Conservation Strategy (WCS), which illustrated that sustainability is a strategic approach to the integration of conservation and development, highlighting the following objectives (IUCN, 1980; Smith, 1993):

- ecosystem management;
- preservation of generic diversity;

- utilization of resources.

Although certain critics protested that the WCS referred only to ecological resources rather than to sustainable development (Lele, 1991), it serves as a platform for the popularization of the concept at the latter stage. This was initially seen in the establishment of WCED in 1982 (Smith, 1993; Glasbergen and Gorvers, 1995), and its study on the assessment of environmental problems, known as the Brundtland Report (WCED, 1987). In this report, sustainable development was defined as 'a development that meets the needs of the present without compromising the ability of future generations to meet their own needs' (*ibid.*: 43).

The Brundtland Report, or *Our Common Future* aimed to interrelate two main concepts: economic growth that is both forceful and socially and environmentally sustainable (*ibid.*: 8). The study concluded that it is impossible to separate the issues of economic growth and the environment, as well as introducing the notion of widening the perspective of economic systems in an attempt to deal with environmental problems (*ibid.*; Pearce *et al.*, 1989, 1990, 1993; Pezzey, 1992; Redclift and Sage, 1994; Glasbergen and Gorvers, 1995; Khan, 1995; Welford, 1995: 6–7; Selman, 1996).

The major strength of sustainable development derived from the WCED 'short definition' is the development of a set of objectives demonstrating that sustainability is a powerful tool for consensus (Lele, 1991). More specifically, the premise of sustainable development incorporates an environmental–society link, which is based upon: environmental degradation, traditional development objectives, and a successful process of development (Lele, 1991).

However, others have claimed that the WCED supported the idea of sustainability from more of a resource base, but not in terms of society, culture, and people (Strong, 1997). Although the review on weaknesses of sustainability in terms of its implementation will be discussed in the next section of this chapter, one important point that surfaced was that although the Brundtland Commission's proposals were practical, they were difficult to implement in the foreseeable future (Redclift, 1987; Davis, 1991). In particular, Redclift (1987) argues that sustainable development can only be achieved through political boundaries, and that environmental management is needed as a way to monitor social movement dedicated to environmental ends. Davis (1991) suggests that there is a consensus on the term 'sustainable development', as it allows the international community to debate modern development goals in a new and radical way.

Despite these weaknesses, sustainable development received wide acceptance during the Earth Summit in 1992 in Rio de Janeiro, Brazil. There were five core outcomes as a result of this conference (UN, 1992, 1993): a framework for the convention on climate change; the Convention on Biological Diversity; forest principles; the Rio declaration on the environment and development; and Agenda 21. The latter action plan, Agenda 21, introduced more than 100 programmes in the field of sustainable development, such as the climate, biodiversity and forest issues (UN, 1992, 1993).

In overall terms, both the Brundtland Report and Agenda 21 provided the basic tenets for the debate on issues regarding sustainability. There were the inevitable discussions on the nature of sustainability, in addition to the fact that its application took the form of a variety of agendas in a variety of industrial sectors (i.e., Local, Global, Agenda 21 for Travel and Tourism, etc.). In order to examine these issues, an overview of the general nature of sustainability is primarily considered, followed by the effects of its application on tourism.

The concept of sustainability

An examination of the meaning and implications of the WCED definition exposes certain constraints. Here, the dilemma arises as to whether to focus on the definitions of sustainability or to illustrate the issues implied by sustainability. On this point, sustainability's elastic nature was confirmed with the viewpoint that this concept was engaged in a 'transcendent tenet', subject to frequent but imprecise usage (Brown *et al.*, 1987). In contrast, Shearman (1990) suggested that the concept does not necessarily require clarification on the definitional perspective but rather on the operational one, which is the implication for any given context to which it is applied. Sherman concluded that it is more appropriate to treat sustainability as a *concept and illustrate the issues implied by sustainability rather than the issues of sustainability (ibid.: 3).*

Furthermore, the discussion of the different perceptions of sustainability (Mitlin, 1992; Pezzey, 1992; Blowers and Glasbergen, 1995; Khan, 1995; Clayton and Redcliffe, 1996), and its conceptual treatments are based on the issues of sustainability (Cocklin, 1989; Jacobs, 1991; Peattie, 1992; Wilbanks, 1994). These issues have been independently debated (Dovers, 1995), but have also been interwoven with the 'core meaning' (see Box 7.1). However, in treating sustainability as a concept, and aligned with its central idea in the Brundtland Report, three main components can be detailed: *development, needs* and *future generations* (Rees, 1988, 1990; Cocklin, 1989; Dovers, 1990; Pearce *et al.*, 1990, 1993; Charter, 1992; Blowers and Glasbergen, 1995).

The concept of development

Part of the debate within this concept involves its similarities with economic growth (Turner, 1988; Dovers, 1990; Jacobs, 1991; Charter, 1992; Smith, 1993; Blowers and Glasbergen, 1995: 167–8; Clayton and Redcliffe, 1996). The concept of economic growth has been treated as a process from which environmental protection can be achieved, and the latter should also be based on a balance of other human goals in order to achieve sustainable growth (ICC, 1990). It seems that environmental protection and economic growth are mutually compatible (Turner, 1988), as economic growth alone is insufficient for the purposes of development (Shearman, 1990), and development can be addressed only through the distribution of scarce resources (Blowers and Glasbergen, 1995).

The issue that surfaced at this stage was the compatibility of sustainable development with economic growth (Hunter, 1997: 852) that may reduce human suffering (Redclift, 1987; Shearman, 1990; Smith, 1993; Redclift and Sage, 1994). As growth has been treated synonymously with wealth, it was proposed that growth addressed more the cost, rather than the marginal issues of the physical dimensions of the human economy (Smith, 1993). Perhaps the commitment to

---

Box 7.1 Issues affecting the concept of sustainability

Nature

- The preservation of resources used, ecological process, and biological diversity (land, water, energy, mineral, wild species, flora, fauna, domesticated species, etc.).
- The distinct interpretation and the substitution efforts of the various components of the natural resource base and issues of pollution (marine, solid waste, air, climate change, land, soil etc.).
- The meaning of the value attributed to the natural world and the needs/wants of non-human species, sentient or otherwise.
- The application and the degree of co-operation in applied environmental monitoring programmes (environmental auditing etc.), in an attempt to achieve environmental protection.
- The degree to which a systems (ecosystems) perspective should be adopted, and the importance of maintaining the functional integrity of ecosystems.
- The effective existence of environmental limits to growth.

Society and economy

- The use of the term economic growth or development in promoting human well-being.
- The impact and significance of human population growth.
- The degree of information provision on the environmental effects of economic activity.
- The level of debt, trade, and poverty of the nations.
- The state of human conditions in terms of security, food security, health, urbanization, and in terms of skills, and educational status.

Source: Peattie (1992); Pezzey (1992); Dovers (1995); Hunter (1997); Khan (1995).

---

economic development, as opposed to the economic growth/welfare syndrome would be more appropriate (Jacobs, 1991; Healy and Shaw, 1993), as those who reject limitless economic growth mainly advocate a strong interpretation of sustainable development (Jacobs, 1991; Hunter, 1997).

Even if the acceptance of economic development is taken into account, there is compelling evidence that economic development did not assist the majority of the poorer Third World countries (Turner, 1988; Smith, 1993; Hunter, 1997). According to the Brundtland Report, the idea is that economic development should take place in Third World countries in order to meet basic needs (WCED, 1987). In all cases, however, the issue which remains unsolved in terms of the development perspective is related to achieving equitable growth, handling uneven development and the inseparable issue of inequality in order to meet both development and basic needs and wants (Blowers and Glasbergen, 1995).

The concept of needs

On examining the concept of needs, part of the debate is based on the issues of equity and distribution of resources (Fox, 1994; Blowers and Glasbergen, 1995; Clayton and Redcliffe, 1996). Theoretically, equity highlights an attempt to meet 'basic needs' for the present, otherwise known as intra-generational equity, and for the future, that is inter-generational equity (Healy and Shaw, 1993; Hunter, 1997). Central to the debate at this stage is the exact procedure for achieving equity, distribution of human well-being (wealth), and conservation of resources both locally and globally and from the inter-generational equity perspective (Healy and Shaw, 1993; Blowers and Glasbergen, 1995; Hunter, 1997).

Although, inevitably, there is commitment to the latter principles, the debate takes an alternative view that this should also take into account the distribution of the cost/benefits of the social/economic/environmental triangle which stem from the usage of resources (Jacobs, 1991; Charter, 1992; Smith, 1993; Fox, 1994; Clayton and Redcliffe, 1996; Hunter, 1997). Within all this, the commitment to equity should also incorporate the invisible needs/wants of non-human species, all assisting in their long-term existence (Hunter, 1997).

Moreover, based on the Brundtland Report's principles, 'sustainable development requires meeting the basic needs of all, and extending to all the opportunity to satisfy their aspirations for a better life' (WCED, 1987: 44). On this point it was claimed that the term 'basic needs' is a relative concept, since in the industrialized, or First World, countries products once regarded as 'luxuries' are now seen as 'necessities' (Blowers and Glasbergen, 1995: 168). It follows that as material standards have improved, capital consumption and pollution levels have risen. On the other hand, in poorer countries meeting basic needs exerts pressure on the environment and consumes resources (Lele, 1991; Smith, 1993; Blowers and Glasbergen, 1995; Hunter, 1997). This imbalance has been termed a 'prevailing pattern of world inequality' indicated by measures of poverty, debt starvation and out-migration (Lele, 1991; Smith, 1993: 3; Blowers and Glasbergen, 1995). Although this pattern is commonly known as the 'North–South' divide (Lele, 1991; Smith, 1993), it not only includes issues of short-term development and prosperity versus poverty, but involves deeper issues of distribution and allocation of resources, all of which are necessary to accomplish intra-generational equity and sustainable development (Smith, 1993: 4; Hunter, 1997: 854).

For example, the International Academy on the Environment conducted a survey in Africa, the South Pacific, Central America, and Asia (Barberis, 1993a, b). In particular, in India, Bangladesh and Myanmar, the negative environmental impacts were a ramification of high population density. In Central America the pressures of a growing population and the need for economic expansion led to unsustainable exploitation of forest resources. In the South Pacific, the problems facing resources are outlined by risks such as a rise in sea level, fragility of fresh water sources, and strong reliance on the natural environment for economic growth. Finally, in Africa the problems primarily stem from desertification, where the population places significant pressures on resources, and inappropriate land use causes soil erosion. The study concluded that there is a need to: re-examine the population–growth resources balance; correct the wasteful use of resources; and seek optimal population growth and distribution patterns in an integrated approach towards sustainability (Barberis, 1993a, b).

However, the side-effect of this aim is that for poor countries it can only be achieved by 'adherence to the constant natural assets rule' (Pearce *et al.*, 1989; Hunter, 1997), as distribution of resources and productivity is essential to such populations. In addition, the associated environmental degradation creates a more direct impact on well-being in poor countries than in the industrialized or rich areas of the world (Lele, 1991; Smith, 1993: 4; Blowers and Glasbergen, 1995; Hunter, 1997).

In overall terms, the core argument within the concept of needs is that both extreme resource exploitation and resource preservation positions ignore principles of intra-generational equity (Hunter, 1997). Here, the exploitation of resources and the distribution of socio-economics, in addition to the development costs and benefits, are mainly non-essential, benefiting the First rather than the Third World countries (Turner, 1988, 1991; Shiva, 1989; Hunter, 1997). Resources preservation is associated with low patterns of economic growth that affects Third world countries who meet their needs through economic growth (Turner, 1988, 1991; Hunter, 1997). Here, both views have been criticized on the basis that they do not include enough ecological and socially equitable criteria, and that these criteria are dictated by a number of external factors such as political or personal preference (Lele, 1991). In addition, irrespective to the recognition that Third World countries should search for economic growth in order to meet their equity standards (WCED, 1987), the way to handle these issues in industrialized countries still remains a mystery.

The question that generally exists is: is economic growth a necessity in industrialized countries, as their basic needs are already met? Here, the current view is that in order to meet the criteria of sustainability, the standards of living in First World countries have to be minimized, in order to position global consumption at a sustainable level (Brundtland, 1994: 244).

Alternatively, the industrialized nations have to reduce their environmental resource usage and simultaneously assist the poor nations to meet sustainable patterns of growth (Lele, 1991; Blowers and Glasbergen, 1995). Conversely, the First World nations should endeavour to promote the idea of *shared responsibility* (Blowers and Glasbergen, 1995: 168), so that all contribute to ensure equitable resource usage and preservation. Although this raises the issue of responsibility, the actual implementation of this principle in order to meet equity requirements remains debatable. This is based on concrete evidence that the total aid from the First World to Third World countries declined in 1995 (People and Planet, 1997: 4). The figures showed that in 1995 (total aid: US$59 billion), there was a decrease of 9 per cent, as 14 out of the 21 countries reduced their aid below the agreed level of 0.7 per cent of their gross domestic product (People and Planet, 1997).

Instead of commitment, the new term currently used by the World Bank is that of 'participation' (Narayan, 1996). Within this context, participation is defined as a 'process through which stakeholders influence and share control over development initiatives and the decisions and resources which affect them' (*ibid.*: 17). The World Bank has proclaimed the pitfalls of their approach in the past, and have outlined 'three lessons' to change its operation: new values and behaviour; new tools and capacities; and new ways of doing business (*ibid.*:

17–19). In all cases, the effectiveness of this new approach is to be tested in forthcoming years, by outlining if the equity meets both present and future generations' needs and wants.

The concept of future generations

The concept of future generations deals with the issues of income and capital bequests (Pearce *et al.*, 1989, 1990, 1993; Blowers and Glasbergen, 1995; Clayton and Redcliffe, 1996). The first concept suggests that the income of future generations should not be made less than that of present generations through actions taken by present generations (Pearce *et al.*, 1989, 1990, 1993; Bartelmus, 1994; Bayliss and Walker, 1996). It is believed that the latter group has economic obligations and raises certain issues of inequality, all highlighted in the previously examined concepts of development and needs. The current conclusion of this concept demands the requirement of equality to occur between individuals' of the current generation, unless inequality disadvantages no one (Brown *et al.*, 1987; Pearce *et al.*, 1989, 1990, 1993; Dovers, 1990; Charter, 1992;, Bartelmus, 1994; Blowers and Glasbergen, 1995; Bayliss and Walker,1996).

Capital bequests involve two interpretations of the resources capital (Hunter, 1995a). First, that of the mechanism by which the current generation transfers a stock of resource capital to their future counterparts no less than its existing capacity of stock (Pearce *et al.*, 1989, 1990, 1993; Bartelmus, 1994; Bayliss and Walker, 1996). The debate on this concept is not resolved through the definitional description of capital (the human-made, natural, and human types), or the so-called 'aggregate capital stock of a nation', but through the handling procedures of such capital (Pearce *et al.*, 1993: 15). Basically, this approach values the natural resources in monetary terms (Pearce *et al.*, 1989), where a form of development which damages the natural environment follows the principles of sustainable development only 'if the wealth-created resultant built assets are of greater "value" than the pre-existing natural environment' (Hunter, 1995a: 61). At this point, although the argument has mainly focused on the role of the natural environment and the relationships between the natural and human types, in terms of capital assets given to future generations (Pearce *et al.*, 1993; Bartelmus, 1994; Bayliss and Walker, 1996), in practice this interpretation does not follow the principles of sustainable development (Hunter, 1995a).

The second interpretation concerns only the concept of the *so-called 'constant natural assets rule'* based on the principles of no-substitutability, uncertainty, irreversibility, and equity (Pearce *et al.*, 1989, 1990, 1993, Hunter, 1995a). Here, the broad rule focuses on the principle that the present generation does not 'own' the natural resource base, and as such they do not have the right to pollute or limit the resources (Pearce *et al.*, 1989; Hunter, 1995a; Bayliss and Walker, 1996). Next, this issue raises the view that if one natural area is polluted in some part of the world, this should be immediately replaced or compensated by another area (Hunter, 1995a). Although this has been criticized on the basis that it is more appropriate to preserve rather than compensate a given area, simultaneously it raises issues of the methodology of monitoring in the form of environmental impact assessment, cost-benefit analysis (Pearce *et al.*, 1989), environmental auditing (Barton, 1996) and environmental indicators (OECD,

1991a, b, 1994; Keddy *et al.*, 1993; Hardi, 1997; Moldan *et al.*, 1997; Brugman, 1997). In addition it implies a meaningful management of stocks, flows and balances of environmental assets, where there are a lot of limitations on the methodology and management models (Bayliss and Walker, 1996: 90).

Based on these limitations, certain sustainability conditions have emerged to illustrate the suitable bequests to future generations for the purpose of maintaining incomes – i.e., *weak* and *strong sustainability conditions* (Healy and Shaw, 1993; Pearce *et al.*, 1993; Bartelmus, 1994; Blowers and Glasbergen, 1995; Hunter, 1995a, 1997; Collins, 1996).

Types of sustainability

Advocates of weak sustainability conditions are optimistic for the future, as they suggest that substitution of human-made capital for natural resources and for environmental quality is acceptable (Pearce *et al.*, 1993; Hunter, 1995a, 1997). In a similar vein, the accumulation of human-made capital, especially if combined with efforts to sustain technological progress and improve human capital through education (Bartelmus, 1994), is a suitable bequest for maintaining the income of future generations (Pearce *et al.*, 1993). It represents a *resource exploitative rule* in that 'provided that the net quantity of the capital stock is conveyed from one generation to the next, the conditions of sustainable development are satisfied' (Selman, 1996: 12). In other words, it is a situation where one form of capital can be substituted by another form without any loss of human well-being, hence meeting the 'constant capital rule' (Pearce *et al.*, 1989; Fyall and Garrod, 1997). Next, from the view of strong sustainability conditions, considerable effort should be made to maintain the existing natural resources and environmental stock (Pearce *et al.*, 1993; Hunter, 1995a, 1997; Selman, 1996; Collins, 1996). This does not necessarily imply that no economic change is permitted which utilizes the natural environment, rather, it suggests that environmental policies should be instituted (Pearce *et al.*, 1993; Hunter, 1995a, 1997; Selman, 1996). Here, it is noted that traditional outcomes of economic growth ultimately lead to economic disaster, which stems from the view that human-made capital is always a suitable substitute for natural environmental capital (Pearce *et al.*, 1993; Selman, 1996; Hunter, 1997). The strong sustainability principle is that of a cautious approach to reducing the stock of natural environmental capital, otherwise known as the *resource preservationist rule* (Pearce *et al.*, 1993), which is, in other words, a situation where natural capital cannot be substituted by any other form of capital except by a form of natural capital. Here, both the aggregate and natural capital stock must be at least constant as they are transferred from one generation to the next (Pearce *et al.*, 1993; Fyall and Garrod, 1997) (see Figure 7.1).

At this stage, although there is an agreement between these two types, certain limitations were highlighted on the spectrum of its practical implementation, especially on issues regarding the willingness of the incremental loss of natural capital, and of the application of the 'environmentally unconstrained patterns of growth' (Selman, 1996: 13).

Furthermore, in terms of the principle of strong/weak sustainability, Turner *et al.* (1994) expanded it into four main types: very weak sustainability; weak sustainability; strong sustainability; and very strong sustainability. In this case, both weak and strong sustainability conditions were kept intact, and the new terms were defined based on an extreme rule (Turner *et al.*, 1994; Hunter, 1997: 852–3). Very weak sustainability was seen as 'extreme traditional resource exploitative', and very strong sustainability was termed 'extreme preservationist' (Turner *et al.*, 1994; Hunter, 1997: 852).

On this point Hunter suggests that due to the lack of implementation at the extreme levels of sustainability, this gives rise to widespread agreement in defining sustainable development (1997: 852). He further criticizes the rejection of the extreme paradigms, due to the lack of definition in attempting to become more environmentally conscious, and the lack of vision in becoming more extreme resource preservationist (Hunter, 1997: 852).

In all the cases, the concept of future generations suggested that both the capital bequests and income concepts require flexibility and diversity of scenarios, otherwise the search for sustainable development will be passed on to future generations instead of any equitable capital transfers from the current generation. This is directly linked to the examination of sustainability where its treatment should be based on the implications of sustainability as a concept rather than focusing on the definitional perspective. Although the adoption of treating sustainability as a concept has been claimed as more appropriate within the environmental agenda (Barbier, 1987; Cocklin, 1989; Court, 1990; Dovers, 1990, 1995; Shearman, 1990; Jacobs, 1991; Peattie, 1992; Smith, 1993; Wilbanks, 1994; Blowers and Glasbergen, 1995; Hunter, 1997; Macnaghten *et al.*, 1997), within tourism research the treatment of sustainability is somewhat different.

Figure 7.1   Capital stocks and human well-being

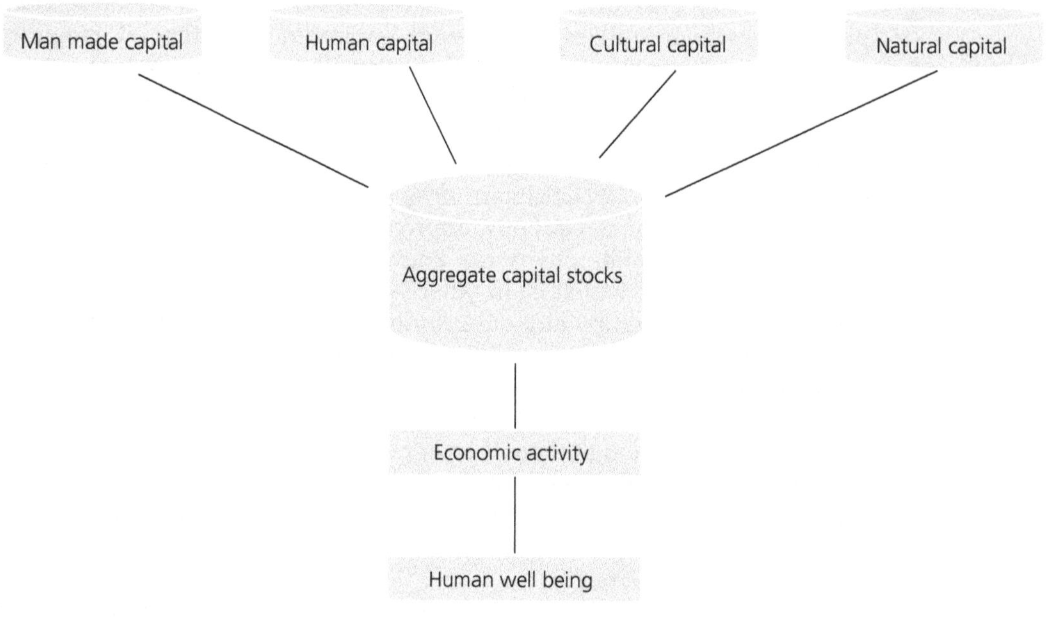

Source: Fyall and Garrod (1997: 56)

The concept of sustainability within the field of tourism

The articulation of the concept of sustainability in the tourism agenda contains both the theoretical contradiction over certain terms, as well as the realism of the importance of the concept. Its application within tourism all over the globe gives a clear indication that the concept has attracted wide attention within non-governmental industry-led bodies in recent years (WTO, 1993, 1995a, b, 1996, 1997; Murphy, 1994; EC, 1995; WTTC/WTO/EC, 1995; Mowforth and Munt, 1998: 105–11).

The transformation of the issues of sustainability within tourism, however, created a situation where most of the approaches became *extremely 'tourism-centric'*, partially divorced from the main principles of the concept of sustainability (Hunter, 1995a, b, 1997; Collins, 1996). In particular, the utilization of the concept of sustainable development in tourism captures the following issues (Hunter, 1995b; Butler, 1998; Milne, 1998; Williams and Shaw, 1998):

- the issue of equity of the local community in terms of living standards and quality of life;
- satisfaction of tourists and tourism industry demands;
- a pot-pourri approach based on the latter two aims in an attempt to safeguard the environmental resource base of tourism (natural, built and cultural aspects);
- maintenance or enhancement of the competitiveness of the tourism industry;
- strong and/or weak sustainability positions;
- sustainable development and/or sustainable tourism. The grassroots of this emphasis within tourism arose from the fact that to some practitioners sustainability concerned the sustainability of products and/or segments, while to others it was a process of development, and to some others it was a principle that should be adopted by all tourism (Godfrey, 1996). Alternatively, the concept of sustainability seems to be an intermediate term, bridging the gap between the developer and the environmentalist (McKercher, 1993; Fyall and Garrod, 1997: 53). The former practitioners are searching for resource exploitation and growth, while the latter practitioners are only looking for resource preservation (Fyall and Garrod, 1997). In addition, the application of sustainability within tourism takes the form of either a tool used for its long-term survival in an attempt to enhance the profitable performance of its operations, or a tool used to maintain the resource base of the tourism enterprises in order to generate more tourism demand (Stabler, 1997). In general terms, however, the consensus which generally exists is that there are two approaches within the application of the concept of sustainability in tourism, those of *sustainable tourism development* and of *sustainable tourism* (Butler, 1993, 1997; Hunter, 1997; Wall, 1997).

Sustainable tourism development

The concept of sustainable tourism development is mainly divided into two general schools of thought, the *product* and the *industry approaches* (Godfrey,

1996: 61). The former school represents the literature on sustainable tourism development or sustainable tourism, where sustainability is seen as an alternative to mass tourism. Generally speaking, the product approach mainly illustrates three general themes: research on the general concepts; research on the development strategies; and research on tourism behaviour (*ibid*.: 62). On the other hand, the industry approach represents the literature in which its practitioners argue that mass tourism is inevitable, and as such the attempt should be made to make all tourism more sustainable (*ibid*.). Further, the industry approach aims to reform the tourism enterprises, and issues of mass tourism development through a comprehensive, systematic, integrative, community-oriented, renewable, and goal-implemented attitude (*ibid*.: 63).

The major difficulty with both these schools of thought is that they represent elusive statements rather than actual cases of meeting sustainability's specifications. The product approach has been criticized on the basis of misleading comparisons between mass versus alternative tourism, and rural tourism versus sustainable tourism (Godfrey, 1996; Slee *et al*., 1997). The same holds true with the industry approach based on the views expressed on the issue of needs, type of resources, clarity of the term conservation and feasibility of destinations to apply sustainable development (Butler, 1997; Hunter, 1995a, b, 1997; Wall, 1997).

More specifically, sustainable development is concerned with the issues of quality, both from the locals' and the tourists' perspectives through economic development (Hunter, 1995a, b, 1997; Pigram and Wahab, 1997). The latter form of development should also take into account the conservation/preservation of resources (Hunter, 1995a, b, 1997). Although sustainable development constitutes the old principle of conservation and stewardship, it details a more pro-active stance (Murphy, 1994: 275). Alternatively, sustainable development has been seen as a component of tourism asset management, where development guarantees the integrity of resources and economic viability (Godfrey, 1996: 62–3).

Furthermore, sustainable development has been defined as:

> tourism which is developed and maintained in an area (community, environment) in such a manner, and at such a scale that it remains viable over an indefinite period, and does not degrade or alter the environment (human and physical) in which it exists to such a degree that it prohibits the successful development and well-being of other activities and processes. (Butler, 1993: 29)

Butler is the main critic of sustainable development, stating that it is necessary to define and manage the base of sustainability (1991, 1993, 1997, 1998; Wall, 1997). In particular, any movement towards sustainable development of tourism should include the co-ordination of policies, pro-active planning, acceptance of limitations, education of all groups, and a commitment to long-range planning (Butler, 1991). He identified four possible solutions to reduce the pressure and associated impacts of tourism on destinations, especially with regard to sustainable development. These solutions included: reducing the number of tourists at over-used sites and limiting visitations to sites before they reach critical levels; changing the type of tourists from 'mass' to 'alternative'; changing the resource to be a more resilient resource; and educating all the actors responsible for tourism (Butler, 1991). However, he states that these tasks face certain limitations due to the following reasons (1996a, 1997, 1998: 120–1):

- the lack of understanding of the needs of present and future generations;
- 'old' destinations face difficulties in becoming sustainable due to their pre-existing structure;
- the form of development is not to make 'new' development sustainable but to attempt to make existing development and destinations sustainable;
- the exceeded carrying capacities of tourism destinations have placed them in a situation where they are unable to meet the equity standards without any redevelopment;
- redevelopment and regeneration of development are more appropriate than small-scale sustainable development strategies.

In a similar vein, Wall (1997) has suggested that the concept of sustainable development is based on the criticism of identification of a responsible body that decides if the development is sustainable. He particularly has expanded on Butler's definition, by suggesting that tourism is not the only activity which consumes resources, and a balance must be formed within the other sectors, hence the *trade-off scenario* must be implemented (Wall, 1997: 45) or *trade-off tourism* (Collins, 1996), or the *view to reflect its multidimensional characteristics* (Wahab, 1997: 137).

Furthermore, Wall addressed the concern of re-conceptualizing the concept of development on the basis that sustainable development is an adaptive paradigm among tourism destinations, capturing the issues of economic viability, environmental sensitivity, and cultural orientation (1997: 46). Similarly, sustainable development has also been seen as a process of balances or the development triangle between economy, environment and society (Farrell, 1992: 116). He added that, although the goal of sustainability is concrete, there are elements that make the concept elusive (*ibid.*: 119). This idea of geometrical figures capturing the concept of sustainable tourism development has been enhanced by the 'magic pentagon', in which a balance must exist between (Muller, 1994: 132–3): economic health; subjective well-being of locals; unspoiled nature and protection of resources; healthy culture; and optimum satisfaction of guest requirements.

However, Muller and Farrell's views have not been criticized on the issue of balanced development (Hunter, 1997: 857). Here, the argument that exists is that there is not a clear interpretation of the issues regarding protection of the environment, as the terms 'protection', 'conservation' and 'preservation' are advocated in the literature simultaneously (Hunter, 1997). In addition, Godfrey's definition of sustainable development raises the issue of the type of resources used (natural, capital, renewable or non-renewable) and the lack of detail and clarity (Hunter, 1997).

Similarly, as with Farrell and Muller's approaches to sustainable development, Cronin (1990) is also a supporter of balanced development. Cronin advocates that sustainable tourism development must follow ethical principles that respect the culture and the environment of the host area; the economy; the traditional way of life; the indigenous people; the leadership of political parties

(1990: 12–13). It follows that the concept of equity should recognize the contribution of the host society through a committed partnership between the local population and government bodies where these stakeholders must share in both the benefits and costs for the present and future (Cronin, 1990). In turn this lays the grounds of the search for 'true sustainable development and use' (*ibid.*).

The issues of equity raised by Cronin give an important insight into the search for sustainable tourism development (Hunter, 1995a; Nepal, 1997; Pigram and Wahab, 1997; Williams and Shaw, 1998). Although meeting equity has been dealt with from a variety of perspectives, even from the travel distribution technologies (Milne and Nowosielski, 1997), at this stage the concern stems from outlining the appropriate balance between the creation of benefits for the present generation and the protection of resources for the future generation, without disadvantaging the poor (Hunter, 1995a: 71).

Issues of sustainable tourism development

A number of limitations have arisen with regard to the general search for sustainable tourism development. Firstly, the issue of *geographical equity*, in that whether the focus is specifically on the destinations or on a particular tourist resort, it has to take into consideration the implications of such equity issues in a general geographical context (Hunter, 1995b; Butler, 1998). The danger which exists is that sustainable tourism development encourages passing on the constraints of development to other provinces of the region, as opposed to dealing with the problems '*in situ*' and addressing them in a wider or sub-national context (Hunter, 1995a: 75, b: 159; McGregor, 1996; Butler, 1998: 30–1). Although this is primarily emphasized on the platform that sustainable development literature is deficient on the issue of scale (Hunter, 1995b), it further outlines that sustainable tourism development should contribute to sustainable development of the region rather than divorce itself from it (Cronin, 1990; Hunter, 1995a, b, 1997; Butler, 1996a, b, 1997; Wall, 1997). This can be achieved through 'a strategic co-ordination and enforcement on a spatially extensive basis, whether community or government led' (Collins, 1996).

Second, sustainable tourism development also has to reject the notion of '*single-sector tourism development planning*' (Hunter, 1995b: 162; Wall, 1997). Here, the concern is that this development is extremely tourism-centric rather than sustainability-centric (Butler, 1991, 1993, 1996a, b, 1997, 1998: 30–2; Hunter, 1995b; Collins, 1996; Wall, 1997). At this stage, the general concept of sustainability and its sub-components of development, needs and future generations, have to be viewed from the broad sectoral perspective rather than from the single tourism stance. On this point, Collins (1996) argues that although the latter principles should be considered, it is more advisable to focus on tourism-free development strategies as an *option* to the environmental/ economic sustainability evaluation. This is because the nature of international tourism does not tally with the long-term objectives of the concept of sustainability, due to the changing usage and nature of tourism destinations, and as such the focus on all sectoral sustainability planning could only initially assist with tourism capital and the preservation of resources (Collins, 1996).

Third, there is the issue of *resources utilization and usage*. This issue initially entails views that sustainable tourism development should 'preserve tourism's future seed corn' (Lane, 1994: 104; Hunter, 1995b). Ironically, this raises the concern that although the general concept of sustainability encourages the stewardship of all natural resources, sustainable tourism development advocates only resources critical to its development and the exclusion of other resources which are not that critical to its development or survival (Lane, 1994; Hunter, 1995b: 157). Again, the issue that arises is that sustainable tourism development should aim to contribute to the preservation of all resources, and not only those used by tourism development (Hunter, 1995b; Collins, 1996). Here, this aim could relate to the issues of carrying capacity (O'Reilly, 1986; Inskeep, 1991; Williams, 1991, 1994; Butler, 1996b; Collins, 1996), environmental control (Butler, 1996b), environmental impact assessment (Williams, 1994; Hunter, 1995a), environmental auditing (Goodall, 1992, 1994, 1995; Stabler and Goodall, 1993; Ding and Pigram, 1995; Diamantis and Westlake, 1997; Diamantis, 1998), resource stewardship (Pigram, 1990) and environmental indicators (WTO, 1995b). Fourth, there is the issue of *type of sustainability* and its implications for tourism destination management.

Types of sustainability within tourism

Types of sustainability within the tourism agenda is an emerging topic of discussion, and, at this point in time, the only example to be illustrated is by Hunter (1997). In particular, he has introduced four different approaches to sustainable development based on the four types of sustainability, which are, in themselves, trade-off scenarios and not tourist-centric (1997: 860–3) (see Table 7.1).

Very weak sustainability type or tourism imperative scenario

With an emphasis on satisfying both tourists and tour operators, this approach is applied in situations where tourism is in its infancy or not developed. It seeks to introduce tourism only in areas where pre-existing economic activities generate more degradation of resources than tourism.

Weak sustainability type or product-led tourism scenario

This scenario outlines the attempt to sustain existing, and create new, tourism products in destinations where tourism is dominant in the local economy. The maintenance of the environment in these tourism destinations receives a secondary priority, simply as a way to sustain the existing tourism infrastructure and its products.

Strong sustainability type or environment-led tourism scenario

This approach suggests that environmental management is at the heart of every destination planning initiative. This scenario includes the creation of new products (i.e. eco-tourism), and the search for niche markets with the authority to solely stress the environmental consequences of the products' consumption rather than their marketing strategies.

Very strong sustainability type or neoteneous tourism scenario

This approach advocates that tourism activity should be small-scale or even discouraged or excluded in circumstances where it generates environmental damage. The term neotenous 'implies that tourism activities would be limited to the very early, juvenile, stages of tourism development' (Hunter, 1997: 862). Here, the aim is to minimize the usage of both renewable and non-renewable resources through the usage of environmental management instruments and techniques.

Hunter's four types of sustainability are essential in broadening the horizons of sustainable development as an *adaptive paradigm* and *non-tourism-centric*. Although the very weak and weak types of sustainability are not ideal for absolute preservation of the destinations' resources, they provide alternative scenarios in circumstances where preservation cannot be implemented. A critical weakness of these four types is that they should include environmental management techniques (i.e. environmental auditing), not just in the neotenous tourism or strong sustainability approaches.

Table 7.1	*Types*	*Characteristics*	
Types of sustainability in tourism	**Very weak** *tourism imperative scenario*	*Status*: *Criteria*: *Benefits*: *Costs*:	Tourism at its early stages Tourism activities do not generate more degradation Tourism is an alternative form of development Creates more employment Increase environmental protection Creates certain antagonistic impacts
	Weak *product-led tourism scenario*	*Status*: *Criteria*: *Benefits*: *Costs*:	Tourism is developed Sustain tourism activities and develop new products Improvement of the local economy and employment Assist preservation practices of surrounding destinations Expansion and diversification of tourism planning Conserve only existing infrastructure and products
	Strong *environmental-led tourism scenario*	*Status*: *Criteria*: *Benefits*: *Costs*:	Tourism at its early stages Environmental management utilization Environmental quality Economic and employment growth Specialized tourism destination Only in circumstances lacking focus and commitment
	Very strong *neoteneous tourism scenario*	*Status*: *Criteria*: *Benefits*: *Costs*:	Tourism at its exploitation and involvement stages Absolute preservation of resources Protection of renewable and non-renewable resources Long-term environmental attractivity Tourism growth is limited Tourism development is abolished to minimize generation of negative environmental impacts Tourism development is sacrificed in cases where other sectors employ better environmental practices

Types of sustainability in tourism

At this stage, critics of these forms of sustainability suggest that it is irrelevant for the tourism industry to support a particular form as, generally, attempts made to measure the capital stocks of the destinations have been done so via an appropriate accounting framework, such as environmental balance sheets, and measurement techniques of the capital flows, such as the travel cost method and the maximum sustainable yield method (Fyall and Garrod, 1997; Goodall and Stabler, 1997). These views are mainly based on the following limitations (Fyall and Garrod, 1997: 57):

- determining whether the industry's efforts in achieving sustainable development are paying off;
- judging whether the industry's efforts are concerned with the most pressing environmental concerns or with the most environmentally damaging activities;
- assessing the industry's progress towards or, potentially, away from the goal of achieving sustainable development.

In all cases, these concerns are absolutely fundamental in the search for sustainable development as there is a lack of understanding of the 'magic' recipe for achieving sustainability. It is quite clear from the literature that there is a *search* for sustainable development at present, which should be addressed through the abolition of the 'tourism-centric' sustainable development paradigm. What seems to be clear is that trade-off scenarios and/or an adaptive paradigm of types of sustainability, and/or a holistic approach, could greatly assist in such a search.

Sustainable tourism

Sustainable tourism is often regarded as part of sustainable tourism development, or used simultaneously by tourism practitioners without any clarification of the similarities or differences between these concepts (Inskeep, 1991; Farrell, 1992; WTO, 1993, 1995a; Gilbert *et al.*, 1994; Lane, 1994; Muller, 1994; Cater, 1995; Orams, 1995a; Godfrey, 1996; Fyall and Garrod, 1997; Goodall and Stabler, 1997; Nepal, 1997; Wahab, 1997). There is certainly a major difficulty in clarifying if there are two distinct concepts or just one that encompasses the other. On this point, Butler argues that there are two distinct concepts where sustainable tourism is defined as: 'tourism which is in a form which can maintain its viability in an area for an indefinite period of time' (1993: 29). Similarly, Wall suggested that there is a distinction between these two concepts, as sustainable development enhances the multiple-sector approach to development and sustainable tourism represents a single-sector approach to development (1997: 44–5). As a result, sustainable tourism is identified as the sole user of resources in the destination and it neglects the other sectors' utilization of resources (Wall, 1997). Although the initial difference between these two concepts derives explicitly from the development perspective, other researchers have regarded sustainable tourism as a product and have drawn comparisons with mass forms of tourism (Lane, 1994; Cater and Goodall, 1997; Godfrey, 1996; Clarke, 1997). Here, there are four positions in the sustainable tourism literature deriving from its comparison with mass tourism (Clarke, 1997: 225–30):

- *polar opposites concepts;*
- *continuum concepts;*
- *movement position;*
- *convergence.*

The first position illustrates the theme of alternative tourism as the antithesis of the mass tourism development movement, or the notion of 'wrong' versus 'right' (Butler, 1990; De Kaft, 1990, 1992; Pearce, 1992; Gilbert *et al.*, 1994; Lane, 1994; Weaver, 1995, 1998; Cater and Goodall, 1997; Clarke, 1997). Initially, the term alternative tourism began to enjoy popularity during the late 1980s, as an optional way of overcoming the threat of mass tourism (Butler, 1990; Jarviluoma, 1992; Pearce, 1992; Romeril, 1994; Weaver, 1998). Alternative tourism is mainly seen as small-scale tourism and it relates to destinations which are rich in traditional cultures, together with fragile environments, and in relation to the destinations concern for the impacts of the sociocultural and environmental consequences of mass tourism utilization (Inskeep, 1991; Jarviluoma, 1992; Ioannides, 1995; Weaver, 1995). In contrast, alternative tourism was treated as a concept with its own features and should be developed, due to the evidence demonstrating that certain resort areas oppose the mass tourism development movement (Butler, 1990). In addition, it is an elitist activity consumed by highly educated and wealthy individuals (Butler 1990), expressing their dissatisfaction with sun-based holidays (Gilbert *et al.*, 1994; Ioannides, 1995). The main principle of this position suggests that alternative tourism aims to replace mass tourism (De Kaft, 1990, 1992) as the small-scale developments and enterprises involved enable the destination to enjoy high degrees of local participation and control (Ioannides, 1995). Hence, the polar opposite position mainly advocates that small-scale tourism is similar to sustainable tourism (Clarke, 1997: 226).

The second position mainly illustrates the phase of a continuum between sustainable tourism and mass tourism based on the polar opposite position theories (Clarke, 1997). It represents the adjustment of the polar opposite position to the continuum from mass tourism to sustainable tourism, based on the simultaneous utilization of the destination's resources by the two concepts (Clarke, 1997; De Kaft, 1990, 1992; Butler, 1990). Critics of the polar and continuum positions however, illustrated that the position of polar opposite 'right' and 'wrong' concepts was misleading and that alternative tourism is an elitist concept (Butler, 1990; Clarke, 1997).

The third position illustrates the movement to make mass tourism more sustainable, or the goal to minimize large-scale tourism through more small-scale sustainable tourism (Clarke, 1997). This position suggests that small-scale tourism products or development become more objective as the whole concept of sustainable tourism becomes a goal for attainment, all supported by the illustration of cases studied which search for such a movement (McGregor, 1996).

The fourth position represents the convergence stage, which is when all forms of tourism aim to become sustainable forms of tourism (Clarke, 1997). According to this position, there is recognition that sustainable tourism incorporates both large- and small-scale interpretations (Clarke, 1997). The former type includes the efforts in the previous position and the latter type offers a 'social slant from a local or destination perspective' (*ibid.*: 229). Hence, the current search is based on converting all forms of tourism towards a more sustainable orientated approach. Although this represents the current stance of sustainable tourism, certain limitations still exist in terms of the definitional relationship between these forms of sustainable tourism.

Consider for instance the idea that alternative tourism is a: 'small-scale tourism development by local people and based on local culture. Alternative tourism pays special attention to environmental and social carrying capacity' (Jarviluoma, 1992: 118). On the other hand, *responsible tourism* 'should lead to more awareness of the problem with tourism, more careful development, more concern for the host community and environment and a more enlightened approach by the tourist' (Gilbert *et al.*, 1994: 35). In both instances, limitations arise not only from the inevitable similarities, but in cases where it is considered as a distinct concept, the questions which then surface are how to achieve such development, concern for local populations, and carrying capacity measures. Similarly, one of the types of sustainable tourism products that attracted considerable attention was eco-tourism (Weaver, 1998; Lindberg *et al.*, 1998). Eco-tourism has been proclaimed to conserve natural areas, enhance small-scale development, educate both tourists and locals as well as provide an incentive for long-term attractiveness of destinations. However, its application illustrates not only the lack of precise definition of eco-tourism (Wheeller, 1991, 1992, 1993, 1994; Orams, 1995a, b), but also that its principles contain numerous direct and indirect costs (Weaver, 1998; Lindberg *et al.*, 1998), all limitations which in part are derived from the lack of a precise nature of eco-tourism management and an understanding of the behaviour of eco-tourists and its links with the other forms of sustainable tourism.

The position of sustainable tourism products

As can be seen in Figure 6.3, initially, eco-tourism may be treated both as a sub-component of alternative tourism and as nature-based tourism, being mainly part of the concept of sustainability. In addition, other forms of sustainable tourism have claimed to have similarities with eco-tourism as well as being part of both nature-based travel and alternative tourism. For example, eco-tourism has claimed to have some similarities with soft eco-tourism (Zalatan and Ramirez, 1996), nature tourism (Wilson and Laarman, 1988), sustainable tourism (Ioannides, 1995; Achama, 1995) and wildlife tourism (Roe et al, 1997).

At the other end of the spectrum, as illustrated in Figure 6.3, both mass tourism and other forms of tourism, such as conference and business tourism, are searching for sustainability in their practices and, as such, are placed outside the sustainability borders. Finally, certain practices of alternative, nature-based, eco-tourism, and sustainable forms of tourism which have practised unsustainable principles, are situated outside the borders of sustainability and have been re-positioned with other tourism products which are searching for sustainable practices.

In general terms, what seems to be occurring within the application of sustainability within tourism is the creation a variety of niches either representing products, forms of development, or consumers. These niche markets are still an elusive goal, not only from the development perspective but, most importantly, from their consumer-based characteristics, and they are searching for these sustainable forms of tourism (Richards, 1996). In overall terms, the theme of sustainable tourism is still an evolutionary paradigm that is seen as a goal to be achieved for small-scale development in the supply environment, and research enhancement on the niche characteristics in the demand and supply sides of the tourism system.

Summary

Implicit in the review of the concept of sustainability is that efforts should be placed on a clearer understanding of sustainability both from the environmental and tourism perspectives. Initially, this includes an agreement on treating sustainability as a concept based on its themes of development, needs, and future generations and the development of methodologies reflecting its multidisciplinary nature. At the heart of this methodological effort is the quest of achieving equitable growth, meeting equity for both present and future generations, and measuring the income and capital bequest of future generations. Arguably, the formulation of methodologies of types of sustainability and environmental indicators has to remain a priority in the sustainability agenda as their success could assist in overcoming the current limitations facing the meaning and effectiveness of sustainability.

Within tourism, there were certain concerns over the mixture of terms used to capture the same phenomenon. Ideally, two different agendas should handle the discussion in tourism, that of sustainable tourism development and sustainable tourism. Within the former, the challenge of achieving sustainability could be enhanced based on an absence of the tourism-centric syndrome, and utilizing methods where trade-off scenarios of different types of sustainability are developed and implemented. These scenarios and/or types of sustainability should be formulated in such a way that the syndromes of tourism-centric geographical equity, single-sector tourism development planning, and tourism-centric resources utilization and usage, should be abolished or at least greatly minimized.

Within the latter case, the challenge to convert mass tourism to sustainable tourism lies in the need to identify the limits of such a transformation, accompanied by the limits of new development and control measures within the tourism industry. Hence, this includes the enhancement of the environmental indicators methodology, and with environmental management techniques applied across the demand, supply and transit route levels of the tourism system. This should also be accompanied by the primary goal of determining the characteristics of the consumers searching for sustainable forms of tourism, and to accumulate the consumers' sustainability knowledge for the tourism industry.

References

Achama, F. (1995) 'Defining ecotourism', in L. Haysith and J. Harvey (eds) *Nature Conservation and Ecotourism in Central America*, Florida: Wildlife Conservation Society, 23–32.

Barberis, M. (1993a) *Issues in Sustainable Development: Population, Poverty and Environment*, Executive Summary, Publication Number A2a, Geneva: International Academy of Environment.

Barberis, M. (1993b) *Issues in Sustainable Development: Population, Poverty and Environment*, Final Report, Academic Paper A2b, Geneva: International Academy of Environment.

Barbier, E.B. (1987) 'The concept of sustainable economic development', *Environmental Conservation*, 14, 2, 101–10.

Bartelmus, P. (1994) *Environment, Growth and Development*, London: Routledge.

Barton, H. (1996) 'The nature of environmental auditing', in H. Barton and N. Brudel (eds) *A Guide to Local Environmental Auditing*, London: Earthscan, 7–24.

Bayliss, D. and Walker, G. (1996) 'Environmental monitoring and planning for sustainability', in S. Buckingham-Hatfield and B. Evans (eds) *Environmental Planning and Sustainability*, Chichester: John Wiley and Sons, 87–103.

Blowers, A. and Glasbergen, P. (1995) 'The search for sustainable development', in P. Glasbergen and A. Blowers (eds) *Environmental Policy in an International Context*, London: Arnold, 163–83.

Bosselman, F. (1978) *In the Wake of the Tourist*, Washington, DC: The Conservation Foundation.

Brown, B. *et al*. (1987) 'Global sustainability: toward definition', *Environmental Management*, 11, 6, 713–19.

Brugman, J. (1997) 'Is there a method in our measurement? The use of indicators in local sustainable development planning', *Local Environment*, 2, 1, 59–72.

Brundtland, G.H. (1994) 'The challenge of sustainable production and consumption patterns', *Natural Resources Forum*, 18, 4, 243–46.

Budowski, G. (1976) 'Tourism and conservation: conflict, coexistence or symbiosis', *Environmental Conservation*, 3, 1, 27–31.

Butler, R.W. (1990) 'Alternative tourism: pious hope or Trojan horse?' *Journal of Travel Research*, 28, 3, 40–5.

Butler, R.W. (1991) 'Tourism, environment and sustainable development', *Environmental Conservation*, 18, 3, 201–9.

Butler, R.W. (1993) 'Tourism – an evolutionary perspective', in J. Nelson, R. Butler and G. Wall (eds) *Tourism and Sustainable Development: Monitoring, Planning and Managing*, Department of Geography, Publication Series No 37 and Heritage Resources Center Joint Publication No 1, Waterloo, Ontario: University of Waterloo, 27–43.

Butler, R.W. (1996a) 'Tourism development and environmental control', paper given at International Scientific Conference on Tourism in the XXI Century, Sharm El-Sheikh, 24–6 September, Egypt.

Butler, R.W. (1996b) 'The concept of carrying capacity for tourism destinations: dead or merely buried?' *Progress in Tourism and Hospitality Research Journal*, 2, 3/4, 283–93.

Butler, R.W. (1997) 'Modeling tourism development: evolution, growth and decline', in S. Wahab and J.J. Pigram (eds) *Tourism Development and Growth: The Challenge of Sustainability*, London: Routledge, 109–25.

Butler, R.W. (1998) 'Sustainable tourism – looking backwards in order to progress?', in C.M. Hall and A.A. Lew (eds) *Sustainable Tourism: A Geographical Perspective*, Essex: Longman, 25–34.

Cater, E. (1995) 'Environmental contradictions in sustainable tourism', *The Geographical Journal*, 161, 1, 21–8.

Cater, E. and Goodall, B. (1997) 'Must tourism destroy its resource base?', in L. France (ed) *The Earthscan Reader in Sustainable Tourism*, London: Earthscan, 85–9

Charter, M. (1992) *Greener Marketing*, Sheffield: Greenleaf Publishing.

Clarke, J. (1997) 'A framework of approaches to sustainable tourism', *Journal of Sustainable Tourism*, 5, 3, 224–33.

Clayton, A.M. and Redcliffe, N.J. (1996) *Sustainability: A System Approach*, London: Earthscan.

Cocklin, C.R. (1989) 'Methodological problems in evaluating sustainability', *Environmental Conservation*, 16, 4, 343–51.

Cohen, E. (1978) 'The impact of tourism on the physical environment', *Annals of Tourism Research*, 5, 2, 179–202.

Collins, A. (1996) *The Limits of Tourism as an Engine of Sustainable Development*, Discussion Paper No. 82, Department of Economics, Portsmouth: University of Portsmouth.

Court, T. (1990) *Beyond Brundtland: Green Development in the 1990s*, London: Zed Books.

Cronin, L. (1990) 'A strategy for tourism and sustainable development', *World Leisure and Recreation*, 32, 3, 12–18.

Davis, D.E. (1991) 'Uncommon futures: the rhetoric and reality of sustainable development', *Technology and Society*, 63, 27–34.

De Kaft, E. (1990) *Making the Alternative Sustainable: Lessons from Development for Tourism*, Brighton: Institute of Development Studies (DP 272).

De Kaft, E. (1992) 'Making the alternative sustainable: lessons from the development of tourism', in V.L. Smith and W.R. Eadington (eds) *Tourism Alternatives: Potentials and Pitfalls in the Development of Tourism*, Philadelphia: University of Pennsylvania Press and the International Academy for the Study of Tourism, 47–75.

Diamantis, D. and Westlake, J. (1997) 'Environmental auditing: an approach towards monitoring the environmental impacts in tourism destinations, with reference to the case of Molyvos', *Progress of Tourism and Hospitality Research*, 3, 1, 3–15.

Diamantis, D (1998) 'Environmental auditing: a tool in ecotourism development', *Eco-Management and Auditing Journal*, 5, 1, 15–21.

Ding, P. and Pigram, J. (1995) 'Environmental audits: an emerging concept in sustainable tourism development', *The Journal of Tourism Studies*, 6, 2, 2–10

Dovers, S.R. (1990) 'Sustainability in context: an Australian perspective', *Environmental Management*, 14, 3, 297–305.

Dovers, S.R. (1995) 'A framework for scaling and framing policy problems in sustainability', *Ecological Economics*, 12, 2, 93–106.

Dowling, R.K. (1992) 'Tourism and environmental integration: the journey from idealism to realism', in C. Cooper and A. Lockwood (eds) *Progress in Tourism Recreation and Hospitality Management*, Volume 4, London: Belhaven Press, 33–46.

EC (1995) *Green Paper on Tourism*, DGXXIII, Brussels: European Commission.

Edgell, D. (1990) *International Tourism Policy*, VNR Tourism and Commercial Recreation Series, New York: Van Nostrand Reinhold.

Farrell, B. and Runyan, D. (1991) 'Ecology and tourism', *Annals of Tourism Research*, 18, 1, 26–40.

Farrell, B. (1992) 'Tourism as an element in sustainable development: Hana, Maui', in V.L. Smith and W.R. Eadington (eds) *Tourism Alternatives: Potentials and Pitfalls in the Development of Tourism*, Philadelphia: University of Pennsylvania Press and the International Academy for the Study of Tourism, 115–32.

Fox, W. (1994) 'Ecophilosophy and science', *The Environmentalist*, 14, 207–13.

Fyall, A. and Garrod, B. (1997) 'Sustainable tourism: towards a methodology for implementing the concept', in M.J. Stabler (ed) *Tourism and Sustainability: From Principles to Practice*, Oxford: CAB International, 51–68.

Gilbert, D.C., Penda, J. and Friel, M. (1994) 'Issues in sustainability and the national parks of Kenya and Cameroon', in C. Cooper and A. Lockwood (eds) *Progress in Tourism Recreation and Hospitality Management*, Volume 6, Chichester: John Wiley and Sons, 30–45.

Glasbergen, P. and Gorvers R. (1995) 'Environmental problems in an international context', in P. Glasbergen and A. Blowers (eds) *Environmental Policy in an International Context*, London: Arnold, 1–29.

Godfrey, K.B. (1996) 'Towards sustainability? Tourism in the Republic of Cyprus', in L.C. Harrison and W. Husbands (eds) *Practising Responsible Tourism: International Case Studies in Tourism Planning, Policy and Development*, Chichester: John Wiley and Sons, 58–79.

Goodall, B. (1992) 'Environmental auditing for tourism', in C. Cooper and A. Lockwood (eds) *Progress in Tourism and Hospitality Management*, Volume 4, London: Belhaven Press, 60–74.

Goodall, B. (1994) 'Environmental auditing', in S. Witt and L. Moutinho (eds) *Tourism Marketing and Management Handbook*, 2nd edn, Hemel Hempstead: Prentice-Hall, 113–19.

Goodall, B. (1995) 'Environmental auditing: a tool for assessing the environmental performance of tourism firms', *The Geographical Journal*, 161, 1, 29–37.

Goodall, B. and Stabler, M.J. (1997) 'Principles influencing the determination of environmental standards for sustainable tourism', in M.J. Stabler (ed) *Tourism and Sustainability: From Principles to Practice*, Oxford: CAB International, 279–304.

Hardi, P. (1997) 'Measurement and indicators program of the International Institute for Sustainable Development', in B. Moldan *et al.* (eds) *Sustainability Indicators: Report of the Project on Indicators of Sustainable Development*, Scope 58, London: John Wiley and Sons, 28–32.

Healy, P. and Shaw, T. (1993) 'Planners, plans, and sustainable development', *Regional Studies*, 27, 8, 769–76.

Hunter, C. (1995a) 'Key concepts for tourism and the environment', in C. Hunter and H. Green (eds) *Tourism and the Environment: A Sustainable Relationship?'* London: Routledge, 52–92.

Hunter, C. (1995b) 'On the need to re-conceptualize sustainable tourism development', *Journal of Sustainable Tourism*, 3, 3, 155–65.

Hunter, C. (1997) 'Sustainable tourism as an adaptive paradigm', *Annals of Tourism Research*, 24, 4, 850–67.

Inskeep, E. (1991) *Tourism Planning: An Integrated and Sustainable Development Approach*, London: Chapman and Hall.

International Chamber of Commerce (ICC) (1990) *The Business Charter for Sustainable Development, Principles for Environmental Management*, Paris: ICC.

Ioannides, D. (1995) 'A flawed implementation of sustainable tourism: the experience of Akamas, Cyprus', *Tourism Management*, 16, 8, 583–92.

IUCN (1980) *World Conservation Strategy*, IUCN, Gland, Switzerland.

Jacobs, M. (1991) *The Green Economy*, London: Pluto Press.

Jarviluoma, J. (1992) 'Alternative tourism and the evolution of the tourist areas', *Tourism Management*, 13, 1, 118–20.

Keddy, P.A., Lee, H.T. and Wisheu, I.C. (1993) 'Choosing indicators of ecosystem integrity: wetlands as a model system', in S. Woodley, J. Kay and G. Francis (eds) *Ecological Integrity and the Management of Ecosystems*, St. Lucie Press, 61–79.

Khan, A.M. (1995) 'Sustainable development: the key concepts, issues, and implications', *Sustainable Development*, 3, 2, 63–9.

Kidd, C. (1992) 'The evolution of sustainability', *Journal of Agricultural and Environmental Ethics*, 5, 1, 1–26.

Lane, B. (1994) 'What is rural tourism?', *Journal of Sustainable Tourism*, 2, 1/2, 7–21.

Lele, S. (1991) 'Sustainable development: a critical review', *World Development*, 19, 6, 607–21.

Lindberg, K., Furze, B., Staff, M. and Black R. (1998) *Ecotourism in the Asia-Pacific Region: Issues and Outlook*, Bangkok: Food and Agriculture Organization, Regional Office for Asia and Pacific.

Macnaghten, P., Grove-White, R., Jacobs, M. and Wynne, B. (1997) 'Sustainability and indicators', in P. McDonagh and A. Prothero (eds) *Green Management: A Reader*, London: The Dryden Press, 148–53.

McGregor, N.C. (1996) 'Investment horizons and sustainable tourism: implications for EU policy', *European Environment*, 6, 6, 194–203.

McKercher, B. (1993) 'The unrecognized threat to tourism: can tourism survive "sustainability"?', *Tourism Management*, 14, 2, 131–36.

Milne, S. and Nowosielski, L. (1997) 'Travel distribution technologies and sustainable tourism development: the case of South Pacific microstates', *Journal of Sustainable Tourism*, 5, 2, 131–50.

Milne, S.S. (1998) 'Tourism and sustainable development: the global–local nexus', in C.M. Hall and A.A. Lew (eds) *Sustainable Tourism: A Geographical Perspective*, Essex: Longman, 35–48.

Mitlin, H. (1992) 'Sustainable development: a guide to the literature', *Environment and Urbanization*, 4, 111–24.

Moldan, B., Billharz, S. and Matravers, R. (eds) (1997) *Sustainability Indicators: Report of the Project on Indicators of Sustainable Development*, Scope 58, Chichester: John Wiley and Sons.

Mowforth, M. and Munt, I. (1998) *Tourism and Sustainability: New Tourism in the Third World*, London: Routledge.

Muller, H. (1994) 'The thorny path to sustainable tourism development', *Journal of Sustainable Tourism*, 2, 3, 131–36.

Murphy, P. (1994) 'Tourism and sustainable development', in W. Theobald (ed) *Global Tourism, the Next Decade*, Oxford: Butterworth-Heinemann, 274–98.

Narayan, D. (1996) 'Learning from the poor: poverty, participation and the environment', *Environmental Matters at the World Bank*, Summer, 17–19.

Nepal, S.K. (1997) 'Sustainable tourism, protected areas and livelihood needs of local communities in developing countries', *International Journal of Sustainable Development and World Ecology*, 4, 2, 123–35.

O'Reilly, A.M. (1986) 'Tourism carrying capacity', *Tourism Management*, 7, 4, 254–58.

Orams, M.B. (1995a) 'Towards a more desirable form of ecotourism', *Tourism Management*, 16, 1, 3–8.

Orams, M.B. (1995b) 'Using interpretation to manage nature-based tourism', *Journal of Sustainable Tourism*, 4, 2, 81–94.

Organization for Economic Co-operation and Development (1980) *The Impact of Tourism in the Environment*, Paris: OECD.

Organization for Economic Co-operation and Development (1991a) *The State of the Environment*, Paris: OECD.

Organization for Economic Co-operation and Development (1991b) *Environmental Indicators: A Preliminary Set*, Paris: OECD.

Organization for Economic Co-operation and Development (1994) *Environmental Indicators: OECD Core Set*, Paris: OECD.

Pearce, D.G. (1992) 'Alternative tourism: concepts, classifications, and questions', in V.L. Smith and W.R. Eadington (eds) *Tourism Alternatives: Potentials and Pitfalls in the Development of Tourism*, Philadelphia: University of Pennsylvania Press and the International Academy for the Study of Tourism, 15–30.

Pearce, D.W., Markandya, A. and Barbier, E.B. (1989) *Blueprint for a Green Economy*, London: Earthscan.

Pearce, D.W., Barbier, E. and Markandya, A. (1990) *Sustainable Development*, London: Earthscan.

Pearce, D.W., *et al.* (1993) *Blueprint 3: Measuring Sustainable Development*, London: Earthscan.

Peattie, K. (1992) *Green Marketing*, London: Pitman Publishing.

People and Planet (1997) 'Rich and poor, *People and Planet*, 6, 2, 4.

Pezzey, J. (1992) 'Sustainability: an interdisciplinary guide', *Environmental Values*, 4, 1, 321–62.

Pigram, J. and Wahab, S. (1997) 'The challenge of sustainable tourism growth', in S. Wahab and J.J. Pigram (eds) *Tourism Development and Growth: The Challenge of Sustainability*, London: Routledge, 3–13.

Pigram, J. (1990) 'Sustainable tourism – policy considerations', *The Journal of Tourism Studies*, 1, 2, 2–9.

Redclift, M. (1987) *Sustainable Development: Exploring the Contradictions*, London: Routledge.

Redclift, M. and Sage C. (1994) 'Introduction', in M. Redclift and C. Sage (eds) *Strategies for Sustainable Development*, Chichester: John Wiley and Sons, 1–16.

Rees, W.E. (1988) 'A role for environmental assessment in achieving sustainable development', *EIA Review*, 8, 3, 273–91.

Rees, W.E. (1990) 'The ecology of sustainable development', *The Ecologist*, 20, 18–23.

Richards, G. (1996) 'Sustainable tourism management education: educational, environmental and industry perspectives', in B. Bramwell, I. Henry, G. Jackson, A.G. Prat, G. Richards and J. Straaten (eds) *Sustainable Tourism Management: Principles and Practice*, Tilburg: Tilburg University Press, 7–22.

Roe, D., Leader-Williams N. and Dalal-Clayton, B. (1997) *Take Only Photographs, Leave Only Footprints: The Environmental Impacts of Wildlife Tourism*, Wildlife and Development Series, London: International Institute for Environment and Development.

Romeril, M. (1994) 'Alternative tourism: the real tourism alternative?', in C. Cooper and A. Lockwood (eds) *Progress in Tourism Recreation and Hospitality Management*, Volume 6, Chichester: John Wiley and Sons, 22–9.

Selman, P. (1996) *Local Sustainability*, London: Paul Chapman.

Shearman, R. (1990) 'The meaning and ethics of sustainability', *Environmental Management*, 14, 1, 1–8.

Shiva, V. (1989) *Staying Alive: Women, Ecology, and Development*, London: Zed Books.

Slee, W., Farr, H. and Snowdon, P. (1997) 'Sustainable tourism and the local economy', in M.J. Stabler (ed) *Tourism and Sustainability: From Principles To Practice*, Oxford: CAB International, 69–87.

Smith, L.G. (1993) *Impact Assessment and Sustainable Resource Management*, Essex: Longman.

Stabler, M.J. and Goodall, B. (1993) 'Environmental auditing in the planning for sustainable island tourism', paper given at the International Conference on Sustainable Tourism in Islands and Small States, Foundation for International Studies, University of Malta, 18–20 November, Valleta, Malta.

Stabler, M.J. (1997) 'An overview of the sustainable tourism debate and the scope and content of the book', in M.J. Stabler (ed) *Tourism and Sustainability: From Principles To Practice*, Oxford: CAB International, 1–21.

Strong, C. (1997) 'The role of fair trade principles within sustainable development', *Sustainable Development*, 5, 1, 1–10.

Turner, R.K. (1988) 'Sustainability, resource conservation and pollution control: an overview', in R.K. Turner (ed) *Sustainable Environmental Management: Principles and Practice*, London: Belhaven Press, 1–28.

Turner, R.K. (1991) 'Environment, economics and ethics', in D. Pearce *et al.* (eds) *Blueprint 2: Greening the World Economy*, London: Earthscan, 209–24.

Turner, R.K., Pearce, D. and Bateman, I. (1994) *Environmental Economics: An Elementary Introduction*, Hemel Hempstead: Harvester Wheatsheaf.

United Nations (UN) (1992) *Earth Summit*, press summary of Agenda 21, New York: UN.

United Nations (UN) (1993) *The Global Partnerships for Environment and Development*, Post-Rio Edition, New York: UN.

Wahab, S. (1997) 'Sustainable tourism in the developing world', in S. Wahab and J.J. Pigram (eds) *Tourism Development and Growth: The Challenge of Sustainability*, London: Routledge, 129–46.

Wall, G. (1997) 'Sustainable tourism – unsustainable development', in S. Wahab and J.J. Pigram (eds) *Tourism Development and Growth: The Challenge of Sustainability*, London: Routledge, 33–49.

Weaver, D.B. (1995) 'Alternative tourism in Montserrat', *Tourism Management*, 16, 8, 593–604.

Weaver, D. (1998) *Ecotourism in the Less Developed World*, Oxford: CAB International.

Welford, R. (1995) *Environmental Strategy and Sustainable Development*, London: Routledge.

Wheeller, B. (1991) 'Tourism's troubled times: responsible tourism is not the answer', *Tourism Management*, 12, 2, 91–6.

Wheeller, B. (1992) 'Alternative tourism – a deceptive ploy', in C. Cooper and A. Lockwood (eds) *Progress in Tourism Recreation and Hospitality Management*, Volume 4, London: Belhaven, 140–45.

Wheeller, B. (1993) 'Sustaining the ego', *Journal of Sustainable Tourism*, 1, 2, 121–29.

Wheeller, B. (1994) 'Ecotourism: a ruse by any other name', in C. Cooper and A. Lockwood (eds) *Progress in Tourism Recreation and Hospitality Management*, Volume 6, Chichester: John Wiley and Sons, 3–11.

Wilbanks, T.J. (1994) 'Sustainable development in geographic perspective', *Annals of the Association of American Geographers*, 84, 541–56.

Williams, P. (1991) *Carrying Capacity Management in Tourism Settings: A Tourism Growth Management Process*, Montreal, Canada School of Resource and Environmental Management, Simon Fraser University.

Williams, P. (1994) 'Frameworks for assessing tourism's environmental impacts', in B. Ritchie and C. Goeldner (eds) *Travel, Tourism and Hospitality Research: A Handbook for Managers and Researchers*, 2nd edn, Chichester: J Wiley and Sons, 425–35.

Williams, A. and Shaw, G. (1998) 'Tourism and the environment: sustainability and economic restructuring', in C.M. Hall and A.A. Lew (eds) *Sustainable Tourism: A Geographical Perspective*, Essex: Longman, 49–59.

Wilson, M.A. and Laarman, J.G. (1988) 'Nature tourism and enterprise development in Ecuador', *World Leisure and Recreation*, 29/30, 1, 22–7.

World Commission on Environment and Development (WCED) (1987) *Our Common Future*, Oxford: Oxford University Press, WCED.

World Tourism Organization (WTO) (1993) *Sustainable Tourism Development: Guide for Local Planners*, Madrid: WTO.

World Tourism Organization (WTO) (1995a) *Sustainable Tourism Development*, background paper by WTO Secretariat in WTO Asian Tourism Conference, Technical Session, Islamabad, Pakistan, 13 January, Madrid: WTO.

World Tourism Organization (WTO) (1995b) *What Tourism Managers Need to Know: A Practical Guide to the Development and Use of Indicators of Sustainable Tourism*, Madrid: WTO.

World Tourism Organization (WTO) (1996) *Tourism and Environmental Protection*, WTO-ETAG, Joint Seminar, Heidelberg, Germany, Madrid: WTO.

World Tourism Organization (WTO) (1997) *Tourism 2000: Building a Sustainable Future for Asia-Pacific*, Madrid: WTO.

World Travel and Tourism Council/World Tourism Organization/Earth Council (WTTC/WTO/EC_ (1995) *Agenda 21 for the Travel and Tourism Industry – Towards Environmentally Sustainable Development*, Oxford: WTTC/WTO/EC.

Zalatan, A. and Ramirez, A. (1996) 'Soft ecotourism: the substitution effect', *The Tourism Review*, 4, 42–8.

8

Competitive analysis of resorts:
A strategic perspective

Strategy formulation: an introduction

At the heart of the Tourism Area Life Cycle (TALC) is the issue of strategy formulation, a topic that has been explored extensively, with the proposal of many theoretical models that can be identified in the literature. The actual approach to formulation of a strategy is often dependent upon the type of tourism or hospitality organization and its leadership. Thus the strategy employed will not determine if the firm's expansion takes place, but rather will determine where it takes place, the phasing of the expansion, the degree of market representation required and the support services needed to maintain and develop a touristic concept.

For any organization to reach its full potential, formulation must be approached from the perspective that it will assist the organization in aligning itself with its environment, a fundamental point made by writers such as Hofer and Schendel (1978); Porter (1980); Dev and Olsen (1989), among others. Thus it is important for organizations to find the optimal pattern or fit between the environment and the organization's strategy. Research evidence from writers already mentioned suggests that tourism and hospitality organizations, which are effective in environmental analysis, do perform better.

The environment as described here can be divided into two areas: general and task. The general environment consists of those broad forces affecting both industry and society. They include trends in technology, politics, economics and sociocultural issues. The task environment relates to those forces working in an industry environment such as changes in the supply of resources, shifts in competitor behaviour, the impact of industry-specific legislation and changes taking place in consumer markets, within which the organization competes.

However, environmental analysis is made more difficult due to the lack of reliable information, the firm's ability to assess it, how current events will affect the organization and the probability that such events will occur. To be successful, the organization must build a network of sources about the environment that are reliable and provide a valid assessment regarding its impact. However, despite the best of sources and probable estimates it is still impossible to predict the exact effect of the environment on an organization.

Competitive strategies in tourism and hospitality

The nature of tourism and hospitality seems to reflect characteristics that fit well into what Porter (1980) describes as a fragmented industry. Specifically, what

Porter means is an industry in which no firm has a significant market share, can strongly influence the industry's outcome, and essentially involves undifferentiated products. Furthermore the industry appears to represent what could be classified as a hostile environment. That is an environment where overall market growth is slow and erratic, there is a significant upward pressure on operating costs and there is intense competition resulting in high market concentration. Clearly, the tourism and hospitality industry possesses many of these characteristics that would classify it as fragmented with a low market share set within the context of a hostile environment. In the face of such conditions strategic positioning is likely to be of particularly crucial significance.

Miles and Snow (1978) argue that organizations can be typified according to their response patterns, they also emphasize that categories of competitive strategy are related to particular industry environments. Table 8.1 shows four different strategic orientations and their respective growth policies.

Strategy implementation

Following the stage of strategic formulation the discussion leads to a decision on the type of strategy to be implemented. The framework for developing strategy developed by Thompson and Strickland (1980) illustrates the key elements necessary to ensure the proper implementation of the organization's chosen strategy, and covers the following four points:

1. Successful performance of the recurring administrative tasks associated with strategy implementation.
2. Creating a fit between the organization's internal processes and the requirements of strategy.
3. Making adjustments for the organization's overall situation in which implementation must take place.
4. Choosing how to lead the implementation task.

These four components recognize that the organization must have in place systems that are designed to match the resources of the touristic organization with its chosen strategy. This suggests that the structure of the organization i.e.,

Table 8.1	Strategic orientations	Growth policy
Strategic orientations and growth policies	Defenders	Growth focus is deeper penetration into current markets
	Prospectors	Growth focus is through the location of new markets, products or services
	Analysers	Growth focus through both market penetration of existing markets and also through market development
	Reactors	Management fails to articulate a viable strategy

Source: Miles and Snow (1978)

its hierarchy, complexity, formalization, allocation and control of resources, must reflect the type of strategy.

Implementing growth policies

Many tourism or hospitality companies' primary growth strategies are similar, as illustrated in Table 8.2, with the growth and quality of products and services supported by technology appearing to be the most favoured approaches. Equally, growth appears to be mainly based on franchising and management service contracts, with some asset-acquiring activity by firms, particularly in the hotel sector. Conversions accomplished through the acquisitions and cherry picking of small chains is also an increasingly popular growth strategy, particularly as it achieves the objective of market share.

There is division among the larger firms as to whether or not segmentation is the way to implement their growth strategies. Companies such as Holiday Inn Worldwide, Choice Hotels International and Marriott believe strongly in the marketing of several brands, whereas the remaining chains focus on the upscale markets. The factor supporting the projected growth in the upmarket luxury segments is increased business travel, with a strong correlation between such travel and economic growth. While economies in the developing world are likely to generate increased business travel, it is questionable whether all the hotel capacity projected will be necessary at the top end of the market. With companies taking more care to control travel expenses, it seems possible that the hotel chains representing more 'value for money' may be better positioned to reflect this trend in business travel expenditures.

While reaction to the environment is better than no action at all, it is preferable to be pro-active and stay ahead of important trends. If management is ahead of emerging trends then it is possible to develop strategies and organizational structures that will permit the firm to achieve maximum performance in the long run.

Defensive strategies

The long-term trends in the environment of the tourism and hospitality industry, have resulted in the emergence of defensive strategies by many corporations.

Table 8.2	Growth strategies	Competitive methods
Growth strategies and competitive methods	Joint ventures	Technology based systems
	Franchizing	Brand development
	Strategic alliances	Product quality
	Management contracts	Sophisticated pricing
	Conversions	Global marketing and advertising
	Sale and leaseback	
	Acquisition of small firms	

A defensive strategy is described as an attempt by a firm to prevent the erosion of its market share. The key characteristics of such defensive strategies are:

- Firms expanding into foreign markets;
- Increased expenditures across the industry for marketing;
- Merger and acquisition activity: consolidation and globalization;
- Regionalization or second-tier chain development;
- The buying back of franchisees by franchisors;
- Privatizing firms using such tactics as leveraged buy-outs;
- Shortening of concept life cycles;
- Price discounting.

Defensive strategies are implemented when a company wishes to reduce the levels of risk that the environment exposes it to. It can be argued that single economy-based businesses need to employ defensive strategies to lower risk, hence the reason why these firms have to expand internationally to reduce the effects of a particular economy on their business. However a defensive strategy can go further with diversification into related industries, i.e., from tourism and hospitality into leisure.

The orientation of corporate firms to expansion

There are tourism and hospitality firms in every country of the world. However, the poor quality of management, inconsistency of facilitates and under-developed markets mean that the full economic significance of the industry will continue to emerge. For instance, corporate hotel companies are represented in 140 countries of the world and are the dominant force in the restructuring of the world-wide hotel industry. If a hotel chain embarks upon a period of growth, the locations they decide to expand to will be determined by their growth orientation. There are two kinds of hotel companies undertaking global expansion: high-density home market companies and low-density home market companies:

1. *High-density home market companies.* The most common pattern to the restructuring of the world-wide industry has been for hotel chains to evolve and expand towards national coverage within their home country before attempting international expansion. This pattern has predominated in the USA, the UK, and France, the three most developed hotel markets in the world. This means that global expansion will only occur once there is saturation of the domestic market. For these companies the global market is of secondary importance to the domestic market in which they have a majority of their interests. These high-density home market companies have been pushed into the global market by the domestic environment failing to give growth opportunities as good as those in other world regions.

2. *Low-density home market companies.* There has been increasing growth in international hotel demand since the end of the Second World War. To

meet this demand, hotel chains have evolved which operate in many countries without necessarily having many hotels in their home country. For these companies global expansion is routine, and the global market is of higher priority than the domestic market in which they have their origins. These companies have not been pushed into the global market by the harsh domestic business environment but were lured by the positive aspects of the international market.

In the development of hotel chains world-wide there is only slight evidence that high-density home market companies are able to capture demand in more than one country, to colonize foreign markets rather than having a token presence. The high-density home market companies are being driven towards international growth as opportunities in their domestic market recede while the low-density home market companies see international growth as a way of life.

Factors determining the implementation of growth strategies

A tourism or hotel firm may decide to implement a strategy for global expansion for a variety of reasons. Once the decision has been made to go global there are still specific factors to consider. There are many determinants that will help achieve growth objectives, operational performance and the general success of expansion. If a company fails to recognize the importance of these factors, the consequences could be disastrous, and only by understanding them can the company really assess the true feasibility of global expansion.

This section of the chapter aims to discuss the role of the most influential factors involved in a global expansion programme and their impact on the feasibility of international growth.

Role of technology

The need for control and support of hotels within a portfolio that is geographically dispersed can be aided through the use of computer reservations systems (CRS). Indeed, this technological link can be essential for survival, therefore corporations looking to expand must be able to use and manipulate a computer system to their needs.

Presently there is increasing use of CRS systems by hotel chains. Internal CRS development was first conducted by Holiday Inn and continual modification to their needs and trading environment have resulted in their latest Holiday Inn Revenue Optimization (HIRO) system. Holiday Inn considers their reservations system to be a major competitive advantage.

The role of CRS is more diverse than a pure sales function. The infrastructure needed for a competent CRS operation can also provide, almost as a by-product, collection and dissemination of financial information and its presentation; sales promotion feedback; customer identification and history; and the means of optimizing rates, yield and/or occupancy across a group. All of these functions are true advantages considering that individual hotels are located huge distances apart and have very little specific regional data supplied to them as would be the case in a domestic hotel chain.

Technology will become one of the most competitive methods that chains will employ to ensure growth. Once the large investment has been made, it will become part of the core technology of each firm and will require monitoring, updating and additional research and development investment in order to remain competitive. Technology will shape the future of marketing programmes, product design and corporate strategies.

Strategic options, evaluation and formulation within tourism and hospitality

At the heart of corporate strategy should be the issue of strategic choice and the first stage in this issue is to consider the strategic options available to the organization that is dependent on that particular firm's circumstances. Three related topics should be discussed regarding this issue of strategic options, namely:

1. The basis on which an organization may seek to achieve a lasting position in the environment, i.e., generic strategies.
2. The alternative directions in which the organization may choose to develop within its generic strategy.
3. The alternative methods by which any direction or strategic development might be achieved, e.g., joint ventures, alliances or acquisition.

These three elements of strategy are not independent of each other and this should be borne in mind when these areas are discussed in this chapter.

Generic strategies

It has already been suggested that specific strategic options can be set within the context of an overall generic strategy and this pulls together many aspects discussed in earlier chapters of this book. One important approach in this view is Porter's (1980) generic strategies; yet despite being widely accepted, problems can be attached to Porter's approach. In order to gain sustainable competitive advantage, Porter suggests that there are three ways in which a firm can achieve that objective:

1. A cost leadership strategy is where a firm sets out to become the low-cost producer in the industry.
2. A differentiation strategy where the firm seeks to be unique within the industry and with this uniqueness it is able to charge a higher than average price. In this sense it is seeking to differentiate itself from the competition.
3. A focus strategy which targets a particular segment group and refines its strategy to serve that segment to the exclusion of others.

It is suggested that with this approach long-term profitability requires the choice of one of these fundamental generic strategies otherwise it is Porter's view that the firm will end up being stuck in the middle.

Problems and constraints

While the framework provided by Porter can be regarded as useful, the problem for the manager is trying to translate this framework into actionable strategies that provide success for the firm in question. Sustainable cost leadership should be regarded as the lowest cost compared with competitors over time, while cost leadership can be achieved through economies of scale, market power and the experience curve effects. Such dominant firms do not automatically have sustainable cost leadership. There are cases of such firms losing market share and others overtaking them. Market share is not the central focus but rather the advantages that it can bestow on the firm, and therefore there is a requirement for managers to manage the business. One important distinction is that cost leadership can be applied to the whole industry or to specific market segments and that Porter uses the terms cost leadership and low price as interchangeable. However, cost should be regarded as an input measure to a firm where its price is an output measure and the cost reduction strategy does not necessarily mean that it would choose a price lower than the competition. A cost-based strategy *per se* does not give competitive advantage, as the opinions of the client or consumer have to be taken into account in order to gain competitive advantage and, in particular, such a consumer view has to be taken *vis-à-vis* the competition.

Porter's view of differentiation is one of a firm selling something so unique that it is in a position to charge a higher price. However one alternative to this approach is that selling a differentiated product or service at a similar price may achieve market share and volume for the firm. It is therefore in this sense possible to differentiate on low prices, i.e., a cost-based strategy that cuts across two of Porter's generic strategies and would be viewed by Porter as being stuck in the middle and therefore dangerous. This differentiation strategy also prompts the question of who the competitors are, and firms even in the same industry may compete on a different basis. Equally, firms may be competing on a range of issues such as ambience, location and levels of service, which suggests that differentiation involves more than just the physical product.

Market-based generic strategies

The approach of Porter (1980) seems in many cases to be based on internal measures as a basis for competitive strategy, but what is perhaps more important is to relate an internal strategy *vis-à-vis* the market or client base. It is this market-based view that needs to be added as a new dimension to Porter's generic strategies.

Price

There is a market segment in many industries that is willing to accept substantially lower-quality goods at very significantly lower prices. Such a segment can be regarded as price-sensitive. Companies could be competing in the same industry but be attempting to appeal to a specific market segment with a low income or a budget-conscious client. Another approach is to reduce price while still maintaining quality of the product or service, but this approach can lead to a price-based battle with the competition. Success with this approach can only be maintained if the firm has the lowest cost base among the competition. A problem leading on from this strategy is that the firm will have to operate with a reduced profit margin and will be unable to reinvest in its product or service. Success with this particular strategy can be achieved if the firm focuses on a specific product market segment and others do not, or cannot, match other firms' cost base.

Differentiation strategies

The essence of this strategy is where the firm offers perceived added value over the competition at a similar or somewhat higher price. In offering what the customer believes is a better product at the same price, or enhancing margins by slightly higher pricing, it is possible to achieve higher market share and therefore higher volume. Such an approach is likely to be successful if the firm can clearly identify who the customer is and what the customer's needs and values are. That the firm must understand what is valued by the customer is an important issue. A major differentiating factor is the ability of the manager to be close enough to the market to sense and respond to customer tastes and values. However, over time, customer values change and therefore the basis for differentiation must change with them. Therefore, a business following a differentiation strategy may have to continually review the basis for differentiation and keep changing its strategy.

Hybrid strategy

It is possible to combine a differentiation and price strategy. Here the success of the strategy depends on the ability to both understand and deliver customer needs while also having a cost base that permits lower prices that are difficult to imitate. Such an approach generates greater volumes and maintains profit margins because of a low cost base.

Focused differentiation

This strategy can be seen as competing in a particular market segment by offering a higher value to the customer at a significantly higher price. In doing so the firm is trying to convince the customer that their product is differentiated from those of their competitors. It is offering a product with a higher perceived value often at a substantially higher price. However, the problem with industry globalization is that the firm may have to choose between taking a broad approach or a more selective, focused strategy. Equally, the market segment the firm wishes to compete in needs to be clearly defined along with the values and needs of the customer. This may create problems as the firm is attempting to compete in different market segments. Also, focused strategies may conflict with the various stakeholder expectations within and outside the firm and such a strategy may be at the expense of a growth. Finally, the advantages of the focused approach may have to be carefully monitored because the market situation may change not only from a customer point of view but also from the response of the competition.

Failure strategies

Increasing price without increasing perceived value or maintaining price and reducing value can in most cases lead to failure. However, in the first case, if the firm is in a monopoly position, it may be that such a strategy can be sustained. This is particularly the case if the organization is protected by legislation or there are high economic barriers to entry.

The comments just made extend Porter's approach to generic strategies by adding the element of a market-based approach. It attempts to relate the product to the perceived value of the client.

Implementation

Having discussed generic strategies, the issue here is to put them into operation and to ensure that they can be sustained over the long term and so produce a profitable long-term advantage. Cost leadership can be related to the different activities within the value chain and any experience curve benefits that can be derived from those activities; for instance, volume purchases may bring with them reduced prices, a build up of experience and knowledge and greater internal efficiencies. An analysis can also be made as to where competitors are vulnerable in terms of costs within their value chain, and therefore it may be possible for the business to drive down its costs in these areas as a further means of gaining competitive advantage.

Sometimes it is the intangible aspects of strategy that suggest that value should not just be related to the product and technology. Service in terms of delivery and after-sales service linked to an understanding of customer needs and values can be one form of differentiation. It is in this way that different phases of differentiation through the value chain can be made. Differentiation in this respect is likely to be achieved not only by one element of the value chain, but by multiple links with all elements of the value chain. If these links can be established, a sustainable basis for differentiation can be found. For instance, a quality image, staff training, information systems, control of suppliers, all will contribute to the strategy of differentiation and the links within the value chain.

Another approach to differentiation and improved competitive standing is to build in switching costs within the strategy in question. If there are actual or perceived switching costs, the firm may achieve a differentiated position in the market. It is therefore important for managers to consider not only their own value chain, but the value chains of others such as buyers and suppliers and they therefore need to consider the links between and within value chains in order to provide a competitive advantage for the firm.

The operationalization and sustainability of these generic strategies poses a number of challenges for managers and require them to identify customer needs and values, either in broad terms or by specific market segments. They then require them to decide on a specific generic strategy appropriate for the firm. The strategy must relate customer needs to a mix of activities achieving a coherent set of links and hopefully differentiating them from the competition. In this approach cost efficiencies can be gained, specifically through the experience curve, and therefore the firm gains an advantage over the competition.

Strategic direction

A number of alternative strategic directions for the tourism or hospitality firm can be determined and set within the context of product and market choices which in many cases can be related to the environmental opportunities for growth available to the firm. However, strategic direction can concern not only growth, but consolidation and efficiency. Four main categories of alternative directions for development can be identified.

Withdrawal consolidation and market penetration

Withdrawal is a course of action, either completely or partially, and may be the most sensible course for a firm to take. For instance, declining performance may be an opportunity for withdrawal from some activities within the organization as a whole in order to raise funds or cut losses and allow the firm to consolidate or grow in other areas. Another example is that large diverse companies may view their subsidiary companies as assets to be bought and sold as part of an overall corporate portfolio.

Consolidation suggests changes in the way that a company operates, although the range of products and markets may remain unchanged. The firm may choose to maintain market share by growing with the market and so maintain a competitive cost structure *vis-à-vis* the competition. As a touristic product moves into the mature stage of its life cycle, the firm may choose to increase its marketing activity in order to highlight perhaps more intangible aspects of the product or service. Equally it may seek to improve its cost structure through productivity gains or higher capital intensity.

The strategy of market penetration may enable the firm to gain market share but will be dependent on the nature of the market and the position of the competition. The relevance of this approach will depend on whether the overall market is growing, static or in decline. For instance, in static markets the issue of the experience curve suggests that market penetration would be difficult since advantageous cost structure of market leaders would normally prevent the incursion of competitors with lower market share. However, this would not prevent firms from adopting the market penetration strategy in mature markets if, for instance, they chose some form of collaboration with other firms.

Product development

A firm may decide to search for alternatives that build upon the company's present knowledge and skills. This may be a viable choice and such an approach can be described as product development. Companies need to follow the changing needs of their customers by a policy of continually introducing new product lines. Although such an approach may raise problems for the firm, new products may be vital to the future of the touristic organization, but the process of creating a new product line is expensive, risky and potentially unprofitable. Most new products never reach the market and for those that do, there are relatively few which succeed. For this reason there has been a trend towards technology transfer and collaborative ventures.

Market development

This approach can be seen when firms with their present products venture into new market areas and exploit new uses for the product or spread into new geographical areas. If the company's distinctive competence lies with a particular product and not the market, continued exploitation of the product by market development would normally be preferable; exporting could also be seen as a method of market development. There may, for instance, be operational or logistical reasons that make the international option more favourable, such as changes in the relative cost of labour, transport or supplies. Organizations might also need to take this approach for defensive reasons such as government-imposed tariff barriers that might have been raised, or import controls introduced in important overseas markets.

Diversification

The term diversification can be used to identify directions of development that take the organization away from both its present products and present market at the same time. A number of diversification types can be identified.

- Related diversification is development beyond the present product and market but still within the broad confines of the industry within which the touristic company operates. It may take the form of backward integration in concerning the inputs to the company's current business.
- Forward integration looks at the company's outputs such as transport or distribution and horizontal integration refers to development into activities that are competitive with or directly complementary to a company's present activities.
- Unrelated diversification is development beyond the present industry into products and markets which at face value may bear no clear relationship to the present product or market. However, it needs to be recognized that increased ownership of more activities within the value chain does not guarantee improved performance for the firm or better value for money for the consumer. Synergy, for instance, is a commonly cited reason for both related and unrelated diversification. Potentially, synergy can occur in situations where two or more activities or processes complement each other to the extent that their combined effect is greater than the sum of the parts. While related diversification may build upon synergies rooted in products or markets, unrelated diversification is also considered synergistic as it is usually based on finance or managerial skills. Other reasons for unrelated diversification may be the aspirations of corporate leaders, the opportunity to employ under-utilized resources in a new field or the desire to move into a different area of activity perhaps because the present one is in decline.

Methods of development

Growing out of the generic strategies just discussed and identified, there are different potential methods of development. For many tourism and hospitality organizations, internal development has been the primary method of strategy development. However, the final cost of developing new activities internally may be greater than that of acquiring other companies, although it may be the case that the spread of costs could be more favourable. This is obviously a strong argument in favour of internal development for smaller companies that may not have the resources available for major investment. Another issue is one of minimizing destruction of other activities. The slower rates of change which internal development brings may make it favourable in this respect. Internal development avoids the traumatic behavioural and cultural problems arising from trying to integrate the two firms involved in acquisition.

Development through acquisition tends to go in waves and has been selective in terms of the supply sector within tourism. One reason to develop by acquisition is the speed with which it allows the company to enter a new product or market area; other reasons could be the lack of knowledge or resources of a particular element or strategy within that particular market area. If the market, for instance, is static, it would be difficult for a new company to enter that market and so entrance by acquisition, reduces the risk of competitive reaction. Another argument is when an established supplier within an industry acquires a competitor, either for the latter's order book to gain market share or, in some cases, to shut down its capacity and help restore a situation where supply and demand are more balanced and trading conditions are more favourable. There are also financial motives for acquisitions, particularly with asset stripping where the main motive for the acquisition is a short-term gain by buying up under-valued assets and disposing of them piecemeal. Another reason may be that the company is buying in to another company that is already a long way down the experience curve and may have achieved efficiencies which would be difficult to match, particularly by internal development. Reasons for mergers as opposed to acquisitions may be similar, although what distinguishes them from acquisitions is that they tend to come about voluntarily.

Joint development and strategic alliances are approaches that have become increasingly popular over the past few years, particularly within the tourism and hospitality industries. Within these categories there are a variety of arrangements which may vary, from formalized inter-organizational relationships to loose arrangements of co-operation between organizations with no shareholding or ownership involved. The form of the alliance is therefore likely to be influenced by:

- Asset management – the extent to which assets do or do not need to be managed jointly;
- Asset separability – the extent to which it is possible to separate the assets involved between the parties;
- Asset appropriability – the extent to which there is a risk of one or other of the parties involved appropriating the assets involved for themselves.

The reasons for these different forms of alliances are varied but usually concern the assets involved in the alliance, be they financial or physical or simply management know-how. Joint ventures are typically thought-out arrangements where organizations remain independent but set up a newly created separate body jointly owned by the parents. Consortia may well involve two or more organizations in a joint venture arrangement and would typically be more focused on a particular venture or project. At the other extreme, networks are arrangements whereby two or more organizations work in collaboration without formal relationships but through a mechanism of mutual advantage and trust. More opportunistic alliances might also arise where they are likely to more focused around particular ventures or projects but again may not be highly formalized. Such arrangements are much nearer to market relationships than to contractual relationships and may exist because the assets do not need joint management or cannot be separated from the firms involved. There are also intermediate arrangements that exist such as franchising, licensing and sub-contracting. All these intermediate arrangements are likely to be contractual in nature but are unlikely to involve ownership and they typically arise because particular assets can be isolated for the purpose of management and these assets can be separated from the parent firm to their advantage. Licensing or franchising are likely to take place, however, where there is a low risk of the assets involved being appropriated.

Strategic suitability

Having identified a variety of strategic options available to the tourism or hospitality firm, the need now is to evaluate those options and to judge their merits. One way of taking this approach is to make a judgement on the basis of suitability, feasibility and acceptability.

In evaluating suitability, the firm is attempting to assess the extent to which a proposed strategy fits the situation identified in the strategic analysis (as identified in a Strengths, Weaknesses, Opportunities and Threats analysis, i.e. SWOT) and how it would contribute to the competitive position of the firm. In this sense, suitability is a criterion for screening strategies before they are assessed for acceptability or feasibility. In this context the strategic manager is asking a number of questions, such as: does the strategy exploit the company's strengths or environmental opportunities? or: does it overcome the company's weaknesses or threats? All this should be set within the context of the organization's purpose, such as profit targets or growth expectations.

To evaluate in terms of feasibility, the concern is whether a strategy can be implemented successfully and whether it is achievable in terms of resources. Some issues to be addressed are:

- Can the strategy be funded?
- Is the organization capable of performing to the required level?
- Are the necessary marketing skills available?

The reaction of competitors needs to be identified and discussed along with whether the firm has the required skills at both management and operational level. It is also important to consider all these issues with respect to the timing of the required changes.

The criterion of acceptability, suggests a relationship with people's expectations and therefore prompts the question: acceptable to whom? Such issues reintroduce the topic of stakeholder theory and in particular stakeholder mapping. The way in which stakeholders express their views is dependent on the particular situation or the strategy under consideration and so an analysis of stakeholders is an acceptable method of testing the acceptability of strategies. In this respect, the evaluation of stakeholder expectations is crucial.

A framework for evaluation

In assessing suitability, a balance needs to be determined between detailed evaluation and the intuition of management. Suitability has been shown to be means of screening options with the three tests being:

1. strategic logic;
2. cultural fit;
3. research evidence.

From this approach a shortlist can be created from which the more detailed use of criteria concerning feasibility and accessibility can be applied.

There are many analytical methods useful both for understanding the current situation of the touristic firm and for evaluating strategic options for the future. They have evolved out of a rational and economic assessment of strategic logic and are primarily concerned with matching specific strategic options with an organization's market situation and its relevant strategic capabilities. Three approaches can be identified:

1. portfolio analysis;
2. life cycle analysis;
3. value system analysis.

The prime concern of evaluation at the corporate level is that of achieving a balanced portfolio and range of strategic business units. Options for the future can be plotted on a matrix with the long-term rationale of business development being highlighted, a well known example being the Boston Consultancy Group Matrix. Taking this approach, two questions to ask are: will the strategy move the company to a dominant position in the markets; and will the funds for investment be available? It is important to have a balance of activities that match the range of skills within the organization, and this is why certain groups are badly overstretched while others remain under-employed. Use of this matrix can help the strategic manager think about an acquisition strategy. This strength is synonomous with attractiveness or the directional policy matrix, discussed previously. This can be used for assigning development priorities among the various strategic business units.

A development of the product portfolio concept is life cycle analysis or product market evolution analysis. The two dimensions to this approach are the market situation described in a number of stages ranging from embryonic to ageing, and a competitive position described in five categories ranging from weak to dominant. The purpose of such a matrix is to establish the appropriateness of particular strategies in relation to these two dimensions. The first stage in this approach is to determine where the organization is currently positioned on the matrix. The position within the life cycle is determined in relation to eight external factors or descriptors of the evolutionary stage of the industry. These are: market growth rate; growth potential; range of product lines; number of competitors; spread of market share between these competitors; customer loyalty; entry barriers; and technology. It is the balance of these factors that determines the life cycle stage.

The competitive position of the organization within the tourism or hospitality industry can also be established by looking at the characteristics of each category or factors. Given the wide variety of strategic options, the main value of this matrix is in establishing the suitability of particular strategies in relation to the stage of industry maturity and the organization's competitive position.

It has already been emphasized that understanding how costs are controlled and value created within the value system is very important when assessing the strategic capability of a touristic organization. It was also noted that the links between the value activities are just as important as the activities themselves. The logic of strategic development can also be tested by the same measure and, in particular, the extent to which the strategy will change the value systems and therefore the competitive position and/or value for money the organization is able to sustain.

The concept of synergy applied in this context is concerned with assessing how much extra benefit can be obtained from providing links within the value system between activities, which either have been previously unconnected or where the connection has been a different type. Synergy can be sought in several circumstances such as market development, product development, or backward integration. Synergy could also arise through many different types of link or interrelationship; for example, in the market by exploiting a brand name, or in the company's operations by sharing purchasing facilities, maintenance and quality control, or in product and process development by sharing information and know-how. Synergy is often used as a justification for diversification, particularly in the tourism and hospitality industry through acquisition or merger.

It has been argued in earlier chapters that firms that diversify by building on their core businesses do better than those who diversify in an unrelated way. However, this can be a difficult argument in practice for a number of reasons. For instance the notion of a core business is not at all clear, as it could be defined by product or market or technology and is often defined in historical terms. It is also important to point out that core competencies are more culturally based and are often difficult to transfer from one situation to another; so it is perhaps wrong to suggest that diversification may be more successful because it builds on core competencies. This at least partly explains the difficulties that many organizations have had with diversification; assumptions are made about the transferability of core competencies when in fact they are not transferable. It has been argued that synergy should not be regarded as necessarily arising from horizontal links within the value system through the sharing of activities or skills, but can also arise from a shared strategic logic between touristic businesses or business units.

Another area where value chain analysis can be useful to an assessment of the suitability of strategies is in the locational decisions of international companies. The logic of gaining competitive advantage through the management of individual value activities suggests that the separate activities of design and marketing may often be located in different countries. This needs to be balanced against the importance of successfully managed links that prove more difficult to achieve if the separate activities become more dispersed internationally. The most successful international companies are those that can develop organizational arrangements to exploit the advantages of specialization and dispersion while managing links successfully.

While strategic logic is important, it is also relevant to review the options within the political and cultural realities of the touristic organization, and so cultural fit focuses on the extent to which particular types of strategy might be more or less simulated by an organization. Indeed, one of the key roles of the leadership within an organization is to shape and change its culture to better fit the preferred strategies. This tension between strategic logic and cultural fit has sometimes been described as a 'head versus heart' issue. However, the key judgement is whether or not such strategies are suitable for the organization's current situation, particularly if significant environmental change has occurred. The purpose of strategic logic analysis is to indicate whether or not the organization's paradigm requires some fundamental change. Whether paradigm changes are required or not, the assessment of strategic options in terms of cultural fit is valuable. If the organization is developing within the current paradigm, this analysis helps to identify those strategies that would most easily be assimilated. In contrast, if the paradigm needs to change, the analysis helps in establishing the way in which the culture will need to adapt to embrace new types of strategy. One of the key determinants of how culture might influence strategic choice is again the stage an organization has reached in the life cycle.

It is possible to discuss the relationship between life cycle culture and strategy and so link it to life cycle models. A combination of these perspectives and different stages in the life cycle can prove valuable in establishing options that fit both the strategic logic and the cultural situation.

In its embryonic stage, the firm's culture will be shaped by its founders. Once the organization survives, such personal beliefs become strongly embedded in the organization and shape the type of development that subsequently occurs. These core beliefs hold the organization together and become a key part of its core competence; organizations will typically seek out developments that fit its culture.

The growth phase of an organization involves a large variety of cultural changes in different circumstances and in some cases cultural developments can dictate strategic choice. The cohesiveness of culture seen in the embryonic stage tends to dissipate into subcultures, each of which may favour different kinds of development. As middle management emerges within the organization, in turn there is a diversity of expectations and the diffusion of a single dominant culture and the preference for one type of strategy. There may also be uncomfortable dilemmas to face as strategic logic may dictate one approach although the original beliefs of the organization may demand another approach.

By the time organizations reach maturity their culture tends to have been institutionalized to the extent that people are not aware of it or even find it difficult to conceptualize culture in a meaningful way. Such organizations tend to favour developments that minimize change and are evolutionary from the current situation. However, whereas incremental developments may be easier from a cultural point of view, they may well prove wholly inadequate if environmental circumstances are changing rapidly.

In decline, a cohesive culture may be seen as a key defence against a hostile environment. Organizations face difficult decisions concerning retrenchment, investment and withdrawal from products and markets that are engrained in their culture. In some situations the difficulties of adjustment can be so great that the organization's owners choose to sell out to another organization that may then be able to instigate radical changes.

So far, this chapter has attempted to suggest the suitability of strategies either by establishing the logic behind them or through assessing their cultural fit. Since the major purpose of strategic change in most organizations relates to the need to sustain or improve performance, this part of the chapter will review the evidence that is available on the relationship between choice of strategy and the performance of a tourism or hospitality firm.

The strategic importance of market power has already been discussed, and in understanding the likely impact of environment on any one organization this market power is a crucial factor in anyone's analysis. Such an analysis has used market share as a measure of market power and there is evidence that market share and profitability are linked. The link between performance and relative market share that is emphasized by the experience curve tends to show that return on investment rises steadily in line with relative market share. An explanation for this link is that they are largely concerned with cost benefits which market share brings. Companies with high market share seem to be able to buy competitively or to produce components more economically in-house. Also, economies of scale benefit firms with high market share. The example being that market overhead costs tend to decline as a percentage of sales with increased share. Indications are that firms with high market share develop strategies of higher price and higher quality than lower share competitors. High-share firms tend to be more profitable, thus providing the cash resources for research and development in order to improve and differentiate products, and thus enhancing their market position and also justifying higher prices, which in turn increase profits.

Another aspect to consider is consolidation strategies with the upgrading of product or service quality. The evidence is that quality is of very real significance and generates improvement of profit performance. The best situation appears to be a combination of high share and high product quality, but even firms with lower market shares demonstrate significantly higher profit performance if they have tourism products of superior quality. It can also be suggested that a reliance on increased marketing spending to consolidate an organization's position in its market is not in itself a satisfactory way of improving performance. Heavy marketing expenditure may actually damage a return on investment for firms with low market share. This does of course pose problems for a firm that is trying to improve or maintain its standing in its existing product market. Trying to do so by increasing marketing expenditure is likely to result in reduced profitability. In other words, attempting to buy market share is unlikely to be successful. Equally, high marketing expenditure is not a substitute for quality – indeed, it appears that high marketing expenditure damages return of investment when quality is low. It must be concluded that simply gearing up marketing expenditure, as a means of consolidating a company's position is not sufficient. Finally, improved productivity through capital investment can be regarded as another consolidation strategy but, also in isolation, capital intensity can damage return on investment. This is particularly true for companies with weak market positions. Also, since high capital investment is a barrier to exit, those suffering from low margins are reluctant to get out, so they continue to battle on and make the situation worse. Indeed, raising capital intensity in an attempt to improve profit returns is most likely to be successful for companies that already have a strong position in the market and are unlikely to meet fierce price competition and are able to make real reductions in layout and production costs. It is for some of these reasons that many organizations prefer sub-contracting as a means of improving productivity.

It has been argued in this chapter that higher relative market share is often of strategic advantage to organizations. However, the processes of building market share and market penetration are not without their costs. Short-term profits are likely to be sacrificed, particularly when trying to build share from a low base. Similarly, product development can bring uncomfortable dilemmas to many organizations, as they may prove expensive and unprofitable particularly in the short run. Product development may require a commitment to high levels of spending on research and development. It is evidence of this type that has convinced many touristic organizations to look seriously at technology transfer or acquisition of similar companies as alternatives to their own research and development efforts.

Diversification is probably one of the most frequently researched areas of business with specialists looking at the relationship between the choice of diversification as a strategy and the performance of the organization in financial terms. The link patterns of diversification and financial performance is unclear apart from one important message, that successful diversification is difficult to achieve in practice. The success of diversification is contingent on the circumstances of an organization's level of industry growth, market structures and the firm's size. The relationship between performance and diversity will also vary with the period of time studied, i.e., the point in the business cycle. Also, a key contingent factor is the resource situation of the organization, particularly the existence of under-utilized resources. It could perhaps be suggested that successful touristic organizations choose diversification if opportunities in their current product market domain are limited. Finally the concept of diversity should not be interpreted too narrowly as related in product terms; diversity is also an issue in other dimensions such as market spread. There is some evidence that profitability does increase with diversity but only up to the limit of complexity beyond which the relationship reverses. This raises the issue of whether managers can cope with large, diverse organizations.

Screening options

One of the benefits that should emerge from the assessment of suitability is an understanding of the underlying rationale behind particular types of strategy. However, within these broad types there is likely to be a range of specific strategies that an organization could follow and the process of evaluation normally requires a narrowing down of these various options before a detailed assessment can be undertaken. This is not to suggest that options eliminated at this stage will not be given further consideration later. The basis for comparison in assessing strategic capability should not only be assessed in absolute terms or against industry norms but should also identify the incentive to change from the present strategy to the new strategy. One particular relevant comparison would be to evaluate what would happen if the strategy was to do nothing and would provide a valuable baseline against which to assess the incentive to change. A useful technique, which incorporates this approach, is GAP analysis that can be used to identify the extent to which existing strategies will fail to meet the performance objective in the future. GAP analysis should also apply to measures other than profitability although some of these may be easily quantifiable such as productivity or volume sales whereas others may be more subjective but none the less very important, such as levels of quality or service. Three contrasting approaches to screening options can be identified:

1. ranking options;
2. decision trees;
3. scenarios.

Ranking is a systematic way of analysing specific options for their suitability or fit with the picture gained from the strategic analysis. Each option is assessed against a number of key factors that the strategic analysis has identified in the organization's environment, resources and culture. One of the major benefits of ranking is that it helps the analyst to think through mismatches between a company's present position and the implications of the various strategic options. More sophisticated approaches to ranking assign a weighting to each factor in recognition that some will be of more importance in the evaluation than others.

Another approach is decision trees. Whereas ranking assumes that all options have equal merits in the first instance, the decision tree approach ranks options by progressively eliminating others. This elimination process is achieved by identifying a few key elements or criteria which future developments are intended to incorporate such as growth, investment and diversification. Decision trees combine the identification of options with a simultaneous ranking of those options although a limitation of this approach is that it tends to be simplistic as it takes very much a Yes or No approach.

Ranking evaluates options against a specific list of items or criteria derived from the strategic analysis, decision trees achieve the same outcome by eliminating options through progressively introduced additional criteria to be satisfied. A third approach to screening is that of scenario planning. Scenarios can therefore be produced to screen strategic options by matching them to possible future scenarios. The outcome of this approach is not a single prioritized list of options but a series of contingency plans that identify the preferred option for each possible scenario. Equally important in taking this approach is the organization's ability to monitor the onset or otherwise of a particular scenario in time to implement the appropriate strategy.

The strategic evaluation of choices

An assessment of the returns likely to accrue from specific options is a key measure of the acceptability of an option. However there are a number of different approaches to the analysis of return:

1. profitability analysis;
2. cost-benefit analysis;
3. shareholder value analysis.

Three common approaches to this traditional financial analysis of profitability can be identified. First, the company can forecast the return on capital employed a specific time after the new strategy is implemented. Second, payback period has been used where a significant capital injection is needed to support a new venture. The payback period is calculated by finding the time at which the cumulative net cashflow becomes zero – the judgement is then whether this is regarded as an adequate outcome and if the company is prepared to wait that long for a return. Managers seek very different rates of return depending on the industry, so such behaviour is better understood if payback is used as a targeting device.

Third, discounted cashflow analysis (DCF) is perhaps the most widely prescribed investment appraisal technique and is essentially an extension of the payback period analysis. Once the net cashflows have been assessed for each of the preceding years, they are discounted progressively to reflect the fact that the funds generated early are of more real value than those in later years. The net present value of the venture is then calculated by adding all the discounted annual cashflows after taxation over the anticipated life of the project. DCF analysis is particularly useful in comparing the financial merits of strategies that employ very different patterns of expenditure and return.

While these three forms of profitability analysis are widely used, it is important to recognize that they do have certain limitations. Financial appraisals tend to focus on tangible costs and benefits and do not set the strategy in its widest context. For example, a new product launch may look profitable as an isolated project but may not make real strategic sense in terms of the market acceptability for the project within the company's portfolio. In reverse, the intangible costs of losing strategic focus through new ventures is readily overlooked. Also, the use of return on capital in evaluating strategic options can be criticized because it is backward- rather than forward-looking. It does not concentrate on assessing the firm's capability of generating future cashflows or value. This discussion has focused so far on the evaluation of strategic options pursued through internal development. However, another common situation in which evaluation is required is strategic development through acquisition. And so the value of the company being acquired needs to be assessed and an assessment of cost savings needs to be determined prior to acquisition, along with likely proceeds from disinvestments or sale of assets and the anticipated impact on the value of the merged companies. There are three key ways in which a company can be valued.

The balance sheet value of the net assets of the firm is one approach, although there is a danger with this that some key assets may not appear and others may be under-valued. If the approach is to continue the business as a going concern, earnings potential may be a key strategic issue and the cost of the business may be rationalized on merger, particularly those of overheads and the relevant synergy gained. Forecasting such cost savings may be difficult.

A third approach is market evaluation that would apply to a publicly quoted company. However, during the bidding period the cost is likely to rise beyond the starting share price.

In many situations the analysis of profit gives too narrow an interpretation of return, particularly where intangible benefits are an important consideration. Cost-benefit analysis attempts to put a money value on all the cost and benefits of a strategic option including both tangible and intangible returns. The basis of quantification used needs to be justified carefully and is likely to be the subject of disagreement from different interested parties. One of the greatest difficulties of such an approach is deciding on the boundaries of such an analysis. Despite such difficulties, cost-benefit analysis is an approach that is valuable if its limitations are understood. Its major benefit is forcing people to be explicit about the various factors that should influence strategic choice. A detailed cost-benefit analysis would proceed to assign weightings to the various items, in order to reflect their relative importance to the decision about whether or not to proceed with a particular strategy. This would also normally be combined with a sensitivity analysis of the key net present value and internal rate of return outcomes in relation to the main assumptions.

It was during the 1980s that shareholder value analysis developed, placing emphasis on the value creation process and the responsibility of directors to create values and benefits for shareholders. Such an approach concentrates on strategies and not just investment projects. Such a financial analysis must be driven by an understanding of the value creation process, and the competitive advantage that the organization derives from the process. In particular, it is critical to identify the key cash generators of the business, the value or cost driver. Assessment of the acceptability of a strategy through net present value is likely to be critically dependent on a relatively small number of these value and cost drivers. They become the key factors which link the analysis of the key competitive strategy to the likely acceptability of that strategy in terms of improvements of shareholder value. It must also be remembered that the value and cost drivers often act in conjunction with each other, so managers need to make judgements on how these interdependencies may work rather than expecting simplistic answers from precise financial measures.

Analysing risk

One measure of acceptability of the strategic options being assessed is the risk that the organization faces in pursuing that strategy. A useful analysis is the projection of key financial ratios that give a measure of the risk that the organization would be taking by pursuing various strategies. For instance, the capital structure of the company may change in pursuing different options. One measure of risk is the extension of long-term loans that will increase the gearing of the company and increase the financial risk. In order to take this approach there needs to be an examination of the likelihood that the company will reach break-even point and the consequences of falling short of the volume of business while interest on loans continues to be paid. Another consideration is the likely impact on the firm's liquidity in assessing the options. Reduced liquidity increases the financial risk of the business. An increasingly important element in this assessment of risk is companies that intend to trade internationally. The nature of the debtors they would have to take on would have to be considered, and whether or not they would be able or willing to take export guarantee insurance to mitigate this risk.

Sensitivity analysis is a useful technique incorporating the assessment of risk. During a strategic evaluation this technique allows each of the important assumptions underlying a particular option to be questioned and changed. In particular, it seeks to test out how sensitive the predicted performance or outcome is to each of these assumptions. Sensitivity analysis asks what would be the effect on performance if, for example, market demand grew by only 1 per cent or by as much as 10 per cent. Would either of these extremes alter the decision to pursue that particular strategy? This process helps management develop a clear picture of the risks of making particular strategic decisions and the degree of confidence it might have in a given decision. In theory, the uncertainty factor surrounding key variables in the evaluation could be assigned probability distributions and statistical analysis used to assess how these uncertainties combine in an overall risk analysis strategy. However, it is difficult to assign a probability distribution to so many variables. Sensitivity analysis has proved to be a good way of communicating to decision-makers the areas of uncertainty underlying the evaluation and allowing them to use their judgement in the choice process.

Decision matrices can be applied when there are many circumstances where specific aspects of strategic choice can be reduced to simple choices between a number of clearly defined courses of action. This is often the case when choosing between different development methods for a particular strategy. In deciding which option to choose, it is necessary before any detailed analysis, to be clear about which type of decision rule will be used to weight the various options against each other. The optimistic decision rule would choose the best outcomes for each option. The pessimistic decision favours the best of the worst outcomes. The regret decision rule would favour options that minimize the lost opportunity that might occur by choosing any particular option. The expected value rule introduces an important new dimension, namely the probability that each outcome would occur. Although decision matrices are helpful in analysing some aspects of the strategic choice, they clearly need to be tempered by other considerations which would not be directly included in such a simplified analysis.

The principle of simulation modelling is a useful one in strategy evaluation in those aspects that lend themselves to this quantitative view. Financial models are often used to assess strategic options. Risk analysis is a technique that seeks to assess the overall degree of uncertainty in a particular option by mathematically combining the uncertainties within each of the elements in the option. However, one of the limitations of the use of strategic modelling is the need for large amounts of high-quality data concerning the relationship between environmental factors and company performance. The danger in all this is that the model will become a gross over-simplification of the reality and will fail to encompass the most important uncertainties and risks, particularly as competitor reactions are difficult to assess and/or incorporate into the model.

Heuristic models are a means of identifying solutions in a systematic way and are most valuable in complex situations where there are many options available to an organization and many different requirements or criteria to be met. Many strategic decisions are concerned with finding a satisfactory option rather than the best option and so the decision criteria to be listed are compared against the various options until one is found which satisfies all the criteria. This is not necessarily the best option. A computer search would be performed to provide a short-list of options that fit the criteria and in that way could be useful for screening.

Analysing stakeholder reactions

Stakeholder mapping is a valuable tool in assessing the likely reactions of stakeholders to new strategies, and helps manage these reactions and hence the acceptability of a strategy. This is important as a new strategy might require a substantial issue of new shares and this could be unacceptable to powerful groups of shareholders since it would dilute their voting power. Also plans to merge with other companies or to trade with new countries could also be unacceptable, for instance, to the unions, the government or some customers. Very often the initial evaluation of a strategy using stakeholder analysis will identify critical mismatches with the expectations of some stakeholders. This evaluation might then proceed to the next stage of the analysis where a number of issues can be addressed. For instance a strategy should or could be amended to better fit the expectations of the stakeholders without unduly sacrificing acceptability as assessed by the other measures of risk and return. It is unlikely that an optimum strategy exists, so successful strategies are those that seek an acceptable compromise between the conflicting interests of various stakeholders. Analysis of stakeholder expectations also assists in determining the likely success of the strategy during implementation. Also there may be a need to try and persuade or encourage existing stakeholders to shift their position in order to give the strategy a chance. The accurate assessment of those political activities that the firm needs to support a new strategy is an important aspect of evaluation and is often neglected in favour of the more numerical and rational analyses already discussed. Both can be seen as necessary.

Analysing feasibility

Having considered the acceptability of strategic options, it is now important to assess the feasibility of those alternatives and whether they are achievable in resource terms. A valuable piece of analysis in assessing financial feasibility is funds flow forecasting which seeks to identify the funds that would be required for any strategy and the likely source of those funds. This approach starts with an assessment of the capital investment needed and the forecast of cumulative profits earned during the period. The working capital required by the strategy can be made with separate consideration of each element of the working capital by using a simple pro rata adjustment related to the forecasted level of increases in sales revenue. Tax liability and expected dividend payments are identified along with any shortfall in funds, which can be funded by a variety of methods. Such funding will incur interest payments that need to be built into the funds flow analysis. This approach would normally be programmed onto a computer spreadsheet that would assist in identifying the timing of any new funding requirements.

Break-even analysis is a simple and widely used technique that is helpful in exploring some key aspects of feasibility. It is often used to assess the feasibility of meeting targets of return and as such combines a parallel assessment of acceptability. It also provides an assessment of the risk within various strategies, particularly where different options require markedly different cost structures.

It is often helpful to make a wider assessment of the resource capability of the organization in relation to specific strategies. This can be done through a resource deployment analysis that is a way of comparing options with each other. The resource requirements of alternative future strategies should be laid out indicating the key resources for each strategy. A resource analysis of the company should then be matched with the resource requirements for possible strategic options. This analysis can be closely linked to the competitive strategy by focusing the analysis on those value activities that must strongly underpin the cost advantage or value creation process and in this way could be part of a shareholder value analysis. It should be pointed out that the real benefit of such an analysis should be the identification of those necessary changes in resources which are implied by any strategy and an analysis of whether these changes are feasible in terms of scale, quality or timescale.

Selection of strategies

It is a widely accepted view that a rational choice of future strategies should occur in relation to objectives. When quantified, the organization's objectives are used as a yardstick by which options are assessed. Evaluation methods are therefore central to the decision-making process and are expected to provide quantified answers regarding the relative merits of various options to indicate the right course of action.

A common way in which the selection of strategies occurs is also by referring the matter to a higher authority. Those managers responsible for evaluation may not have the authority to give the go-ahead to the solution. Equally, those senior managers who must decide on a strategy may not have participated in the evaluation of the options, thus the evaluation process can be seen as a means of raising the level of debate which occurs among senior managers when they are making their judgement on the selection of strategy. In large, diversified organizations there will be different types of evaluation occurring at the centre from those in the divisions and the subsidiary companies.

There are many circumstances where the uncertainties that an organization faces are such that evaluation processes leave the choice of directions for the future very finely balanced. Nevertheless, some organizations will need to come off the fence and commit their resources and efforts to a particular strategy. Deferral of an overall final decision on a strategy may be implemented, at the same time committing some resources to partial implementation, thus allowing the firm to gain more experience and understanding of the suitability of each strategy. This testing and learning approach becomes an important precursor to the bid for resources to higher authorities that might follow. However, the weakness of this approach is that the organization may only ever develop by tinkering around the edges in a very minimalist way and never really making a fundamental reassessment of its present situation and future opportunities. This would be incrementalism at its worst.

There is often disagreement on strategy between stakeholders who have similar power within the company. This may be between management and unions or between two different groups of managers. In these circumstances it is not unusual for an outside agency such as a consultant to evaluate the situation for the company. Often this process of evaluation is described as objective and rational by virtue of the consultant's detachment from the situation. In practice, consultants are aware of the political reasons for their involvement.

Summary

Strategy evaluation has often been presented as an exact science while such analytical methods are really only useful as a source of information to strategic decision-makers. It has been seen that the contribution which various analytical methods made to improving the quality of strategic decision-making will differ quite considerably. However even the most thorough strategic evaluation cannot possibly anticipate all the detailed problems and pitfalls which might be encountered in the implementation of a strategic change. So it is necessary to recognize that strategic decisions will be refined or even reversed as part of their process of implementation.

References

Dev, C. and Olsen, M.D. (1989) 'Operating environment and strategy: the profitable connection', *Cornell Hotel and Administration Quarterly*, 30, 2, 9–14

Hofer, C.W. and Schendel, D. (1978) *Strategy Formulation: Analytical Concepts*, St Paul, Minnesota: West Publishing.

Miles, R E., and Snow, C C. (1978) Organisational strategy: structure and process, McGraw-Hill.

Porter, M. (1980) *Competitive Strategy*, New York: The Free Press.

Thompson, A.A. and Strickland, A.J. (1980) *Strategy Formulation and Implementation*, Boston: Irwin.

Further reading

Christopher, M. (1988) 'Logistics and competitive strategy', *Logistics World*, December, 152–82.

Christopher, M. (1986) *Effective Logisitics Management*, London: Gower.

Das, T.K. (1991) 'Time: the hidden dimension in strategic planning', *Long Range Planning*, 24, 3, 49–57.

Eildon, S. (1981) 'Zero-based budgeting: promise or illusion?', *Omega*, 9, 2, 107–12

Fombrun, C., Tichy, N. and Devanna, M. (1990) *Strategic Human Resource Management*, Chichester: John Wiley and Sons.

Glautier, M.W.E. and Underdown, B. (1991) *Accounting Theory and Practice*, 4th edn, London: Pitman.

Hardaker, M. and Ward, B. (1987) 'Getting things done', *Harvard Business Review*, 65, 6, 12–20.

Howard, K. (1975) *Quantitative Analyses for Planning Decisions*, New York: McDonald & Evans.

Knowles, T. (1996) *Corporate strategy for hospitality*, Harlow, Pearson Education.

Kotler, P. (1991) *Marketing Management: Analysis, Planning, Implementation and Control*, 7th edn, Englewood Cliffs, NJ: Prentice-Hall.

Lumby, S. (1991) *Investment Appraisal and Financing Decisions: A First course in Financial Management*, 4th edn, London: Chapman and Hall.

Peters, R. and Waterman, R. (1982) *In Search of Excellence*, New York: Harper and Row.

Phyrr, P.A. (1973) *Zero-based Budgeting: A Practical Management Tool for Evaluating Expenses*, Chichester: John Wiley and Sons.

Pizan, A., and Mansfield, Y. (1996) *Tourism, crime and international security issues*, London, John Wiley and Sons.

Scholes, K. (1991) *Learning to Live with Devolution*, Sheffield: Sheffield Business School.

Scholes, K. and Klemm, M. (1987) *An Introduction to Business Planning*, Basingstoke: Macmillan.

Steiner, G A. (1979) *Strategic Planning*, New York: The Free Press.

Torrington, D. and Hall, L. (1986) *Personnel Management: A New Approach*, Englewood Cliffs, NJ: Prentice-Hall.

Vesey, J.T. (1991) 'The new competitors: they think in terms of speed to the market', *Academy of Management Executives*, 5, 2, 23–33.

Wild, R. (1984) *Production and Operations Management*, 3rd edn, New York: Nelson.

Institutional pressures and operational aspects of investment in travel and hospitality

Introduction

Investment in travel and tourism is an important aspect of its development and planning. Often investments are made by international organizations such as the World Bank, the European Union, and the World Tourism Organization, as well as the governments of specific countries. Generally speaking, investment in travel and tourism services shows a considerable diversity from country to country, not only in terms of the level of revenue earned from tourism, but also in terms of government funding for tourism. Such monetary variations are a clear reflection of the policies and priorities of governments and the relationship between the private and public sectors on a country-by-country basis. Against this background this chapter aims to provide an overview of the issues that influence investment decisions in general as well as specifically in travel and tourism. As such, two main themes will be discussed.

First, the institutional aspects of investments that arise from the impact of certain agreements, such as the General Agreement on Trade in Services (GATS), agreements in Latin America, and the European Currency (Euro), which will influence the decision-making at tourism destinations and country level.

Second, the operational aspects of investment decisions from a financial accounting perspective, such as the cashflow analysis, risk management and detailing decision-making techniques that will influence tourism and hospitality enterprises. Overall the chapter will highlight the issues that ought to be considered when managing the investment agendas for the sectors of tourism and hospitality.

Institutional aspects for investment

Any investment decision within tourism and hospitality enterprises currently has to consider a number of external and internal issues that will influence such a decision. One of the most important issues in this era of globalization is trade agreements and, more specifically, the role that they play within the territory that they are practised.

Types and roles of trade agreements

Trade agreements have created an ever-shrinking world, which has been moving towards a global market. On a daily basis, consumers buy goods and services that are produced in countries other than their own and local companies produce goods that are consumed by people in other places. This increase in trade can be attributed to a number of factors including the reduction in the cost of communication and transportation, as well as other socio-economic factors, which have led to higher world-wide disposable income. Another key factor is an almost century-long series of continuously involving international negotiations that have led to numerous agreements to reduce barriers to trade. The act of reducing trade barriers by reducing tariff rates, reducing the variance in protection across industries and increasing the transparency of trade policy is often referred to as trade liberalization.

The main approach to trade is based upon a principle referred to as most-favoured nation (MFN) status, whereby any access to a domestic market given to one trading partner has to be extended to all countries. In general there are two categories of agreements: equal treatment and preferential treatment. Under equal treatment, all countries are given access to a domestic market, while under preferential treatment only certain countries are given access (WTO, 2002a). This principle is also applied in accordance with the number of sectors involved. At the preferential extreme a single market or commodity is protected, while at the other extreme all goods are traded freely.

There are currently four levels of economic integration based on trade agreements: free trade area; customs union; common market; and economic union. Trade agreements can also be classified by the number of countries involved as unilateral, bilateral or multilateral.

Free trade area

A free trade area is the most straightforward, simple and least restrictive form of integration, considered the first step towards economic integration. Generally, under free trade agreements, participating nations eliminate all barriers, including tariff and non-tariff barriers (TAWC, 2002a). Examples include:

- G-3 – composed of Mexico, Venezuela and Colombia.
- NAFTA (North American Free Trade Agreement) – composed of Mexico, Canada and the USA.
- FTAA (Free Trade Area of the Americas) – composed of 34 countries, currently under negotiation.

Customs union

These agreements are pursued by countries in the hope of creating a larger economic region in which producers can obtain economies of scale. Ideally, nations can eliminate all tariff barriers between them and establish a common external tariff for trade in goods and services with third parties. However, in many cases these agreements included a complex system of regulations and are frequently structured on a product-by-product basis. During the 1980s most of the agreements were modified, following the MFN principle, encouraging greater trade and access to the world market (WTO, 2002). As examples in the case of Latin America the customs unions that exist are (TAWC, 2002):

- MERCOSUR (Southern Common Market) – composed of Argentina, Brazil, Paraguay and Uruguay.

- Andean Community – composed of Bolivia, Colombia, Ecuador, Peru and Venezuela.
- Central American Economic Treaty – composed of Costa Rica, El Salvador, Guatemala, Honduras and Nicaragua.
- CARICOM – Caribbean Community and Common Market.
- CACM – Central American Common Market.

Common market

Some of the customs union agreements grow into common markets, where eliminating barriers hindering the free movement of productive goods and labour strengthens the customs union. This might create impartiality within a country, and while the process is longer and complex, it is a more complete arrangement. One example is the European Common Market.

Economic union

The most advanced form of economic integration is economic union. An example is the European Union, which recently introduced the Euro (€) as the common currency. There are few trade restrictions within an economic union, nevertheless, under special conditions, countries can still protect some industries (WTO, 2002c).

Unilateral agreements

Unilateral agreements represent the decision of a single country to open its home market to foreign investment. Yet, this country does not expect other countries to open their markets.

Bilateral agreements

Bilateral agreements are typically established between two nations or organizations that want to eliminate or minimize trade barriers. For instance (TAWC, 2002):

- Chile with MERCOSUR;
- Mexico with Bolivia, Costa Rica and Nicaragua individually;
- Bolivia with MERCOSUR.

Multilateral agreements

Multilateral agreements are arrangements established among several nations. One example is the Latin American Integration Association (ALADI) which is composed of Argentina, Bolivia, Brazil, Chile, Colombia, Ecuador, Mexico, Paraguay, Peru, Uruguay and Venezuela (TAWC, 2002).

General Agreement on Tariffs and Trade (GATT)

A country that gains membership into GATT automatically gains access to the rest of the members of the trading system on an MFN principle. Through GATT a number of changes in the world trading system have occurred, related to the use of tariffs. At the outset of GATT, the average tariff rate was over 100 per cent among industrialized countries. By 1993, tariff rates had fallen to less than 5 per cent (WTO, 2002).

Moreover, the agreement creates an incentive for member countries to specialize in an industry in which they have a competitive advantage. GATT has led to greater competition and reduced costs of production for industries across countries. As a result, consumption patterns have changed and trade among countries has increased, creating new business opportunities for companies and enhancing living standards across the world.

General trade issues covered by GATT include (Biederman and Zuckerman, 1998):

- Total elimination of foreign tariffs on items.
- Establishment of trade-related investments measures, which should facilitate foreign investment.
- Establishment of new standards and procedures in regard to anti-dumping and countervailing issues.
- Increased protection for intellectual properties such as copyright and trademarks.

From 1948 to 1994 GATT provided the rules for much of world trade. Through those 47 years it was more a provisional agreement than an organization. GATT was a major player in accelerating and promoting trade during the 1950s and 1960s. However, during the economic crises and recessions of the 1970s and 1980s, governments started to seek other types of arrangement, such as bilateral agreements, in order to protect their home markets. This, as a result, undermined GATT's credibility. Therefore, during the latest round of negotiations in Uruguay, from 1986 to 1994, GATT was replaced by the World Trade Organization (WTO) (WTO, 2002). The GATT's secretariat no longer exists; however, its key principles are used as a foundation for other agreements such as the GATS, which is part of the WTO.

General Agreement on Trade in Services (GATS)

Trade tensions in the global marketplace between the mega-markets of North America, Europe and Asia prompted a response by the WTO of drawing up the General Agreement on Trade in Services (GATS).

The GATS constitutes one aspect of the Uruguay Round of negotiations on world trade and was finally agreed by 118 member countries. GATS is the first multilateral, legally enforceable agreement to cover international trade and investment in services, establishing rules and disciplines on policies affecting access to service markets. GATS main objective is also to create a framework of multilateral principles and rules for the liberalization of trade in services, with due respect for national policy objectives and the level of development of each member state (Alan, 1985; IIE, 1996; EU, 1999).

The end result of the Uruguay Round on services showed a schedule of specific commitments from each member country. A country cannot become a member of GATS without having accepted at least some specific commitments that, once undertaken, are conditioned by the basic principles to ensure effective market access. There are disciplines relating to market access and national treatment, and various regulatory matters that have to be respected by members. Looking at the schedule of specific commitments, the industrialized countries as well as developing countries adopted the majority of those commitments at the end of the Uruguay Round (see Table 9.1). Each of these commitments applies as follows to 12 main service sectors:

1. business services, including professional services;
2. communication services, including telecommunications and audio-visual services;
3. construction and related engineering services;
4. distribution services;
5. educational services;
6. environmental services;
7. financial services, including insurance and banking;
8. health-related and social services;
9. tourism and travel-related services;
10. recreational, cultural and sporting services;
11. transport services, including maritime, waterways, air and road transport services;
12. other services not included.

Since countries are free to decide in which sectors they will offer market access, the number of sectors covered by national schedules varies widely, although the majority of the commitments were made in tourism and financial services (see Figure 9.1).

Scope of GATS

The GATS agreement is a long-term undertaking in which all significant trading countries are likely to become members. Its importance lies not so much in any liberalization that might take place immediately, but in the fact that it enables

Table 9.1		Number of countries	Number of services commitments	Commitments as share of maximum possible (%)
Commitments on services at the end of the Uruguay Round	Industrial countries	25	2,423	53.8
	Developing countries	81	2,159	17.2
	Latin America	–	738	15.3
	Africa	–	396	9.8
	Middle East	–	106	16.5
	Asia	–	796	26.0

Source: WTO (1999)

liberalization to occur via a continuing process of detailed negotiation between countries (Jamws and Rai, 1987; John and Chris, 1991; Peter, 1992; OECD, 1996; Ferndez, 1997; Mia, 1998).

The detailed negotiations are about reducing barriers, which restrict the freedom of service suppliers to operate in foreign markets either through establishing a facility there with the necessary foreign personnel or through cross-border trade. The barriers to such trade derive from restrictions on market access and national treatment.

In terms of market access restrictions, the GATS deals with trade restrictions such as:

- maximum foreign ownership limitations;
- restrictions on the establishment of some kind of local representation – for instance, a foreign company's ability to acquire a presence in the market is blocked;
- restrictions on the ability of service suppliers to choose the type of business (e.g. company or partnership) through which they operate;
- limitations on the overall number of service suppliers allowed to operate in the market because of a quota system or a monopoly situation.

  (UNCTAD and the World Bank, 1994; WTO, 1995, 1996, 1998, 1999; UNCTAD, 1996, 1998; OECD, 1996).

Figure 9.1   Number of countries undertaking commitments in each sector ($billion – 1990 values)

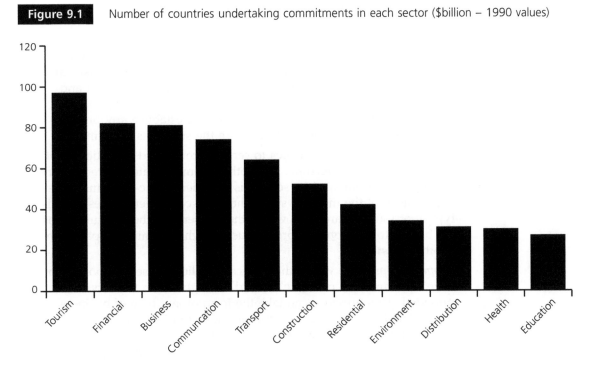

Source: World Trade Organization (1999)

National treatment limitations essentially relate to measures or practices that restrict competitive opportunities for foreign suppliers. These include limiting use of a company's well-known logo or title, discriminatory restrictions on the mobility of foreign personnel, an obligation to involve local personnel in all projects, or nationality requirements in order to carry out specific types of work.

The Uruguay Round was primarily about the clear identification and subsequent gradual reduction of such barriers. What this means in practice is that countries have begun the multilateral process of exchanging concessions relating to market access and national treatment among themselves, or, in other words, the elimination of barriers to trade in services (UNCTAD and the World Bank, 1994; WTO, 1995, 1996, 1998, 1999; UNCTAD, 1996, 1998; OECD, 1996).

According to the European Union, the GATS has an extremely wide scope of application. It applies to measures imposed by a member state to the agreement that affect the consumption of services originating in other member states. Measures include those taken by 'central, regional or local governments and authorities' and by non-governmental bodies in the exercise of powers 'delegated by central, regional or local governmental authorities' (WTO,1999).

This raises one of the most critical issues with regard to the definition of trade in services. GATS does not define 'services' but does define 'trade in services'. The definitions given cover not only the cross-border supply of services but also transactions involving the cross-border movement of capital and labour. This is necessary because services must very often be supplied through a commercial presence in the export market or through the presence of an individual service supplier. There are also many situations, as in tourism, where the consumer purchases the service abroad. Overall, there are four ways in which a service can be supplied, often referred to as the four modes of supply. These modes are:

1. *Cross-border*: where the trade takes place from the territory of one member state into that of another. Only the service itself crosses the border, without the movement of people, such as information and advice passing by means of fax or electronic mail, or cargo transportation. The service supplier does not establish any presence in the territory of the member state where the service is consumed.

2. *Consumption abroad*: this relates to services consumed by nationals of a member state in the territory of another member state where the service is supplied. Essentially, the service is supplied to the consumer outside the territory of the member state where the consumer resides. This is typical of tourism, and also where the property of the consumer crosses the border to be serviced abroad, such as when a ship is repaired in another country.

3. *Commercial presence*: where the service supplier crosses the border to have a 'commercial presence' abroad through which the service is provided. This presence can take the form of any type of business or professional establishment, including incorporation, branches, representative offices, joint ventures, and so on.

4. *Presence of natural person*: this mode applies to natural persons only, when they stay temporarily in the market, for the purpose of supplying

services, for example the self-employed, and employees of service suppliers.

The main purpose of defining the supply of a service according to these methods of supply is to facilitate the identification of regulations affecting them in the 12 service sectors, one of which is tourism and related services.

GATS and tourism

The GATS has many implications for tourism, particularly for tourism policy-makers. These were detailed in a 1994 report entitled *Tourism Services and the GATS* commissioned by the World Tourism Organization, the United Nations Conference on Trade and Development (UNCTAD) and GATT. The report concluded that the GATS has a range of impacts upon tourism and hospitality company including:

- promoting free movement of labour globally;
- enabling the international development of, and access to, computer reservation systems;
- removing barriers to overseas investment.
  (WTO, 1995, 1996, 1998, 1999; UNCTAD, 1996, 1998; OECD, 1996).

The report defines tourism services as products or outputs resulting from the activities of economic units, whether profit-making or non-profit-making, which are destined for final or intermediate tourism consumers, provided that the value of these activities can be measured in economic terms. Tourism differs from other services in that it is a final consumer-orientated activity. Unlike other services, tourism is not a specific type of service, but an assortment of services consumed by the visitor.

Accordingly, at an international level, trade in tourism services (i.e. the provision of tourism services) occurs when a supplier of one country sells a service:

1. in his own country, to a visitor (consumer) who is resident in another country or to a supplier of another country, either through cross-border movement of the foreign supplier or via the foreign supplier's commercial presence or establishment in the first country;

2. in another country, to a supplier or resident of, or visitor to, that country, either cross-border, via an agent, through a commercial presence or by the establishment in the other country.

The key to achieving effective liberalization in any particular sector like tourism is contained in the obligation to allow market access and national treatment. These are defined as follows:

- *Market access*: this means granting foreign service suppliers access to domestic markets. It includes allowing the provision of services cross-border or through some kind of commercial presence or through the movement of foreign service suppliers into the market.

- *National treatment*: this means that countries are obliged to treat foreign tourism service suppliers in the same way as domestic service suppliers.

According to the World Trade Organization, instead of 'tourism services' the GATS classification introduces the term 'tourism and travel-related services'. By such wording, the term corresponds partly to the United Nations/World Tourism Organization definition of tourism that is described as comprising 'the activities of persons travelling to and staying in places outside their usual environment for not more than one consecutive year for leisure, business and other purpose provides'.

Tourism and travel-related services (TTRS), category 9 of the Services Sectoral Classification List of GATS, is distinctly limited in scope. The category is divided into four sub-sectors, the first three of which have associated listing under the United Nations 'Provisional Central Product Classification' (CPC). These sub-sectors are as follows:

A Hotels and restaurants (including catering)
B Travel agencies and tour operators services
C Tourist guides services
D Other.

No further sub-classifications are currently provided for under TTRSs. Tourism activities which are part of more general services activities, most notably many transport services, but also including certain business services, distribution services, and recreational, cultural and sporting services, have typically been placed within these general services categories.

Commitments in tourism and travel-related services

According to the World Bank, the number of commitments made by members varies widely by sub-sector. Sub-sector A (hotels and restaurants) shows the greatest number, with 112 members all making commitments, followed in order by sub-sector B (travel agencies and tour operators services) with 89, sub-sector C (tourist guides services) with 54, and sub-sector D (other) with only 13 commitments. Under 'other', a number of members have given no description in their GATS schedule of what is included; other members have listed specific activities, in one case including transport-related commitments (see Table 9.2)

Of the 112 members making commitments: ten have made them in all four sub-sectors; 45 have made them in three sub-sectors; 36 in two sub-sectors; and 21 in only the first sub-sector. In other words, nearly one-half of the members making commitments have done so in three or more sub-sectors.

With regard to the level of market access and national treatment provided within member state schedules, commitments by mode of supply also vary widely for the tourism sector as a whole (see Table 9.3). The percentage of members placing no restriction on market access is highest for consumption abroad (at 49 per cent), and lowest for the presence of natural persons (at 1 per cent) and commercial presence (22 per cent). Many countries attempt to constrain some commitments on commercial presence (77 per cent).

Table 9.2	Countries	09.A.	09.B.	09.C.	09.D	Total
Summary of specific commitments in the Uruguay Round	Angola	X				1
	Antigua and Barbuda	X				1
	Argentina	X	X	X	X	4
	Australia	X	X	X		3
	Austria	X	X	X		3
	Bangladesh	X				1
	Benin	X				1
	Bolivia	X	X			2
	Botswana	X	X			2
	Brazil	X				1
	Bulgaria	X	X			2
	Burkina Faso	X	X			2
	Burundi	X	X	X		3
	Cameroon	X	X			2
	Canada	X	X			2
	Central African Republic	X	X	X	X	4
	Chad	X	X			2
	Chile	X	X	X		3
	Colombia	X	X			2
	Congo	X	X	X		3
	Congo R.P	X	X	X		3
	Costa Rica	X	X	X		3
	Côte d'Ivoire	X	X	X		3
	Cuba	X	X	X		3
	Czech Republic	X	X	X		3
	Djibouti	X				1
	Dominica	X				1
	Dominican Republic	X	X	X		3
	Ecuador	X	X			2
	Egypt	X	X	X	X	4
	El Salvador	X	X	X		3
	European Community	X	X	X		3
	Fiji	X				1
	Finland	X	X	X		3
	Gabon	X	X			2
	Gambia	X	X	X		3
	Ghana	X	X			2
	Grenada	X				1
	Guatemala	X	X	X	X	4
	Guinea	X		X		2
	Guinea-Bissau	X				1
	Guyana	X	X			2
	Haiti	X				1
	Honduras	X	X	X		3
	Hong Kong	X	X			2
	Hungary	X	X			2
	Iceland	X	X	X		3
	India	X	X			2
	Indonesia	X	X		X	3
	Israel	X	X	X		3
	Jamaica	X	X			2
	Japan	X	X	X		3
	Kenya	X	X	X		3
	Korea, Republic of	X	X	X		3
	Kuwait	X	X	X		3
	Lesotho	X	X	X		3
	Liechtenstein	X	X	X		3
	Macau	X	X			2
	Malawi	X	X	X	X	4

Countries	09.A.	09.B.	09.C.	09.D	Total
Malaysia	X	X			2
Mali	X				1
Malta	X	X			2
Mauritania	X	X	X		3
Mauritius	X	X	X	X	4
Mexico	X	X	X		3
Mongolia	X	X	X		3
Morocco	X	X	X	X	4
Myanmar	X	X			2
Namibia	X	X			2
New Zealand	X	X	X		3
Nicaragua	X	X	X		3
Niger	X	X	X		3
Nigeria	X	X	X		3
Norway	X	X	X		3
Pakistan	X	X			2
Panama	X	X			2
Papua New Guinea	X				1
Paraguay	X	X	X		3
Peru	X	X			2
Philippines	X	X			2
Poland	X	X			2
Qatar	X				1
Romania	X	X	X		3
Rwanda	X				1
St. Kitts & Nevis	X				1
St. Lucia	X				1
St. Vincent & Grenadines	X				1
Senegal	X	X			2
Sierra Leone	X	X	X	X	4
Slovak Republic	X	X	X		3
Slovenia	X	X			2
Solomon Islands	X				1
South Africa	X	X	X		3
Sri Lanka	X	X			2
Suriname	X	X			2
Swaziland	X				1
Sweden	X	X	X		3
Switzerland	X	X	X		3
Tanzania	X				1
Thailand	X	X		X	3
Togo	X	X	X		3
Trinidad and Tobago	X	X			2
Tunisia	X	X			2
Turkey	X	X			2
Uganda	X	X			2
United Arab Emirates	X		X		2
Uruguay	X	X	X		3
USA	X	X	X	X	4
Venezuela	X	X		X	3
Zambia	X	X	X	X	4
Zimbabwe	X	X	X		3
Total	112	89	54	13	268

Source: World Trade Organization (1998)

Key: 09.A   Hotels and restaurants   09.B   Travel agencies and tour operators services
      09.C   Tourist guides services   09.D   Other

Regarding national treatment, the pattern is similar, with the percentage of members having no restrictions on their commitments at 52 per cent for consumption abroad and 11 per cent for the presence of natural persons.

Regarding 'unbound' modes of supply – i.e. those for which no commitments are made – the level with respect to both market access and national treatment is highest for cross-border supply, due primarily to a lack of technical feasibility, at 27 per cent and 24 per cent, respectively (see Tables 9.2, 9.3, 9.4 and 9.5).

Benefits of GATS to tourism

The principle benefit of GATS to tourism is the liberalization of international exchange of tourism services. GATS will help:

- the production of tourism services;
- the movement of people linked to these services;
- the global development of tourism.

Table 9.3 — Number of countries by mode of supply – tourism and travel-related services	Mode of supply	Market access			National treatment		
		Full	Part	No	Full	Part	No
	Cross Border	33 / 29%	49 / 44%	30 / 27%	37 / 33%	48 / 43%	27 / 24%
	Consumption Abroad	55 / 49%	47 / 42%	10 / 9%	58 / 52%	42 / 38%	12 / 11%
	Commercial Presence	25 / 22%	86 / 77%	1 / 1%	49 / 44%	61 / 54%	2 / 2%
	Presence of natural person	1 / 1%	105 / 94%	6 / 5%	12 / 11%	90 / 80%	10 / 9%

Source: World Trade Organization (1998)

Table 9.4 Percentage by sector and mode of supply – tourism and travel-related services (market access) (%)

Market Access	Cross border			Consumption abroad			Commercial presence			Personal mobility		
	Full	Part	No	Full	Part	No	Full	Part	No	Full	Part	No
09.A.	31	23	46	54	37	9	27	72	1	3	91	6
09.B.	49	19	31	56	20	15	27	67	6	1	88	11
09.C.	56	7	37	78	13	9	41	54	6	0	85	15
09.D.	38	31	31	38	54	8	23	69	8	0	92	8

Source: WTO (1998)
Key: 09.A Hotels and restaurants   09.B Travel agencies and tour operators services
09.C Tourist guides services   09.D Other

The production of tourism services

There are several obstacles to business that tourism service suppliers share with other service and manufacturing businesses. The key resources of any service business are the human, intellectual and financial capital, which are needed to solve business problems, exploit opportunities and compete in the marketplace. What this agreement does is tackle those basic impediments to a company's ability to deploy those key resources or, in other words, to move people, information and money across borders.

This would help to ensure that suppliers of tourism services are not frustrated in their ability to take advantage of market access commitments inscribed in another party's schedule. Tourism enterprises generally need to install, maintain and interconnect with terminal and communication equipment in order to supply tourism services in another country, for example, when a travel agent in one country makes arrangements for holidays in another.

The movement of people linked to tourism services

GATS facilitates the movement of people supplying services. Tourism services are also people-intensive in the sense that the provision of such services often requires close personal contact between supplier and client. It is clear, therefore, that the ability to move key personnel into and out of markets can be a crucial component of business strategy for tourism enterprises with international operations. The reality, however, is that virtually every country imposes visa and work permit restrictions, which inhibit, delay or render uncertain the movement of professional, managerial and technical personnel to where they are needed. The GATS can be of use to tourism services because it provides a framework for negotiating temporary entry (meaning without intent to establish permanent residence) of service personnel into the territory of other parties.

The global development of tourism

GATS contributes to the world-wide development of tourism. It provides *increased transparency* by way of clear and detailed information on conditions of access and operation in all services markets of GATS members.

Table 9.5 Percentage by sector and mode of supply – tourism and travel-related services (national treatment) (%)

National treatment	Cross border			Consumption abroad			Commercial presence			Personal mobility		
	Full	Part	No	Full	Part	No	Full	Part	No	Full	Part	No
09.A.	37	21	42	58	30	12	51	46	3	11	79	10
09.B.	55	15	30	70	13	17	64	27	9	17	69	15
09.C.	59	4	37	85	4	11	76	15	9	13	67	20
O9.D.	54	23	23	62	38	0	54	46	0	23	69	8

Source: WTO (1998)
Note: percentages may not add up to 100 due to rounding; basis of total is listed sectors
Key: 09.A Hotels and restaurants   09.B Travel agencies and tour operators services
      09.C Tourist guides services   09.D Other

It also constrains – and should over time eliminate – government discrimination towards foreign service companies. A *dispute settlement mechanism* would provide rights of compensation or retaliation in cases of violation of the national treatment principle.

The increasing participation of developing countries in world services trade is provided for in the GATS through the negotiation of specific market opening commitments. This development objective relates to three main areas:

1. Strengthening the domestic services capabilities of developing countries through access to technology on a commercial basis. Specifically greater access to knowledge and technology could be realized by developing countries attaching conditions to their market opening commitments, for example, minimum requirements for training and employment in foreign-owned hotels.

2. Improving the access of developing countries to distribution channels and information networks. In the tourism sector, this refers above all to access to computerized information and reservation networks managed and owned by entities in industrialized countries.

3. Liberalizing market access in sectors and modes of supply of export interest to developing countries. For instance, this refers to the freedom to deploy abroad not only key personnel but also regular personnel in places where developing countries are supplying tourism services.

Apart from GATS, the second agreement that will influence investment decisions for European tourism destinations, arises from the introduction of the single currency.

The impact of the single currency on tourism

The introduction of the single European currency (Euro) in 2002 was the most important project of economic integration ever undertaken in the European Union. One of the sectors with special interest in this process is travel and tourism, as the sector is unique in the way in which the final consumer and therefore the most widespread user of the single currency goes to the product rather than the other way round.

So far, the process of the European Monetary Union (EMU) is not changing the national cultural differences which affect holiday tastes of consumers in member states or the national regulations, tax or social security structures within the EU which are barriers to a single market or to a competitive tourism industry. Generally speaking, EMU still has certain benefits and costs attached to its framework.

Benefits

It is still early to see the true benefits that EMU will have for the tourism industry. The most documented benefit of EMU for travel enterprises is the elimination of transaction costs from foreign exchange dealings. These transaction costs are estimated to be from 0.4 per cent to 1 per cent for European economies and the extent to which travel enterprises will achieve these savings depends on their business structure (Bywater, 1997).

In addition, trade among participating countries in the Euro area is expected to increase, as small and medium-sized travel enterprises that were unable to manage foreign exchange transactions will enter the Single Market. On the other hand, consumers will be able to make bookings direct as the difficulties of cross-border booking will disappear and so will benefit by not losing money from converting one currency to another.

These savings on transaction costs will not be immediate either for the consumer or the travel companies and charges for transactions are possible. The Association of British Travel Agents (ABTA) in their report *The Euro and ABTA Members*, prepared by the Centre for Economics and Business Research (CEBR), published a comprehensive analysis of the Euro on the travel and tourism business. It predicts that if the Euro succeeds, its impact on market integration in the euro zone will boost business travel to all Euro zone destinations.

Costs

Examination of the benefits of the EMU highlights some issues of concern for the travel companies. The consumer savings from the exchange transactions translates into a loss of revenue from the traveller's cheque operations of the travel companies. Companies such as Thomas Cook and American Express might lose a significant source of income as a result of the EMU.

Operational aspects of investment: a financial accounting perspective

Traditionally, the operational aspects of any investment decision relate to the financial statements used by any business operation, including the profit and loss account (P&L) and the balance sheet (BS).

The balance sheet shows the financial position of a business on a given date, and usually by the time it's available to the public it is out of date. It fails to show the value of location, reputation, human resources and the current market value of a business. On the other hand, the income statement shows operational results for a stated period of time, but it fails to address questions such as:

- How much cash was actually provided by operations?
- What amount of fixed assets was purchased?
- How much debt was either paid or borrowed?
- What amount of dividends was actually paid?
- What amount of funds was raised through the sales of capital?

The cashflow statement (CFS) is designed to answer these questions and many more. The Financial Accounting Standards Board (FASB), which is the current accounting rule-making body in the USA has mandated that the CFS be included with the other financial statements issued to external users since 1988. Other statements like the statement of changes in financial position or the statement of fund flows were generally focused on working capital rather that cash.

In any investment decision, the CFS is the base on which financial decisions are made, therefore it is of utmost importance that all managers are able to read it and use it. Without being able to measure and predict inflows of cash, projects cannot be taken on and companies cannot expand or grow. When examining financial statements, the CFS is often given minor attention next to the P&L and the BS. When one thinks of quarterly or yearly reports, the P&L and the BS are considered immediately. This occurs because a number of people who receive financial reports often do not read the CFS; therefore they are not aware of the advantages it brings ('Here is Something', 1997).

Essentially, the CFS shows the movement of cash in a business during a certain period of time. In doing so, it also denotes the value of a company at any point in time. The CFS indicates a tourism and hospitality company's ability to continue to operate by identifying where the company's money came from and where it has gone. For example, a cash increase is seen under securities if the company has sold common stock for cash. Similarly, if the company has bought assets, then there will be a cash deficit under assets. A CFS analyses a company's potential to generate enough cash to cover its expenses.

A successful company should focus on cashflow, which is what it currently manages, rather than on assets and profits, which are aftermath analyses (Allen, 1994). Cashflow is affected each time an exchange occurs between buyer and supplier, and as such the CFS requires no reconciliation and therefore is quicker to compile. Some even go so far as to say that a CFS appropriately tailored for a company should replace all other accrual accounting systems (Jones, 1998).

The CFS is roughly divided into three sections:

1. *Operating activities*: the first is cash arising from operating activities. The money can come from sales throughout the year or from working capital. A company needs strong cashflow from sales, but it must also continue to increase investment – this will represent a decrease in cash. A company must learn to balance these elements so that it will not find itself tied up when in need of cash. Included in the cash from operating activities is working capital. Working capital is very liquid, but it is not paper money. For example, inventories, short-term government bonds or investments make up working capital. In essence, it is the current assets and the current liabilities.

2. *Investing activities*: the second part of the CFS is cash arising from investing activities. This involves the purchase or sale of marketable securities and/or investments. This includes the purchase or sale of fixed assets.

3. Financing activities: the final part of the CFS is the cash arising from financing activities. Primarily, this shows a company's ability to pay dividends to its shareholders. Financing activities also include the payment of long-term debt and any impacts of consolidation.

A detailed description of the preparation of the CFS follows.

Cashflow statement: preparation

To prepare and complete an analysis of flows of cash, you will usually be presented with the following information:

- condensed income statement;
- comparative balance sheets;
- additional notes to the accounts.

All that is being done in a CFS is the justification of a change in cash balance from one year to the next – looking at where money has come from and where it has gone. So at the end the 'change in cash' figure should reconcile back to the comparative balance sheets.

The following brief steps describe the completion of a statement of cash flows. In preparing the first section, the operating activities, companies have a choice between two methods. Both methods will be presented below.

Operating activities

In this section of the CFS we include transactions related to revenue and expenses accounts. The result of this section will determine the ability of top management to generate cash for the core purpose of that particular business.

Operating activities – direct method

The procedure for preparing the operating activities section of the CFS using the direct method differs from that using the indirect method. Under the direct method, the operating activities section does not begin with net profit; instead, it shows cash collected from customers and cash used for various operating expenses. Obtaining cash basis information requires an analysis of the transactions of each revenue and expense account or a conversion of year-end information from the accrual basis to cash basis accounting. This process is relatively time consuming and requires advanced financial accounting knowledge.

Operating activities – indirect method

The indirect method has been gaining considerable attention and use lately. This is primarily due to its simplicity and step-by-step approach.

First, we focus on the income statement or P&L. We start with the net profit or net income, then we adjust this figure for any items included in this total which have not used or provided cash, i.e. depreciation or amortization. These items are the so-called non-cash expenses which are subtracted from sales and therefore served as a reduction of the taxable income. Nevertheless, these amounts are not a cash outflow so we need to add them back to our net profit. Any gains/losses on the sale of assets need to be adjusted as well because these are not operating activities. A company is in business to make money from providing products or services to clients not from the sale of assets which are the means of providing those services. Although sales of assets do result in a cash inflow they are not operating activities so we will account for them at another section of the CFS. These two steps will complete the use of the P&L account and the next step will be the use of the balance sheet.

We are looking at the current account of the balance sheet, and any additional notes that we have been supplied with, to account for any changes in current accounts (current assets and current liabilities) between balance sheet dates. To do that we need to prepare a comparative balance sheet with the change from last year's figure and the current amounts. This helps determine if we have experienced an increase or decrease among the different lines of a balance sheet. Obviously the first current asset account, namely cash and cash equivalence, will be ignored as the change in cash from last year to this year is the actual cash inflow or outflow. This line will serve as a control line at the end to determine if, at least mathematically, a company has correctly prepared the CFS.

The second group of current assets which are ignored are changes within the marketable securities and short-term investments sections. For example, the purchase of government bonds, treasury bills or any other valuable securities that the company intends to keep for a time less than 12 months from the balance sheet date are not considered as operating activities accounts. Companies usually invest in such securities due to unnecessary large amounts of available cash. The prime objective is to get a return on these amounts which is higher than the interest a bank would pay for a normal demand account. But nevertheless, any cash inflows or outflows for this purpose are not part of operating activities as, again, a company is in business to make money from operations by providing services to guests and not sales or purchases of marketable securities, unless that is the prime activity of that company.

A brief explanation follows of a typical current asset account to illustrate the reasoning behind any adjustment. Debtors accounts represents the credit sales of a business – when customers promise to pay for services or products already received by a business within 12 months of the balance sheet date. Debtors accounts relate directly to sales. Sales amounts on an income statement increase regardless of cash being immediately received or on an open debtors account. That is due to the accrual accounting principle. By using the following current assets section of a comparative balance sheet we can first determine the change within the debtors account.

The balance table below shows an increase in debtors in comparison to the previous year of 10,000. This increase reflects an increase in credit sales. By considering that all sales, regardless of being cash sales or credit sales, were recorded and accounted for during the preparation of the P&L account we have to subtract this amount from the net income amount so we can reflect the actual cash inflow. This will imply that an increase of current assets needs to be subtracted from the net income and a decrease needs to be added to that balance.

Balance Sheet			
Current Assets	**2000**	**2001**	Change in A/C balance
Debtors	**30,000**	**40,000**	10,000 (increase)

The following illustrates this logic:

Increase in current assets accounts	Subtract the increase in balance
Decrease in current assets accounts	Add the decrease in balance

Current liabilities accounts will follow exactly the opposite logic. The following example will give more value to this assumption. Creditors represent the current obligations of a business. Let's assume that the comparative analysis of the current liabilities section of a company showed the following results:

Balance Sheet

Current Liabilities	**2000**	**2001**	Change in A/C balance
Creditors	**30,000**	**40,000**	10,000 (increase)

The above illustration shows an increase in the creditors account in comparison to the previous year of 10,000. This increase is the product of an additional 10,000 current obligations for the company. This might be due to a purchase of a product or service, perhaps advertising, which has not yet been paid. The matching principle dictates that all expenses should be recorded in the same period as the revenue they help to generate. Thus, an amount of (unpaid) advertising expense appears on the income statement and is subtracted from sales to arrive at the profit line. Because we did not actually pay that amount, obviously, we have to add it back to the net income amount. So the following logic will apply when analysing and adjusting net cashflows from operating activities under the indirect method (see Table 9.6).

The second step is to determine the net cashflows from investing activities (see Table 9.7). This activity relates to cashflows from sales or purchases of marketable securities as well as cash inflows or outflows from sales of acquisitions of non-current assets. For example, cash used to purchase property and equipment or cash proceeds from the sales of such assets. The following section illustrates the logic in preparing this activity.

Table 9.6

Operating activities – indirect method

Income statement

Net Income	Starting point
Depreciation/amortization	Plus
Loss on sales of assets	Plus
Gain on sales of assets	Minus

Balance sheet

Current assets	Increase in account balance	Decrease in account balance
Cash	Not applicable	Not applicable
Marketable securities	Not applicable	Not applicable
Remaining current assets	Minus	Plus
Current liabilities	Increase in account balance	Decrease in account balance
Dividends payable*	Not applicable	Not applicable
Current portion of LTD**	Not applicable	Not applicable
Rest current liabilities	Plus	Minus

* The actual amount paid for the current year will be used at another section of the CFS as a company might declare a dividend this year but actually pay it next year.
** Part of the 'financing activities' section of the CFS.
The total either plus or minus will be the net cash flows from operating activities.

The third step in preparing a CFS is the preparation of the financing activities section. This includes any activities that are related to cashflows, retirement of debt and the re-purchase of capital stock. Also any payment of cash dividend to a company's shareholders will be considered.

To determine the net cashflows from financing activities, we must turn our attention to the non-current liabilities and equity accounts. Table 9.8 will illustrate the preparation of this section. The balance of the above will give the net cashflows from financing activities.

The last step in preparing the CFS is to provide supplementary schedules of non-cash financing and investing activities, as well as supplementary disclosures of cashflow information that might be necessary for the user of this statement to have a fair and clear picture of the cash inflows and outflows. To conclude, the following section will present the relationship of the CFS to the other main financial statements by presenting their sections and how they are linked with each other.

Table 9.7	*Cash in-flows*	
Investment activities	Proceeds from sales of Marketable securities	Plus
	Proceeds from sales of Investments	Plus
	Proceeds from sales of Fixed Assets	Plus
	Proceeds from sales of Other Assets	Plus
	Cash out-flows	
	Purchases from sales of Marketable securities	Minus
	Purchases from sales of Investments	Minus
	Purchases from sales of Fixed Assets	Minus
	Purchases from sales of Other Assets	Minus

Note: Only the actual cash received or paid will be considered and not the book value of the above-mentioned asset accounts.

Table 9.8	*Cash in-flows*	
Financing activities	Proceeds from cash borrowing	Plus
	Proceeds from sales of capital stock	Plus
	Proceeds from sales of debentures	Plus
	Cash out-flows	
	Purchase of treasury stock	Minus
	Payment of dividends	Minus
	Payment of debt	Minus

Note: To prepare the investing and financing activities we need to have access to any notes and disclosures that involve transactions related to these balance sheet accounts.

The balance sheet (BS)

In the past, importance has been placed on the assets and liabilities of a tourism and hospitality company, making the BS a major tool in assessing a tourism and hospitality company's worth (Tucker and Tucci, 1994). The weakness of this is that the BS can only be compiled after the month end closing and must be reconciled each month. The BS shows a company's assets equal to the sum of their liabilities and equity. The principal dilemma with the BS is that all of the figures are recorded at cost and do not adjust for inflation or time. A company will always prove under-valued on its BS, and will therefore have to revert to other ways of finding its current value.

The profit and loss (P&L) statement

Over time financial statements have concentrated on a company's earnings performance thereby utilizing the P&L as the major financial statement (Tucker and Tucci, 1994). The P&L lists all the forms of revenue and subtracts from it all of the expenses incurred to achieve that revenue. As with the BS, this must be reconciled each month, proving the P&L to be a lengthy and tedious statement to compile.

The important point to take notice of is that bottom-line profit/loss and cash move independently from each other (Cultera, 1998). This is because the bottom line comes from the P&L, which shows the difference between income and expenses for a specific period of time. A tourism and hospitality company can make a profit and yet suffer a loss of cash inflows. The two are entirely different issues and not to be confused.

Risk

No one can be sure of what the future will bring, therefore decisions on future occurrences or events create uncertainty and, furthermore, risk. Technically, uncertainty is a situation where there are a variety of possible outcomes and little, if anything, is previously known to guide a well-rounded decision. Risk is a situation where there are a variety of possible outcomes and all of the possibilities are known before any final decisions are taken (Dixon, 1994). The higher the variability of these possible outcomes, the greater the risk. Since the difference between them is so minor, the terms are used almost interchangeably.

Risk is a complex and still undefined issue and there exists considerable debate on how to define risk, what risk is relevant, on how to assess and measure risk, and how to summarize or characterize risk (Groth, 1992). Below are some common terms that attempt to identify the various types of risk.

- *Pervasive or systematic risk* is present at all times and in all situations. Systematic risk cannot be diversified, that is, it cannot be broken down or contained. This type of risk affects all sectors of all industries. No matter what kind of investment is being considered, systematic risks are present and must be carefully weighed (Jones, 1991).
- *Interest rate risk* involves the variability in the return of a security due to fluctuation in interest rates. This affects bonds more than common stock because these tend to move inversely to interest rates (Jones, 1991).

- *Market risk* involves the variation of returns of all types of stocks due to fluctuations in the stock market. This directly affects the prices of common stock although all securities face market risk. Market risk encompasses issues that are external to the stock market itself, such as economic fluctuations or political instability (Jones, 1991).
- *Risk dealing with purchasing power* within a market is synonymous with inflation risk, which is directly linked to interest rate risk, since inflation moves parallel to interest rates (Jones, 1991).
- *Specific or unsystematic risk* is present in varying degrees depending upon the investment situation and is not directly related to market performance, as is pervasive risk. Specific risks can be diversified in order to be contained. These risks tend to affect parts of industries and therefore may pose a problem in individual aspects of the investment decision (Jones, 1991).
- *Business risk* is the risk of doing business in a certain environment or within a certain industry. Business risk also encompasses uncertainty in the amount of pre-tax profits due to an inability to effectively forecast levels of demand (Jones, 1991). Business risk also includes any risks taken when generating cash or, in other words, operating income (Groth, 1992).
- *Financial risk* is the risk of acquiring debt to finance a project or investment. Financial risk deals with the varying levels of fixed interest financing within a capital structure (Jones, 1991).
- *Liability risk* is the risk of liquidating short-term common stock (Jones, 1991).
- *Total risk* measures the risk within an entire portfolio (Jones, 1991). Business decisions are constantly being taken, but the most crucial relate to investments because these determine the future of the tourism and hospitality company. Investing means having to forego present consumption in order to increase the total amount that can be consumed at a future time. This is the reason why such decisions are only taken at the highest levels of a tourism and hospitality company (Sirpal, 1998). As a result, they are almost always impossible to reverse and prove even more expensive to amend.

Risk has been gaining a lot of attention in recent years. Until recently, it has always been viewed in a negative light, as something to avoid, as a danger. The greater part of a tourism and hospitality company's risk tactics as of late has been on how best to avoid it. Risk is now being looked at as the integral connection between being able to manage and improving performance because it generates shareholder value. Risk management embraces risk as being inherent to business and providing the opportunity to maximize wealth (International Management Accounting Study, 1999). Correct risk management 'establishes, calibrates and realigns the relationship between risk, growth and return' (*ibid.*).

Investment appraisal techniques

Strategic financial decisions are based upon a company's cashflow position. Fundamentally, if a company has excess cash, it is free to make investments. In contrast, if a company cannot even cover its short-term debt, it should refrain from making any investments. The availability of cash gives a company the freedom to make choices to improve its financial situation, whether it is to invest, to reinvest or to sell. Risk plays an indispensable role in financial decisions and cash remains a constant preoccupation.

Payback

Payback relates to how quickly a new project or investment will generate cash in order to payback the original investment and is used when large upfront investments are made. Although not all companies use this method to take a final decision on whether or not to continue with a proposed project, it is important to calculate it because it provides an overall time frame. The most important issue to look at, which payback does not calculate, is the length of time after which the initial investment is paid back and how much cash will be generated then.

The payback method also proves useful when measuring risk. The longer the payback period the higher the risk. This is especially true of companies that can only look a couple of years down the line. Even if the necessary cash is available for the initial payment, a tourism and hospitality company has to be sure it will have enough cash inflows to safely continue its day-to-day operation. A similar argument stands when going to the opposite extreme of a very short payback period. A short payback period means there is high return on investment, and the higher the risk in an investment, the higher the returns (Dixon, 1994). Payback serves two main purposes. First, it is used as a filter because it allows a tourism and hospitality company to see quickly and clearly which investments will provide the adequate returns within an acceptable period of time. Second, the payback method is also used to rank or prioritize projects. The investment that quickly provides an acceptable amount of return is given first priority.

However, payback also has its drawbacks. It ignores all cashflows generated from the investment itself and is only concerned with the time up to when the original investment is recovered, therefore making it a short-sighted technique. For example, Table 9.9 considers three projects, each with an initial investment of US$5000.

Strictly in terms of payback, Project X would have to be accepted. Its payback period is three years while Project Y does not reach the investment cost and Project Z takes almost four years. But, in reality, would a tourism and hospitality company invest in a project that after only three years gives no returns? Or

Table 9.9	Cashflows	Project X ($)	Project Y ($)	Project Z ($)
Payback investment 1	Year 0	(5000)	(5000)	(5000)
	Year 1	1000	500	1200
	Year 2	1500	1300	1200
	Year 3	2500	1300	1300
	Year 4	0	1300	1400
	Total	5000	4400	5100

would such a company invest in a project without making a profit but just paying back the original investment? Based on the same basic variables, another example is given in Table 9.10.

	Cash flows	Project X ($)	Project Y ($)	Project Z ($)
Table 9.10	Year 0	(5000)	(5000)	(5000)
Payback investment 2	Year 1	1900	1800	1700
	Year 2	2000	2200	2100
	Year 3	2500	2500	2600
	Year 4	2600	2500	2600
	Total	9000	9000	9000

The three projects have the same return after four years and have approximately the same payback time of two and a half years. Because of the complexity of projects and investments, companies have to look to other more detailed techniques in order to get more precise answers. With the above two examples, it can be seen how a tourism or hospitality company can use payback as its first filter, so as to let the projects with the desired payback period continue for further screening.

Discounted cashflow techniques

Cashflow in itself covers only the present time. Forecasted, or discounted, cashflow is based on estimates for the future. They are carefully compiled by anticipating future cash inflows and outflows. Because time and money values change as time moves forward, cashflows must be discounted to adjust for those changes. Discounting, therefore, is giving the present value to money receivable at a future point in time: the reverse of compound interest.

Net present value

When discounting is applied, the capital being used to fund the investment is costed. Net present value (NPV) is used to value an investment's positive and negative cash flows. It is the total of the cashflows expected, net of the initial investment made (Damodaran, 1992). NPV builds on the payback method by showing the amount of cash investors can immediately take as a result of the investment. It looks for the maximization of the present value of the cashflows of an investment, where the discount rate used is the return required by the investors.

Positive NPV gives the go-ahead for an investment to be made, while negative NPV leads the tourism or hospitality company to look at other methods of evaluating investment possibilities (Higson, 1995). A positive NPV means that the project will make more than the rate of return required by the investors. A positive NPV where the investment decision is taken will consequently increase the value of the tourism or hospitality company by that same amount. Similarly, if a current project with a negative NPV is sold or terminated, the value of the company will increase by the NPV amount (Damodaran, 1992).

Although NPV is a very strong appraisal method, it too has its weaknesses. The NPV of a project may seem 'two-dimensional' due to changes in the discount rate used. The original discount rate used to calculate the NPV is the true cost of capital. Often, the discount rate is risk adjusted, thus no longer representing the true cost of capital. It is here that the problem arises. The adjusted discount rate does not result in the actual return of the project but the return and the risk adjustment for it. The first dimension is the actual amount of return, equivalent to the original discount rate used. The second dimension is the excess amount over the minimum required to cover all costs of capital adjusted for risk. This alone often causes managers to turn to internal rate of return rather than the NPV method (Lefley and Morgan, 1999).

Internal rate of return

The internal rate of return (IRR) method is an alternative discounting technique that facilitates the comparison of various investments because it is quoted as a percentage. The IRR is the point at which the cash inflows equal the cash outflows of an investment. At this point the NPV of the investment is zero, neither a gain nor a loss. The IRR represents the rate of return on the amount of money initially invested, which is now tied up in the project.

If the IRR exceeds the required rate, then the project should be accepted; if not, then the project should be rejected. This method has two major defects. First, if the NPV does not follow a straight line, crossing the horizontal axis at one single point, the IRR cannot be found. Second, IRR and NPV do not always work together and can result in different alternatives for the same investment decision (Andrew and Scmidigall, 1993). Although IRR has proven to be less effective than NPV, it is none the less used more often; managers find it easier to calculate (Arnold and Turley, 1996). Analysts are more familiar with rates of return than present values and this, unfortunately, may lead managers into taking the wrong financial decision.

When NPV and IRR conflict

NPV and IRR do not always give the same results. There are times when the NPV of a project is high, yet the IRR is low and vice versa. When this occurs, a choice has to be made of either the project with the highest NPV or the project with the highest returns – but which? It must be remembered that NPV compares all additional cashflows to the cost of capital, simply by discounting. IRR, on the other hand, does not. This therefore means that NPV takes into account the size of an investment, whereas IRR, because it is a percentage number, does not. For example, it is better to have a return of 50 per cent per year on an investment of US$1000 than a 100 per cent return per year on an investment of US$100 (Arnold and Turley, 1996). Therefore, it is not the percentage on its own that makes a difference, but rather the NPV of the money being invested.

Sensitivity analysis

Sensitivity analysis shows how sensitive an outcome is to change by breaking down the investment into its components and measuring how each one reacts to change. Components can be: variable costs, selling price, volume of sales, and the original investment itself. This analysis highlights areas in which a small variance to the planned component will cause an influential change in the entire project (Arnold and Turley, 1996).

By making the NPV of a project equal to zero, the sensitivity of the components can be clearly seen. With an NPV of zero, a project will certainly be rejected, therefore the variation of the components between the planned value and the value that gives a zero NPV represents how sensitive the component is.

Sensitivity analysis can be calculated in various ways, either with a single formula, for an entire investment, or with a string of formulas, one for each component. The latter method uses break-even annual contribution, whereas the first method uses NPV directly. Both methods require the use of annuity tables, therefore assuming that cashflows every year are similar. This makes the calculations simple, yet it is not realistic to forecast the same cashflows each year throughout the life of a project. It is possible to calculate sensitivity when yearly cashflows differ, yet the calculations become lengthy because annuity tables can no longer be used (Arnold and Turley, 1996).

The most significant fault of this method, whether it be with a single formula or with a string of them, is that it takes each component into account separately. In reality, all of the components of a project are interdependent, yet this method considers each in isolation. Again, like payback, this method can be used to indicate areas where problems may arise, but it should not be the sole deciding factor.

Current changes in risk and investment decisions

Unlike other fields of study, finance has undergone few changes. From the beginnings of the P&L to the introduction of the computer, new methods and techniques undertaken by industries have been few and far between. Academics have also been making small adjustments here and there, perfecting the existing and functioning models. None the less, in reality, companies have been slow to follow. Surprisingly, company reporting and decision-making has lagged behind these developments. Companies still rely on IRR for investment appraisal whereas NPV has proven to be most appropriate (Arnold and Turley, 1996).

Net present value profile

In order to optimize NPV and provide managers with another sound investment appraisal technique, Lefley and Morgan (1999) have created the NPV Profile (NPVP). This model takes NPV one step further by including discounted payback (DPB), discounted payback index (DPBI) and the marginal growth rate (MGR). The NPV, DPBI and the MGR indicate the returns of an investment, while the DPB measures the risk in time of the project. This model therefore provides a solution for differentiating between projects with the same NPV (Lefley and Morgan, 1999).

First, the present values (PV) are calculated in order to arrive at an NPV. By using the PV of the cashflows the DPB is calculated. Like payback, the DPB looks at time and risk, by determining how long it takes to recover the original investment; the difference here is that instead of using accounting cashflows, discounted cashflows are used. The DPB encompasses a time value, and measures liquidity and time risk of an investment. Time risk is the risk of uncertain returns, which increases with time. In other words, the longer a project takes to recover the original investment, the higher the risk of it never materializing. Because DPB incorporates a risk factor, it is important to note that the cashflows used are discounted at the unadjusted cost of capital. Had it not been so, risk would be accounted for twice (Lefley and Morgan, 1999).

Next, the DPBI is found. The DBPI is a number that indicates the number of times the original cost of an investment will be recovered throughout the life of a project. This figure is therefore a sign of the project's profitability. The DPBI is calculated by dividing the sum of the discounted cashflows by the cost of capital of a project. The higher the index, the more profitable the project is deemed to be. By including the DBPI the major weakness of the payback method is eliminated. The DPBI takes into account all the cashflows of a project, not just those up to the payback period (i.e., the point when the investment is recovered) (Lefley and Morgan, 1999).

Finally, the MGR is calculated. The MGR is essentially the marginal return of a project. That is to say, the additional amount of returns, over the minimum required, each year. The MGR delineates a project's economic life. The longer the life of a project, the lower the MGR. This can be correlated to compound interest. If a compound interest rate equal to the MGR is applied to the initial cost of a project for the entire life of that project, the result will be the same as the sum of the PV's of the project (Lefley and Morgan, 1999). At this point, a project is ready to be reviewed by management. All of the information has been gathered and calculated to produce an optimal result.

The FAP model

One of the newest financial models incorporates NPVP, risk, benefits and even sensitivity analysis to produce the most sound investment decision. The Financial Appraisal Profile (FAP) was introduced in 1997 and created by Frank Lefley at Imperial College in London. This model not only uses financial values, but also assigns numbers to benefits that are often ignored in accounting, such as strategic value. These values make a difference when making investment decisions, but do not have a numerical value *per se* (Lefley, 2000).

Before anything else, a corporate risk threshold (CRT) has to be determined. This can be compared to the break-even point of the sensitivity analysis. Any potential risk higher than the CRT will cause the project to be rejected. The CRT is used when calculating the percentage change an element of the FAP model can undergo before the project must be rejected (Lefley, 2000). Project risks are taken into account by using a risk index (RI). The RI is the measurement of the probability of occurrence of a specific risk multiplied by the impact of that risk. It is important to note that the effect of a high probability and low impact of a risk is not the same as a low probability and high impact of a risk. The RI highlights whether the overall risk of a project lies mostly in the probability or impact sectors. The RI measures the amount of risk within parts of a project too, thus allowing the whole project to be valued piece by piece and as a whole.

Riskier areas of a project will easily be identified and thus can be handled more effectively (Lefley, 2000).

Strategic benefits are those that play a vital role in the future of a tourism or hospitality company, such as competitive advantage, responding to customer needs, goodwill within the community and flexibility. These benefits are often taken into account by management when the actual decision to undertake the project is made, but they do not have any numerical value as such. A strategic index (SI) is a formulated number assigned to the benefit or benefits identified. The project is divided into its strategic benefits and these are ranked by order of importance to the tourism or hospitality company. The strategic benefits are given a second score according to how they rank within the project itself. The two rankings are then multiplied to achieve a single SI for each strategic benefit. Their weighted average is then the final SI for the project as a whole (Lefley, 2000).

When it comes time to accept or reject a project using the FAP model, the decision becomes more complicated, but also more complete. Not only is the financial side important, but also the risks and the benefits brought about in the project. Because greater returns imply greater investment, a tourism or hospitality company might be willing to accept a greater RI. On the other hand, a company might be willing to accept a project with small returns because it has a high SI which will benefit them as a whole in the long run. The FAP model encompasses all parts of the investment decision and involves both facts and opinions (Lefley, 2000).

The most outstanding aspect of the FAP model is the combination of financial facts and management opinion. For example, when compiling the RI, the management of the company will rank the risks identified from 0 to –10. The lowest number (–10) is the highest amount of risk in an area of the project that the company is willing to accept. The project area with the highest risk is used as the overall risk of the entire project, i.e., the RI of the project (Lefley, 2000).

Again, when deciding on the SI, management input is crucial. For example, it is management that must rank, in order of importance, the strategic benefits of the project to the tourism or hospitality company. The first ranking, corporate ranking (CR) is on a scale of 1–10, with 10 being the benefit of the highest strategic importance to corporate management of the company. The second ranking, project strategic score value (PSSV), is also on a scale of 1–10, with 10 being the most strategic benefit for the project. Risk is ranked negatively, while strategic benefits are ranked positively simply to show the adverse effects of risk compared to the attractive effects of strategic benefits (Lefley, 2000).

Project budget model

The project budget model deals with the actual accounting part of project management. The two models above are directed at project managers and planners, yet they ignore the fact that projects, their costs and returns, must eventually be recorded and thus placed into accounting periods. This creates a divide between planners and accountants. The planners are concentrating on the project as a whole, whereas the accountants see things in periods (for example, one month or one year). This issue alone complicates the time factor, making it difficult to split the numbers accurately across accounting periods (Arthur, 2000).

This model attempts to link both the project planners and managers with the accountants and produce a viable result for both. To create the model there are three general stages.

The first stage is to take the project and divide it into tasks based on relevant cost; for example, personnel, materials and equipment. Tasks that begin or end on the same day or that use the same resource can be grouped into one. In other words, salaries and wages are grouped together because they rely on the same resource (Arthur, 2000). The second stage is to build a task-based budget. This calculates all of the costs of the relevant tasks based on 'assumptions' or information on those tasks. Information about the tasks includes start and finish dates, duration and the actual costs. The last stage is the construction of a spreadsheet that allocates all of the costs into time periods based on the 'assumptions' from the previous step. The following formula is used to calculate tasks within periods:

$$[ABS (PS - TF - 1) - ABS (PS - TS) - ABS (PF - TF) + ABS (PF - TS + 1)] / 2$$

where PS is the period starting date
PF is the period finishing date
TS is the task starting date
TF is the task finishing date
ABS is the absolute value of a number. Therefore it is the absolute value of the result of the equation in parenthesis.

This formula results in the exact number of days of a task within an accounting period. If the task and the period do not overlap, the answer will be zero. If the result is then divided by the duration of the entire task, the proportion of the task that falls into the accounting period is found (Arthur, 2000).

Summary

This chapter reviewed the institutional pressures and the operational aspects for investment for tourism destinations and enterprises. Initially, the importance of GATS and the Euro were reviewed to highlight the issues that ought to be considered for future investment in the sector. Here, the main benefit embodied in the GATS is an increase in the economic efficiency of the service sectors of the signatories brought about by an improvement in domestic resource allocation and greater access to lower-cost/higher-quality service inputs. GATS also aims to liberalize trade in all services and all modes of their supply. This approach is beneficial for the tourism sector because of the multitude of tourism services and their links with other sectors.

Further, one the most important benefits to tourism is that GATS will propel the travel and tourism industry internationally. It will ease the flow of people, information and capital across boundaries. Equally, employees with special expertise will be able to move freely around the globe, sharpening their skills and adding value. In addition, GATS could reduce restrictions on foreign investment and the transfer of funds that will bring new investors into the market and fuel new projects. This, in turn, will help spread travel and tourism investment and growth far and wide.

The second half of this chapter considered the operational aspects of investment in tourism and hospitality sectors that have relied solely on financial and statistical data. With the FAP and the NPVP models, companies can better assess the risks and the benefits of a future project with the direct input of its management. But if managers currently lack the understanding to use already established methods like NPV, what are the chances that they will be willing to convert to even more complex models such as the FAP, NPVP or the project budget model? It seems that although these methods are available, companies in travel and tourism sectors will still rely on the traditional investment decision-making structures. Having said this, in this era of globalization and free trade, pressure is mounting for these enterprises to change their tactics and apply cutting edge techniques of investment appraisal. As a result, the issues surrounding investment decisions for travel and hospitality enterprises and destinations are not only on how they generate and allocate investments, but most importantly how they assess these investments.

This chapter provided a platform of discussion on how investments appraisal should be considered in the future as well as the institutional pressures that arise from GATS and the Euro that will influence investment decision-making.

References

Alan, L. (1985) 'International Economics', London: George Allen & Unwin.

Allen, D. (1994) *Strategic Financial Decisions*, London: Biddles Ltd, 133.

Andrew, W.P. and Scmidigall, R.S. (1993) Financial Management for the Hospitality industry, Lansing: Educational Institute of the American Hotel and Motel Association, 220–2.

Arnold, J. and Turley, S. (1996) *Accounting for Management Decisions*, London: Prentice-Hall, 293, 270–2).

Arthur, A. (2000) 'How to build your own project budget model', *Management Accounting*, 78, 20–2.

Biederman, A., and Zuckerman, D. (1998) *Exporting and Importing – Negotiating Global Markets*, 2nd edn, New York: AMACOM (American Management Association).

Cultera, P. (1998) 'What pays the bills?', on-line, www.emerald-library.com

Damodaran, A. (1992) *Applied Corporate Finance*, New York: John Wiley and Sons, 157, 158, 165.

Dixon, R. (1994) *Investment Appraisal*, London: Biddles Ltd, 157, 158, 165.

EU (1999) *GATS 2000*, Luxembourg: European Commission.

Ferndez, R. (1997) *Returns to Regionalism: An Evaluation of Non-traditional Gains from Regional Trade Agreements*, working paper, New York: World Bank.

Groth, J.C. (1992) 'Common sense risk assessment', on-line.

Here is Something (1997) 'Free cash flow', on-line, available at www.worth.com/articles

Higson, C. (1995) *Business Finance*, 2nd edn, London: Butterworths, 57, 58, 60.

International Management Accounting (1999) Enhancing Shareholder Wealth by Better Managing Business Risk, London: International Federation of Accountants and PricewaterhouseCoopers.

IIE (1996) Competitive Liberalization and Global Free Trade, New York: Institute for International Economics.

Jamws, K. and Rai, A. (1987) *International Business Operating in the Global Economy*, New York: Holt, Rinehart & Winston.

John, W. and Chris, M. (1991) *The World Economy*, London: Harvester Wheatsheaf.

Jones, C.P. (1991) *Investment Analysis and Management*, 3rd edn, New York: John Wiley and Sons, 57, 58, 60.

Jones, S. (1998) 'An evaluation of user ratings of cash vs accrual based financial reports in Australia', on-line, www.emerald-library.com

Mia, M. (1998) *International Trade*, London: Macmillan.

Peter, D. (1992) *Global Shift*, London: Paul Chapman.

Lefley, F. (2000) 'The FAP model of investment appraisal', *Management Accounting*, March, 28–31.

Lefley, F. and Morgan, M. (1999) 'A creative way of looking at the NPV', *Management Accounting*, 77, 39–41.

OECD (1996) *Market Access for the Least Developing Countries: Where Are the Obstacles?*, Paris: Organization for Economic Co-operation and Development.

Sirpal, S. (1998) 'Strategic planning, risk-taking and reward systems for managers in multi-divisional companies – an empirical study', on-line.

TAWC (2002) 'The Americas in a world context: trade and cooperation', on-line, available at www.eia.doe.gov/emeu/cabs/chapter6a.html

Tucker, J.J. and Tucci, L.A. (1994) 'Why traditional measures of earnings performance may lead to failed strategic marketing decisions', on-line, www.emerald-library.com

WTO (1996) *Questions and Answers about GATS and Tourism*, Geneva: World Trade Organization.

WTO (1995) *Seminar on GATS Implications for Tourism*, Madrid: World Tourism Organization.

WTO (1998) *Tourism Sector*, Geneva: World Trade Organization.

WTO (1999) *World Trade Report*, Geneva: World Trade Organization.

WTO (2002) 'The World Trade Organization statistics: international trade statistics – trade by region', on-line, available at www.wto.org/english/res_e/statis_e/tradebyregion_e.htm

World Tourism Organization (WTO) (1999) 'Marketing tourism destinations on-line', Madrid: WTO.

UNCTAD and The World Bank (1994) *Liberalizing International Transactions in Services: A Handbook*, New York and Geneva: United Nations.

UNCTAD (1996) *Promoting Growth and Sustainable Development in a Globalising and Liberalising World Economy*, New York: United Nations Conference for Trade and Development.

UNCTAD (1998) *The Tourism Sector in Developing Countries, with Particular Focus on Tour Operators, Travel Agencies and Other Suppliers*, New York: United Nations Conference for Trade and Development.

Further reading

'Business man of the century', (1999) *Fortune*, 140, November 22, 66–76.

El Amin, A. (1999) 'Keep your eyes on the cash flow', on-line, www.bermudasun.org

Harris, P. (1995) *Accounting and Finance for the International Hospitality Industry*, Oxford: Reed Elsevier PLC, 105.

Higgens, R.C. (1989) *Analysis for Financial Management*, 2nd edn, Illinois: Irwin, 209.

McKenzie, W. (1998) *The Financial Times Guide to Using and Interpreting Company Accounts*, 2nd edn, London: Pitman Publishing, 12, 308.

Weston, J.F. and Copeland, T.E. (1995) *Managerial Finance*, London: Redwood Books, 93, 96, 97.

Key Internet sites

http://www.ilo.org/

http://laborresearch.org

http://www.world-tourism.org/

http://www.wttc.org/

http://www.isn.ethz.ch

http://www.oecd.org

http://gopher.undp.org

http://gopher.unesco.org

http://ue.eu.int

http://www.worldbank.org

http://www.wto.org

http://www.nafta-sec-alena.org

http://www.rau.edu.uy/mercosur/pre26.merco.htm

http://www.globalissues.org

http://www.hrw.org/press/2001/04/nafta0416.htm

Globalization within tourism and hospitality: Strategic implications

Background

The impact of globalization upon labour issues in the hotel, catering and tourism markets can be simply stated as follows: to cope with the international intensity of competition brought about by globalization, a knowledge-based economy has emerged to replace the previously dominant 'Fordist' mode of production. This knowledge-based economy utilizes the skills of the workforce to the full, so creating a new way of thinking about human resources, and also new responses to the management of human resources by organizations.

This new paradigm for human resource management (HRM) and organizational behaviour is characterized by speed, flexibility, integration and innovation. The process of globalization not only reduces borders and barriers for trade between nations, but it also renders these boundaries permeable both within and between organizations. This increased permeability of boundaries has been brought about by a series of drivers operating on a global scale. Some assert that globalization goes beyond the idea of permeating boundaries between nations and organizations, but also crosses the traditional borders of time, space, scope, geography, functions, thought and cultural assumptions. This, in turn, demands both a different perspective and position to be taken on the human resource management and operation of tourism organizations. Of course, while hotel, tourism and catering organizations themselves are affected by globalization, so too they enhance and sustain the process of globalization in terms of their own responses to the phenomenon.

With each wave of global forces, competition has intensified and structural adjustments have been needed. This is because drivers of globalization are often outside the control of individual enterprises or nations, creating both opportunities and threats and demanding a response by enterprises, governments and communities. Many of the forces and consequences of globalization will benefit tourism and the service sector. Technology, information and the reduction of boundaries have created new forms of service company, not only the large transnational corporations (TNC) such as the Disney Corporation, but also the small niche specialist that can take advantage of the Internet, international communications, and market positioning/targeting. This has clear implications for both the training and management of human resources. Table 10.1 demonstrates the growth of employment in services in the post-war years.

However, much of the writing on globalization is focused not on services, but on manufacturing, and the concepts are derived from traditional economic theory. The service sector's response to the challenges of globalization is quite different. Service organizations internationalize through overseas market presence while also demanding the right conditions within which to deliver the service – in terms of labour, technology and government regulation. It is more difficult to separate the enterprises' delivery of the service from management functions as the service is 'produced where it is consumed'. This enhances the role of labour responsiveness at the national level, while ensuring strict quality control through head office HRM, training and quality management procedures.

An important strategy in making openness work is for a country to develop its own internal, open complementary policies and institutions, such as a regulatory apparatus for capital flows, transparency for trade rules, civil and political liberties, free trade unions, non-corrupt bureaucracies, independent judiciaries and social safety nets.

Drivers of globalization: impacts upon hospitality and tourism

Creation of a global society means that tourism businesses have the ability to operate globally and many have opted for a competitive strategy of internationalization. Global enterprises view the world as their operating environment and establish both global strategies and global market presence. Globalization of the tourism sector has brought a significant expansion in the scope of workforce management and a host of organizational challenges including:

- the ability to deliver products and to transform ideas into services through innovative human resources policies and the training of staff, in particular, training models adopting international standards and delivered with local application;
- deployment and flexible hiring policies;
- knowledge and information dissemination;
- talent identification and development.

Destinations in the global market

Destinations compete with other destinations in the global market for international tourists. Seaton and Bennett (1996) explain that destinations are

Table 10.1	Year	USA	Canada	Australia	Japan	France	Germany	Italy
Percentage	1960	58.1	54.7	N/a	41.9	39.3	40.2	33.4
distribution of	1970	62.3	62.6	57.3	47.4	48.0	42.8	40.1
employment in	1980	67.1	67.2	64.8	54.8	56.4	51.9	47.7
services by selected	1990	72.0	72.1	70.7	59.2	65.3	57.6	58.6
countries, 1960–98	1998	74.6	73.9	73.9	63.2	71.4	63.1	61.4

Source: US Bureau of Labor Statistics

both physical entities and sociocultural entities and their tourism image is influenced deliberately by contact with the human resources based at the destination, as well as the marketing efforts of the authorities and tourism firms (induced sources) and by personal experience of consumers, word of mouth, history, the media, and so on (organic sources).

The international marketing of destinations occurs on several levels. The public sector is usually involved at national level but also at regional and local level. Cooper (1998) states that:

> At these levels the lead agency tends to be the public sector and this in turn has a number of implications for the marketing process. For example, the public sector often is not able to sell products, rather it relies on overall promotion of the destination to *pull* consumers to points of sale provided by the private sector.

There is also an issue here in terms of the fact that the public sector is poorly equipped to take leadership in this field. From the point of view of the human resources employed in the public sector there is a need for retraining in terms of marketing awareness and capability, and technology awareness and capability.

The private sector has it own interests to put forward, but as 90 per cent of tourism firms are small or medium-sized enterprises (SMEs) with limited resources, they benefit from and often rely on education, training and marketing efforts co-ordinated and directed by the public sector.

Successful destination policy rests on strong partnerships between the different stakeholders and on a coherent, consistent and collaborative marketing approach to create identities that are unique. Destinations must find identities that differentiate them from other destinations in the global marketplace. Therefore all public sector and private sector organizations must work in partnership to pursue differentiation strategies.

Partnerships can also be created at international level. For instance, the tourist boards of Scandinavian countries collaborate to bring tourists to the region by joint marketing actions. Once the tourists have decided to come to the area, then the countries compete with each other to convince them to visit their respective countries. In other words, they collaborate to create a market and compete to divide it up.

Globalization

Globalization, deregulation and technological advances

Globalization is more than just internationalization of firms. Borders are becoming increasingly difficult to define or to maintain. The world is shifting from distinct national economies to a global economy. Technological advances in areas such as transport and communications are helping to overcome physical distance and barriers and sustain the trend towards a global economy. The global movement towards deregulation and anti-protectionism championed by institutions like the World Trade Organization (WTO) has meant that barriers to entry into most markets in the world for international businesses are declining.

Capital flows freely between most countries, advances in technology have reduced communication costs, production is internationalized and populations are travelling to other countries for work and leisure. As a result, business is internationalizing and tourism is a leading industry in this globalization process. The most successful tourism businesses are those that understand how to operate in the international arena.

The impact of technological advances on the hotel, catering and tourism sector has been well documented in an ILO (International Labour Organization) Tripartite Report published in 1997. The report concludes that technological progress in the sector has developed at a rapid rate in the last few years and has resulted in increased labour productivity, a rise in demand for skilled workers but a fall in demand for other staff, higher salaries for skilled workers, a gradual standardization of the equipment and a significant reduction in equipment cost.

Technology in the hotel sector contributes to improving the quality of services and increasing the efficiency of the operation. Hotels' rooms are being equipped with computerized equipment familiar to customers and increasingly expected by them. Back office equipment allows managers to obtain speedy, accurate and comprehensive billing information; to provide detailed guest profiles to help improve service; to facilitate the analysis and control procedures; and to assist in the elaboration and monitoring of forecasts and budgets.

Probably technology has had the most profound effect on tourism distribution channels, notably the travel agency sector. Electronic on-line distribution, mainly controlled by the airlines that own global distribution systems (GDS), is changing the role of travel agents and the way they operate. Increasingly, airlines are distributing their products directly to the consumer, bypassing the travel agent altogether, for instance to the PC via the Internet, WAP Mobile telephones, through kiosks at airports or by developing a ticketless travel system where the consumer pays at the moment of travel. However, fears that the travel agent sector will disappear have not been realized. Rather, there has been a paradigm shift and the travel agency sector is re-evaluating its functions, providing a greater range of services and gradually adopting new methods of payment instead of merely relying on commissions, which principals are increasingly trying to avoid. This is particularly true for the corporate travel industry which may give away their commissions to their clients and bill them a service fee per ticket or a monthly fee for their services.

The public sector is also using new technology to manage and promote destinations in both the regional and global arena. Destination management systems (DMS) enable public sector organizations like local tourist boards to publicize and distribute products in a region through a central facility that provides on-line information and reservation facilities at representative offices in the home country and abroad and on the Internet. This means that even the smallest destinations can advertise their tourism products alongside major players at a minimal cost. The system allows the public sector to co-ordinate the activities of local stakeholders and therefore provides an important management tool for analysis of demand and supply.

Technology and increased competition are changing the way tourism firms are managing their human resources and this is having both positive and negative impacts on the tourism labour force. Tourism is prone to seasonality and new methods of human resources management implemented by tourism firms are largely based upon adapting working time to market fluctuations. While flexibility and the demand for skills are favouring certain categories of workers, a trend towards greater job insecurity and a rise in part-time contracts, irregular working time and consequently diminished remuneration and high rates of turnover is increasing. On the other hand, technology is replacing some of the mundane and routine jobs and has created new, more challenging jobs for some workers. The flexibility brought by the introduction of new technology and changes in human resources management has benefited certain categories of employees who can combine other activities (e.g. taking care of children) with their working lives.

Technology has introduced labour-saving equipment that has meant a reduction in labour requirements for certain departments (e.g. kitchen porters and service staff in hotels). On the other hand, the introduction of sophisticated equipment and of IT requires skilled operators and this leads to higher labour unit costs.

Employees in travel agencies are required to cope with sophisticated computer-based technology. There is evidence of an increase in small agencies and therefore an increase in job opportunities but the introduction of technology in larger enterprises is reducing the size of the workforce rapidly. Advances in e-commerce will seriously affect the size of the labour market for the sector. The traditional brick and mortar players are also fearful and predict that some 25 per cent will lose their jobs. Commissions will go down, although airlines will find other ways of giving credit to their best players. Reservations employees and customer service employees are most likely to suffer job losses. On the other hand, new jobs will also be created around IT needs, consulting and call centres.

Training staff to cope with new technology is proving to be a problem in the hotel, catering and tourism sectors. These are dominated by SMEs, which tend to regard training as a cost rather than an investment.

Globalization and international competition

Deregulation has strongly increased competition between firms and states. Firms do not base their policies only on the individual countries they operate in but also on pursuing global policies. These policies rely on free access to the market in each country. For this reason, the air transport sector has been transformed since deregulation.

Advances in communication technology, which enable firms to pursue global strategies, have greatly intensified international competition. These innovations are particularly significant for the tourism and hospitality sectors.

Globalization and industrial strategy

To cope with globalization and intensive competition, tourism and hospitality companies are adopting new industrial strategies and adapting traditional methods and techniques for the global arena. Diversification and sectoral strategies are no longer just applied within countries but also across borders.

Large tourism firms such as American Express follow globalization strategies. For example, American Express focuses on diagonal integration – developing a range of products in related sectors. The company operates in 130 countries, employs 73,000 staff and had a turnover on US$17.1 dollars in 1997. American Express developed its strategy focusing on two core businesses:

- Its travel agency network which comprises 3200 outlets world-wide including those that it acquired from Thomas Cook, Havas Voyage in France, Nyman & Schultz in Sweden, Schenker Reinus in Germany, Life Co in the USA and a joint venture with BBL Travel Amex in Belgium.
- Its financial services (such as travellers cheques and credit cards) with the American Express Bank and the American Express Financial Advisors. American Express has been involved in the tourism industry for a long time and has offered travellers cheques for many years.

American Express has become the largest business tourism operator in the USA, Australia, Canada, Mexico and France. It also has an important position in the United Kingdom and Germany.

The company's focus has been on a leadership strategy in national markets, aiming for at least 30 per cent of the sector; it has succeeded in reaching its objectives in 25 countries around the world. By following this strategy, American Express has become a global company.

Globalization and alliances

In recent years, one aspect of this discussion has been that it is increasingly difficult for individual companies to grow organically in the global arena without seeking partners and allies to develop their strategies. Quite simply, alliances are in a better position to control the market. With an increase in equity participation between firms, alliances can result in concentration and growth on a global scale. The impact of alliances on employment and labour relations is further developed in the section on collective bargaining.

Globalization and marketing

It is becoming increasingly apparent that globalization can lead to monopolies by giving alliance partners the power to set prices and conditions that can result in closing the market to competition. For instance, in the air transport sector, rules have been introduced to control the operation of GDS to prevent certain companies or alliances enjoying unfair advantages over their competitors. Here, the EU package of air transport deregulation was designed to avoid both pure monopoly and pure free market competition by creating a deregulated system with limits. This was as a direct result of observing the US experience of deregulation.

Paradoxically, a return to regulation will make it more difficult for firms to pursue globalization strategies, which is what made them very profitable in the first place. As Brown (1998) observes, if true globalization is to take place, future patterns will feature the downscaling of companies so that core large firms are increasingly unable to dominate the producers marketing globally.

Globalization and social inequality

An ILO report prepared in 1995 concluded that globalization boosts economic growth but risks widening social inequalities. On one hand, trade liberalization and increased investment stimulate economic activity, the production of goods and services and boosts productivity. Globalization holds the prospect of rising standards of living although the ILO warns that the process is neither instantaneous nor painless.

On the other hand, globalization and trends in global policies bring a number of social problems and create social gaps between workers that are in a position to benefit from increased competition and those that are left behind; these social issues include the following points:

- Increased competition and the adoption of new technology affects the lives of working people. According to the report, there will be increased demand for skilled workers, to the disadvantage of unskilled workers.
- It could be argued that trade is associated with greater labour market turnover, that may have detrimental consequences for workers with only modest transferable skills.
- The global trend is for a reduction in taxes for higher wages earners. The study carried out for the ILO report found that 67 out of 69 countries had witnessed a decline in the maximum tax rate on high incomes. This means that governments find it increasingly difficult to redistribute income to address rising income inequalities through the tax system.
- Developing countries with narrow export bases are vulnerable to changes in terms of trade.
- The ILO warns that there is a danger that short-term capital flows, far from being a mere reflection of economic fundamentals, will determine exchange rate fluctuation and, consequently, output and employment. Countries where the internal financial institutions are weak are particularly exposed to the volatility of short-term capital flows.

Few countries argue for protectionist policies to counter the effects of globalization, yet at the same time they want the benefits of globalization while minimizing its costs. The way forward is the strengthening of globalization's social pillar via education and training, social safety nets, the adoption of labour legislation that combines the need for economic adaptability with that of protection of vulnerable groups and observance of core international labour standards.

Liberalization of air transport

As a core sector of the tourism industry, the air transport sector has been at the forefront of creating competitive, open global markets, and freeing distribution and delivery channels (WTTC, 1999). In the last decade, changes in the global structure of the sector have been remarkable. To quote the United Nations Conference on Trade and Development (UNCTAD): 'The air transport industry is undergoing structural change due to the processes of liberalization, privatization, internationalization, consolidation and concentration of air carriers' (UNCTAD, 1998).

International Air Transport Association (IATA) passenger forecasts for the period 1999–2003 suggest a cautious growth forecast of a +5.02 per cent increase in passenger traffic. However, growth patterns do vary regionally depending on economic conditions; Latin America for example has had its growth rates downrated.

Background to the airline industry

At the Chicago Convention in 1944, legal guidelines were set for the international operation of airlines. The basic aim of the Chicago Convention was to facilitate international operation by fixing bilateral air services agreements between countries and, on occasions, at a regional level. The Chicago principles were based on the five freedoms of the air concerning air transport relations:

1. The first freedom concerned the right of an airline company of one state to fly over the territory of another state.
2. The second freedom concerned the right of an airline company of one state to land on the territory of another state for non-commercial reasons.
3. The third freedom related to the right of an airline company to carry passengers, mail and goods from its own state to another state.
4. The fourth freedom concerned the right of an airline company of one state to embark passengers, mail and goods in another state and carry them to its own state.
5. The fifth freedom related to commercial transport between two states other than the airline companies' own country's. This is a key condition for the growth of international air transport competition and liberalization policies based on multilateralization.

Although fifth freedom rights were agreed at the Chicago Convention, to date they have never really come into force. There have, however, been a number of bilateral agreements, such as the Bermuda agreement between the UK and the USA, introducing fifth freedom rights.

Today, liberalization of air transport is largely dependent on market access for private carriers and on cabotage rights. Cabotage is the right of an airline company of one country to embark passengers, mail and goods in another country and carry them to another point in the same country for a fee or for a leasing contract. Cabotage introduces competition between domestic and international carriers and is one of the most contentious issues of air transport liberalization.

Two international organizations play regulatory roles in the international air transport market: the ICAO and IATA.

- The International Civil Aviation Organization (ICAO) is a United Nations organization involved in air transport security, operational and safety requirements and technical regulation. However, it has limited control of the economics of air transport.
- The International Air Transport Association (IATA) is a non-governmental organization and its membership is a requirement for airline companies. It

complements the role of the ICAO and is concerned with the economics and finance of air transport (tariffs, operating conditions, facilities and the operation of a clearing house for inter-airline debts). It also arbitrates in inter-airline and airline–travel agency conflicts. IATA's main function has always been to set tariffs and trade agreements, although this role has reduced since deregulation.

Deregulation of the airline industry first appeared in the USA at the end of the 1970s and has had far-reaching consequences for the policies and strategies of all airline companies. Since that period, transformation of the industry can be attributed to three main factors:

1. Deregulation of the domestic market in the USA; the catalyst for a general lowering of domestic and international prices.
2. Strategies of airline companies towards tourism radically changed after the competition introduced by the charter companies in the 1980s. Companies like Laker, Wardair and Capitol, although they failed, transformed the industry.
3. Introduction of general discounts on scheduled airlines. Tour operators can now sell seats at very competitive prices to cover tourism demand, thus generating a new clientele for the airlines (this amounts to selling charter seats on scheduled airlines at an advantageous price).

These three trends have transformed the structure of the air transport market by reinforcing a process of deregulation first in the USA, then in Europe, and gradually to the other regions of the world.

In contrasting the American and European experience of airline deregulation, matters have been very different. In the USA deregulation saw a return of the airlines to a free market and Europeans watched with interest. They put into place a more conservative package of deregulation having learned the lessons of the US experience.

US Open Skies policy

The definition of 'Open Skies' adopted by the North American Department of Transportation principally concerns the establishment of links with European partners and aims to spread deregulation to all routes to Europe and within Europe. The five main clauses of 'Open Skies' include:

1. *Free access to all routes*: this is the keystone of all liberalization and deregulation air transport policies. It allows airlines to operate freely between different airports with the only limitation involving issues of security, financial guarantees and the availability of airport slots. Airlines can pursue strategies that will introduce new services to satisfy demand (i.e. the opening of new routes), close down routes or change prices and schedules.
2. *No restriction on capacity and frequency on any route*: this clause allows airlines to establish *hubs* without restrictions. The strategy rests on the freedom to greatly increase frequencies so that both transit and direct-

route passengers can be accommodated. Following deregulation in the USA, hubs have been established by the main US airline companies for domestic as well as international routes leaving the US, notably in Dallas, Atlanta, Chicago, New York, Miami and Denver.

3. *No restriction on operation in all international markets*: this reinforces the strategy based on creating hubs by allowing airlines to service intermediate points and to use an unlimited number of smaller aircraft to and from international gateways. The clause particularly favours airline companies with large fleets who can establish themselves quickly in new markets.

4. *Flexibility of tariffs*: airlines are able to fix their own tariffs, this being one of the most important conditions for the liberalization of air transport. The best performing airlines can service new routes and increase their market share. However, seat dumping must be prohibited to guarantee the long-term interests of the customer. Flexibility of tariffs has been mainly implemented by US airlines on North Atlantic routes.

5. *Liberalization of charter rules and elimination of restrictions on charters*: non-scheduled air transport plays a very important role in the development of tourism, in certain regions of the world, such as the Mediterranean region. It allows companies to address traffic problems during peak periods and to maintain pressure on keeping air fares competitive. Hence, 'Open Skies' also concerns charter companies, which must also have the same access to the market.

Faced with a restructured air transport market, European companies and companies from other regions in the world do not have the means to enter the domestic market of the USA. The policy of certain European airlines has been to buy into already established North American airlines, for instance KLM with NorthWest and Lufthansa with Continental.

Air transport liberalization in EU countries

In May 1992, transport ministers of the then 12 EU countries agreed to drop restrictions on air fare tariffs within the EU and, in April 1997, European deregulation moved one step closer to coming into existence when the 15 EU countries agreed to allow cabotage rights. These measures are designed to eliminate protectionist barriers within the EU. Prior to this date, airline companies in the EU had been required to have their fares approved by a supervisory authority. They are now able to set their own prices.

These measures have gone a long way to eliminate protectionist barriers within the EU. However, a compromise had to be reached between the more liberal countries, who wanted the measures implemented immediately, and those, such as France, Spain and Italy, who favoured a long transition period of six years. This deregulation process of air transport in Europe covers three main areas:

1. From 1993, airline companies could set tariffs freely. However, these can be opposed by the civil authorities of the countries concerned, particularly if they do not relate to the real cost of flying a particular

route. This regulation is to avoid the air fare wars that followed deregulation in the USA. Furthermore, certain European governments, like the UK's, also wanted to avoid extreme variations in prices.

2. The second area relates to the standardization of operating conditions for all airline companies in Europe. From 1993, all carriers in the EU could trade from any country within the EU if they conform to three conditions:

   • at least 51 per cent of the company's capital should be owned by citizens of member countries of the EU;

   • a minimum capital investment of 100,000 ECUs;

   • the aircraft should be registered in the country that issued its certificate of airworthiness.

   The objective behind setting these conditions is to prevent companies from non-EU countries setting up operation in the community.

3. The third area concerns *cabotage rights* (the right to operate domestic flights in other EU countries and to operate flights originating from other EU countries), which was allowed from 1 April 1997. The cabotage right is a fundamental step in European deregulation as it places European airline companies in a similar competitive environment to that of the USA.

The impact of airline liberalization

By removing barriers for entry, air transport liberalization has brought down the price of air fares for the consumer. Globally, air fares have declined 40 per cent in real terms – after adjusting for inflation – in the past 20 years. Cheaper and more efficient air transport has been the driving force behind the globalization of business and the development of long-distance tourism (Air Transport Action Group, 1994).

In Europe, this has resulted in the creation of new carriers known as 'low cost' airlines such as EasyJet from the UK and Ryanair from Ireland providing inexpensive 'no frills' services on popular routes. Ticket prices offered by these companies are up to 80 per cent below the prices of those offered by the major airlines. As a result, the major airlines with their strong financial backing have also entered the low cost market by either creating new airlines to compete or entering into partnership with local companies. BA has now become the second largest company operating domestically in France with its partnerships with the airline companies TAT and Air Liberté, and in addition its subsidiary airline – Deutsche BA – controls nearly 40 per cent of the German domestic market.

Air transport liberalization and employment

With this liberalization, there is a clear trend towards the creation of new jobs in the airline sector, even though technology is reducing the number of jobs in airline offices (see Table 10.2). There is also evidence that the impact of deregulation of airlines for human resources varies regionally. For example, although most European airlines have gone through a drastic downsizing and have laid off thousands of employees in order to cut costs, productivity per employee is still not up to the level of carriers in the USA or the Far East. On the other hand, the introduction of new carriers has created a number of direct and indirect tourism jobs, particularly in the regional carriers and the regional airports. For example, German estimates suggest that for each job created at an airport, a further two jobs are created in the neighbourhood, generating regional economic benefits.

In the period 1998–2008, the air transport sector is forecast to generate an extra 100,000 jobs. Many of these jobs will be generated in regional airlines, as liberalization encourages the growth of such routes. Future trends in the smaller airlines will be to increase employee motivation, and thus both retention and service quality.

Air transport liberalization and General Agreement on Trade in Services (GATS)

The air transport sector is governed by a global system involving 185 countries and 'hundreds of airlines, big and small, serving over 1.5 billion passengers a year' (IATA, 1999). The liberalization process, achieved by multilateral conventions such as the Chicago Convention, relies on a complex combination of 3500 bilateral agreements between nations. Traffic rights are based on 'reciprocal exchange of rights between states on the basis of fair and equal opportunity'. The GATS involves 135 countries committed to the 'most-favoured nation' (MFN) principle that ensures that all member countries receive at least the same treatment as that accorded to other countries with which they may have agreements but which may not be signatories of GATS.

It was felt at the Uruguay Round of GATS in 1994 that the inclusion of traffic rights in the agreement would allow states that had not opened their markets to other countries through bilateral agreement to automatically benefit from market access to countries committed to GATS obligations. Governments and airline companies were unwilling to upset a regulatory system based on

Table 10.2

Employment statistics (IATA) for 1987 and 1997

Employment category	1987	1997
Flight attendants	72,697	96,198
Mechanics	51,233	65,500
Aircraft and traffic service personnel	198,892	269,581
Office employees	40,690	38,354
All other	43,333	45,729
Total	457,349	586,509

Average compensation per employee ($)	1987	1997
Salaries and wages	35,205	49,972
Benefits and pensions	5,461	9,710
Payroll taxes	2,491	3,541
Total compensation	43,157	63,223

Source: IATA

bilateral agreements and controlled by the UN agency ICAO: in other words, that aviation rather than trade interest should continue to play the predominant role at state level (IATA, 1999).

There would seem to be no question that the air transport industry will continue to liberalize. The main concern is that liberalization will proceed in a manner, which produces the best balance of benefits to consumers, airlines and the public interest. Presently, just three ancillary services are included in the GATS in a separate Annex on Air Transport Services (IATA, 1999):

- aircraft repair and maintenance;
- selling and marketing of air transport services;
- computer reservation system services.

The main organizations responsible for air transport are now examining ways in which GATS could contribute to future air transport liberalization. According to IATA:

- There is a need to educate trade negotiators about air transport, and airlines about the GATS.
- The ICAO should continue to be the intergovernmental agency dealing with air transport.
- The Seattle Round offers the opportunity to clarify what is covered by the GATS and to develop better trade definitions for the air transport sector.
- Potential obstacles to market access, such as congestion, environmental measures and taxation, should be identified and addressed.
- The airline industry prefers to be dealt with on a sectoral basis and not as part of a package of services and goods.
- GATS is not the vehicle for fundamental reform at this time. Applying the MFN principle could even hold back liberalization if liberal treatment was not granted on a reciprocal basis.
- Finally, there is a belief that a hybrid system could emerge that would allow multilateral and bilateral arrangements to co-exist depending on national and regional preferences and needs.

The European Union

Tourism in the European Union (EU) comprises 2 million businesses generating 5.5 per cent of GDP, 6 per cent of employment and 30 per cent of external trade in services. According to the EU, there are 9 million people employed in tourism in the region. The EU has a number of initiatives and activities through programmes such as the Structural Funds, the sustainable development programme, the fifth research and development framework programme, the information society and the training and enterprise policy. These initiatives represented an investment via the European Regional Development Bank of €4.7 billion for the period 1994–9.

In October 1998, the High Level Group on Tourism and Employment concluded that with the right mix of policies and initiatives another 2.2 to

3.3 million jobs could be created in the tourism industry by 2010. This forecast will depend on the creation of a positive climate for investment, and the creation of conditions in which all stakeholders, including the social partners, can work together with a common aim.

The EU has selected the tourism sector as a pilot for the implementation of European employment strategy in the services sector, which centres on: 'Employability', 'Entrepreneurship', 'Adaptability' and 'Equal opportunities'. The strategy aims include:

- the pooling and dissemination of qualitative and quantitative information, including best practice;
- the development of user-friendly information tools on EU programmes and initiatives of interest to tourism;
- the development of a structured platform of consultation and co-operation with public authorities, the tourism industry and other interested parties.

(*Source*: European Commission – Web page dated 28 April 1999)

However, the rigid labour markets encouraged by trade blocs such as the EU with their market intervention on minimum wages, job protection legislation and social benefits are said to encourage high unemployment. In the EU the main concern of social policy is to combat this effect upon the labour market by focusing on those excluded from the labour market and the unemployed. The strategy involves investing in training, technology and quality production processes.

Community labour laws and social policy are impacting upon the tourism sector through the imposition of benefits for both seasonal and part-time workers via the Maastricht Social Protocol. This is challenging the previously *ad hoc* personnel policies of tourism companies across the community and in particular is impacting upon small businesses. The EU's policies on economic convergence are also attempting to integrate people excluded from the labour market. Policies stress the need for training, and the creation of jobs in new economic sectors such as technology.

Other EU policies include the ability to compete in global markets through the free movement of workers across Europe, harmonization of qualifications and tax incentives for education/training.

None the less there is evidence that in the UK, the degree of casual employment in the tourism sector severely restricts workers' rights and that employers manipulate legislation to their own advantage. Small organizations appear to go to greater lengths to avoid the legislation than do larger organizations.

The North American Free Trade Agreement

The substantial trade bloc formed by the USA, Canada and Mexico has had major impacts upon the labour market. For example, the North American Free Trade Agreement (NAFTA) is estimated to have cost the USA nearly 500,000 jobs between 1994 and 1998 due to imports from Mexico and Canada.

On balance, manufacturing jobs were hit the hardest, while NAFTA is estimated to have increased jobs in the service sector. Employers were also able to gain wage concessions from workers by threatening to relocate to Mexico. This impact of NAFTA is despite the inclusion of a 'side agreement' on labour designed to protect workers from the effect of competitive economic pressures from NAFTA. A Commission for Labour Cooperation has been established with offices in each country.

MERCOSUR

MERCOSUR brings together the economic power of four Latin American countries – Argentina, Brazil, Paraguay and Uruguay, with associated members Chile and Bolivia. In economic terms, it is the fourth largest trade bloc in the world with a population of 205 million people. Economic integration within this trading bloc is increasing the flow of labour across borders and encouraging the flow of goods and investment. The two basic principles of the union are:

1. Free trade with no tariff nor pre-tariff restrictions between the member States.
2. A common external tariff for third countries.

It was agreed to use the methodology created by the General Agreement on Tariffs and Trade (GATT) for the treatment of services. MERCOSUR is committed 'to accelerate its economic development processes with social justice', 'in order to improve living conditions of its inhabitants'. To tackle the impact of economic integration on labour, MERCOSUR has appointed a committee (Subgroup No. 11) to take charge of labour relations, employment and social security. This Subgroup is to tackle 'the undeniable occupational and social issues brought about by MERCOSUR' (MERCOSUR website, 1999). It recognizes that there will be some short-term negative effects of integration on labour. As with the Association of South East Asian Nations (ASEAN), there is real concern that economic advance and increased wealth will impact upon the environment.

ASEAN

ASEAN comprises ten member countries: Brunei Darussalam, Cambodia, Indonesia, Laos People's Democratic Republic, Malaysia, Myanmar, Philippines, Singapore, Thailand, and Vietnam.

The Fifth ASEAN Summit held in Bangkok in December 1995 set the current direction for ASEAN member countries to focus on:

- promoting sustainable tourism development;
- preservation of cultural and environmental resources;
- the provision of transportation and other infrastructure;
- simplification of immigration procedures;
- human resources development.

(Plan of Action on ASEAN Cooperation in Tourism).

In 1996, ASEAN published its strategy to develop a critical pool of tourism labour-power. This included the following issues:

- Travel and tourism is a human resource-intensive industry and the availability of a skilled and trained workforce is a crucial element in the success of any tourism development plan or programme. More importantly, people make a vital difference in the attractiveness of an ASEAN member country as a destination, in addition to the natural and cultural tourism assets, and thus investment in human resource development (HRD) is an integral part of any tourism plan or programme;

- For 1997, travel and tourism is expected to generate employment for 260 million people across the global economy. By the year 2007, the employment forecast is about 383 million, or well over 100 million new jobs created world-wide over the next decade. Regional analysis shows that Asia-Pacific generates the most travel and tourism-related jobs – 173 million, with an additional 21 million new jobs created by 2007 in Southeast Asia, with, e.g., Indonesia having 1.9 million new jobs.

- Against this backdrop, continued emphasis on tourism education and training is necessary, not only to sustain ASEAN's competitive advantage, but for the upgrading of skills to address the demand for improved levels of quality, service and professionalism in the tourism and travel industry.

The actions necessary for the implementation of these programmes will include the following:

- Co-operate in HRD activities (tourism) education and training), by sharing resources, skills and training facilities, e.g., networking of tourism training centres/institutes, provision of technical assistance and experts, emphasis on new job skills and new technologies, training of trainers, etc.

- Intensify public–private partnership in HRD activities, through relevant training bodies, the Association of South East Asian Tourist Associations (ASEANTA) and other regional/international tourism organizations such as Pacific Asia Tourist Association (PATA), World Travel and Tourism Council (WTTC) and the World Tourism Organization (WTO), etc.

- Conduct training needs assessments, to ascertain workforce needs and tourism HRD and skills requirements.

  (ASEAN web site, 1999).

Transnational business integration: foreign investments

Alliances

One of the consequences of an industry without boundaries like tourism is the opportunity to work with other organizations to pool resources, overcome limitations of resources and thus to gain competitive advantage in a fast-changing environment. This does not necessarily mean that tourism organizations will dispense with the advantages of limiting their operations as such boundaries provide an opportunity to focus. In fact, the process of forming alliances and co-operation provides a relational view of competitive advantage, to complement the traditionally held models of resource-based or industry-structure view. Here the concept of the *value chain* is pivotal. Traditionally the value chain has been seen as one in which each organization maximizes its own success across the value chain. In this traditional model information, strategies and resources are not shared and the chain is inefficient. However, in a globalized society the value chain represents the process by which organizations and enterprises are linked together to create products and services that have more value combined than separate. In other words, organizations look outside their own boundaries and aim to strengthen the whole web, not simply their own part of it.

Foreign market entry strategies: foreign investments, mergers and acquisitions, strategic alliances, franchising

Firms entering foreign markets are concerned with a variety of issues such as:

- which markets to enter, and the sequence and timing of entry;
- how to enter these markets;
- which competitive marketing strategies are to be adopted for success in the market.

Economic and sociocultural factors must be taken into consideration before a firm decides on a foreign market strategy. It must understand the barriers to free trade that may impede its entry into certain markets. This means that firms often enter markets sequentially, beginning with those where they have the most knowledge and progressively widening their geographic portfolio. However, there are also a number of barriers to entering new markets. For example, according to the World Tourism Organization (1998), 40 years ago international tourism was effectively free of taxation, but taxes in the tourism industry are now increasing in number and impact. Nowadays, taxes on tourism are seen as an easy source of income for governments. But this can seriously damage the competitive positioning of a destination and affect a foreign firm's decision to invest in a country.

Other factors, known as non-tariff barriers, should also be taken into account. These include:

- barriers to entry such as visa restrictions; document charges; ease of access;
- exchange controls; differential exchange rates;
- international regulations; technical standards (e.g. EU package holiday directives);
- health and safety regulations;
- government subsidies for local or competing firms.

International agreements such as GATS are aimed at liberalizing the international exchange of services and reducing trade barriers which restrict the freedom of service providers to operate in foreign markets and which restrict market access. GATS also facilitates the movement of people supplying services who require temporary entry to work in the tourist industry of another country.

There are also a number of social and cultural difficulties facing firms entering the foreign market. Obviously, an understanding of the language and of the culture is essential as well as knowledge of local conditions. One way around this is by employing local staff, but the skills needed to understand and operate the firm's business are not always available locally. Then there is the problem of adverse discrimination in situations where customers, suppliers and/or the authorities favour local firms over foreign firms. There are several ways for firms to enter a foreign market:

- direct investment or acquisitions;
- licensing/franchising;
- management contracts;
- joint venture;
- strategic alliances;
- exporting;
- build operate transfer

Direct investment and acquisitions

The advantage of direct investment over other methods of entry is that competitive advantage achieved by the firm in other markets, such as the technological leads it has over competitors, are not shared with local firms and can therefore be kept away from the competition for as long as possible. Furthermore, the foreign firm does not have to share profits with local firms, as it is obliged to when it grants licences to operate under its name.

On the other hand, this approach is the riskiest method of entering foreign markets and is costly in terms of capital and management resources. A foreign firm may also be at the mercy of the host government, which can erect hurdles in the form of supplementary taxation, the obligation of partnerships with local players and the compulsory hiring of local labour even if the necessary expertise is not available locally. Furthermore, a foreign firm will generally not have the local knowledge and contacts of a local firm.

One way of overcoming these obstacles is by taking over local firms already established in the domestic market. The international firm obtains 100 per cent ownership as well as a presence in the market, contacts in industry and with the authorities and benefits from the local expertise offered by the staff already employed by the acquired firm.

Therefore, the decision to pursue a full-ownership strategy in a foreign market will hinge on whether the firm's priority is on the ability to determine strategy without having to rely on the approval of partners or on the security of sharing risks. The UK tour operator Airtours has in recent years expanded in the international market by acquiring firms or merging with foreign firms.

From a human resources point of view, this type of arrangement can be beneficial where the acquiring organization leaves the management of the human resource (HR) function to local managers. In this way, local custom and practice prevail. However, if the acquiring organization decides to manage the HR function from a distance and to impose central principles and systems, this can lead to problems.

Licensing/franchising

Licensing is a contractual agreement whereby a firm allows another to sell and use its products for a fee. According to Terpstra and Sarathy (1991): 'a licensing agreement is an arrangement wherein the licensor gives something of value to the licensee in exchange for certain performance and payments from the licensee'. The licensor (the international company) may give the licensee (the national firm) one or more of the following things:

1. patent rights;
2. trademark rights;
3. copyrights;
4. know-how on products or processes.

In return for the use of the know-how or rights received, the licensee usually promises:

1. to produce the licensor's products covered by the rights;
2. to market these products in an assigned territory;
3. to pay the licensor some amount related to the sales volume of such products.

Licensing presents a number of advantages over direct investment. Products are introduced to a new market with little risk to the licensor. The licensee has the advantage of being able to sell a proven product already endowed with a reputation, which has been established abroad. This method of market entry is favoured by some international hotel corporations, e.g., Holiday Inn. Their international reputation guarantees licensees a ready-made market. Often, the licensor will also sell a management contract to provide the expertise to run the hotel.

The main disadvantage of licensing is that the licensor has less control over how the product is produced and delivered. However, from a local HR perspective licensing has the advantage of local management and hiring of personnel with the added benefit of the expertise of the franchiser and any good international practice that is passed on.

Management contracts

Some well-established international companies provide their expertise by leasing out management teams to run local firms. The contracting firm benefits from the knowledge and experience of the international firm as well as from their reputation for quality and good service. However, if the expertise is not transferred to the local firm, it will always be dependent of foreign management to operate. Ankomah (1991) showed that the tourism industry in certain regions of the world is subject to a dependency culture. In 1979, 72 per cent of all hotels in Sub-Saharan Africa were operated under a management contract, in Asia the figure was 60 per cent, in Latin America 47 per cent compared with just 2 per cent in Europe. These proportions are likely to have increased with globalization and the implications for labour in the sector are negative as management practices are often imposed, and expatriate management is hired to the detriment of local opportunities. None the less a number of countries have now put into place policies to ensure the gradual indigenization of the hotel sector and companies have to conform to certain local/foreign ratios of personnel.

Joint ventures

The difference between a joint venture arrangement and licensing is that the international firm takes an equity stake in the local firm. As a partner, it also has a say in how the business is run. Because of the capital investment and its management involvement the international firm's risk increases so it has a greater commitment to the business. The firm's foothold in the country is stronger because it is linked with a local firm. Furthermore, if the local firm has a strong interest in the partnership, the threat of expropriation from the authorities because of changes of circumstances decreases. Terpstra and Sarathy (1991) note that for this reason Club Méditerrannée takes minority ownership in the villages that it operates abroad. They always make sure that local interests are big enough so that if Club Med is thrown out, those interests will suffer first.

The rules governing the structure of joint ventures vary from country to country. Some countries will not allow international firms to have wholly owned operations on their territory and insist that local firms own over 50 per cent of shares in joint venture operations.

The international firm brings capital, technology, management and marketing expertise, training and consulting, and often a finished product, which can be introduced immediately to the market.

National firms bring local market knowledge such as language, culture and local business conditions; local marketing skills; and local contacts. They are often in a better position to break down barriers to entry in the market than their foreign counterpart because they are usually already well-established in the local market. Generally, the implications for labour are positive, although this is dependent upon the rate of technology transfer.

Strategic alliances

A strategic alliance is a co-operative relationship between businesses. It can be informal, such as a pooling of information, or contractual. It may focus on a business function such as marketing or research and development or be comprehensive and involve all the functions in the businesses.

Joyce and Woods (1996) define strategic alliances as 'partnership agreements (formal or informal) between two firms who may agree to co-operate in a variety of ways – including joint ventures, joint-product development, transfer of skills, etc. Horizontal alliances are where the partnership is between competitors'.

A strategic alliance is often created to enter a market. An agreement with a firm that has access to a foreign market may be the best strategy to gain a foothold in that market. Airline companies frequently adopt this strategy in order to build networks across different markets. Marketing alliances allow several airlines to act in some ways as a single carrier, sharing schedules and even profits in what amounts to a virtual merger without any of the financial and employment consolidations of a traditional corporate merger. By not actually merging, the airlines enjoy the benefits of their new consolidated markets without the need for regulatory approval or having to combine their workforces.

Exporting

Countries lacking the required skills base to develop and run their tourism industry often rely on expertise from abroad. Consultants in economic development, construction, architects, land use, marketing, management, banking, and so on, provide know-how and professional services. These services may be imported directly by governments or provided by international institutions in the form of technical assistance such as the World Tourism Organization. Hotel corporations export services and labour at all professional levels to firms in countries that do not have the available expertise to run and operate establishments aimed at the international clientele.

Labour is also exported as a commodity. For instance, several international hotels in the Middle East employ operational staff from Asia, particularly from the Philippines, because of their reputation for providing good service and for their technical ability. In all of these projects the transfer of expertise and technology is crucial if the HR sector in the host country is to benefit.

Build operate transfer (BOT)

This financing method was developed to encourage the private sector to invest in infrastructure development, for instance for the construction of power plants and roads, and their maintenance and refurbishment. The first BOT scheme was run in Turkey to implement a thermal power generation project. The concept allows the financing organization to set up a revenue-producing venture, operate it and reap profits for a limited amount of time – the payback period. At the end of the payback period, the operation is transferred to the community.

The BOT model is a way of mobilizing foreign capital and expertise. BOT allows developing countries with shortages of development capital to develop an economic sector. For instance, foreign firms are invited to build hotels in resorts and operate them for a number of years. There may be conditions attached such as training of local staff or building a facility for the community, but clearly this is an ideal arrangement from the point of view of transferring expertise, opportunity and technology to the host country.

The advantages and disadvantages of TNCs

A number of authors have highlighted the advantages and disadvantages of TNCs on the local economy and on local labour. These are summarized in Table 10.3. It is important to introduce policies aimed at maximizing the benefits brought by transnational corporations and minimizing the problems that they may cause.

Summary

This chapter has shown that the process of globalization not only reduces borders and barriers for trade between nations, but it also renders these boundaries permeable both within and between organizations. This increased permeability of boundaries has been brought about by a series of drivers operating on a global scale. The discussion has shown that some assert that globalization goes beyond the idea of permeating boundaries between nations and organizations, but also crosses the traditional borders of time, space, scope, geography, functions, thought and cultural assumptions. This in turn, demands both a different perspective and position to be taken on the human resource management and operation of tourism organizations. Of course, while hotel, tourism and catering organizations themselves are affected by globalization, so too they enhance and sustain the process of globalization in terms of their own responses to the phenomenon.

With each wave of global forces, competition has intensified and structural adjustments have been needed. This is because drivers of globalization are often outside the control of individual enterprises or nations, creating both opportunities and threats and demanding a response by enterprises, governments and communities. Many of the forces and consequences of globalization will benefit tourism and the service sector.

Table 10.3	Disadvantages of TNCs	Advantages of TNCs
The advantages and disadvantages of TNCs	Knowledge & skill transfer may be inappropriate and undermines competitive advantage of home country	Knowledge and skill transferred and industrialization promoted
	Local jobs destroyed and inappropriate jobs supported	Jobs created in the TNC and stimulated in other economic sectors
	Local competition eliminated, particularly SMEs	Competition stimulated to improve standards – exposure to international hotel chains requires locally-owned hotels to raise standards
	Destroys local culture and imports management approaches – The Disney Corporation was criticized for imposing its culture on the French for example	Effective management and 'modern' attitudes promoted
	Leakage of financial benefits to head office	Foreign exchange earned or saved by host nation
	Demand distorted and social inequalities promoted	Demand stimulated locally in terms of domestic tourism
	Interferes with host country politics creating a neo-colonial relationship – for example in terms of tour operators and destinations	

Source: Livingstone (1989), Kinsey (1988) and Smeral (1998)

References

Ankomah, P. (1991) 'Tourism skilled labour: the case of Sub-Saharan Africa', *Annals of Tourism Research*, 18, 433–42.

Brown, F. (1998) *Tourism Reassessed: Blight or Blessing?*, Oxford: Butterworth-Heinemann.

Cooper, C. (1998) 'Strategic perspectives on the planning and evolution of destinations: lessons for the Mediterranean', paper presented to the seminar: Tourism in the Mediterranean, University of Westminster, December.

ILO (1995) *In the Twilight Zone – Child Workers in the Hotel, Tourism and Catering Industry*, Geneva: ILO.

ILO (1997) *New Technologies and Working Conditions in the Hotel, Catering and Tourism Sector*, Geneva: ILO.

Joyce, P. and Woods, A. (1996) *Essential Strategic Management: From Modernism to Pragmatism*, Oxford: Butterworth-Heinemann.

Kinsey, J. (1988) *Marketing in Developing Countries*, London: Macmillan.

Livingstone, J.M. (1989) *The Internationalisation of Business*, London: Macmillan.

Seaton, A.V. and Bennett, M.M. (1996) *The Marketing of Tourism Products: Concepts, Issues and Cases*, London: International Thomson Business Press.

Smeral, E. (1998) 'The impact of globalization on small and medium enterprises: new challenges for tourism policies in European countries', *Tourism Management*, 19, 4, 371–80.

Terpstra, V. and Sarathy, R. (1991) *International Marketing*, Florida: The Dryden Press.

UNCTAD (1998) Expert meeting on strengthening the capacity for expanding the tourism sector in developing countries, June.

World Tourism Organization (1998) *Tourism Taxation: Striking a Fair Deal*, Madrid: WTO.

WTTC (1999) *Travel and Tourism. A White Paper*, London: WTTC.

Further reading

Anon (1997) 'NATOUR pushes for privatisation', *Travel Asia*, 11 April, 6–8.

Arthur Andersen (1997) 'Hospitality and leisure', *Executive Report*, Fall, 4, 2, 5–6.

Ashkenas, R., Ulrich, D., Jick, T. and Kerr, S. (1995) *The Boundaryless Organization*, San Francisco: Jossey Bass.

Baldacchino, G. (1997) *Global Tourism and Informal Labour Relations*, London: Mansell.

Baum, T. (1993) *Human Resources Issues in International Tourism*, Oxford: Butterworth-Heinemann.

Boudreau, M.C. *et al.* (1998) 'Going global', *Academy of Management Executives*, 12, 4, 120–8.

Bradley, F. (1991) *International Marketing Strategy*, Hemel Hempstead: Prentice-Hall.

Bradley, S.P., Hausmann, J.A. and Nolan, R.L. (1993) *Globalization, Technology and Competition*, Boston: Harvard Business School Press.

Buhalis, D. (1998) 'Information technology', in C. Cooper *et al.* (eds) *Tourism Principles and Practice*, Harlow: Addison-Wesley Longman.

Campbell, A.J. and Verbeke, A. (1994) 'The globalization of service sector multinationals', *Long Range Planning*, 27, 2, 95–102.

Canada News Wire (1998) Air Canada Press Release: Air Canada develops self check-in for airports, focuses on technology to simplify travel experience, available at /www. newswire. ca/April 1, 1998.

Cherrington, D.J. and Middleton, L.Z. (1995) 'An introduction to global business issues', *HR Magazine*, 4, 6, 124–30.

Coburn, C. (1995) *Partnerships: A Compendium of State and Federal Cooperative Technology Programs*, Columbus: Battelle.

Crotts, J.C. and Wilson, D.T. (1995) 'An integrated model of buyer–seller relationships in the international travel trade', *Progress in Tourism and Hospitality Research*, 1, 2, 125–40.

Dicken, P. (1992) *Global Shift*, 2nd edn, London: Paul Chapman.

Donaghue, J.A. (1999) 'Better bargaining', *Air Transport World*, 36, 3, 9.

Dunning, J.H. (1988) 'The eclectic paradigm of international production: a restatement and possible extensions', *Journal of International Business Studies*, 19, 1, 1–32.

Dyer, J.H. and Singh, H. (1988) The relational view: co-operative strategy and sources of inter-organizational competitive advantage', *Academy of Management Review*, 23, 4, 660–79.

European Commission (1999) *Enhancing Tourism's Potential for Employment – Follow-up to the Conclusions and Recommendations of the High Level Group on Tourism and Employment*, Brussels, 28.04.1999 COM (1999) 205 final.

Geller, L. (1998) 'The demands of globalization on the lodging industry', *Florida International University Hospitality Review*, 16, 1, 1–6.

Ghoshal, S. and Bartlett, C.A. (1990) 'The multinational corporation as an inter-organizational network', *Academy of Management Review*, 15, 4, 603–25.

Go, F. (1996) 'A conceptual framework for managing global tourism and hospitality marketing', *Tourism Recreation Research*, 21, 2, 37–43.

Hufbauer, G.C. (1994) 'The coming boom in services trade: what will it do to wages', *Law and Policy in International Business*, 25, 2, 433–8.

IATA (199) 'Liberalisation of air transport and the GATS', discussion paper, October, London: IATA.

ICFTU (1998) *A Possible Framework for Multilateral Investment: A Discussion Paper*, Brussels: ICFTU.

IH&RA Human Resources Think-Tank (1999) *Organizational and Workforce Challenges for the 21st Century*, Paris.

ILO Hotel, Catering and Tourism Committee (1989) *Productivity and Training in the Hotel, Catering and Tourism Sector*, Geneva: International Labour Office.

ILO (1994) *Backgrounder*, April, Geneva: ILO.

Johnson, J. and Valhi, J.E. (1977) 'The internationalisation process of the dirm: a model of knowledge development on increasing foreign commitments', *Journal of International Business Studies*, 2, 23–32.

Juyaux, C. (1999) 'Quality of service and working conditions in the European tourist and hospitality industry', *Cahiers Espaces*, 61, 25–9.

Kanter, R.M. (1995) 'Thinking locally in the global economy', *Harvard Business Review*, September/October, 151–60.

Kappor, T. (1999) 'The new hospitality', *Workplace Lodging*, November, 105–8.

Keller, P. (1996) 'Globalization and tourism', *Tourist Review*, 4, 6–7.

Korten, D.C. (1995) *When Corporations Ruled the World*, London: Earthscan.

Kotler, P., Bowen, J. and Makens, J. (1996) *Marketing for Hospitality and Tourism*, Englewood Cliffs, NJ: Prentice-Hall International.

Lazear, E. (1999) 'Globalization', *Economic Journal*, 109, 454, C15–C40.

Lee, B.J. (1993) 'NAFTA', *Business Korea*, 1, 6, 28–9.

Makridakis, S. (1989) 'Management in the 21st century', *Long Range Planning*, 22, 2, 37–53.

Marray, M. (1999) 'Small is beautiful', *Air Finance Journal*, 216, 60–1.

Melin, L. (1992) 'Internationalisation as a strategy process', *Strategic Management Journal*, 13, 2, 99–118.

Morrison, A. (1989) *Hospitality and Travel Marketing*, New York: Delmar.

Morrison, A. (1998) 'Small firm statistics: a hotel sector focus', *Service Industries Journal*, 18, 1, 132–42.

Normann, R. and Ramirez, R. (1993) From value chain to value constellation: designing interactive strategy', *Harvard Business Review*, July–August, 65–6.

Office for National Statistics (1997) *Business Monitor*, PA 1003, London: Stationery Office.

Organization for Economic Co-operation and Development (1997a) *Economic Globalization and the Environment*, Paris: OECD.

Organization for Economic Co-operation and Development (1997b) *Local Economies and Globalization*, Paris: OECD.

Organization for Economic Co-operation and Development (1997c) 'Partnership in tourism: a tool for job creation', issues paper for the conference in Rome, 27–8 October.

Organization for Economic Co-operation and Development (1998) *Globalization and the Environment*, Paris: OECD.

Paliwoda, S.J. and Thomas, M.J. (1998) *International Marketing*, 3rd edn, Oxford: Butterworth-Heinemann.

Palpacuer, F. and Parisotto, A. (1998) 'Global production and local jobs: issues for discussion', international workshop, Geneva, 9–10 March, ILO, Geneva.

Parker, B. (1998) *Globalization and Business Practice: Managing Across Boundaries*, London: Sage.

Pekar, P. and Allio, R. (1994) 'Making alliances work – guidelines for success', *Long Range Planning*, 27, 4, 54–65.

Poon, A. (1993) *Tourism, Technology and Competitive Strategies*, Wallingford: CAB.

Porter, M. (1990) *The Competitive Advantage of Nations*, New York: The Free Press.

Rosewarne, S. (1998) 'Globalization and the liberalisation of Asian markets', *World Economy*, 21, 7, 963–79.

Shaw, G. and Williams, A. (1994) *Critical Issues in Tourism – A Geographical Perspective*, Oxford: Blackwell, 143.

Shulze, G. (1999) 'Globalization and the economy', *World Economy*, 22, 3, 295–352.

Szivas, E. (1999) 'The influence of human resources on tourism marketing', in F, Vellas and L. Becherel (eds) *The International Marketing of Travel and Tourism*, Basingstoke: MacMillan Press.

Teare, R. *et al.* (1997) *Global Directions: New Strategies for Hospitality and Tourism*, London: Cassell.

Thomas, R. (1996) 'Assessing and influencing the policies of the European Union' in R. Kotas, R. Teare, J. Logie, C. Jayawardena and J. Bowen (eds) *The International Hospitality Business*, London: Cassell.

Thomas, R. (ed) (1998) *The Management of Small Tourism and Hospitality Firms*, London: Cassell.

Urry, J. (1990) *The Tourist Gaze: Leisure and Travel in Contemporary Societies*, London and Newbury Park: Sage.

Vernon, R. (1966) 'The product cycle hypothesis in a new international environment', *Quarterly Journal of Economics*, May, 190–207.

Wheatcroft, S. (1992) Airlines: reaping the rewards of globalization', *Transport*, 13, 6, 1–3.

Wilson, K. and Worland, D. (1993) 'Australia', in T. Baum (ed) *Human Resources Issues in International Tourism*, Oxford: Butterworth-Heinemann.

World Tourism Organization (1998) 'Government role in tourism management and promotion', *WTO News.*

World Tourism Organization (1999*) Marketing Tourism Destinations On-Line*, Madrid: WTO.

Key internet sites

http://www.abacus.com

http://www.aseansec.org

http://www.air-transport.org

http://www.barig.org/

http://www.british-airways.com/

http://www.cf.ac.uk//ccin//union/tuinter.html

http://epinet.org/

http://www.galileo.com

http://www.iata.org

http://ideas.uqam.ca/

http://www.ilo.org/

http://laborresearch.org

http://www.mercosur.org

http://www.quantas.com

http://star.arabia.com/

http://stats.bls.gov/

http://www.summersault.com

http://www.sabre.com/

http://www.world-tourism.org/

http://www.wttc.org/

http://atta.indian.com

http://www.prit.bc.ca/learning

http://www.ih-ra.com

http://www.isn.ethz.ch

http://www.oecd.org

http://www.nbbd.com/ecotourism
http://www.icomos.org/tourism
http://www.uvm.edu/~mmarquar/index
http://www.dfee.gov.uk/skillsforce
http://www.green-travel.com
http://www.iatm.co.uk
http://www.unicc.org/unctad
http://gopher.undp.org
http://gopher.unesco.org
http://ue.eu.int
http://www.worldbank.org
http://www.ecotourism.org

Globalization in tourism and hospitality:
Costs and benefits

Background

While inevitably discussion on tourism and hospitality centres around the major firms, it is the smaller family-owned or independently owned operations that dominate the market. Taking a European perspective, the European Commission has formulated an enterprise policy to support small and medium-sized enterprises (SMEs) and counter the advantages that the single market will bring to the larger operators at the expense of the smaller ones. The policy aims to (Thomas, 1996):

1. create a favourable business environment via the removal of unnecessary and costly administrative, physical and legal burdens (deregulation);
2. encourage cross-border co-operation between enterprises;
3. commit to providing business information and support.

EU Tourism Employment Policy

Based on the European Employment Strategy, a number of measures have been introduced to support tourism employment in SMEs:

- *Taxation*: in the White Paper on *Growth, Competitiveness and Employment* published in 1993 (Chapter IX), the EU pointed out the need to reduce the tax burden on labour to exploit the large potential for job creation in businesses offering local services and to reintegrate into the tax system 'businesses which have drifted into the black economy'. This has culminated in a proposal for a Council Directive (62 of 17 February 1999), which allows businesses in member states, meeting certain specific conditions and requirements, to apply for a reduction of the VAT rate on labour-intensive services for a period of time.

- *Labour market transparency*: the EU set up the European Employment Network (EUREN) to assist job seekers and tourism businesses to match demand and supply in tourism jobs and to improve worker mobility.

- *Greater recognition of education, training and work experiences in tourism across the Union*: The EU has introduced several directives to encourage the mutual recognition of professional qualifications acquired in EU member states. The EUROPASS training is one of the European Commission's projects to 'promote mobility in work-linked training, including apprenticeship'. It is a system which allows hospitality and tourism employers to understand the value and recognize different qualifications that exist in the EU as well as 'experiences acquired during work-linked training abroad' (Council Directive 1998/51/EC of 21 December 1998 in OJL 17 of 22 January 1999 p.45).

- *The European Social Fund (ESF)*: The ESF is guided by the priorities of the European Employment Strategy to develop 'employability, entrepreneurship, adaptability and equal opportunity'. The fund is allocated to develop human resources and improve the functioning of the labour market in the EU. The coming programme (2000–6) focuses in particular on initiatives to 'prevent and combat unemployment'. Countries which adopt National Action Plans of Employment (NAP) may benefit from certain incentives:

  - to improve the quality of training and the efficiency of employment services;
  - to develop closer links between the world of work and education and training institutes;
  - to foster systems for forward planning and for anticipating employment and skills needs, in particular in the case of new forms of work organization.

- *Dialogue between social partners*: this is a key priority of the European Commission and a framework agreement has been drafted on fixed-termed work, which is relevant to seasonal employment in the tourism industry. This has been particularly successful in the hotel and restaurant sectors under the 'HORECA' initiatives. The commission hopes to encourage similar platforms for dialogue for other sectors of the tourism industry (COM – 1998; 322 of 20 May 1998).

- *The EU Joint European Venture (JEV) Programme*: this is designed to encourage European SMEs to set up joint transnational businesses in the EU and to take advantage of the single market. The EU has created the JEV initiative to finance transnational joint venture projects up to a maximum of €100,000. The programme continues to develop with 45 projects submitted to the European Commission; 25 have been accepted, although until now these have mainly been in the manufacturing sector (EuroInfo Monthly 118/EN, April/May 1999).

Government support for SMEs

One example of government support originates from Austria where the government has introduced a set of policies to support SMEs and family-owned tourism businesses in order to provide a favourable framework for tourism development and reduce barriers for growth. These policies include subsidies to ensure that local capital is invested in the industry to counter the high share of foreign investment capital, and the promotion of co-operation to develop local synergistic networks to implement pilot projects such as multiple distribution channels, destination management schemes, joint offers and joint brand development. In Austria, the government is also promoting consultation and training to develop a more varied form of tourism in the country. However, it is up to the private sector to take advantage of the framework conditions put in place by the government and implement the initiatives (World Tourism Organization, 1998).

A second example comes from the UK. In its new strategy 'Tomorrow's Tourism', released in 1999 the British government claims that it is committed to creating the appropriate economic climate for enterprise and investment. It has introduced a number of measures to this effect including:

- the establishment of Regional Development Agencies (RDAs);
- the 'New Deal' where employers receive subsidies and training grants from the government if they employ the young and the long-term unemployed;
- changes to the benefit and tax system.

There is a particular concern that SMEs should be supported, and a number of measures have been introduced to help them stay competitive. These include:

- a new Enterprise Fund which provides £180 million over three years to help small firms with loan guarantees and venture capital arrangements;
- the development of Business Angels networks which bring together small firms needing funds with private individuals wanting to invest in growth businesses;
- the Enterprise Investment scheme;
- the identification of innovative ways in which banks might build partnerships with successful businesses.

Tourism and hospitality partnerships: a critique

At the heart of this discussion is the topic of partnerships. In an effort to contextualize this section of the chapter, prior research on partnerships has led to valuable insights into the behaviour of firms and the consequences for performance. Central to this critique is the need to explore two questions:

1. What factors influence the success of partnerships?
2. What is the effect of partnerships on the performance of firms/ organizations entering into them?

Researchers, Selin and Chavez (1995: 844) in an effort to encapsulate the term 'partnership' define it as 'an arrangement devoted to some common end among otherwise independent organizations'. Equally, a partnership can also be regarded as a voluntary pooling of resources between two or more parties in order to accomplish collaborative goals – in part, a mutual self-help group (Gulati, 1998). Analysis by Smallbone (1991) suggests six categories of activity for such agreements, namely basic activities (i.e. consultancy), finance, education and training, property, marketing and promotion, other activities (i.e. advice networks). He goes on to develop his study by presenting a typology of partnerships on the basis of three perspectives: strategic; intermediate; and local. In furthering Smallbone's discussion, the key dilemma emerging for the effective operation of partnerships is the matter of accountability, or lack of it. In order to attract a broad base of support, local democratic accountability may be regarded as necessary for success which would require a genuine sharing of control and decision-making, absent in many initiatives. In reviewing the literature, it would seem from the comments so far that three methodologically related themes run across these prior efforts (Gulati, 1998).

First, the unit of analysis is either the firm or the partnership. For instance, researchers have tried to identify the attributes of firms that influence their proclivity to enter into such an agreement, their choice and characteristics.

A second related theme has been examining the formation and performance of partnerships in an asocial context. This approach takes into consideration the role of the external environment (both general and industry), usually encapsulated within measures of competitiveness in product or supplier markets. For instance, from a transaction costs standpoint this translates to the argument that with increased competition, it is more likely that a firm will be exposed to bargaining and other forms of opportunistic behaviour, hence the desire to join tourism partnerships (Williamson, 1985). Resource dependence theorists, similarly, make the case that at intermediate levels of industry concentration, firms experience high levels of competitive uncertainty and frequently enter into partnerships (Pfeffer and Nowak, 1976).

Finally, prior research on partnerships has focused primarily on firm and industry level factors that impel firms to enter into such agreements. For instance, Andrews (1971) notes that the strategic actions of firms are the outcome of the match between a firm's existing competence and the availability of new opportunities. It would seem that researchers have primarily focused on the existing competence (or lack thereof) that may propel firms to enter into partnerships, and have generally paid less attention to the opportunities that lie in such agreements.

Evolving from these three research themes, a fourth category can be added that a facet of an organization's environment is its social network of external contacts. While economic factors have a tendency to be emphasized in the literature, such action does not take place in a barren social context. Underlying this fourth view is a quest for information to reduce uncertainty, a quest that has been identified as one of the main drivers of organizational action (Granovetter, 1985). There have been four broad foci of prior research on the influence of social networks: inequality, embedding, contagion and contingency. The essence of these foci is that the informational benefits from social networks can have ramifications for the development and ultimate success of the partnership itself.

Placed in a UK historical context, tourism partnerships between the public and private sectors are not a new concept. The idea goes back to Victorian times when many amenities, such as parks, gardens and promenades, were taken over by local authorities because the private sector could no longer run these loss-making businesses. In the 1980s, UK resorts in their decline stage attempted to rejuvenate by forming partnerships with the private sector. Today, these partnerships embrace policy, strategy formulation, development projects and marketing initiatives.

Selin and Chavez (1995) observe that partnerships have become a popular management strategy for accessing scarce resources in a time of financial constraint. However, they have also found that, in order to sustain and nurture partnerships, special skills are necessary with constant feedback and the reshaping of issues before they begin to lose their importance.

The consensus from the literature seems to be that 'partnerships' are the way forward, but what of the potential impacts of these partnerships? What are the real benefits, and what do they actually mean for resorts? What sort of problems are likely to be encountered?

Over the last few years this type of agreement of co-operation and collaboration has been actively sought by both the private and public sectors in the tourism industry. Partnerships are presently seen as a way to stimulate investment, creating both wealth and jobs. However, some cynics feel that the private sector is trying to get its hands on the local authority budget and the local authority is trying to supplement its declining revenue by taking more from the private sector than property rates.

As Selin and Chavez (1995) note, the importance of forging partnerships has become popular in tourism management circles, although very little empirical research has been conducted to explain the concept. There is potential for joint public and private sector co-operation, which must follow the formulation and acceptance of policy and strategy. Provision of basic infrastructure and the establishment of a system of consultation and co-ordination, which links the public and private sector areas of action are central to the process. Therefore, consultation between the public and private sectors is crucial. Each has a role to play since each contributes market knowledge and expertise.

Globalization and human resources

A key issue for the operation of transnational organizations is the means by which they transfer their corporate practice, philosophy and culture from headquarters to subsidiaries overseas. This is critical in the hotel, tourism and catering field where the essence of the product is international and the encounter with the consumer is intercultural. The rationale behind this comment is that global tourism organizations are dependent upon the delivery of the tourism product at individual destinations in culturally specific settings. In other words, while transnational corporations may appear to act as monolithic forces, their products depend upon delivery of the tourism service by personnel based at the destination, whether it be the hotel, the restaurant or the attraction. From a human resource management (HRM) perspective, the global tourism company is a caricature, where the reality is of locally derived management structures, behaviour and labour practice.

However, a global economy must be increasingly culture- and context-sensitive, not only in terms of delivering the product, but also in terms of flexible labour practices and the increasing likelihood of employing foreign nationals. In part it is through the medium of the informal labour markets that cultures and contexts will be preserved in the face of globalization. Globalization therefore poses two key problems for the labour market:

1. To gauge the balance between international HRM procedures and locally specific practices. Here, the HRM strategies of global corporations can be characterized as:

   - ethnocentric – characterized by central/corporate control across the organization, irrespective of context;
   - polycentric – characterized by a *hands-off* approach where each subsidiary develops its own approach, guided by local conditions and practice;
   - geocentric – characterized by a compromise between the two approaches above – subsidiaries engage with the corporate approach, yet are allowed sufficient latitude to deliver products within the local context.

2. To gauge the balance between internal *organization-driven* HRM procedures and the local/regional market *customer-driven* needs of the HR function. Here we can envisage the corporate culture of training manuals, standardized requirements of employees, corporate culture, corporate ethics and in-house literature cascading down from head office to meet the local informal organization. At the local level, traditions and social practices of the employees activate the global corporations' products and projects. For the hotel sector, the bottom line is derived from customer satisfaction levels elicited from quality audits where local nuances in service, menus and entertainment may be more sought after than homogenized international cuisine and cabaret.

The development of an informal labour market and set of practices is particularly prevalent in small-island/small-state destinations in response to the entry of hotel chains, international airlines and food franchises. Baldacchino (1997) has researched the informal labour markets in Malta and Barbados concluding that jobs in the informal economy are characterized by:

- the need to develop a network of contacts both within and outside the organization;
- the need to develop a set of specialist *indispensable* skills;
- striving to enlarge the scope of the job;
- an ability for multi-skilling or role multiplicity;
- the ability to manipulate organizational structures.

He also maintains that recruitment within the informal labour market is characterized by:

- word of mouth;
- personal recommendation;
- internal advertising within the firm; and more unusually
- external advertising.

Here, management avoids expensive recruitment costs through an informal labour market operating in tourism destinations through a market of personal recommendation and referrals. In other words there is an extended internal labour market where companies can save on training costs and staff turnover is low. This situation occurs typically in small-scale island destinations or small states such as Malta or Barbados.

Industrial relations in the informal sector are characterized by a dearth of research, not surprising given that the sector is by definition non-unionized and where the relationship between worker and manager is a flexible and personalized one. However, such social situations where personalization of the labour relationship develops between manager and managed does create problems in terms of discipline and over-familiarity. In other words, labour–management relations appear to be more prone to person-specific rather than office-specific negotiations.

Personnel policies: impact on productivity

Productivity in the services sector is difficult to measure and definitions and approaches vary internationally. The most comprehensive data are found in the USA where, generally, productivity is increasing, meaning that workers can achieve wage increases without fuelling inflation, although this will demand strong worker bargaining power. In the hotel, catering and tourism sectors, productivity is not showing the same pattern, and in certain sectors it declined in the late 1990s (see Table 11.1).

In part these figures can be explained by:

- changes in the measurement of productivity over the two decades;
- the fact that airlines have reached a technology frontier whereby previous productivity gains could not be sustained;
- weak bargaining power of the employees in the tourism sector leading to over-hiring and reliance on immigrant labour; and
- technology has not delivered the productivity gains expected.

Although technology can be identified as a key driver of globalization, there is an increasing debate as to the 'productivity paradox' related to the increased investment in IT in the tourism sector, set against a decline in productivity. This is particularly the case in contrast to manufacturing. In manufacturing, IT has been used to replace labour, whereas in services it is often utilized in conjunction with highly-paid personnel. To quote Shaw and Williams (1994: 143): 'This is

Table 11.1	SIC Code	Industry	1987–1997 output per hour	1996/1997 % change output per hour
Productivity in the US economy	4512/13/22	Air transport	1.1	0.9
	58	Eating/drinking place	−0.6	−1.6
	701	hotels/motels	0.8	−0.6

Source: EIU

not to say that there is possibility of substitution of capital for labour. Bagguley (1987) argues that in the UK there have been two technological revolutions with catering in recent decades. The first was the introduction of automatic dishwashers in the 1950s and 1960s, which led to a reduction in the number of kitchen assistants' jobs. The second revolution was the introduction of sophisticated methods of pre-preparing foods, such as dull-cook technology and microwaves, in the 1970s and 1980s. This led to the de-skilling of kitchens and an increase in the number of kitchen assistants at the expense of chefs. Linked to this, there has been an enormous growth of fast-food outlets based on both technology and new work practices which, for example, have allowed companies such as McDonald's to reduce their labour costs to, reputedly, no more than 15 per cent of sales'.

In the different sectors of the hotel, tourism and catering industry productivity rates vary. For example, in the airline sector globalization will encourage convergence of both productivity and wage rates among workers internationally – for example, it will be increasingly difficult for Air France workers to be half as productive as United Airlines employees and yet be paid higher wages. Companies will expand their operations in locations where productivity is good and desert those where the balance of productivity and wages is seen to be poor. In 1999, employee productivity in the airline sector grew by 3.1 per cent, and inflation-adjusted remuneration per employee grew. In the late 1990s, the reduction of in-flight catering through such innovations as budget airlines has impacted upon the structure of employment in the airlines.

Personnel movements

In a globalized economy, the skills of the workforce are going to be the key competitive weapon. Brainpower will create new technologies, but skilled labour will allow enterprises to employ the new product and process technologies being generated. At the same time, transnational corporations (TNCs) will run their various operations from the point at which there is the greatest pool of expertise. Globalization has generated new concepts and terminology for the HR sector through some of the obvious impacts of creating:

- a culturally diverse workforce and the changing composition of the workforce;
- changing work patterns including telecommuting, electronic workplaces and use of the Internet;
- greater awareness of ethical and legal issues in the workplace.

This means that globalization is thus driving personnel and HRM departments to obtain and retain an effective workforce by:

- valuing and properly managing workforce diversity;
- accommodating a highly diverse workforce in terms of work arrangements, child care, dependent care, job sharing, dual-careers, disabilities;
- the need to offer alternative work schedules, employee assistance and other service programmes;

- the need to balance employee rights and business requirements;
- the need to comply with an increasing number of government regulations in human resources;
- the need for increased human capital investment;
- the need to link HRM and its contributions to the bottom line of the organization.

Personnel policies for TNCs in the hotel, tourism and catering sector, for example, have to recognize that the previous approach of standardizing procedures and training policies and applying them to hotel units, restaurants and other subsidiaries overseas is increasingly outmoded in a new climate of empowerment and retention of staff. This is particularly the case given that in many parts of the world where the industry is expanding there is an acute shortage of qualified staff to fill positions. New personnel approaches will:

- empower staff;
- reward and reinforce performance;
- enable employees to perform;
- enhance the customer experience;
- generate useable data; and
- provide each employee with the responsibility to do the job.

TNCs increasingly trade internally and move assets around the world internationally. However, their very size and the fact that increasingly key functions are outsourced mean that the organization of the future is likely to be a loose network of smaller businesses working together on project-based assignments. This allows the mobilization of both talent and information to achieve the organization's objectives. An internationally focused HR policy must therefore:

- educate the workforce in cultural sensitivity and global orientation;
- educate and orientate senior management on the international strategy of the TNC;
- encourage staff to adopt and utilize IT;
- adopt flexible HR training and implementation strategies in terms of software development, language translation and extranets;
- ensure transfer of information and technology through networks from HQ to subsidiaries;
- recognize the various stages of internationalization that companies go through;
- create and implement policies for hiring of expatriate staff and foreign workers;
- train staff to manage international assignments, be aware of cultural differences in overseas locations (for example, in negotiation styles and dress codes), and different labour laws and legislation in the workplace.

Globalization also leads to the demand for highly skilled labour, generating 'world-class quality'. TNCs can only succeed by developing the skill base of their employees through empowerment and training. In the long term, chasing cheap labour around the world is both costly and counterproductive. Globalization, combined with competitive recruitment environments and government legislation, is leading to a new generation of personnel policies. This means that such a process is impacting upon the operation of personnel departments. Increasingly, personnel managers have to be aware of global demographics, skill shortages, training needs and supply, unemployment patterns and wage rates, as well as the variations of national policies on health and safety, occupational standards, dismissal, discrimination and workers' rights.

An important issue is the location of the international personnel function, whether at corporate headquarters or in each of the local companies. Internationalization strategies demand a change in personnel policies and strategies. In particular, this implies:

- management commitment to transnational strategies;
- worker education in the tactical procedure necessary to achieve transnational operations;
- development of IT skills and procedures to support transnational operations through knowledge and information transfer to create the virtual learning organization.

Specific issues faced by HR departments in the face of global companies are:

- consolidation of the workforce;
- development of national contracts;
- on-site management of staff;
- changing recruitment practices – e.g., use of the Internet;
- temporary hiring solutions.

Mergers and acquisitions: impacts on HRM

In both the accommodation and the airline sector, transnational business integration has grown significantly during the last ten years due to globalization. For the accommodation sector, internationalization has allowed companies to grow at a rate acceptable to shareholders, while not over-building in their domestic markets. In the late 1990s, Latin America and Asia have seen significant developments by international hotels companies, with the consequent squeeze on the labour market for trained personnel. The consequences for the labour market are:

- the need to upgrade training institutions and programmes;
- employee retention schemes are being put into place including cash incentives, day care schemes for children and educational assistance, and board-level recognition of the value of employees.

It is increasingly evident that international companies are specializing in short-term international placements for staff, identifying international training needs. In part, this is also in response to an increasing number of workers making themselves available for temporary assignments. Globalization has led to mergers and acquisitions across the tourism sector. In the airline sector the implications for labour are both positive and negative. On the positive side, mergers and alliances create an internationally aware and mobile workforce where international standards can be set. On the other hand, the use of engineering hubs in regions of cheap labour and the manipulation of labour laws internationally are creating concerns among unions.

It is therefore clear that globalization has prompted a range of innovative personnel training strategies and approaches to complement these trends:

- Company performance is entirely dependent upon the expertise and attitude of its staff. Their personnel policy has three pillars:
  - put in place the right organization to deliver business strategy;
  - support, develop and train staff to deliver the strategy;
  - create an organizational culture that recognizes and rewards performance.
- A range of customer contact skills courses and training packages have been developed in different countries. These are now acceptable on an international basis through such programmes as the Canadian Superhost Face to Face programme designed to reflect the realities of the tourism industry in the twenty-first century. Other countries have adopted the programme as in the UK where the programme is known as Welcome Host.
- The Swiss leading hotels group has developed an interactive training approach based on interactive CD-ROMs to improve staff attitude.
- Sheraton have developed an intercultural communication training package designed to familiarize employees with the needs of the Japanese language and culture to build guest satisfaction.
- In Aruba, the Costa Linda Beach Resort has taken the international principles of quality management and implemented them to incorporate the basic habits, values and culture of the island.
- Continental Airlines have used training and performance-based payment schemes to raise its service levels from one of the worst rated airlines to one of the best. The pay-for-performance scheme operates through profit sharing and equitable distribution, providing employees with a sense of ownership of the change process.
- Ansett, the Australian airline, has put into place an HR policy to attract and retain senior management through reward, development and succession planning programmes.

Effects of transnational business on small enterprises

Its been stated that the SME sector has demonstrated that it contributes positively to economic and social development by supplying goods and services, providing necessary avenues for self-employed workers, mobilizing savings and accelerating regional development. In tourism and hospitality, small firms are in the majority. According to the European Union conference, Agenda 2010, held in May 1998:

> In European tourism, SMEs account for 90 per cent of all businesses and more than 94 per cent of them are micro operators employing less than 10 individuals. There are some 2.7 million SMEs in tourism (West Central and Eastern Europe) employing some 17 million people. This compares with a only a few hundred large organizations defined as employing more than 250 people each, although collectively the turnover of large firms represents an important share of most tourism markets.

Smeral (1998) warns that globalization is increasing the pressure on SMEs. He explains that the potential of SMEs for realizing economies of scale is very low and the use of computer reservation systems (CRS) has not spread significantly. Many restaurant and hotel businesses are sources of side income for people engaged in the agriculture sector. Furthermore, SMEs are disadvantaged because of their high unit average costs with respect to production.

Because of the preponderance of SMEs in the industry, European tourism is particularly vulnerable. International receipts per arrival in Europe are approximately 20 per cent lower than the world average. Although Europe is the largest of the world's tourism regions, it is losing market share. The region's share of world tourism arrivals will have fallen from 73 per cent in 1960 to 45 per cent by 2020 (World Tourism Organization, 1998).

Smeral explains that this is a result of the market expanding. In the last two decades, many new destinations have entered the tourism market and developed their industries. The traditional customers of the European SMEs – originating from domestic and the (neighbouring) foreign markets – have more options on how to spend their vacation (mostly in the form of the consumption of standardized mass products with a rough degree of differentiation). He points out that it is the destinations with the highest number of SMEs that are suffering the most. In terms of international revenues (tourism exports) Denmark (–27 per cent), Austria (–23 per cent), Germany (–17 per cent), and Switzerland (–16 per cent) suffered in the period from 1990 to 1996 with the greatest losses in market share; Europe as a whole lost only 10 per cent of its market share in the same period.

As well as coping with the effects of globalization, SMEs need to adapt to new business conditions. Here, technology is a further issue, as SMEs will increasingly benefit from IT through using the Internet and its advantages in providing 'market reach' for SMEs, and alliances with IT companies and providers who design e-commerce services tailored to SMEs.

SMEs are under pressure to install new systems and to train their staff to use these. However, in terms of HRM, SMEs find it difficult to invest in training or staff development because they not only see this as a cost rather than an investment, but also their investment resources are limited, and many in the hotel, tourism and catering sector are managed by a generation who have had no formal training in the sector.

Strategies for SMEs' competitiveness

SMEs need to pursue strategies to ensure that they survive in a globalized market. In the manufacturing sector SMEs form global networks where production activities are performed at various locations. In other words, SMEs in an area may specialize in producing certain complementary elements for an overall product, for example, businesses specializing in producing software or computer chips in Silicon Valley, California. The benefits of co-operating include (Pyke, 1994: 3–4):

- the advantage of achieving economies of scale;
- the sharing of information about the latest techniques and technologies might be an essential mechanism for keeping small firms up to date and competitive;
- more rational and efficient distribution of activities, thus increasing the size of productive capacity;
- facilitating political cohesion among small firms allowing them to press for their specific interests whether at regional or national level.

These associations are known as *clusters* or, in the hotel industry, *consortia*. A cluster is a grouping of related business by either geographical region or industry. There are several types of clusters. Porter (1990) identified the *industrial cluster* where businesses are related because they are buyers and suppliers of each other, or they use common technologies, distribution channels or labour pools. *Regional clusters* are geographic agglomerations of firms in the same or closely related industries.

Compared with the manufacturing sector where goods may be produced globally, tourism services are consumed where they are produced, at the local level. The fragmented and interdependent nature of the tourism product means that various agents with influence on the product offer must co-ordinate their operations to provide the overall experience. Porter's concept of the value chain presents the notion of interlinked economic activities that may belong to different industries, i.e. the different sub-sectors of the tourism industry: hotels, restaurants, shops, local transport, and so on. It is important for each stakeholder to consider the development of the network as a whole as a primary objective. Competitive advantage depends on organizational competences and capabilities, and in most networks lead firms play an important role. These are generally the larger, wealthier firms in the network and often have political influence. In a tourism resort, the lead firm, for instance a big hotel, may support the costs of developing and running a public facility, sponsor local events or provide marketing actions for the area.

In tourism, the public sector has a co-ordinating role to support the activities of the private sector. To compete in the global tourism market, SMEs must be integrated in a destination management system that is supported by public tourism policies. Smeral concludes that:

> In order to alleviate the impacts of globalization on SMEs, the public and private sector should implement flexible production technologies, as well as holistic destination management policies aimed at delivering innovative and

"commodifiable" experiences to meet "post-modern" tourism demand. The support for building highly integrated destinations with flexible operating network alliances is an important measure to help SMEs compete with global players and restore their capabilities to deliver significant contributions to income and employment creation.

Overseas firms and local SMEs

When a well-established foreign firm chooses a site or area to develop business activities, it may influence the way local firms operate in a number of different ways. A large investor may oblige the authorities in a potential area of the investment to comply with certain conditions or even change local laws before going ahead with the development. For instance, when Ryanair, the low cost airline, opened up the London to Carcasonne (South of France) route, it insisted that the local authorities in Carcasonne improve infrastructure at the airport, organize transit facilities and provide new services (e.g. to deal with the transport of skis) for the expected volume of passengers it would bring.

Large tour operators have strong (maybe too strong) influence on the way hotels operate in the destinations they feature and the prices that they charge, particularly in mass market beach resorts and in short-season resorts (e.g. ski resorts). In general terms, as the presence of a tour operator grows at the destination, the greater its influence becomes.

Tour operators may also impose conditions on local suppliers. For example, Explore Worldwide, the adventure tour operator from the UK, has a strong commitment to protecting the environment of the destinations it features. Part of that commitment includes ensuring that their suppliers comply with their norms *vis-à-vis* protecting the environment and use environmentally friendly equipment, products and materials.

However, developments brought by foreign firms can seriously affect local communities and local businesses. The destruction of a series of villages, as took place on certain coasts in India or in the Calabarzón region in the Philippines and in many other places, creates a detrimental and irreversible situation; self-sufficient local populations are simply expelled, and receive very little compensation (Valayer, 1999).

Foreign companies that operate a franchise system can also maintain control over how local franchisees run their business. Uniglobe Travel has developed a world-wide travel agency franchise system with over 1150 franchises in 16 countries. Uniglobe provides tools, systems and support, such as professional training, a business consultation service from 18 regional offices, software programs, automation agreements with computer reservation system providers and a preferred supplier programme in which a package of incentives and commissions are negotiated with principals. A franchise owner association allows Uniglobe franchisees to meet and exchange ideas.

Employment and working conditions

Employment in the tourism and hospitality industry is notoriously insecure because of seasonality, fluctuations in demand, high numbers of part-time and temporary jobs (ILO, 1989; Jafari, 1990) as well as a substantial proportion of jobs in the shadow or grey sector (Szivas, 1999). However, there is evidence of greater job stability for core tourism workers at management and supervisory levels than for peripheral semi-skilled and unskilled workers.

Atkinson (1984, cited in Shaw and Williams, 1994) suggests that the internal labour market of companies consists of two main categories of workers: core workers and peripheral workers. Core workers are full-time permanent employees enjoying job security and high earnings. They tend to be managers or professionals in short supply externally and therefore in great demand by employers who pay well to retain them. They are able to perform several functions and Atkinson attributes to this group the characteristic of *functional flexibility.*

Another group identified by Atkinson form the secondary labour market comprises generally semi-skilled full-time workers – this he termed the peripheral group. There is a large turnover of staff in this group. Employers have a greater pool of potential workers to recruit from and therefore have an advantage in pay negotiations. This means that jobs in this category tend to be less secure, with few promotion and career prospects. They are therefore according to Atkinson *numerically flexible* (see Figure 11.1).

A second peripheral group, also numerically flexible, includes:

- workers on short-term contracts;
- temporary workers;
- part-time workers;
- workers on government sponsored training schemes;
- job-sharers;
- people working from home.

Figure 11.1

Functional and numerical flexibility

Self employment

Agency temporaries

First peripheral group
Secondary labour market
Numeral flexibility

Core group
Primary Labour

Second peripheral group

Subcontracting

Shot-term Public subsidy Delayed recruitment Job-sharing Part-time

Increased outsourcing

Source: Atkinson (1984), quoted in Shaw and Williamson (1996)

Tourism relies heavily on the flexibility offered by the secondary market, particularly in seasonal destinations. Many of these jobs are only available during the tourist season and employers can hire and cut back when needed.

Employers also have the option of sub-contracting work to other companies (e.g. tour operators may often sub-contract elements of the tour to other tour operators to perform – like meeting and greeting clients at an airport). They may also hire self-employed people to perform certain functions (tour managers are usually hired by tour operators on a tour-by-tour basis) or bring in temporary workers from specialized agencies (in peak season, travel agents often need more qualified staff to operate the telephone lines).

However, Urry (1990, cited in Shaw and Williams, 1994) suggests that Atkinson's model does not completely relate to the tourism industry. First, he explains that core workers in tourism do not tend to be functionally flexible. They normally perform very specific jobs such as receptionist or food and beverage manager and cannot perform other job functions. Second, temporary workers often do the same job as core workers and are brought in at peak periods.

An alternative way of looking at labour markets in tourism is provided in the Simms *et al.*'s model (1988), which identifies the characteristics of strong internal markets and weak internal markets. The structural features of strong and weak internal labour markets are as follows (*ibid.*: 6; also in Shaw and Williams, 1994):

- specified living standards;
- single port of entry;
- high skill specificity;
- continuous on-the-job training;
- fixed criteria for promotion and transfers;
- strong workplace customs;
- pay differentials remain fixed over time.

The standard features of weak internal labour markets are:

- unspecified hiring standards;
- multiple ports of entry;
- low skill specificity;
- no on-the-job training;
- no fixed criteria for promotion or transfer;
- weak workplace customs;
- pay differentials vary over time.

Research conducted by Simms *et al.* (1988) found that tourism is characterized by:

- weak labour internal markets;
- high levels of on-the-job training;

- small numbers of promotions and transfers;
- *ad hoc* management practices;
- high use of labour from the external labour market;
- a high degree of labour turnover.

Unskilled workers and pay

A number of authors have noted that in the hotel and catering industry, low pay predominates (Riley 1993; Baum, 1993). A survey conducted by Riley showed that 64 per cent of the workforce falls into the operative or semi-skilled and unskilled category (cited in Baum, 1993). Riley notes that at that level there are a number of downward pressures on pay. The high pool of workers seeking unskilled jobs in the hospitality industry means that it is a buyers' market with managers/owners holding power in wage negotiations. Management is also more likely to *deskill* when demand fluctuates. To quote Riley: 'As it is easier to adjust the supply of unskilled labour than that of skilled, it is always in the interest of management to deskill. The ever-present fluctuation in customer demand creates an ever-present incentive to deskill'. He further explains that productivity does not improve with permanent status. Seniority in the job is therefore rarely rewarded and this also contributes to keeping wages low. Riley listed the following forces as downward pressures on pay in the sector:

- the likelihood of a surplus of unskilled labour;
- the need for short-term adjustment in labour supply;
- the opportunities to deskill labour;
- mobility for those wishing to learn or advance encouraged by the hierarchical structure of the industry;
- the supply of skilled labour from vocational education;
- the transferability of skills, allowing workers to emigrate to other markets without loss of material benefit;
- a lack of incentive to reward long service as productivity is not related to job tenure.

According to research conducted by Manchester Metropolitan University, UK, there is a higher incidence of worker dismissals in the hotel sector than in other sectors. The study showed that in 1996, 67 per cent of hotels surveyed dismissed staff compared with 43 per cent for all industries. The common reasons for sacking staff were misconduct followed by lack of ability. Just 20 per cent of workers dismissed attempted to get the dismissal overturned through the courts. The study identified the causes as:

- high percentage of casual and part-time staff in the industry;
- low trade union representation;
- lack of employment rights means that few ex-workers pursue claims through industrial tribunals.

Legislation

Although employment laws differ from country to country, most countries abide by international standards such as the ILO's Conventions and Recommendations. A convention is a legal instrument regulating some aspect of labour administration, social welfare or human rights, and a recommendation is similar to a convention except that it is not subject to ratification, and provides more specific guidelines (ILO, 1994). In 1994, there were 174 conventions (6000 ratifications) and 181 recommendations.

Member countries of economic trade blocs may abide by common conventions. Member states of the EU, except for the UK, adopted the Social Charter in 1989 which aimed at achieving social as well as economic cohesion in the EU. The commitments in the charter include, among others, combating every form of discrimination; equal treatment in access to employment, working conditions and social protection; improvement in working and living conditions for workers; rights to social protection; freedom of association and collective bargaining; minimum working age for children; protection of older workers; and rights of people with disabilities to programmes that help them in their social and professional life.

Employment laws in a country will depend on the political system and the political group in power. For instance, the conservative governments in the UK and the USA in the 1980s adopted 'supply-side' economics which advocates withdrawing from economic intervention policies, allowing a 'free market' where impediments to investment are removed, thereby creating jobs. This meant that laws protecting and supporting businesses were relaxed. In the UK during the Conservative governments of the 1980s and 1990s, gradual changes to the Employment Act, the Trade Union Reform and the Employment Rights Act systematically eroded the rights of both employees and the collective rights of trade unions established in the 1970s. These were felt to be too restrictive and a constraint on competitive enterprise. These changes included:

- extending the service qualification needed to make an unfair dismissal claim from six months to two years thus reducing job security;
- tightening the description and classification of what constitutes legitimate industrial action in order to deter and limit strikes;
- providing 'new rights' for trade union members to limit the power of union officials, i.e., to deter union pressure in cases of non-striking union members;
- providing legal safeguards for employees denied employment because of refusing to join a union;
- allowing employers to provide incentives to employees who opt out of collective bargaining or leave a union;
- disallowing actions in defence of the closed shop;
- prohibiting secondary actions and secondary picketing during strikes.

Some of these actions were challenged by the EU and, when all the members of the EU adopted the Social Charter in 1989, the UK refused to sign because it was felt that the provisions would impose higher labour costs, leading to bankruptcies and job losses.

The Labour government elected in 1997 reversed or changed some of the policies of the previous government. It imposed a minimum wage, opted to sign up for the EU Social Charter and restored some union rights.

Full-time employees in the hotel, catering and tourism industries will generally benefit from the same employment rights as other full-time employees in other sectors in the country. However, workers in non-standard employment do not usually enjoy the same rights although laws are now being introduced in some countries to provide some protection and rights.

Turnover of personnel

The turnover of personnel in the hotel and catering sector is legendary in terms of its scale.

In Asia, for example, labour turnover is estimated at 30 per cent annually and there is a critical shortage of skilled labour. According to a Hong Kong Hotel Association Survey, labour turnover in Hong Kong hotels is over 50 per cent because there has been a significant rise in the construction of new hotels and therefore greater opportunities for promotion and higher salaries in recent years; the labour market remains very tight and there is little unemployment; there are new entrants from other industries but who leave within one year; and in a highly materialistic society such as Hong Kong, people do change jobs even for small increase in benefits package (Heung, 1993).

In other countries such as the UK, experience in some London hotels suggests that labour turnover approaches 100 per cent annually. This is clearly problematic in terms of continuity of quality in the organization, as well as wasteful in training and other types of investment.

A survey in the UK in 1997 by the Institute of Personnel and Development revealed that the hospitality industry had, at 42 per cent, the second highest labour turnover of all sectors after wholesale and retail (43.5 per cent). Construction follows well below with 25 per cent of workers moving jobs and the average for industry at large was 20 per cent.

The survey identified the reasons for this high turnover of labour as:

- low pay;
- prevalence of part-time workers;
- long, unsocial hours;
- high proportion of low-skill jobs.

The Institute of Personnel and Development recommend improving staff training and development and weighing up the cost of higher wages against recruiting and retraining staff. Replacing a single worker in the hotel and leisure industries cost £1922 on average and it takes an average ten weeks to fill jobs compared to five weeks in other industries.

In a survey carried out by the Educational Institute of the American Hotel and Motel Association and KPMG Peat Marwick with 229 full-service hotels from ten companies world-wide, they found that turnover in the hospitality industry is increasing at an alarming rate. The survey looked at both voluntary and involuntary turnover and found annual employee turnover at:

- 158 per cent for line employees;
- 136 per cent for supervisors;
- 129 per cent for managers.

Despite the high turnover of staff, in many parts of the world there is an acute shortage of labour-power to enter the hotel, tourism and catering sector. This can be due to:

- lack of training opportunities;
- negative perceptions of work in the sector;
- cultural issues attached to working in the service sector;
- demographics.

A survey conducted by Arthur Andersen in 1997 of 500 executives in the Americas, Asia-Pacific, and 'Europe, the Middle East, India, Africa' (EMEIA) regions elicited the responses to questions relating to labour shortages in the sector given in Tables 11.2 and 11.3.

In response to these worrying trends just discussed, globalization in the hotel sector has meant that companies are increasingly providing employee benefits – such as education and crèche services, as well as having to endorse minimum wage agreements. In addition, there is increased incidence of 'interest-based' wage bargaining in the airline sector. Globalization is increasing the trend towards motivational pay awards or performance-related pay as a key to attracting and keeping staff in competitive international environments. However, the introduction of internationally transparent innovations such as

Table 11.2		Overall	EMEIA	Americas	Asia/Pacific
The hospitality industry faces continuing shortages of labour? (%)	Agree	74	62	81	82
	Disagree	11	15	9	8
	Neither	13	21	9	10
	Don't know	2	1	1	–

Source: Arthur Andersen (1997)

Table 11.3		Overall	EMEIA	Americas	Asia/Pacific
The following issues currently contribute to the shortage of qualified labour in the hospitality industry? (%)	Competition from better paying industries	78	74	81	74
	Low compensation levels	67	60	73	54
	Low acceptance of service culture	55	66	56	54
	Industry image	44	53	39	33
	Inadequate hospitality education	42	44	37	54
	Poor growth opportunities	29	31	29	21

Source: Arthur Andersen (1997)

the Euro will expose domestic companies to international comparison and also expose national variations in wage rates and remuneration packages.

One area highlighted by Austin Knight Company in the UK was ageism: they found it to be the most common form of discrimination in the workplace. In a sample of 967 employees over one-third felt discriminated against. The British government has asked employers to sign a voluntary code of practice, although if this approach does not succeed, legislation may follow.

One example in this area is the hotel chain Choice Hotels, which owns, manages and franchises 241 hotels. They found that employing older workers makes good business sense and specifically recruit the over-50s. Management points out the advantages of employing this age group as being:

- less absenteeism;
- they stay longer in the job;
- they have better customer care skills;
- they have greater confidence in dealing with guests.

Summary

The focus of this chapter has been on the smaller family-owned or independently owned operations that dominate the tourism and hospitality market, and has adopted an HRM bias. The discussion has illustrated the approaches that have been developed to create a favourable business environment via the removal of unnecessary and costly administrative, physical and legal burdens (deregulation). It has also shown how a number of measures have been introduced to support tourism employment in such businesses. The areas considered were: labour market transparency; greater recognition of education, training and work experiences; issues concerning employability, entrepreneurship, adaptability and equal opportunity; and finally, a dialogue between social partners.

References

Arthur Andersen (1997) 'Hospitality and leisure', *Executive Report*, Fall, 4, 2, 1–6.

Augustyn, M.M., and Knowles, T. (2000) 'Performance of tourism partnerships: a focus on York', *Tourism Management*, 21,4, 341–52.

Bagguley, P. (1987) 'Gender and labour flexibility in hotel and catering', *Services Industries Journal*, 10, 105–18.

Baldacchino, G. (1997) *Global Tourism and Informal Labor Relations*, London: Mansell.

Baum, T. (1993) *Human Resources Issues in International Tourism*, Oxford: Butterworth-Heinemann.

Granovetter, M. (1985) 'Economic action and social structure: the problem of embeddedness', *American Journal of Sociology*, 91, 3, 481–510.

Gulati, R. (1998) 'Alliances and networks', *Strategic Management Journal*, 19, 293–317.

Heung, V. (1993) 'Hong Kong', in T. Baum (ed) *Human Resources Issues in International Tourism*, Oxford: Butterworth-Heinemann Ltd.

ILO Hotel, Catering and Tourism Committee (1989) *Productivity and Training in the Hotel, Catering and Tourism Sector*, Geneva: International Labour Office.

ILO (1994) *Backgrounder*, April, Geneva: ILO.

Jafari, J. (1990) 'Research and scholarship: the basis of tourism education', *Journal of Tourism Studies*, 1, 1, 33–41.

Pfeffer, J. and Nowak, P. (1976) 'Joint venture and interorganisational interdependence', *Administrative Science Quarterly*, 21, 3, 315–39.

Porter, M. (1990) *The Competitive Advantage of Nations*, New York: The Free Press.

Pyke, F. (1994) *Small Firms, Technical Services and Inter-Firm Co-operation*, Geneva: International Institute for Labour Studies.

Riley, M. (1993) 'Labour market and vocational education', in T. Baum (ed) *Human Resources Issues in International Tourism*, Oxford: Butterworth-Heinemann Ltd.

Selin, S. and Chavez, D. (1995) 'Developing and evolutionary tourism partnership model', *Annals of Tourism Research*, 22, 4, 844.

Shaw, G. and Williams, A. (1994) *Critical Issues in Tourism – A Geographical Perspective*, Oxford: Blackwell, 143.

Simms, J., Hales, C. and Riley, M. (1988) 'Examination of the concept of internal labour markets in UK hotels', *Tourism Management*, 9, 1, 3–12.

Smallbone, D. (1991) 'Partnership in economic development: the case of UK Local Enterprise Agencies', *Policy Studies Review*, 10, 2–3, 89–98.

Smeral, E. (1998) 'The impact of globalization on small and medium enterprises: new challenges for tourism policies in European countries', *Tourism Management*, 19, 4, 371–80.

Szivas, E. (1999) 'The influence of human resources on tourism marketing in F. Vellas and L. Becherel (eds) *The International Marketing of Travel and Tourism*, Basingstoke: MacMillan Press.

Thomas, R. (1996) 'Assessing and influencing the policies of the European Union' in R. Kotas, R. Teare, J. Logie, C. Jayawardena and J. Bowen (eds) *The International Hospitality Business*, London: Cassell.

Urry, J. (1990) *The Tourist Gaze: Leisure and Travel in Contemporary Societies*, London and Newbury Park: Sage.

Valayer, D. (1999) 'The human dimension of an expanding sector', *The ACP-EU Courier*, May–June, 47–8.

Williamson, O. (1985) *The Economic Institutions of Capitalism*, New York: The Free Press.

World Tourism Organization (1998) *Government Role in Tourism Management and Promotion*, Madrid: WTO News.

Further reading

Ankomah, P. (1991) 'Tourism skilled labour: the case of Sub-Saharan Africa', *Annals of Tourism Research*, 18, 433–42.

Anon (1996a) 'A full-time approach to part-timers', *Leisure Week*, 9 February.

Anon (1996b) 'Ageism tops world discrimination survey', *Financial Times*, 2 February.

Anon (1997a) 'Flexible hours mean bad news for fast food staff', *Caterer and Hotel Keeper*, 18 September.

Anon (1997b) 'Growing acceptance drives trends in staffing', *Services Industry Supervision*, 58, 10, 6–8.

Anon (1997c) 'Hotels hold high rate of staff sacking', *Caterer and Hotel Keeper*, 27 November.

Anon (1997d) 'NATOUR pushes for privatisation', *Travel Asia*, 11 April.

Anon (1997e) 'Unions cross international boundaries', *Hotel and Motel Management*, 3 March, 3, 38.

Anon (1998a) 'Hospitality suffers huge losses from high staff turnover' *Personnel Management: Hotel and Catering*, 21 January, 6.

Anon (1998b) 'Hotel discovers that oldies are also goldies', *Asian Caterer and Hotel Keeper*, April.

Anon (1998c) 'Industry hit by increasing staff exodus', *Express Hotelier and Caterer*, 15 June.

Anon (1999a) 'Disabled students caught in the benefit trap', *Caterer and Hotelkeeper*, 25, 7 February.

Anon (1999b) 'Hospitality suffers huge losses from high staff turnover', *Caterer and Hotel Keeper*, 21 January.

Ansett Holdings Limited (1999) *Annual Review*, Melbourne: Ansett Holdings.

Ashkenas, R., Ulrich, D., Jick, T. and Kerr, S. (1995) *The Boundaryless Organization*, San Francisco: Jossey Bass.

Ashton, D. and Green, F. (1996) *Education, Training and the Global Economy*, Cheltenham: Elgar.

Bamford, R. (1998) 'New government, new expectations', *The Hospitality Yearbook 1998*, Guildford: University of Surrey.

BC Stats (1998) *Direct Tourism Employment – 1998*, Vancouver: Ministry of Finance and Corporate Relations.

Black, M. (1995) *In the Twilight Zone – Child Workers in the Hotel, Catering and Tourism Industry*, ILO Child Labour Collection, Geneva: ILO.

Bontron, J.C. *et al.* (eds) (1997) *Rural Employment: An International Perspective*, Wallingford: CAB.

Boudreau, M.C. *et al.* (1998) 'Going global', *Academy of Management Executives*, 12, 4, 120–8.

Bradley, F. (1991) *International Marketing Strategy*, Hemel Hempstead: Prentice-Hall.

Bradley, S.P., Hausmann, J.A. and Nolan, R.L. (1993) *Globalization, Technology and Competition*, Boston: Harvard Business School Press.

Bratton, J. and Gold, J. (1999) *Human Resource Management: Theory and Practice*, Basingstoke: MacMillan Press Ltd.

Brown, F. (1998) *Tourism Reassessed: Blight or Blessing?*, Oxford: Butterworth-Heinemann.

Buhalis, D. (1998) 'Information technology', in C. Cooper *et al. Tourism Principles and Practice*, Harlow: Addison-Wesley Longman.

Burgess, J. and Strachan, G. (1990) 'The expansion of non-standard employment in Australia and the extension of employers control', in A. Felstead and N. Jewson *Global Trends in Flexible Labour*, Basingstoke: MacMillan Press.

Campbell, A.J. and Verbeke, A. (1994) 'The globalization of service sector multinationals', *Long Range Planning*, 27, 2, 95–102.

Campbell, L.M. (1999) 'Ecotourism in rural developing economies', *Annals of Tourism Research*, 26, 3, 534–53.

Canada News Wire (1999) Air Canada Press Release 'Air Canada develops self check-in for airports, focuses on technology to simplify travel experience, available at www.newswire.ca/April 1, 1998

Cherrington, D.J. and Middleton, L.Z. (1995) 'An introduction to global business issues', *HR Magazine*, 4, 6, 124–30.

Coburn, C. (1995) *Partnerships: A Compendium of State and Federal Cooperative Technology Programs*, Columbus, OH: Battelle

Collingsworth, T. (1997) 'Child labour in a global economy', *Foreign Policy in Focus*, 46, 2, 52–65.

Conway, H. (1997) 'Dry white season for Scots hotels', *Caterer and Hotel Keeper*, 16 October, 25–8.

Cooper, C. (1997) 'Strategic perspectives on the planning and evolution of destinations: lessons for the Mediterranean', paper presented to the seminar: Tourism in the Mediterranean, University of Westminster, December.

Crotts, J.C. and Wilson, D.T. (1995) 'An integrated model of buyer–seller relationships in the international travel trade', *Progress in Tourism and Hospitality Research*, 1, 2, 125–40.

Dawkins, P. (1985) 'Non-standard hours of work and penalty rates in Australia', *Journal of Industrial Relations*, 28, 564–87.

Department for Culture, Media and Sports – Tourism Division (1999) *Tomorrow's Tourism: A Growth Industry for the New Millenium*, London: DCMS.

Dicken, P. (1992) *Global Shift*, 2nd edn, London: Paul Chapman.

Donaghue, J.A. (1999) 'Better bargaining', *Air Transport World*, 36, 3, 9.

Dunning, J.H. (1988) 'The eclectic paradigm of international production: a restatement and possible extensions', *Journal of International Business Studies*, 19, 1, 1–32.

Dyer, J.H. and Singh, H. (1988) 'The relational view: co-operative strategy and sources of inter-organizational competitive advantage', *Academy of Management Review*, 23, 4, 660–9.

European Commission (1999) *Enhancing Tourism's Potential for Employment – Follow-up to the Conclusions and Recommendations of the High Level Group on Tourism and Employment*, Brussels, 28.04.1999 COM (1999) 205 final.

Frazee, V. (1998) 'World business leaders target top workforce issues', *Workforce*, 3, 2, 8.

French, W.G. (1996) 'Global trade', *Human Resources Professional*, 9, 6, 25–8.

Gee, C. (1994) *International Hotel Development and Management*, Michigan: Educational Institute of the American Hotel and Motel Association.

Geller, L. (1998) 'The demands of globalization on the lodging industry', *Florida International University Hospitality Review*, 16, 1, 1–6.

Ghoshal, S. and Bartlett, C.A. (1990) 'The multinational corporation as an inter-organizational network', *Academy of Management Review*, 15, 4, 603–25.

Gill, G.A. (1991) 'The effects of on farm tourism', *Tourism Recreation Research*, 16, 1, 69–71.

Go, F. (1996) 'A conceptual framework for managing global tourism and hospitality marketing', *Tourism Recreation Research*, 21, 2, 37–43.

Haywood, M. and Pickworth, J. (1993) 'Canada', in T. Baum (ed) *Human Resources Issues in International Tourism*, Oxford: Butterworth-Heinemann Ltd.

Head, J. and Lucas, R. (1998) 'The impact of unfair dismissal rights on the employment relationship in the hospitality industry', *International Journal of Hospitality Management*, 17, 3, 243–51.

Hudson, K. (1999) *No Shortage of Non-Standard Jobs*, Washington, DC: EPI, Economic Policy Institute Briefing Paper.

Hufbauer, G.C. (1994) 'The coming boom in services trade: what will it do to wages', *Law and Policy in International Business*, 25, 2, 433–8.

IATA (1999) 'Liberalisation of air transport and the GATS', discussion paper, London: IATA.

ICFTU (1998) *A Possible Framework for Multilateral Investment: A Discussion Paper*, Brussels: ICFTU.

IH&RA Human Resources Think-Tank (1999) *Organizational and Workforce Challenges for the 21st Century*, Paris, August.

ILO (1995) *In the Twilight Zone – Child Workers in the Hotel, Tourism and Catering Industry*, Geneva: ILO.

Johnson, J. and Valhi, J.E. (1977) 'The internationalisation process of the firm: a model of knowledge development on increasing foreign commitments', *Journal of International Business Studies*, 2, 23–32.

Joyce, P. and Woods, A. (1996) *Essential Strategic Management: From Modernism to Pragmatism*, Oxford: Butterworth-Heinemann.

Juyaux, C. (1999) 'Quality of service and working conditions in the European tourist and hospitality industry', *Cahiers Espaces*, 61, 25–9.

Kanter, R.M. (1995) 'Thinking locally in the global economy', *Harvard Business Review*, September–October, 151–160.

Kappor, T. (1999) 'The new hospitality', *Workplace Lodging*, November, 105–8.

Keller, P. (1996) 'Globalization and tourism', *Tourist Review*, 4, 6–7.

Kinsey, J. (1988) *Marketing in Developing Countries*, London: Macmillan.

Korten, D.C. (1995) *When Corporations Ruled the World*, London: Earthscan.

Kotler P., Bowen, J. and Makens, J. (1996) *Marketing for Hospitality and Tourism*, Englewood Cliffs, NJ: Prentice-Hall International.

Lazear, E. (1999) 'Globalization', *Economic Journal*, 109, 454, C15–C40.

Lee, B.J. (1993) 'NAFTA', *Business Korea*, 1, 6, 28–9.

Livingstone, J.M. (1989) *The Internationalisation of Business*, London: Macmillan.

Makridakis, S. (1989) 'Management in the 21st century', *Long Range Planning*, 22, 2, 37–53.

Marray, M. (1999) 'Small is beautiful', *Air Finance Journal*, 216, 60–1.

Melin, L. (1992) 'Internationalisation as a strategy process', *Strategic Management Journal*, 13, 2, 99–118.

Morrison, A. (1989) *Hospitality and Travel Marketing*, New York: Delmar.

Morrison, A. (1998) 'Small firm statistics: a hotel sector focus', *Service Industries Journal*, 18, 1, 132–42.

National Bureau of Economic Research Working Paper Series NBER, Cambridge, MA: NBER.

Normann, R. and Ramirez, R. (1993) 'From value chain to value constellation: designing interactive strategy', *Harvard Business Review*, July–August, 65–6.

Office for National Statistics (1997) *Business Monitor*, PA 1003, London: Stationery Office.

Organization for Economic Co-operation and Development (1997a) *Economic Globalization and the Environment*, Paris: OECD.

Organization for Economic Co-operation and Development (1997b) *Local Economies and Globalization*, Paris: OECD

Organization for Economic Co-operation and Development (1997c) 'Partnership in tourism: a tool for job creation', issues paper for the conference in Rome, 27–8 October.

Organization for Economic Co-operation and Development (1998) *Globalization and the Environment*, Paris: OECD.

Paliwoda, S.J. and Thomas, M.J. (1998) *International Marketing*, 3rd edn, Oxford: Butterworth-Heinemann.

Palpacuer, F. and Parisotto, A. (1998) 'Global production and local jobs: issues for discussion', international workshop, Geneva 9–10 March, ILO, Geneva.

Pannozo, G. (1998) 'Operational strategies for employment policies in tourism', *Espaces Paris*, 149, 28–31.

Pan-Suk, K. (1999) 'Globalization of HRM', *Public Personnel Management*, 28, 2, 227–43.

Parker, B. (1998) *Globalization and Business Practice: Managing Across Boundaries*, London: Sage.

Pekar, P. and Allio, R. (1994) 'Making alliances work – guidelines for success', *Long Range Planning*, 27, 4, 54–65.

Poole, M. (1998) 'Human resource management and the theory of rewards', *British Journal of Industrial Relations*, 36, 2, 227–47.

Poon, A. (1993) *Tourism, Technology and Competitive Strategies*, Wallingford: CAB.

Poulin, L. *et al.* (1997) 'Some thoughts on the working conditions of women in the accommodation and catering sectors', *TEORUS*, 16, 3, 19–20.

Ramrayka, L. (1996) 'A full-time approach to part-timers', *Leisure Week*, 9 February, 12–15.

Roberts, K. *et al.* (1998) 'Managing the global workforce', *Academy of Management Executives*, 12, 4, 93–106.

Rosewarne, S. (1998) 'Globalization and the liberalisation of Asian markets', *World Economy*, 21, 7, 963–79.

Seaton, A.V. and Bennett, M.M. (1996) *The Marketing of Tourism Products: Concepts, Issues and Cases*, London: International Thomson Business Press.

Shulze, G. (1999) 'Globalization and the economy', *World Economy*, 22, 3, 295–352.

Slaughter, M.J. (1999) 'Globalization and wages', *World Economy*, 22, 5, 609–29.

Smith, E.L. (1997) 'Sow entrepreneurship, reap employment', *Black Enterprise*, 27, 11, 222–30.

Sussens-Messerer, V. (1998) 'Globalization and jobs', *Finance Week*, 76, 27, 20–2.

te Kloeze, J.W. (1994) 'The benefits of rural tourism, the role of the state, and the aspects of training and co-operation', formal speech at the Central and East European Federation for the Promotion of the Green-Soft-Rural Tourism Conference, 'Rural Tourism Development in Bulgaria and in the Balkan Countries', Karlovo.

Teare, R. *et al.* (1997) *Global Directions: New Strategies for Hospitality and Tourism*, London: Cassell.

Thomas, R. (ed) (1998) *The Management of Small Tourism and Hospitality Firms*, London: Cassell.

Travelab (1999) *The Report on the Scandinavian Travel Industry on the Web*, Helsingborg: Travelab.

Terpstra, V. and Sarathy, R. (1991) *International Marketing*, Florida: The Dryden Press.

UNCTAD (1998) 'Expert meeting on strengthening the capacity for expanding the tourism sector in developing countries', June.

Vandenbusche, H. (1998) 'Globalization', *World Economy*, 21, 8, 1151–77.

Vernon, R. (1966) 'The product cycle hypothesis in a new international environment', *Quarterly Journal of Economics*, May, 190–207.

Weiermiar, K. and Peters, P. (1998) 'The internationalisation behaviour of small and medium-sized service enterprises', *Asia Pacific Journal of Tourism Research*, 2, 2, 1–14.

Wheatcroft, S. (1992) 'Airlines: reaping the rewards of globalization', *Transport*, 13, 6, 1–3.

Wilson, K. and Worland, D. (1987) *Employment and Labour Costs in the Hospitality Industry*, Research Report No. 1, John Read Faculty of Business Research Papers, Footscray: Footscray Institute of Technology.

Wilson, K. and Worland, D. (1993) 'Australia', in T. Baum (ed) *Human Resources Issues in International Tourism*, Oxford: Butterworth-Heinemann Ltd.

World Wildlife Fund (1990) *Ecotourism – The Potentials and Pitfalls*, Baltimore: WWF.

World Tourism Organization (1997) *Rural Tourism: A Solution for Employment, Local Development and Environment*, Madrid: WTO.

World Tourism Organization (1998) *Tourism Taxation: Striking a Fair Deal*, Madrid: WTO.

World Tourism Organization (1999) *Marketing Tourism Destinations On-Line*, Madrid: WTO.

WTTC (1997 onwards) *Steps to Success: Human Resources Good Practices from WTTHRC*, London: WTTC.

WTTC (1999) *Travel and Tourism. A White Paper*, London: WTTC.

Key Internet sites

http://www.abacus.com

http://www.air-transport.org

http://www.barig.org/

http://www.british-airways.com/

http://www.cf.ac.uk//ccin//union/tuinter.html

http://epinet.org/
http://www.galileo.com
http://www.iata.org
http://ideas.uqam.ca/
http://www.ilo.org/
http://laborresearch.org
http://www.quantas.com
http://star.arabia.com/
http://stats.bls.gov/
http://www.summersault.com
http://www.sabre.com/
http://www.world –tourism.org/
http://www.wttc.org/
http://atta.indian.com
http://www.prit.bc.ca/learning
http://www.ih-ra.com
http://www.isn.ethz.ch
http://www.oecd.org
http://www.nbbd.com/ecotourism
http://www.icomos.org/tourism
http://www.uvm.edu/~mmarquar/index
http://www.dfee.gov.uk/skillsforce
http://www.green-travel.com
http://www.iatm.co.uk
http://www.unicc.org/unctad
http://gopher.undp.org
http://gopher.unesco.org
http://ue.eu.int
http://www.worldbank.org
http://www.ecotourism.org

12

Global trends in tourism and hospitality:
A focus on South America, Asia-Pacific and the Middle East

This chapter reviews key trends within the tourism and hospitality industries of Europe, South America, Asia-Pacific and the Middle East.

South America

Background

Within the main tourism and hotel sectors of South America, regional growth is set to slow somewhat in 2002–3 as political and economic conditions deteriorate in Argentina, yet considerable variations will continue to exist within and between countries. Equally, economic activity will remain fairly robust in some countries, in particular Brazil and Chile. Domestic demand gains momentum and structural reforms are put in place, most notably in Brazil. These have left it better placed to weather adverse global conditions. In summary, growth in Argentina, Brazil and Chile will be influenced by five key points.

1. Economic growth in the Pacific Rim and tourism feeder countries.
2. The heavy dependence on certain incoming markets, particularly neighbouring South American countries.
3. The ability to effectively market key destinations to North American and European tourists.
4. The real cost of air transport and the near monopolistic control of certain national carriers.
5. The quality of local infrastructure, superstructure and the balance of hotel supply with demand.

The potential growth within the tourism and hotel industries of Argentina, Brazil and Chile is heavily dependent on intra-regional travel throughout South America, increasing in many cases by over 50 per cent of arrivals to the three chosen countries. It is therefore regional economic trends over the medium term that will dictate tourism arrivals, hotel occupancy and average daily rate. In addition, the relatively high cost of airline travel between Europe, North America and these South American countries will continue to constrain opportunities to develop alternative or emerging markets – an ongoing barrier to growth. Equally, the near monopolistic national carrier control of internal flights within Argentina, Brazil and Chile will continue to have cost implications for the non-South American traveller once he or she arrives at the destination.

Regional economic trends

Argentina

The country's economy has not fully emerged yet from the recession that began in 1999. Indeed, the political turmoil during 2002 will unfortunately not improve current depressed expectations from investors and, above all, consumers. GDP growth was −3.4 per cent in 1999, −0.5 per cent in 2000, −0.8 per cent in 2001 and −15.0 per cent in 2002. A prediction for the future is conditional on a successful resolution of the current political problems and a benign international environment.

The current interrelationships between the key countries of South America can be seen to emerge from the devaluation of the Brazilian currency in January 1999, which provoked a 15 per cent appreciation of the Argentine real effective exchange rate. Within Argentina, such an appreciation of the currency *vis-à-vis* Brazil was only partially offset by price deflation. In addition, another important factor weighing down on Argentina's competitiveness is the continuous strength of the US$D/€ exchange rate, given that a higher share of its exports are destined for Europe rather than the USA. Also, Argentina was and remains vulnerable to a worsening of the international economic context, especially a possible rise in interest rates, given its sizeable financing needs.

Brazil

The country's stability-oriented monetary and fiscal policies over the last three years have successfully contributed to a strong recovery since the devaluation crisis of 1999. However, the devaluation of the Argentine peso at the start of 2002 and Argentina's subsequent default on its foreign debt have been just the latest in a series of blows to the regional economy, causing many international institutions to withdraw from the region. The Argentine crisis, coupled with political uncertainty, pushed the real to a low of US$4.1 during the summer of 2002; it recovered to a level of US$3.5 by the end of 2002. In 1997 it was just below parity.

Strong growth, however, has led to a widening current account deficit in Brazil, which has started to cause concern among investors. Therefore, while foreign direct investment continues to flow in, and the recent US rate cuts have and will improve the financing environment for the country, volatility in the Brazilian currency is likely to prevail in the months ahead, and the room for further domestic interest rate cuts will be limited. The integration of Brazil into international capital markets means that it must pay the price of external shocks, be it last year's crisis in Argentina, or negative sentiment in US markets.

Chile

While Chile's economy has recovered since the 1999 recession, manufacturing and service sectors still have some way to go. Nevertheless, GDP growth was above 5 per cent in 2000–1 and the country was expected to take the lead in South America in 2002. In view of its good fundamental data, Chile has growth potential of an estimated 6 per cent. However, this potential cannot be fully exploited at present because of the slowdown in the global economy and factors weighing on the domestic investment climate.

The new Socialist government (which took office in March 2000) has been pursuing a prudent fiscal policy in line with its promises. Against this backdrop and the international trend of falling interest rates, the Chilean central bank has been given scope for monetary easing.

After a nominal depreciation of 7.5 per cent in the course of 2000, the Chilean currency in the first weeks of 2001 appreciated up to 3 per cent, but by early March had lost 5 per cent again. In the course of 2002 it was expected to move sideways by and large, which could have implications for tourism in terms of the cost of visiting the country.

Although consumer price inflation was high at above 4 per cent in 2000, the central bank was rightly confident that the inflation target of 2–4 per cent for the end of 2002 could be met. As a small, open economy (with exports at 26 per cent of GDP), Chile has a significant exposure to the risks of the global growth slowdown. On the other hand, it benefits relatively little from the decline in international interest rates as its foreign debt is moderate. The continuing strong dependence on copper exports (40 per cent of all goods exports) and fluctuations in copper prices pose a special risk.

Tourism in South America

For most South American countries, tourism represents an unrealized developmental potential, be it Patagonia, the Incas in Peru, or the Amazon forest of Brazil. Only recently has it attracted the attention of policy-makers as it has the potential to contribute towards alleviating the major political, social, and economic problems that characterize many parts of the region. In an effort to raise their general level of prosperity, some nations have embraced tourism as a strategic alternative. In fact, in countries such as Argentina, Brazil and Chile, tourism has taken on a new dimension in recent years, contributing significantly to those countries' balances of payments and providing millions of jobs.

Taking a historical perspective, the performance of the South American tourism industry in the 1960s was mediocre, despite the tourism boom experienced elsewhere, in a reflection of the political, economic and social situation of the region. This depressing period was further aggravated in the 1970s by serious social and political disputes, which contributed to creating a poor reputation (incorrectly in many cases) that still causes many tourism feeder countries to define South America as a region of political and economic instability to which it is relatively unsafe to travel. The overall consequences of these contextual issues were low investment in tourism and a decreasing interest in the international tourism market throughout the region.

Many countries within the region saw increasing internal and external debts, hyperinflation and social and political uncertainties throughout the 1980s, which all helped to guarantee that both tourists and tourism investment remained absent from most countries in the region. However, towards the end of the 1980s major changes, such as the process of democratization and economic reform, have become a growing influence within significant regional players, especially Argentina, Brazil and Chile, in terms of tourism attractiveness. The reforms implemented in this period have positively influenced many neighbouring countries and have paved the way for a more promising tourism industry.

The major structural changes experienced by most Latin American countries in the 1990s, such as the transition to democracy in many previously oppressed countries, the consolidation of economic blocs, the improvement in trade with major markets around the world and the improvement in basic services such as health and education, among other factors, have contributed to the development of a positive environment for tourism in the region, with the sector emerging as an important promoter of economic development. Indeed, the World Travel and Tourism Council –(WTTC) predicts regional travel and tourism GDP growth of over 6 per cent per annum for the coming decade, which is double the world average. Such rates could be even higher in Argentina and Chile.

By the year 2010, travel and tourism in South America is expected to produce US$347.1 billion worth of economic activity and 15.3 million jobs. These prospects were unimaginable a few decades ago, when South America was submerged in regional disputes, chronic economic problems, major social problems and was ruled mainly by dictatorial or military regimes.

However, some limiting factors, such as the great distance from the most important generating markets, poor co-ordination and planning, and a lack of resources for investment in tourism infrastructure, will continue to limit potential growth and expansion. The relatively low level of charter flights to the region will continue to have major negative implications for the cost of travel to the three countries. A significant increase in tourist arrivals from the USA and Europe will only occur when this key point is addressed.

Over the past decade there has been an increase of about 50 per cent in the number of arrivals to South America. Intra-regional travel represents by far the greatest proportion of international arrivals in the area, a point illustrated by Tables 12.1 to 12.11 which analyse the Argentine, Brazilian and Chilean markets.

The WTTC notes that Argentinian tourism is expected to generate US$30.6 billion in economic activity (total demand) in 2001, growing to US$53.7 billion

Table 12.1 Foreign tourists' expenditure in Argentina, 2001

Country of origin	Arrivals	Average length of stay (days)	Total expenditure ($)	Average daily expenditure ($)	Average purchase per tourist ($)	Total expenditure per tourist ($)
Bolivia	113,234	15.4	81,412,795	43.3	52.2	719.0
Brazil	333,012	7.1	300,451,577	114.8	91.9	902.2
Chile	520,316	8.2	353,521,469	69.4	109.2	679.4
Paraguay	469,191	7.6	346,302,024	84.7	97.8	738.1
Uruguay	392,450	6.0	185,940,916	58.0	128.4	473.8
Rest of Latin America	149,156	13.6	197,182,181	85.4	163.6	1,322.0
North America	179,832	19.3	384,888,091	91.5	373.5	2,140.3
Europe	370,933	18.8	500,810,000	83.5	187.9	1,759.2
Rest of World	92,340	13.8	136,692,533	90.6	225.8	1,480.3
Total	2,620,464	10.7	2,487,201,587	80.9	141.9	1,007.0

Source: Country reports No 1 (2003)

by 2011. Demand is expected to grow by 4.2 per cent per annum in real terms between 2001 and 2011.

The industry is expected to contribute 3.3 per cent to GDP in 2001 (US$9.3 billion), rising to US$15.1 billion (3.2 per cent of total) by 2011.

In Brazil, according to the WTTC, tourism is expected to generate US$58.2 billion in economic activity (total demand) in 2001, growing to US$164.0 billion

Table 12.2	*2000*	*1999*	*1998*	*1997*	*1996*	*1995*
South America	3,036,169	2,961,684	2,810,101	1,520,367	1,405,583	1,106,063
Europe	1,305,674	1,227,829	1,144,599	701,684	671,152	509,153
North America	744,270	647,807	607,852	459,553	406,265	254,566
Total	5,313,463	5,107,169	4,818,084	2,849,750	2,665,508	1,991,416

Brazil: international visitor arrivals by global region, 1995–2000

Source: Country reports No 1 (2003)

Table 12.3	*2000*	*1999*	*1998*	*1997*
South America	57.1	58.0	58.3	53.3
USA	12.2	10.9	10.9	14.0
Europe	24.6	24.1	23.7	24.6
Germany	5.46	5.53	5.45	4.93
Italy	3.81	3.48	3.52	4.32
France	3.10	2.58	2.52	2.96
UK	2.40	2.48	2.44	2.18

Share of Brazilian tourist market, 1997–2000 (%)

Source: Country reports No 1 (2003)

Table 12.4	*Nationality*	*Total*	*Comments*
	South America	1,238,462	Argentina represented the largest section of the market at 851,465, particularly in January and February. Peru was second at 137,700.
	North America	177,555	USA was the largest sector at 137,700.
	Central America	8,113	
	Caribbean	3,756	
	Europe	237,856	Germany, Spain, France, UK and Italy represent the top four source markets.
	Oceania	16,846	Australia is the main market at 13,399 visitors.
	Africa	2,631	The main source market was South Africa
	Asia	21,587	The main source market was Japan
	Middle East	13,243	Israel dominates this market
	Other	1,651	
	Total	1,723,107	

Number of foreign visitors to Chile, 2001

Source: Country reports No 1 (2003)

by 2011. Demand is expected to grow by 3.8 per cent per annum in real terms between 2001 and 2011.

The industry is expected to contribute 3.4 per cent to GDP in 2001 (US$21.2 billion), rising to US$60.9 billion (3.4 per cent of total) by 2011.

WTTC data suggests that Chilean tourism is expected to generate 8.6 per cent of total exports (US$2131.9 million) in 2001, growing to US$4,343.0 million (6.1 per cent of total) in 2011. The industry is expected to generate US$9065.9 million in economic activity (total demand) in 2001, growing to US$20,374.6 million by 2011. Demand is expected to grow by 5.4 per cent per annum in real terms between 2001 and 2011. Tourism is expected to contribute 3.9 per cent to GDP in 2001 (US$2811.5 million), rising to US$5547.7 million (3.6 per cent of total) by 2011.

The hotel sector

Argentina

In Argentina's capital city Buenos Aires, international and domestic chains, as well as independently managed hotels, have significantly increased supply, by over 1200 rooms in the four-star category (including NH, Meliá and Holiday Inn), and by over 600 rooms in the five-star category (Hilton, Starwood and Holiday Inn), since 1999. With this commentary, it is interesting to highlight the development of the Spanish chain NH, which appears as a leading investor and operator in Argentina at the four-star level, in which it currently owns and operates approximately 500 hotel rooms, 350 of which were opened in 1999.

Table 12.5

Foreign visitors to Chile, selected ranking by country, 2001

Nationality	No of visitors	No days	Expenditure per day $	Total expenditure $
Total	1,723,107	10.3	44.4	787,750,268
America	1,429,293	9.2	39.3	517,024,140
1. Argentina	851,465	8.6	30.3	222,202,575
2. USA	137,700	12.3	68.5	116,087,270
3. Peru	137,077	7.4	29.0	29,457,029
4. Bolivia	94,973	7.3	26.3	18,223,671
5. Brazil	72,462	10.9	59.5	46,962,728
Europe	237,856	16.0	57.9	220,258,287
1. Germany	44,800	17.0	53.0	40,363,774
2. Spain	36,231	16.0	66.8	38,699,493
3. France	36,221	16.3	55.9	32,990,888
4. UK	35,944	13.4	62.5	30,098,382
5. Italy	19,323	10.1	63.9	12,475,028
Australia	13,399	12.9	53.9	9,320,196
Asia	21,587	14.7	80.5	25,552,251
Rest of the world	20,972	14.7	50.6	15,595,394

Source: Country reports No 1 (2003)

However, in certain upmarket hotel categories supply may be starting to outstrip demand.

The problem with these developments, according to consultants Horwath International, is that the upward trend prevailing during the five years preceding 2000, both in average occupancies as well as in room rates, seems to have reached a temporary standstill, due mainly to the increase in hotel rooms during 1999–2002 and the country's political and economic slowdown.

In order to have a better understanding of the situation in the country's hotel industry, it should be mentioned that international hotel chains are currently constructing more than 1450 rooms in three-, four- and five-star categories in secondary locations throughout the country. This creates the situation that Argentina's hotel market could be at a point of inflection considering that new actors now entering the market may guide their business actions by developing new markets yet, simultaneously, aggressively competing in the current one – a choice between competition for market share or the development of market growth. For the future, the approach in this market will be highly competitive, and a sustained improvement of quality in facilities and services shall be an imperative for all players in the sector, both for international chains and local groups. Indeed, the strength of internationally recognized brands with their perceived lower purchase risk for the foreign visitor represents a competitive threat to the domestically owned hotel sector. The trend for the latter may be an increase in hotel affiliation, either through franchising or consortia such as Best Western.

However, Inter-Continental, Caesar Park, Starwood, Marriott, Hyatt and Hilton (which opened up a spectacular hotel at Puerto Madero where corporate rates start at US$220) have all entered into a wild race for a piece of the upper-tier segment of the Argentine hotel industry. All this investment from major international hotel firms in Argentina is, in turn, putting pressure on local hoteliers. The highly sophisticated Alvear Palace – the only fully Argentine-owned property among the big hotels – had a lot of investment, refurbishing and modernization to do in order to remain competitive in this new and highly competitive environment. The hotel fully succeeded, and today it is widely considered one of the top 20 hotels in the world.

From a marketing perspective, it would seem from this discussion that there are two distinct types of hotel in Buenos Aires. For example there are the Alvear Palace and the Hyatt, which are comparatively small hotels with only about 160 rooms each. Then there are larger hotels like the Starwood, Inter-continental and Marriott. Both categories are directing their promotional efforts at different segments, including business and leisure, attracted to the city.

But, while the supply of five-star rooms in Buenos Aires has risen dramatically in just a few years, few investors have set their eyes on the variety of world-class tourist attractions Argentina has to offer, from the Iguana Falls in the north, to the breathtaking mountains and lakes of Bariloche, to the Perito Moreno glacier and the penguin and whale watching sites of Patagonia. This leaves enormous room for further hotel building – not the huge, ultra-modern Marriotts and Hiltons now so ubiquitous in Buenos Aires but, rather, mid-priced lodgings more in tune with their regional location, according to analysts.

The European and North American tourists correctly treat Argentina as a long-haul destination and seek to access the vast array of natural attractions the country offers. In terms of hotels, great scope exists to develop high-quality three- to four-star hotels that blend into the settings of the respective regions. Tourists are seeking an escape from the bland uniformity of the major five-star hotels which are found in any major city and instead seek the relaxed charm of the kind found in English country hotels, a Scottish lodge or a German gasthof. In response to this view, Accor, France's largest hotel chain, plans to build 35 three- to four-star units in a US$230 million venture. The company has already opened the first two Ibis – one in the western city of Mendoza in January 1999, and a second in Buenos Aires in May 2001 – and is targeting several tourist spots throughout the country. So far, the company has no major problems in implementing its development plan. Needless to say, it is not happy with the current economic stagnation in the country, but it is confident the situation will improve over the period 2002–5.

As the preceding discussion shows, many hotels have been built in recent years in Argentina, but there is one that stands out in terms of telecommunications and high technology – the Buenos Aires Hilton. Inaugurated in April 2000 within the Puerto Madero area of the city, the US$85 million Buenos Aires Hilton has been equipped with the latest in communications gadgetry, including broadband Internet connectivity and high-speed lines throughout the whole building, in every bedroom and in meeting facilities.

With 421 rooms, it also is the largest hotel to be built in Buenos Aires in the past 25 years.

The Hilton derives 55–60 per cent of its revenues from corporate travellers, 15–18 per cent from conventions and congresses, and 8–10 per cent from the leisure market. In turn, half its business travellers come from the USA, one-quarter from Europe, and the rest from elsewhere in the world, mostly Brazil and Chile. While the Hilton has added 20 per cent more rooms to the corporate segment of the market, the company is confident that the city is far from reaching a glut – an optimistic view perhaps.

In addition to this development, Hilton, not just in Buenos Aires, is currently evaluating other locations throughout the country, mostly for regional travellers and the leisure market at tourist destinations.

Brazil

The recovery of the Brazilian economy in the second half of 1999 sparked a sustained increase in demand for hotel accommodation throughout the country. This trend continued in 2000–2, with Brazilian GDP expected to grow by over 4 per cent. However, Horwath International (as cited in Knowles, T., Felzenstein, C. and Garces, A. (2003)) note that due to the increase in hotel supply, occupancy for 1999 (at 59.3 per cent) decreased when compared with the prior year (at 61.7 per cent) on average. The average rates in local currency increased 16.6 per cent between 1998 and 1999, however, when comparing performance in US dollars, average rates declined significantly from US$92.0 to US$68.80. This 25 per cent decline is directly attributable to the currency devaluation which occurred in January 1999. The conclusion to be drawn is that increases in supply and exchange rate fluctuations significantly affected the Brazilian hotel market.

All this new room supply is occurring predominantly in the country's major commercial centres, for the most part, in the condo-hotel sector, due to a heavy dependence on the business and conference market, and less so leisure. Although condo-hotels are not generally perceived as full-service hotels, due to the level of sophistication in their design, development, branding and management, they have become formidable competitors to the more traditional full-service hotels. Investor interest in this sector continues to increase, given the minimal investment required to purchase a unit, their low variable cost base and their level of sophistication in an environment where interest rates are declining.

Table 12.6

Argentina: accommodation by type and province, 2000

Province	1 Star	2 Star	3 Star	4 Star	5 Star	Apart hotel	Other	Total
Ciudad de Buenos Aires	27	40	39	48	11	42	243	450
Buenos Aires	358	289	180	41	3	99	1,198	2,168
Catamarca	2	1	9	1		1	98	112
Chaco	12	6	6	1		1	25	51
Chubut	9	14	11	5		12	179	230
Cordoba	217	154	50	16	3	12	547	999
Corrientes	41	14	11	3			173	22
Entre Rios	24	14	16	3	2	14	221	294
Formosa	2	2	5			1	37	47
Jujuy	11	9	3	3			60	86
La Pampa	4	3	4	2			103	116
La Rioja	6	2	3	3		2	37	53
Medoza	29	26	13	6		14	156	244
Misiones	10	4	11	3	4		99	131
Neuquen	14	19	13	2	1	18	259	326
Rio Negro	41	16	22	9	5	2	357	452
Salta	11	13	16	8		3	94	145
San Juan	2	5	4		1	8	76	96
San Luis	24	8	10	3			175	220
Santa Cruz	13	9	6	2		6	145	181
Santa Fe	17	22	24	13		8	98	182
Santiago del Estero	40	34	16	5		35	86	216
Tierra del Fuego	2	2	7	4	1	5	33	54
Tucuman	11	11	12	4	1	1	55	95
Total	927	717	491	185	32	284	4,554	7,190

Source: Country reports No 1 (2003)

Table 12.7

Brazil: hotel occupancy rates, 1995–2001 (%)

	1995	1996	1997	1998	1999	2000	2001
Luxury	61.3	64.4	66.0	63.5	62.5	63.0	47.0
Superior	56.0	59.0	62.0	61.3	60.5	61.9	60.0
Economy	64.7	51.6	59.1	59.8	55.9	57.0	55.0

Source: Country reports No 1 (2003)

Given the unique financing mechanism of these properties, the balance between supply and demand is not often considered when contemplating their development. As such, many believe that ongoing development of this product sector will result in an increasing supply and demand imbalance, suggesting further deterioration in occupancy and average daily rates for full-service hotels between 2002 and 2005. For example, in metropolitan São Paulo approximately 70 condo-hotels with 17,000 rooms opened in the past three years, increasing the city's supply nearly four-fold.

As a result of these supply trends, hotel affiliation, particularly for locally owned properties, has become and will continue to be increasingly necessary to effectively market properties in Brazil and internationally. Given the strong expansion of hotel supply, which began after the stabilization of the country's economy in 1994, the industry is starting to show signs of a supply and demand imbalance. While an increasing number of hotels are being professionally developed and managed, due to the significant increases in supply, financial performance will be largely dependent on operational efficiencies as opposed to market growth. As a result, it is becoming increasingly important for asset managers or owners' representatives, who have specialized expertise in the industry, to assist hotel owners in assessing market positioning and identifying operational efficiencies in order to ensure that management is enhancing revenues and minimizing expenses with the objective of maximizing owners' profit.

Turning to the luxury/first-class segment in Brazil, several new properties are under construction or have recently opened, both in urban and resort areas. In São Paulo such hotels include the Palacio Rangara, Grand Hyatt, Kempinsky and Hilton. In Rio de Janeiro, Marriott International developed the first new luxury hotel in the city for 20 years, opened in 2001. In Porto Alegre the city's first international chain affiliated hotel (Starwood) has opened. Regarding resort destinations, seven properties with 2200 rooms opened between 2000 and 2003. These properties include five hotels as part of the Costa do Sauipe resort. This is the first integrated, self-contained resort destination in South America, and includes Marriott, Renaissance, Sofitel Convention, Sofitel Suites and Super-Clubs Breezes. Other hotels proposed to open during this period include the Blue Tree Park, Angra dos Reis, Rio de Janeiro, and Inter-Continental Muro Alto, Pernambuco.

Chile

The fall in foreign tourist numbers experienced in Chile in 2001 can be linked very closely to that of Argentina, whose size in the past has historically

Table 12.8		1995	1996	1997	1998	1999	2000	2001
Brazil: hotel room rates, 1995–2001 (US$)	Luxury	110.0	160.9	160.0	168.2	146.3	141.9	120.5
	Superior	64.7	75.0	71.9	71.5	59.6	59.3	55.2
	Economy	41.2	42.7	39.7	39.9	36.1	31.6	34.0

Source: Country reports No 1 (2003)

contributed to around 50 per cent of the total. In addition, the overwhelming dominance of the domestic air carrier Lan Chile will inevitably suggest high costs in holidaying within the country as air transport is the main method of visiting the key destinations within Chile. This point, together with the fact that there is a virtual absence of charter flights to Chile, means that travel to the country, and holidaying within it, is expensive. Segmentation of the main Chilean tourism arrivals market in 2001 was as follows: 71.9 per cent from South America; 13.8 per cent from Europe; and 10.3 per cent from North America.

Hotel capacity in Chile grew by over 6.0 per cent during the period 1997–2001, as a result of strong business and leisure tourism activity. International hotel chains together with local entities and businessmen have been looking at expanding to the regions outside the capital city – the Santiago Metropolitan area – and are targeting the executive segment through major five-star hotel projects. In addition to the increase of business travel to Chile as a result of its economic success of recent years, Chile has the potential to develop its leisure tourism sector. This has created a high demand for hotel capacity throughout the country.

Within the capital city, three large properties in the five-star category are the Hilton, Marriott and Sol Melia. They are all located in the same residential/commercial area of Avenidas Kennedy and Americo Vespucio, which is the emerging and central development magnet in upper Santiago. These three projects have added 1000 rooms and triggered strong competition in the sector over the past five years.

Large international chains, such as Hyatt, Starwood, Radisson, Choice, Holiday Inn, Best Western, Kempinski, Inter-Continental, and Hampton Inn, are already present in Chile.

After years of centralized investment in Santiago, the hotel industry has commenced expansion to the regions, based on their economic growth and capacity demand. Prior to this expansion, important cities throughout Chile would typically have one good hotel. Holiday Inn has opened four 'Holiday Inn Express' properties in Temuco, Concepcion, Iquique and Antofagasta, with plans for more. It would seem that this trend in developing mid-market hotels outside Santiago is set to continue over the next five years.

According to the tourist board SERNATUR (2001) and the National Institute of Statistics (INE 2001) there are 1631 'tourist accommodation units' in the country, representing a growth in provision from the 1405 available in 1998. The 2001 figure equates to 363,308 rooms and 730,224 beds. This figure is distributed as follows:

- hotels 48.8 per cent;
- apart-hotels 4.8 per cent;
- motels 19.7 per cent;
- residences (hostels) 17.5 per cent;
- camping 8.9 per cent
- complementary 0.3 per cent – most of these premises are located in the Lake District region (20.3 per cent) and the Valparaiso region (19.3 per cent).

In 2001 the numbers of visitors (national and international tourists) staying in tourist residences were down by 3.4 per cent compared to 2000. This was mainly because of the national and international economic downturn and, in particular the economic recession of some South American countries.

According to SERNATUR (2001) the average capacity of the hotel industry in Chile is 30.3 rooms. However, in the Santiago Metropolitan region the average capacity in the hotel industry is 70.8 rooms, in the Tarapaca region it is 34.6 rooms and in the Bio-Bio region it is 33.5 rooms, all above average. The average number of beds per accommodation unit in the country is 59.3. However, this average is higher in the Santiago Metropolitan region with 115.3 units, and in the Tarapaca region with 70.8 units.

During 2001, 1,912,257 visitors spent one night or more in a tourist residence (hotel, motel, apart-hotel, hostel, cottage or camp), which represents a downturn of 12.3 per cent compared to 2000. Analysis shows that 46.1 per cent of this total is concentrated in the metropolitan region of Santiago. Other regions of relevance in 2001 were Valparaiso with 11.4 per cent, the Lake District region in the south with 10.1 per cent, and Tarapaca region in the north with 8.2 per cent. Finally, the most relevant cities where foreign visitors spent one night or more in 2001 were:

- Santiago (879,433)
- Vina del Mar (163,216)
- Iquique (82,004)
- Arica (73,197)
- La Serena (61,307)
- Puerto Varas (54,194)
- Pucon (51,465)
- Puerto Montt (50,061)
- San Pedro de Atacama (41,683).

Turning to domestic tourism, during 2001 a total of 3,871,892 Chileans spent one or more nights in a tourist residence (hotel, motel, apart-hotel, hostel, cottage or camp). This figure is 1.4 per cent less that in 2000. The regional distribution of this sector was:

Table 12.9 Accommodation capacity, number of rooms, 1998–2001

	Total	Hotel	Residential	Motel	Apart-hotel	Camping sites	Camping cabins	Others
1998	346,849	249,863	30,483	25,439	16,590	21,070	3,037	367
1999	353,645	255,647	31,209	25,307	17,462	20,284	3,456	280
2000	364,188	261,599	32,369	28,867	17,063	21,430	2,565	295
2001	363,308	260,053	32,657	28,737	17,890	21,187	2,604	180

Source: Sernatur (2001)

- 13 per cent in the Coquimbo and Bio-Bio regions;
- 12.1 per cent in the Tarapaca region;
- 11.5 per cent in the Santiago Metropolitan region;
- 11.2 per cent in the Lake District region;
- 10.4 per cent in the Valparaiso region.

The other regions attracted less than 10 per cent of this market. In terms of cities, the most important for this domestic market were:

- Santiago (over 400,000 Chilean visitors that spent one night or more);
- Iquique, La Serena, Vina del Mar, Concepcion and Coquimbo (more than 200,000 'Chilean visitors that spent one night or more');
- Arica, Antofagasta, Calama, Pucon and Valdivia (more than 100,000 'Chilean visitors that spent one night or more').

Summary on South America

Based on the available data it would seem that Brazil and Chile will probably lead the region's growth in tourism and hospitality over the period 2003–5, and Argentina will only very slowly emerge from its current political and economic problems.

Table 12.10 Occupancy of domestic and foreign tourist residences, 1998–2001 (actual numbers)

	Total	Hotel	Residential	Motel	Apart-hotel	Camping sites	Camping cabins	Others
1998	3,167,091	2,403,049	195,341	265,503	156,309	123,070	22,595	1,224
1999	2,835,930	2,142,475	166,565	255,639	147,053	102,763	20,802	633
2000	2,881,950	2,161,634	159,340	273,440	130,287	130,905	25,465	879
2001	2,783,382	2,088,299	153,238	244,651	162,764	112,130	21,711	589

Source: Sernatur (2001)

Table 12.11 Room occupancy rates by accommodation category, 1998–2001 (%)

	Total	Hotel	Residential	Motel	Apart-Hotel	Camping sites	Camping cabins	Others
1998	35.0	37.8	25.4	30.2	42.0	18.8	21.3	11.3
1999	30.2	32.5	19.3	28.0	38.1	17.2	15.3	7.8
2000	30.8	32.9	19.7	27.8	39.1	19.4	32.0	9.6
2001	32.5	34.1	21.0	31.7	43.9	21.7	30.6	15.9

Source: Sernatur (2001)

In Argentina, confidence has been badly affected by political and economic uncertainty. The markets investing in tourism and hospitality are increasingly concerned about the country's deteriorating fiscal position and the authorities' ability to meet their external obligations.

The problems in Argentina have affected sentiment towards the region, restricting access to international capital markets. So far, however, the effects have been relatively muted. Brazil is not badly placed to deal with these problems. Its move to a floating exchange rate and inflation targeting policy regime, and progress in limiting the fiscal deficit, give the authorities greater flexibility in economic policy, thus encouraging hotel investment.

On the positive side for Brazil, destinations such as São Paulo, an important convention city, is home to the fifth largest convention centre in the world – the Anhembi Complex, and is ranked 27th among world convention cities by the International Congress and Convention Association. Of all visitors to São Paulo 60 per cent are there for business, they stay an average of 3.7 days and spend an average of US$311 per day including hotel accommodation. In addition to this business segment, the devaluation of the Brazilian real in 1999, encouraged an increase in domestic leisure travel and there is hope that international leisure travel will also grow significantly. With 12,000 restaurants, 70 museums, 200 cinemas, 23 parks and over 16,000 rooms, São Paulo is well positioned to tap into the international leisure travel industry.

However, on the negative side, international air fares remain high, charter flights are limited, and tourist visa requirements pose a significant deterrent to leisure travellers. These key issues need to be resolved in order to fully open up the Brazilian tourism and hotel market.

Turning to Chile, the country will suffer slower growth in tourism and hospitality over the 2003–5 period, especially in relation to Asia, Japan and its heavy dependence on neighbouring Argentina, but the economy is set to remain one of the region's best economic performers. The problem for this country is the disparity between its capital city Santiago and internal destinations, the lack of international hotel brands outside Santiago, and the near monopolistic position of the airline carrier Lan Chile for internal flights. All these points imply higher costs for the traveller and, outside Santiago, restricted access to established international branded hotels.

The relative stability of the Brazilian and Chilean economies over the 2001–3 period, in contrast to Argentina, has heightened investor confidence, and many international hotel companies have announced major developments over the next five years. However, there is some concern that supply will soon outstrip demand in certain locations. Hoteliers' concerns about oversupply may be valid as evidenced by hotel performance. Hoteliers are already witnessing falling average daily rates (ADRs) and occupancy, especially in the luxury sector. The data suggest that the future will see an increased emphasis on the mid-market hotel sector.

In addition, during the past two decades access to hotel financing have been relatively restricted in the three countries; however, this has changed with the stabilization of the economies in Brazil and Chile, and a wealth of new investors are moving into the market. There is also a well-established leisure tourism base as a result of domestic travellers, which will aid in the effort to attract more international leisure tourism business. However, issues of adequate airlift and non-prohibitive air fares need to be overcome before this leisure sector can be fully developed. It is perhaps this final point which will determine the long-term success of these tourism and hotel markets.

Asia-Pacific

Setting the scene

Asia-Pacific destinations are expected to dominate economic growth in the travel and tourism industry over the next few years, but the cost of 11 September 2001 to the region's industry has been severe. In the view of many analysts, 2003–5 will be a period of initial stabilization followed by recovery, though this process requires continued partnership between the private and public sectors on a national and regional basis. Growth in the Asia-Pacific hotel industry is closely linked to the economic success of countries within the region, and in particular to property and land values which have fallen dramatically over the past few years, increasing the debt burden of hotel firms and affecting bank lending policies.

In economic terms, the overall health of Asia-Pacific continues to recover from the financial meltdown that crippled it in mid-1997. However, most of the area's domestic economies continue to perform well below their pre-crisis levels. While economic conditions improve from market to market, the pace of the recovery varies widely, thus affecting the wider tourism industry and specifically the hotel sector.

The WTTC in 2002 published its annual travel and tourism economic research findings which report that the dramatic impact of 11 September 2001 on tourism will stabilize and recovery will begin during 2002–3. The WTTC report also accurately forecast record growth for 2003 with a massive rebound for the travel and tourism industry.

Through its research, WTTC estimates that the impact of 11 September 2001 caused a 7.4 per cent decline in travel and tourism-related demand world-wide in 2001 and 2002 combined, but it is confident that this downward trend will bottom-out and an upturn will begin in the second half of 2002. The upturn will continue into 2003 with global travel and tourism demand forecast to increase in real terms by 6 per cent (see Figure 12.1).

When these world-wide figures are analysed on a regional basis, the trends illustrate a mixed picture, particularly in 2001 (see Figure 12.2). Both East Asia-Pacific and South Asia registered growth in the first 6 months of the year at 9.9 and 1.2 per cent respectively. This trend went into reverse in the second half of the year. Data from the WTTC estimates that 85 per cent of these declines within the two regions were attributable to the events of September 2001 and 15 per cent to independent recessionary events; in 2002 the ratio was put at 70 per cent to 30 per cent.

Taking the example of Southeast Asia drawn from the WTTC, the data clearly illustrate that the fall in growth clearly came from a significant drop in business travel, with a consequent knock-on effect for both the industry's contribution to GDP and a significant fall in employment.

While the average growth in tourism in 2003 is expected to be 6 per cent for the USA and 5.5 per cent for Europe, with a world average of 6.0 per cent. The

Figure 12.1   World travel demand, 1998–2003

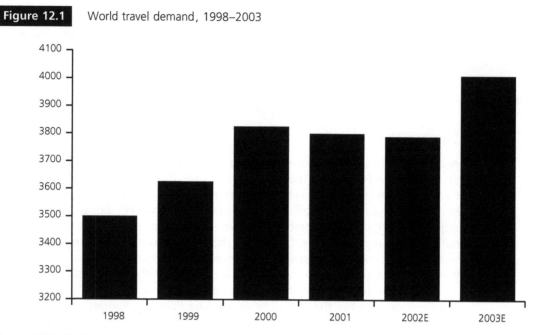

Source: WTTC (2002)
Figures for 2002 and 2003 are estimates

Figure 12.2   International tourist arrivals: regional trends, 2001

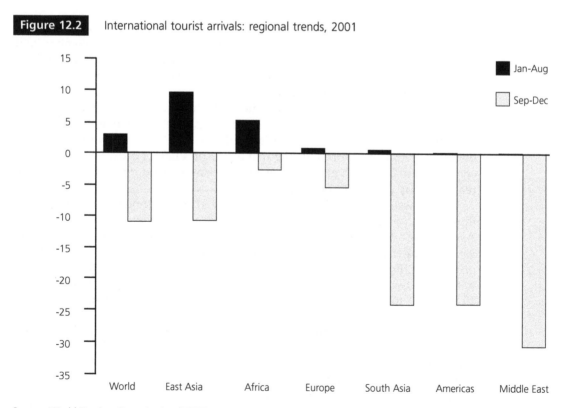

Source: World Tourism Organization (2002)

longer-term trend for 2002–12 in a number of countries is even more positive. Table 12.12 illustrates that four of the top ten countries in terms of growth are from the Asia-Pacific region, namely India, China, Laos and Vietnam.

Over the coming decade, it is forecast that traditional tourism markets such as France, the USA and the UK will continue to take a backseat to emerging growth markets in travel and tourism. Table 12.12 illustrates that Turkey is projected to be the top growth country in the world over the next decade, achieving 10.2 per cent annualized growth in travel and tourism-related demand. In second and third ranking are India and China, with 9.7 per cent and 8.5 per cent respectively. In another important category – job creation – China is ranked first, with growth in travel and tourism employment expected to create a phenomenal 9.3 million full-time job equivalents over the next decade.

Asia-Pacific: a macro economic overview

Economics

Powered by booming exports, a low risk of inflation and falling interest rates, GDP growth for Asia-Pacific reached 6.2 per cent in 2000. South Korea lead the way with 8.3 per cent GDP growth for 2000, while Singapore, Malaysia, the PRC and Taiwan all recorded growth rates above 6 per cent. GDP growth rates of between 4 per cent and about 5 per cent for Thailand, Indonesia and Hong Kong were recorded, while only 3 per cent growth occurred in the Philippines.

Private consumption throughout the region in 2000–1, despite increasing 8 per cent, was still 15 per cent below 1996 levels in US dollar terms. At this rate, pre-1997 crisis levels of economic strength would not have been matched until late 2002. The trend over the period 2002–4 will be driven by externally focused market sectors (primarily technology) and the global economy, while sectors dependent on bank credit – e.g. real estate and specifically hotels – will recover at a much slower pace.

Table 12.12			
Travel and tourism demand, top ten industry growers, 2002–12 (annualized real growth (%))	1	Turkey	10.2
	2	India	9.7
	3	China	8.5
	4	Laos	8.2
	5	Botswana	8.1
	6	Mexico	7.7
	7	Vanuatu	7.7
	8	Uganda	7.7
	9	Vietnam	7.5
	10	Nigeria	7.5

Source: WTTC (2002)

More than four years after the economic crisis that hit the region, banking systems are either impaired, as in South Korea, Thailand, Indonesia and the PRC, or have simply more conservative lending policies, as in Hong Kong, Singapore and Malaysia. However, without bank credit, property price inflation should remain modest, which will encourage inward investment into the hotel market.

Dividing Asia-Pacific in two, developing and developed, GDP growth declined by 3.9 percentage points and by over 2 percentage points respectively during 2001. The poorer GDP outcome in 2001 was associated with a sharp downturn in world trade growth, from over 12 per cent in 2000 to 1 per cent in 2001. However, some economies and sub-regions, such as China, India, Australia, New Zealand and the economies in transition in northern and Central Asia, remained relatively immune. The slowdown was not restricted to inter-country trade and subsequently spread to a broader range of manufacturing activities and services. The events of 11 September 2001 significantly intensified the downturn, yet translated into only slightly higher inflation in many countries. Among the developed countries of the region, Japan experienced deflation, Australia recorded lower inflation and New Zealand experienced only modest price pressures.

The dramatic suddenness of the global downturn in 2001 meant that as it intensified, fiscal measures were supported by more relaxed monetary policies in the form of lower interest rates in most economies of the region, with a few minor exceptions.

As of late 2002, signs of a global and regional upturn were mixed, although evidence of a rebound in recovery is becoming more discernible. While the majority of the economies in the region were expected to exceed their 2001 GDP growth rates in 2002, the improvement was modest, about 1.1 percentage points higher in 2002 than in 2001 for the region's developing economies as a whole. Any upturn in the region's developed countries in 2002 was moderate and restricted to Australia.

The nature of the recovery in 2002 was conditioned by both external and domestic factors. Externally, the overall economic environment in the USA, by and large, remains uncertain despite some positive signs on the horizon, such as improved consumer confidence and an increase in output in the last quarter of 2001. The EU, on present evidence, is unlikely to have matched its 2001 performance in 2002, while Japan is in the throes of yet another recession, the third in the last decade.

Asia-Pacific is particularly vulnerable to external developments on account of the high trade-to-GDP ratios of several economies, and this concentration on exports has meant the national economies were particularly vulnerable to the global slowdown.

Tourism

The fortunes of tourism and hotels in Southeast Asia in 2002 were directly linked to developments in the global economy. The events of September 2001 and their fallout have almost certainly worsened the global outlook, thus necessitating a stronger regional stimulus than would not otherwise have been needed. In addition, in some countries of the sub-region, slow progress in the reform and restructuring of the corporate and enterprise sector is likely to hinder the growth of domestic economic activity. Many of the least developed countries were directly affected by both the combination of the global slowdown in 2001 and the September 2001 events, with the global slowdown having a negative impact on commodity prices and earnings, and on tourism revenue. The majority of these countries rely on commodity exports or tourism, or both, for a major share of GDP.

The medium-term challenge for tourism and hotels is to stimulate growth. This will require certain policy initiatives that can be best promoted at the regional level. For instance, the regional perspective on sustainable development, adopted at the High-Level Regional Meeting for the 2003 World Summit on Sustainable Development, held at Phnom Penh in November 2001, is a good example. Greater regional co-operation in terms of marketing and promotion could also offer a means for economies of the region to counter some aspects of the global slowdown. However, not all sub-regions and countries are experiencing the present downturn to a similar degree. China and India appear relatively immune, while the economies of Australia, New Zealand and the Republic of Korea are still growing at a reasonable rate. They could therefore provide a useful stimulus to other economies by partially offsetting the decline in external demand from within, e.g. Japan, and outside the region. In this context, the region as a whole could move forwards with growth-enhancing trade agreements that boost both trade flows and investor confidence. For instance, China's intended participation in a free trade arrangement with ASEAN is a case in point.

Every country in Asia-Pacific recorded an increase in tourist arrivals from 1998 to 1999, with an average increase across the region of 9 per cent, according to statistics from the Pacific Asia Travel Association (PATA) – a similar trend continued in 2000. China led the way in 1999 with an 18.6 per cent increase in arrivals, followed by Hong Kong at 11.5 per cent; Singapore at 11.4 per cent, and Thailand with 10.3 per cent. Taiwan and the Philippines recorded the smallest increases, of 4.9 per cent and 1.0 per cent respectively. Yet the data for 1998 and 1999 also show that only two countries – Thailand and South Korea – have recorded three consecutive years of arrivals growth.

In comparing 2001 with 2000, international arrivals to East Asia and the Pacific grew by less than 4 per cent, although the pre-September 11, growth rate was more than twice that much. The best performing destinations included China (+6 per cent), Hong Kong (+5 per cent), Malaysia (+23 per cent), and Thailand (+4 per cent). Several destinations were affected by economic problems in Japan, which accounts for 17 per cent of the region's tourism. Japanese outbound tourism fell by an estimated 4.6 per cent in 2001, especially impacting Guam (–10 per cent), Indonesia (–4 per cent), the Republic of Korea (–3 per cent), and Australia which showed a decrease of 1.6 per cent for the first 11 months of the year.

Overall for the year, international arrivals to the region fell by 6 per cent. The period September–December 2001 resulted in a drop of 24 per cent in tourism to the region. Countries such as Nepal (–22 per cent) and Sri Lanka (–16 per cent) were also affected by civil unrest throughout the year. Even the initial bright spot in the region, the Maldives, which achieved strong growth of 9 per cent in the first half of the year, ended the period with a loss of just over 1 per cent.

Undoubtedly, as the economies of Asia-Pacific develop and the region's middle class grows, a rise in intra-regional travel will follow. Here, it is reasonable to believe that strong regional chains may be able to capture this market ahead of global operators because their products and services are distinctly 'more Asian'. Indeed, international brands that do not make a greater attempt to adapt culturally may be missing out on a significant opportunity. However, this change in market mix would not necessarily be a change for the better, because Asians generally stay fewer days and spend less than travellers arriving from long-haul destinations such as Europe and the USA.

Hotel sector

With more than 45,000 rooms and 178 hotels in the region, London-based Six Continents maintains the largest brand portfolio in Asia-Pacific. Six Continents is followed by three other global players: Marriott International, with about 30,000 rooms at 80 hotels; Accor Asia-Pacific, with about 28,000 rooms at 168 properties; and Starwood Hotels and Resorts, with more than 25,000 rooms at 68 hotels (see Table 12.13).

But, among these four global hotel firms, data show that only between 8 per cent and 12 per cent of their total room count managed world-wide is within Asia-Pacific – a relatively small proportion when coupled with the fact that 75 per cent of the hotel stock in the region is non-branded; there is clearly an opportunity for global brand operators to grow in the region.

One of the ways this growth could be achieved is by establishing partnerships with strong, local hotel operators. Interestingly, some of the best candidates for joint ventures in Asia-Pacific already have global aspirations of their own. The Mandarin Oriental Hotel Group, Shangri-La, The Peninsula Group, Raffles and CDL's Millennium and Copthorne brands are among those testing their market acceptance outside Asia-Pacific.

Contrasting hotels with tourism, the positive changes in tourist arrivals within the Asia-Pacific region do not translate into significant increases in hotel operating performance. Here, the relationship between supply and demand determines the outcome from market to market. According to industry commentators, in 1998 virtually every Asia-Pacific market covered recorded

---

Table 12.13

Hotels in Asia-Pacific	Accor Asia-Pacific	168
	Marriott	80
	Starwood Hotels and Resorts	68
	Prince Hotels	75
	Tokyo Hotel Group	93
	Shangri-La Hotels and Resorts	37
	Hyatt Hotels and Resorts	42
	Nikko Hotels International	46
	Hilton International	34

Source: company reports

negative growth in revenues per available room (revPAR). In 1999, the hotelbenchmark survey, which covers 550 hotels in 24 markets, revealed four cities that registered double-digit positive revPAR growth: Seoul, up 30 per cent; Bali and Tokyo, up 16 per cent; and Bangkok, up 10 per cent. However, this bounce-back in results was from a very low base.

Although the economic recovery in Asia-Pacific is clearly underway, it has not yet hit every country in the region. Despite changes in business arrivals, three markets that managed to record negative revPAR growth in 1999 were Beijing (–14 per cent), Shanghai (–17 per cent) and Jakarta (–24 per cent). In Jakarta, which recorded negative revPAR performance for a third consecutive year, the decline is linked to local politics. The market has been so unstable that travellers simply avoid it. In Beijing and Shanghai the issue clearly is oversupply. Both cities have become primary targets of foreign investors, and global hotel chains with the hope an early entry into these two markets will pay huge dividends in the longer term. Indeed, designs for Shanghai are to make it the central commercial hub for China. Unfortunately, over-building there will probably prevent investors from receiving any returns for three to four years. At this time, Shanghai simply cannot attract the number of corporate or leisure travellers necessary to support the vast increases in supply. The market has also been very dependent on the Japanese, who have been travelling less because of their own economic problems. Until new source markets are found, this poor performance is expected to continue.

Selected countries: a review

China

The evidence from China is that international hotel groups have stepped up the fight to win market share in the country. Accor has teamed up with the Beijing Tourist Group to develop Accor brands across China. Meanwhile, Starwood is working with Discovery Group to develop the Four Points brand and initially aims to open ten properties over the next two years.

Domestic consolidation has been seen in the merger of the Jinjiang and Huating Groups, creating the biggest hotel group in mainland China with 27 hotels (13,000 rooms). The new group has a portfolio of three- to five-star hotels but is also targeting the domestic tourist market estimated at 71 million people. It is rolling out its budget hotel concept and will open the first hotel in Shanghai.

Thailand

The trends within the Asia-Pacific hotel industry in 2001 were negative, with the Thai tourist authority registering a fall of 6 per cent in the number of visitors from the USA, while the Thai Farmers' Research Centre estimates that the tourist industry could lose an estimated US$158 million in revenue if American tourists continue to stay at home. In 2001 Bangkok's biggest hotel, the Imperial Queen's Park, had three major conferences postponed, with the hotel operating at less than 60 per cent capacity. The central reason for this was a global reluctance to travel because of safety concerns associated with September 11.

In addition, nearly 30 per cent of bookings in the second half of 2001 at seaside holiday resorts, such as Puket and Ko Samui, were cancelled, mostly from the USA and Japan. The Japanese are very sensitive about security issues and cancellations from there are a close second to the Americans.

Singapore

In contrast, Singapore was not so badly affected. This is largely because many of the island's visitors are business people whose travel arrangements are less flexible than those who might be travelling for leisure. In 1999, Singapore recorded the highest increase in tourism arrivals over 1998 levels, compared with other markets in the region. The 11 per cent increase was attributed primarily to the improved economic environment in Association of South East Asian Nations (ASEAN) countries, which are major source markets for Singapore. According to the Singapore Tourism Board, arrivals from these countries were up 17.8 per cent over 1998 levels. Indonesia, Japan and Malaysia represented the largest markets in terms of visitor arrivals. However, consistent growth was seen in visitor arrivals from China and Japan.

Although substantial marketing resources were invested in 1999, notably in the MillenniaMania campaign, the full impact has emerged from 2000 onwards. Other notable tourism developments include the opening of the Singapore Exhibition Centre and the development of a theatre and concert complex, completed in 2003. This is expected to boost conference and meeting visitor numbers in the long term.

Singapore's reputation as an efficient and corruption-free business hub with sound economic fundamentals and a highly skilled labour force provides an encouraging outlook. Favourable economic conditions characterized by low inflation rates and healthy GDP growth are expected to prevail.

For the hotel industry the outlook is equally promising. The regional economic recovery has put Singapore back in the spotlight as one of the key financial centres in Asia-Pacific and the city looks set to consolidate this position. In addition, Singapore continues to offer an abundant supply of four- to five-star hotel accommodation as well as first-class conference facilities. Consequently, this destination expects to see the continued strengthening of demand from both corporate and MICE (Meetings, Incentive, Conference, Exhibitions) business in 2003.

Hong Kong

In Hong Kong (here treated separately from mainland China) the number of visitors dropped at one brief stage by over 50 per cent in 2001 as a result of September 11. While occupancy within this market has remained buoyant over the past 12 months, evidence from trade sources suggests there is a strong culture of discounting, although this cannot be confirmed from official sources. The sector is still struggling with high levels of debt as a result of high property values which in part has encouraged management to focus on occupancy as opposed to revPAR. While interest rates remain low, the lending institutions continue to be conservative in advancing any form of real estate finance, and that includes hotel properties. As part of the strategy of establishing an economically sustainable tourism industry, the city secured a deal to build a second Disney World in Asia. The Disney park will open on Lantau Island in 2005 and will incorporate up to four hotels, adding from 2000 to 2500 rooms to hotel supply in

Hong Kong. Other projects aimed at generating increased tourism demand include the Snoopy Park in Sha Tin (New Territories), which opened in 2000 and the Madame Tussaud's waxworks located on the Peak. Table 12.14 illustrates trends in tourism arrivals and occupancy for the period May 2001–April 2002. Unfortunately, revPAR data for the period were not available and so a clearer view on discounting within the hotel industry cannot be established.

Japan

As a major supplier of visitors to the region, Japan saw cancellations by half of those people planning to travel overseas from the country in the last two quarters of 2001, according to the Japan Association of Travel Agents. The marketing response from travel authorities throughout the region was to plan to concentrate on encouraging tourism within the region. Firms want to encourage prospective tourists to consider ASEAN countries and Australasia as good alternatives to the USA.

In terms of hotels in Japan, since the early 1990s, when the country's economic bubble burst, real estate values have been declining. Hotel properties have under-performed and, given the deflationary conditions, inflation in property values can no longer be relied on to put real estate assets back into credit. Corporate re-structuring among hotel groups is forcing the divestiture of hotel assets. For example, JAL Hotels is looking to divest overseas resort properties from its portfolio to improve its balance sheet.

Although the hotel market in Japan is changing, domestic players still dominate and international groups have limited presence. The top ten Japanese brands account for approximately 18 per cent of total hotel room stock in Japan, compared with international hotel brands (including management contracts, franchises and other affiliations) which account for a mere 3 per cent. It would seem that the problem for the region's hotels are their dependence on the Japanese economy. Figures for 2001 show that unemployment in the country is

Table 12.14		
Hong Kong: tourism and hotel performance	**Month**	**Visitor arrival**	**Average hotel occupancy rate (%)**
	May 2001	1,165,933	80
	June 2001	1,108,185	76
	July 2001	1,174,565	79
	August 2001	1,246,197	81
	September 2001	1,052,860	74
	October 2001	1,154,817	76
	November 2001	1,141,992	81
	December 2001	1,305,185	84
	January 2002	1,180,540	81
	February 2002	1,115,853	75
	March 2002	1,297,219	86
	April 2002	1,403,041	87

Source: Travel and Tourism Analyst (2002)

at a post-war high of 5.3 per cent and getting worse every month. The problems of the Japanese hotel sector are epitomized by the Tsuraya Hotel, south of Tokyo, that pioneered tourism in Atami, once a fashionable hot-spring resort. Now it has become the 16th hotel in the town to close down in the space of a few years. The economic slump has meant a sharp decline in the number of high-paying corporate customers. The Tsuraya was also saddled with enormous debts dating from the collapse of the property market in 1990. The hotel was once valued at US$240 million but the site was sold in 2001 for just $12 million to a foreign investor.

In addition to these economic trends there are demographic trends which are seeing Japanese customers getting older. Competition is getting harder all the time, there are fewer customers and they spend less than they used to.

South Korea

In South Korea, as part of its effort to restructure the corporate sector, the government opened its markets to foreign investors and record-breaking amounts of foreign investment poured into the South Korean economy in 1999–2000. Despite recording an increase in international tourism arrivals, receipts dipped mainly due to shifts in market segmentation to lower-spending visitors, as well as a decrease in the average length of stay since 1997.

South Korea's tourism campaigns are based on varying themes. Other than promoting the country's unique arts and culture, the Korean National Tourism Organization launched the Korea Grand Sale 2000 campaign that aims to promote South Korea as a shopping destination. South Korea also jointly hosted the World Cup 2002 with Japan and ten South Korean cities were venues for the event. Opened in 2001 at a cost of US$5.6 billion, a new airport at Inchon (56km west of Seoul) is expected to replace Seoul's congested Kimpo Airport for international flights and will have an annual handling capacity of 27 million passengers.

In spite of a remarkable economic recovery, the South Korean economy remains susceptible to factors that can hinder further economic growth, such as an increase in interest rates to temper inflationary pressures, or a weakening in the Japanese yen, which would weaken South Korea's export competitiveness. In addition, South Korea's strong economic rebound could also remove the perceived urgency for reform and restructuring. However, with continued foreign direct investment in South Korea, corporate demand should continue to strengthen. Growth in tourist arrivals is likely to continue, which bodes well for the hotel industry, both in terms of occupancy, revPAR and the positive hotel supply situation.

Malaysia

This country recorded just over 8 per cent growth in international tourist arrivals in 1999 to 6 million, after three consecutive years of decline. A marketing campaign, 'Malaysia – Truly Asia', aimed at promoting Malaysia as a multifaceted and culturally diverse destination, has been ongoing for the past four years. Events such as Formula One, World Cup golf and the Asian Shooting Championships have placed Malaysia on the map as a venue for sporting events. Malaysia's Tourism Promotion Board marketing strategy is focusing on targeting regional markets such as Singapore, Thailand, Japan, China, India, Hong Kong and Taiwan, as well as Europe.

In the hotel investment arena, a number of owners of highly leveraged hotel projects have been pressured to divest, in the event that loans cannot be restructured. Faber Group Bhd, which is 60 per cent owned by Malaysia's biggest conglomerate Renong Bhd, has been working on restructuring its debt for some time. Danaharta, the asset management vehicle approved by the Malaysian government to handle non-performing loans (NPL), has acquired RM1.5 billion (Mayalasian Ringgits) of NPL, secured against 26 hotels in Malaysia. At present, too much emphasis is being placed on improving occupancy and less on revenue management. Danaharta is reportedly lobbying to lift the foreign investment restriction of 30 per cent for hotel ownership.

New Zealand

The unique environmental and cultural characteristics of New Zealand provide the foundation for tourism product development, with consideration given to sustainability of both types of resources in the country's strategic tourism planning. A two-tiered government system sees local tourism associations cater for regional idiosyncrasies under the strategic direction set by central government.

New Zealand's economic growth during the first half of 2001 was buoyed by a competitive exchange rate and strong commodity exports, although growth began slowing noticeably before the terrorist attacks in September. Since this time, weakened international economies, declining export prices and a sharp drop in long-haul travel have threatened to slow the New Zealand economy. Domestic business confidence levels have dropped and investment spending is expected to slow.

On a world stage however, the New Zealand economy remains comparatively healthy, aided by strong economic performance during the first half of 2001 and the benefits of a competitive exchange rate. Nevertheless, the continued global slowdown and reliance on inter-regional and global trading partners is likely to further impact the New Zealand economy in the period 2002–4.

New Zealand's Tourism Satellite Account (TSA) provides an official measure of the impact of tourism on the New Zealand economy. According to the latest available data, tourism made a direct contribution of 4.9 per cent to GDP during 2000, with 94,000 full-time equivalent employees directly engaged in tourism. Including indirect contributions, the figure rises to about 9.3 per cent of GDP (the indirect estimate relates to 1997 data). Although the Asian economic crisis impacted tourism growth potential during 1997 and 1998, TSA data for 1998–2000 shows renewed growth in tourism's contribution to GDP, with a 15 per cent rise between 1997 and 2000.

Domestic tourism demand in New Zealand accounts for 73 per cent of total tourism expenditure, with international demand accounting for the remaining 27 per cent. Between 1990 and 2000 international demand grew by 85 per cent (albeit from a low base) and, as a result, significant investment and attention has been targeted at this lucrative market segment.

New Zealand received 1.94 million international visitors during the year ending September 2001, a growth of 12.2 per cent relative to the previous year.

Australia provides one third of all international arrivals to New Zealand. The UK, USA and Japan also contribute significant volume to international arrivals, at 11 per cent, 10 per cent and 8 per cent respectively. Despite relatively strong growth in international visitor numbers in the past two years, the events of 11 September 2001 and the shift in the global economies have affected tourism industry performance. Inbound travel has been noticeably influenced by dampened consumer sentiment, as global economies adjust to the weakened US economy. For New Zealand's Australian market, the additional influences of an unstable aviation landscape, a recent federal election and more strict corporate travel policies have served to further reduce cross-Tasman demand.

Although international visitors contribute just 27 per cent to total tourism expenditure, their economic contributions to accommodation services is substantially higher at 55 per cent. New Zealand's five primary markets, Auckland, Rotorua and Wellington on the North Island, and Christchurch and Queenstown in the South Island, attract a unique mix of visitors, impacting positively on market performance. Data from the New Zealand Hotel Industry Benchmark Survey illustrate weakened revPAR performance in Auckland, primarily influenced by supply additions, and likely to be further impacted if the anticipated decline in inbound tourists continues. Stronger revPAR performance for 2001 was recorded for Rotorua, Christchurch and Queenstown, where both domestic and inbound demand has improved. Wellington still commands the strongest room rates across all markets, driven by a strong exposure to corporate and government demand, which elevate mid-week occupancies in particular. Competitive performance in 2003 is likely to favour those properties where business and nationality mix is diversified across a range of markets or less exposed to the long-haul inbound markets of the USA and Japan in particular.

Australia

Australia is in a unique position. Part of the reason behind a peak in Chinese visitors is Australia's 'Approved Destination Status' (ADS). Of the 19 countries allowed to promote group travel directly in China, Australia and New Zealand are the only Western nations. In the two and a half years since ADS was granted, arrivals from China have almost doubled, but the number of tour guides has not. That is due, in part, to the Australian government's immigration policy, which does not allow overseas tour guides to qualify for long-stay business visas. By 2020, it is estimated that 100 million Chinese people a year will travel overseas. Growth in the Australian market alone is forecast to be at 20 per cent per annum. By 2012, 50 per cent of all tourists to Australia are expected to come from Asia.

Results for the first six months of the year 2001 according to Deloitte & Touche indicate that both occupancy levels and average room rates are growing at over 2 per cent, resulting in an overall rooms yield increase across the country of 5 per cent. Melbourne maintained its position as the highest yielding market with a rooms yield just over AUD130. The city also enjoys the highest occupancy of all the markets monitored, with demand levels for the first half of 2001 at 78 per cent. Sydney achieved pre-Olympic rate growth as expected, although demand unexpectedly softened in the last two months of 2001. Occupancy levels in Perth are on the increase as inbound demand from Asia returns. Hotels in Perth recorded a 10 per cent increase in occupancy to reach 74 per cent in 2001, however average rates remained under pressure. Although the Adelaide market performed particularly well in June 2001, the first six months of the year saw occupancy levels only grow by 1 per cent, while growth in average room rates out-performed the country average at 3.5 per cent.

Few significant construction starts are expected in the Australian market over the period 2002–4 following the significant increase in room supply seen in the last three years. Although new hotels are set to enjoy positive trading with peak occupancy and average room rates in 2002/2003, the medium-term outlook is somewhat subdued as new supply continues to be absorbed into the market and competition for market share is likely to increase between domestic and international groups as more global brands have recently entered the Australian market.

India

Despite recent political problems, as a growing tourist destination India needs to encourage tour operators to take a more long-term approach to the planning of tourist ventures. India has had particular problems of unsustainable tourism, where tourist centres had suffered due to environmental degradation and the erosion of traditional social values. But the country is now ready to reach its true potential as a tourist destination, with high investment in infrastructure and the development of tourist routes. India will also explore the possibility of joint packages to ensure that visitors visit more than one country in the region. The major problem for the country's hotel industry is the major brands' location in certain 'honeypot' destinations and a virtual absence outside these areas.

Fiji

Fiji is one of the most popular tourist destinations in the region, but despite all its virtues, Fiji's tourism industry, a core of the national economy, was hit hard by the shock of September 11 and, before that, of a military coup in 2000. According to the National Visitors Bureau, tourist numbers to the South Pacific islands exceeded 380,000 in 2001, up some 14 per cent from the previous year, when the coup led by failed businessman George Speight frightened tourists away. In 2000 the number of visitors fell to just a fraction of the 1999 level, which was a record year, after Australia and New Zealand, Fiji's core markets, had advised their citizens to stay away from the islands because their security could not be guaranteed. Tourists from Europe, Japan and the Americas also avoided Fiji.

The terrorist attacks in the USA in September 2001 cast their shadow on the industry as well. There are no official numbers for Fiji, but French Polynesia, the second most popular destination in the region, suffered a 9.7 per cent slump in arrivals after the attacks. Overall, the Fiji tourist industry lost more than 40 per cent of its customers.

However, two years after the coup, tourists are returning to Fiji. Visitor numbers from Australia and New Zealand soared 35 per cent and 28 per cent respectively for the year 2001–2. More tourists are coming from Japan and the USA, with only Europeans still staying away, whose numbers are down a further 7 per cent.

Summary on Asia-Pacific

Hotel operators in several Asia-Pacific markets continue to 'cut each other's throats', discounting room stock despite the recent recovery in average occupancy rates. One would assume that once occupancies rise to a certain level, operators will start squeezing out higher rates. Three markets where this heavy discounting still occurs are Hong Kong, Manila and Singapore, where occupancies rose 10 per cent in 2002 but heavy price discounting continued. There are two reasons for this trend:

- Many property owners are still focused strictly on the utilization rates – that is, the occupancies – of their hotels. So, rather than focusing on revPAR or gross operating profits (GOP), operators are forced to discount to increase occupancies, because that is the directive they are getting from hotel owners.

- The market may not be well balanced – that is, supply does not match demand, not only in size, but also in terms of market mix. Singapore is a prime example. Here, there are too many five-star hotels and not enough five-star travellers. As a result, five-star operators are having to reach down to grab four-star market share. They do this by lowering their rates.

While the typical four-star business traveller resists the five-star segment, they will upgrade if it is made attractive to them. What ultimately happens is that three- and four-star hotels suffer most because they reach down for business on the bottom rungs, but find that there is none. Not surprisingly, these middle segments in some markets have been hit harder in revPAR terms than the five-star sector.

While the path to a complete recovery of the hotel markets in Asia-Pacific will be full of obstacles, there are a few key improvements that can be made to help recover shareholder value in the region:

- *Asset management*: more attention needs to be paid to the overall hotel performance, focusing on revenue management and improving GOP, rather than strictly trying to increase occupancies. Owners have already gained more leverage as they have become more prudent, demanding shorter management contracts with performance-based fees from hotel operators.

- *Brand and distribution*: shareholder value is associated with distribution. While hotel companies in the USA and Europe have been looking for incremental business in Asia-Pacific, they would also be wise to revisit the impact of global distribution systems (GDS) and the Internet on driving regional business through effective distribution and proper revenue management practices.

- *Customer relationship management*: the hotel industry in Asia-Pacific will need to raise its level of sophistication with regard to utilizing customer data. To date, hoteliers have been good at collecting the data, but less so at using it to the best effect, such as in target marketing.

- *Benchmarking*: the collection of business information – costs, revenues and other operational data – in the region is also in its infancy. For the benefit of all, knowledge sharing must be encouraged.

Middle East

The Middle East offers a remarkable collection of centres of great touristic appeal, creating a natural visitor magnetism. Indeed, many people rank the region's attractions among the most important places to visit in the world. The opportunities for expansion of cultural tourism, given the region's concentration of religious and historic sites, can hardly be overestimated. At the same time, there are tremendous opportunities in leisure tourism development that capitalizes on the region's superb climate and other natural gifts.

An honourable and just regional peace – and a willingness to work co-operatively – are among key factors that will dictate the strength of tourism growth and the success of private hospitality ventures in the future.

One of the few constraints to the development of a substantial increase in tourism will be adequate infrastructure. For the Middle East to fully realize its promise, collaboration among tourism agencies and the easing of travel restrictions will also be of paramount importance. Middle Eastern countries with mature tourism sectors can be of great assistance to others with less-developed industries. In such a process the nations of the Middle East will all benefit as they co-operate to promote the region and its gifts to the world. However, while tourism arrivals to the region are increasing, this cannot be taken for granted. The political instability of the past may prove a threat to this highly sensitive industry.

Specifically, demand in much of the Middle East region continues to grow, including Saudi Arabia, Bahrain, Kuwait, Damascus and Casablanca. Hoteliers report that both leisure and business demand (notably in Saudi Arabia and Bahrain) have shown growth. This positive trend provides comfort to hotel companies that are expanding in the region. Egypt for instance has shown a remarkable recovery with occupancies almost at the same levels as in 1997 before the Luxor attack on tourists. However, until the charter business returns, regions outside Cairo will continue to struggle. In addition, although Cairo has seen an improvement in occupancy, average rates have suffered as a consequence, a situation exacerbated by new hotel supply.

Syria, for instance, has experienced good growth in tourist arrivals with figures at around 3 million. The Syrian government recently announced that 2500 internationally managed four- and 5-star hotel rooms are anticipated to open over the next few years. However, the approval process for foreign investment projects, controlled by the Syrian Ministry of Tourism, may delay the development of these projects.

Dubai's beach resorts continue to see rises in occupancy as its status as a winter holiday destination increases. This has enabled Jumeirah Beach to cope with a significant increase in supply, although average rates have dropped a little. Meanwhile, city centre hotels are struggling with the increasing supply and the greater appeal of the beach-located luxury hotels.

Despite the region's economic setbacks in recent years, new investment shows no sign of slackening. Hotel companies Oberoi, Sheraton, Radisson SAS,

Bass Hotels and Resorts, Starwood, Four Seasons, Hyatt and Choice are operators planning major investment and expansion in the region. The hotel industry remains confident that this market is far from saturated and a number of companies have the Middle East at the forefront of their hotel development strategy. This said, oversupply remains second only to political instability as a threat to the region's hoteliers.

Middle East tourism in a world context

The substantial growth of tourism activity world-wide clearly marks the sector as one of the most remarkable economic and social phenomena of the past century. The number of international arrivals shows an evolution from a mere 25 million international arrivals in 1950 to over 700 million in 2003, corresponding to an average annual growth rate of 7 per cent.

In addition to strong overall expansion, the development of modern tourism is characterized by an ongoing spread of tourists over the globe, together with a diversification of the tourism product and increasing competition between destinations. More and more destination countries have succeeded in earning a share of the growing tourism pie. By region, this trend of deconcentration is illustrated by above average growth in the number of international tourist arrivals to East Asia-Pacific, South Asia, Africa and the Middle East, and below average growth of more traditional tourism-receiving regions, such as Europe and North America.

Growth patterns of emerging destinations are normally very dynamic with double-digit increases for a number of years in a row. On the other hand, emerging destinations tend to be more vulnerable than mature destinations to the political and economic climate and possible threats to their image in the source markets. Because of this, periods of fast growth often alternate with years of little growth or decline. In general, however, tourism tends to be very resilient.

The main tourist-receiving regions have been, and continue to be, Europe and North America. The Middle East (as defined by the World Tourism Organization) is one of the world's smallest regions, receiving only 18 million tourists in 2002, but it also had the fastest growth rate. Egypt, which represents half of the regional total, posted a spectacular growth rate and a record number of tourist arrivals that far exceeds totals achieved before the Luxor attack. Syria also fared well, with arrivals increasing substantially.

The performance of economic variables in recent years within the main generating markets has favoured tourism development for many countries. However, on the world scale the positive effects of this have been largely offset by the economic downturn in East Asia and the Pacific, in South America and in the Russian Federation. According to major economic bodies, such as the International Monetary Fund, the OECD and Eurostat, world economic prospects for 2003 and beyond are bright.

Regional potential

After decades of political instability, the peace process in the Middle East continues to very slowly bear fruit with one of the chief beneficiaries being increased travel to a region with a unique abundance of natural, historic and cultural assets. Modern jet-age tourism is a relatively new phenomenon in many parts of the Middle East, although the region has been a magnet for travellers for millennia. Many existing hotels were developed in the late 1970s and early 1980s to serve the needs of business travellers. In recent years, a wave of development in a number of other destinations in the region has brought new hotel resorts and leisure attractions associated with the growth in regional and international recreational tourism.

Notwithstanding political and military conflict – coupled with a lack of cohesive regional marketing initiatives – the Middle East has posted growth in visitor arrivals of almost 10 per cent annually over the last five years. Egypt is one of the cornerstones of tourism by virtue of the volume of visitors. Of the 10 million visitors to the Middle East each year, the countries of Egypt, Israel, Jordan and Lebanon together represent just over 50 per cent of all arrivals. Egypt is the dominant market with approximately 3 million visitors.

What is clear is that there is much room for growth. The World Tourism Organization reports that the region has approximately 150,000 hotel rooms, just over 1 per cent of the world's supply. Total visitor arrivals to the Middle East annually amount to 2 per cent of world arrivals, similar to Greece. For the hospitality industry in the Middle East, the challenge lies in tapping the broad opportunities for cultural tourism, as well as other types of leisure and recreational travel, and further developing the infrastructure and services to enrich and extend visitations.

However, there is a significant imbalance of hospitality infrastructure relative to growth potential in certain parts of the region – notably Syria, Jordan and Lebanon. After 15 years of conflict, for example, Lebanon – and its capital city, Beirut – are undergoing a massive rebuilding effort with major hotel development in planning and under construction. Transportation access continues to be an issue in tourism growth. Inter-regional travel has been constrained by virtue of political barriers raised by countries. Lowering of these barriers as the peace negotiations progress would be a boon to tourism, allowing more fluid movement of travellers throughout the Middle East.

As peace comes to the region, the hospitality industry stands to gain significantly as it fulfils the potential for dramatic growth. The Middle East is an emerging market for tourism investment and development. Already far-sighted investors, both regionally and internationally, are capitalizing on the current status of the peace talks in the region. The trickle of investment could well become a flood during the next few years. For countries without the benefit of substantial oil reserves for the next century – including Egypt, Jordan and Lebanon – tourism may become an important engine of their national economies.

In terms of culture and heritage, a rich history of religious, Hellenic, Roman, Byzantine, Crusader and Ottoman occupations has left its mark at scores of archaeological sites, shrines and holy places throughout the Middle East. The Dead Sea, the pyramids of Giza, the temples of Luxor, Petra and Jerash in Jordan, and the historic and religious sites of Jerusalem represent just a few of the many superb visitor attractions in the region. Damascus in Syria is the oldest continually inhabited city in the world. Jerusalem held its 3000 year anniversary in 1996. In addition, the aquatic attractions of the Red Sea, the region's desert landscapes, beaches, sunny winters and other natural resources could conceivably make the Middle East the world's newest tourism 'hot spot'.

Because of these cultural and heritage issues, the Middle East has earned increasing attention as a centre for tourism from international bodies. The World Tourism Organization named 1995 the Arab Tourism Year. The World Bank has helped to fund a number of important tourism development initiatives in the Middle East, among them Tourism Master Plans and loans for infrastructure, including airports and road networks, and water and power utilities.

The potential for substantial international tourism growth is evidenced by that fact that almost 60 per cent of all tourists in the region come from within the Middle East. The traditional major international tourist markets of Europe and North America – which together make up almost 80 per cent of all world tourist arrivals – currently account for only 30 per cent of arrivals to the region. This suggests major potential for expanding the number of international tourists. In addition, as the economies of the region mature and changes in the population demographics result in a more leisure-conscious and affluent middle class, inter-regional tourism will continue to grow.

Hotel industry overview: the Middle East

With the crises in Asia, Russia and Iraq, as well as the oil crisis in the past few years, it is a wonder that anybody has stayed in hotels in the Middle East at all. While, as many believe, half of the world's economic analysts have talked themselves into recession, there have been many economies in the Middle East that have experienced GDP growth. The impact of these crises on regional economies, however, has been felt, resulting in many government infrastructure projects either being put on hold or slowed down. Economic forecasts for oil-based economies are not encouraging, and governments are rapidly embarking on economic diversification and privatization programmes. The high population growth rates experienced in many countries, leading to a potential unemployment time-bomb, have also helped to push the diversification issue to the forefront of the economic agenda.

Despite disagreements among some of the region's politicians that have led to violence and the threat of violence, tourism remains a growing industry. Dubai has experienced some growth in rooms sold in the quality hotel market, and demand levels at some of Egypt's key tourist destinations are almost level with those experienced before the attack on tourists visiting Luxor in November 1997.

With the key fundamentals of sun, sand, sea and a rich cultural past, the region has an advantage over many competing tourism destinations. Growth in arrivals to the region has occurred and, with a new tourism infrastructure being developed in many countries, this appears likely to continue.

While there have been some spectacular declines in room yields, notably in destinations such as Luxor, many destinations continue to achieve yield growth. The somewhat unique markets of Mecca and Medina continued to perform well over the period 1998–2002, with yield growth of more than 20 per cent in US dollar terms. Beirut and Alexandria also both managed to achieve growth. Some resort destinations on Egypt's Red Sea coastline, the 'Red Sea Riviera', are now reporting monthly growth in occupancy levels. However, performance for the Luxor, Hurghada and Giza (Cairo and the pyramids) markets continue to disappoint, with room yields declining.

Hotel development in the region continues, driven both by generous government incentives and confidence that the natural tourism fundamentals, coupled with quality hotel development, will be enough to generate sufficient demand to underpin investment returns. In many destinations, demand statistics tend to support this view; to date, Sharm el-Sheikh and Dubai are good examples.

Economic growth in the Middle East is likely to remain patchy, and demand from the corporate visitor is not expected to show significant gains. Occurring with little or no warning, regional disputes and political tensions are likely to have a continuing impact on tourism to the region.

This market has proved to be particularly resilient in the past, and is expected to show continued growth. With increases in the supply of quality hotel accommodation due to occur over the short- to medium-term, a general softening of occupancy and, in particular, average rates in many markets is anticipated.

There also are many destinations in the region that have yet to tap into the tourism market. Some observers believe that while these countries may be slow in attracting tourists they actually have more to offer. With destinations such as Oman, Fujairah, Yemen and Iran still hiding spectacular coastlines, mountain ranges, and history which predates the birth of Christ, the potential to build tourism remains significant.

International hotel chains dominate

The established international hotel chains, such as Sheraton, Hyatt, Hilton, Meridien and Inter-Continental, currently dominate the management of upscale hotels in the region with more than 90 per cent of the total rooms available in the Middle East being managed by these major groups.

With the easing of restrictions and slow developments in the peace process, new hotel companies in the Middle East are rushing to acquire suitable sites and management contracts. Particularly active are Marriott, with the first new hotel in Beirut, and hotels in Sharm El-Sheikh in Egypt. The Swiss group, Mövenpick, has also been particularly active in Jordan, with new hotels in Petra, the Dead Sea, Amman and Aqaba. Hyatt International, too, has been active throughout the region with new hotels in Amman and Sharm El Sheikh. Other active companies include the deluxe Four Seasons chain currently looking at hotels in Cairo, Beirut and Amman, and the Howard Johnson and Days Inn groups, which are looking at motel-style properties in Jordan.

Tourism profile by country

Egypt

Long the dominant tourism market of the Middle East, Egypt captures nearly 30 per cent of all arrivals to the Middle East. Visitor arrivals, room supply and revenue generation from tourism have risen steadily since 1989. Arrivals are split almost equally between business travellers and leisure tourists. Of all visitors 50 per cent come from Europe, while 28 per cent arrive from other Middle Eastern countries.

The country's tourism industry in the future will be strongly influenced by the government's encouragement of tourism development away from Egypt's more traditional heritage sites. Such development zones include the Red Sea Riviera of Taba, the Sinai region, and Sharm El Sheikh and the Hurghada-Safaga area of the Red Sea. A major challenge for the government will be to limit the damage caused by religious tensions in upper Egypt. Possible future co-operation between Egypt, Israel and Jordan will be an element in boosting tourism in the area overall, as these countries benefit from the peace process and improved inter-regional co-operation.

Hotel occupancies have remained stable in the largest hotel market in the Middle East. The attack on tourists in Tahrir Square in September 1997 caused a number of flight and hotel booking cancellations, but terrorist activity has had less effect on the numbers in Cairo, in comparison to Luxor and the Red Sea destinations.

The number of corporate room nights sold in the Cairo hotel market illustrates the city's focus as a business destination. The city is used as an entry and exit point, from which the leisure traveller moves onto the resorts along the Nile and the Red Sea coast, as evidenced by the significant room-night demand generated by the group/tour and leisure sectors. Travellers from the Middle East and Europe accounted for 70 per cent of the rooms sold in Cairo in 2002. Domestic business has decreased since 1999, whereas the number of rooms from the North American market increased.

In spite of Cairo being the largest hotel market in the Middle East, the city's room stock is generally tired and in need of regeneration. In 1997 the 561-room Sheraton Heliopolis opened, being the first addition to supply at the top end of the market since the Semiramis Inter-Continental opened in 1987. Extensive development is now taking place on the outskirts of the city, in the emerging districts of New Cairo to the east and west of the city.

Egypt is a resilient market – despite the sharp downturn between 1992 and 1995, hotel performances bounced back and they will do so again.

Much of the hotel development in Egypt over the past few years has been concentrated in the Red Sea and Sinai areas, leaving the number of hotel developments in Luxor limited. It is also expected that recent events may discourage future investment. The outlook for the hotel market in Luxor is temporarily bleak. Hotels, particularly the five-star properties, will struggle to build up room rates once more and will need to work hard to encourage European tour operators to resume selling package holidays to the area. It is hard to imagine, however, that visitors will stay away from the wealth of historic sites in the long term.

Jordan

Tourism to Jordan has grown steadily, with visitor arrivals up between 1989 and 1999. The future outlook for Jordan includes co-operative projects with Israel and Egypt to develop the Red Sea Riviera at Aqaba. A major tourism development zone is planned south of Aqaba, with a total of 5000 rooms under discussion. Development planning also is underway for the 'Lowest Park on Earth' on the

Dead Sea, including several hotel projects by major chains (i.e., Holiday Inn, Mövenpick, Hilton). Future development of hotel accommodation is planned in Petra, with between 800 and 1000 rooms in various stages of development.

In addition, there are numerous private sector companies established to take advantage of the anticipated boom in tourism in the region, including Zara Investments and Al Dawliyah – companies with a variety of projects that involve international hotel groups, such as Marriott, Hyatt, Sheraton, Movenpick and Hilton.

However, 2001–3 was not a good period for hoteliers in Amman. The stalled peace process and the unstable political situation in the region were the main reasons for a continuous drop in occupancy. Room rates also decreased and Amman became the cheapest destination in the Middle East after Egypt. The leisure segment, which accounted for 50 per cent of all rooms sold in quality hotels in 2002, diminished in comparison to 1997. In 2001, Amman was predominantly visited by corporate travellers from Europe. For many corporate travellers based in the Middle East, Amman is also a transit destination for undertaking business in the West Bank and Gaza. As the Palestinian National Authority continues to slowly develop in its own right as a functioning independent economy, a knock-on increase in corporate visitation could be positive for the city's hoteliers.

Hyatt opened 80 of its 312 rooms in late 1998. This is the first of many new hotels due to open in the coming years. As a result of this increasing competition, both the Marriott and the Inter-Continental hotels have been undergoing what is regarded by many as long overdue refurbishment programmes.

With the increasing number of new hotels under development – stimulated by the peace process started in 1995 – the market may be entering a period of sustained pressure on performance. This said, the potential for significant economic and tourism growth under a new/reinstated peace process has already been demonstrated across the region, and it is only this that is likely to save the performance of the city's new hotels.

Collectively, the tourism markets of the Middle East constitute what may soon be one of the most dynamic regional destinations in the world. The Middle East might be described as one of the world's first 'tourist' destinations, having served an extraordinary role in the confluence of cultures and religions for thousands of years. Restoring peace offers the exciting prospect of the region regaining its historic prominence with visitors from the 'four corners' of the world.

Bahrain

Bahrain is still seeking to diversify its economy by improving its financial, transport, tourism and trade sectors. In 2001, the country moved forwards in its democratization programme and is increasingly trying to promote itself as a regional free trade hub with the most liberal economy in the Gulf region. Due to the decline in oil prices, GDP growth has decreased slightly, from 5.2 per cent in 2000 to 5.0 per cent in 2001. Additional efforts are being planned to create jobs for Bahrainis, whose country has an official unemployment rate of 6 per cent. Attracting additional international capital will remain one of the country's main policies aimed at boosting the economy and ensuring international exposure, and plans exist for the expansion of infrastructure.

Bahrain is becoming increasingly attractive to business and leisure visitors. In 2001, the quality hotel market in Manama achieved a market-wide occupancy level of 62 per cent, an increase of approximately 3 percentage points. However, average rates in the city declined to approximately US$103 in 2001, compared to US$105 in 2000. The decline was attributable mainly to the global economic slowdown, combined with the events of 11 September 2001, which forced hoteliers to lower their prices for fear of losing market share. Yet the increase in occupancy offset the decline in average rate for quality hotels in Manama, as revPAR experienced an overall increase of approximately 3 per cent, to US$64.

The country is increasingly encouraging investment in the tourism sector. Some of the major investments in the area include a probable US$80 million Formula 1 racetrack. In addition, Gulf-based investors plan to put around US$1billion into the development of a tourist resort on constructed islands located off the Bahrain coast. This project is similar to Dubai's Palm Island, and will include luxury hotels, residential apartments, retail stores and leisure facilities. Furthermore, Accor is planning to manage the Al Dana Resort project (due for completion in 2003) under the Novotel brand. In addition, a multi-million dollar project is planned for the northern shores of the island and will include a marina, a golf course and villas. In 2003 Mövenpick opened a 120-room hotel near the airport and a four-star hotel is planned for Juffair in 2003.

Kuwait

In 2001, the government officially relaunched an economic privatization plan that it had suspended in 1998. The aim of the plan is to reform and revive the economy. Fluctuations in the volume of oil production and oil prices will continue to dominate Kuwait's growth prospects. According to the EIU, GDP growth declined to 0.8 per cent in 2001, from 4 per cent in 2000. Falling oil prices are likely to cause GDP growth to decline further in 2002, after which a turnaround should increase growth to 3.5 per cent in 2003. The current account surpluses are expected to decrease due to a dampening of oil prices and large investment-related imports. The economic and political outlook is uncertain due to concerns about Iraq.

Kuwait attracts few leisure tourists because of its complicated visa regulations, its lack of major attractions and the ban on the sale or consumption of alcohol. Nearly all visitors to the country are business people. Tourism in the country is not likely to experience strong growth in the near future as little effort or investment is being made to improve this sector.

Occupancy levels in Kuwait's five-star properties increased by 3 percentage points to 49 per cent in 2001. Average rates increased from US$178 in 2000 to US$182 in 2001, and still remain high. Although occupancy levels in the five-star hotels remain low, there are a number of projects under construction. These include a 150-room Hilton hotel located on the beachfront, which opened in 2003, a 150-room Four Points, an 80-room Taj and a 300-room Courtyard by Marriott. The increase in supply is likely to have a detrimental effect on hotel performance in Kuwait unless the government makes more effort to promote business tourism. However, as all the hotels are government-owned, there is little pressure to do this.

Oman

According to the Economist Intelligence Unit (EIU), GDP growth increased from 4.7 per cent in 2000 to 5 per cent in 2001, an increase which was driven mainly by the development of the gas sector. An economic contraction is anticipated in 2002 due to the global economic slowdown and the decline in oil earnings and foreign investment inflows. In 2003, an expected increase in public capital spending, combined with stronger oil earnings, is likely to accelerate the economic performance of the country.

Oman's internal political stability appears assured, despite some uncertainty regarding the successor to the ruling sultan, Qaboos bin Said al-Said. Following the events of September 11 the country maintained its close ties with the West.

The government is making further efforts to encourage the expansion of the tourism sector. In 2001, it decided to ease the restrictions on tourism visas for residents of Gulf Cooperation Council (GCC) countries. The new law will mean that GCC residents will no longer have to pay for a sponsorship visa. In addition, Oman has signed an agreement with the United Arab Emirates which eases visa requirements for cross-border visitation between the two countries. The country has also set in place a five-year plan, which recognizes the potential of the tourism sector. The plan is likely to encourage the private sector to lead the growth in the tourism sector. In addition, plans exist to establish a tourism college near Muscat.

In January 2002, a 92-room Ramada opened in Muscat. In addition, the Al Bustan Palace Inter-Continental underwent a four-month renovation in 2001, and the hotel is currently developing a spa and a health club on the premises. New hotel supply includes a 150-room Ritz Carlton, a 300-room Hilton, a 250-room Le Méridien and a 714-room Barr al Jissah Resort, which will be managed by the Shangri La Group. In addition, a 100-room Shedi and a 60-room Serai (both GHM hotels opened in 2003).

Qatar

Qatar will continue to focus on gas-based industries as it seeks to diversify its economy away from the oil sector. According to the EIU, GDP growth showed an increase from 4.3 per cent in 2000 to 5.7 per cent in 2001, which was driven largely by the country's exports of natural gas. While lower oil prices are likely to result in a slowdown in the country's economic prosperity in 2002, Qatar's rapid expansion in the gas sector is likely to result in a significant economic acceleration in 2003.

Qatar will continue to enjoy political stability. The Emir's political reforms have earned him domestic popularity. On the international stage, the country maintains its strong relations with the USA.

Qatar, like its neighbours, is looking to develop an international tourist industry in order to diversify its economy. The government is using tax incentives to encourage local private companies to build tourism-related projects and sporting facilities. A new law was approved allowing foreigners to have up to 100 per cent ownership in tourism projects in the country. To encourage tourism further, Qatar has relaxed its visa regulations by allowing visitors from 33 countries across Europe, the Americas and the Far East to obtain visas upon arrival in Qatar. In addition, Qatar and Oman agreed to allow business visa holders of either country to fly to the other and obtain a visa upon arrival. Furthermore, travel restrictions between Qatar and neighbouring Bahrain have been eased. A major infrastructural project is being planned between the two countries and will feature a bridge which will link them together.

A decrease in hotel performance has been associated mainly with the increase in hotel supply, with the opening of the 374-room Ritz-Carlton and the 154-room Mövenpick. Qatari leaders have created a US$1 billion fund to develop tourist projects. These projects include: the US$15 million Al-Ghariya eco-heritage project; the Al-Bida Park Marketplace, including the development of a village on the Doha corniche; the Aladdin's Kingdom redevelopment near the West Bay Lagoon; the Doha Golf Club resort; and the development of some beaches.

Saudi Arabia

Saudi Arabia is becoming increasingly aware of the need to diversify its economy away from its sole reliance on oil exports. In 2001, according to the EIU (as cited in www.hotelbenchmark.com), GDP growth dropped to 1.7 per cent, from 4.1 per cent in 2000. The main dampener of growth occurred in the crude oil sector, with a squeeze on production throughout the year reflecting OPEC's attempts to boost prices by reducing oil output quotas. Given the deteriorating outlook for global oil demand, particularly in the aftermath of the September 11 attacks in the USA, it will be very difficult for Saudi Arabia to maintain this level of economic growth in 2002. Based on the EIU's latest forecasts, GDP growth is expected to decline further in 2002 to 0.3 per cent, but it is envisaged that GDP growth will recover to 4 per cent in 2003.

While continued efforts are being made by the Saudi government to attract foreign investment to the country, political and religious sensitivities will slow these economic reforms. Domestic unease about Saudi Arabia's close relationship with the USA is also likely to remain as regional and international tensions continue.

Saudi Arabia has a good infrastructure in terms of ports, airports and roads. However, telecommunications need considerable investment. Insufficient investment has been made in information technology and the government still monitors the use of the Internet.

Tourism in Saudi Arabia can be divided into three categories: the Hajj (pilgrimage), commercial visitors, and leisure tourists from other GCC states and from inside the Kingdom. The government is increasing its efforts to boost tourism revenues by means of touristic investments and a relaxation of visa requirements. A major breakthrough has been to allow Hajj pilgrims to visit the country at any time during the year, rather than restrict visitation to certain periods.

Attitudes towards internal tourism are now changing and many new leisure developments are being undertaken to encourage Saudis to take holidays in the country. In general, the effects of the events of September 11 on visitation to Saudi Arabia were less profound than they were on other Arab countries. This was due mainly to the nature and source of the visitations to the country. The vast majority of visitors to the Kingdom are either pilgrims visiting Mecca and Medina or Arabs from neighbouring countries.

There were some additions to hotel supply in Riyadh in 2001 with the full opening of the 224-room Rosewood Al Faisaliyah hotel and the 177-room

Holiday Inn Olaya. In addition, some quality hotels, such as the 372-room Marriott, completed their renovation programmes. The 302-room Riyadh Palace was rebranded as a Golden Tulip during 2001.

Syria

In December 2001 President Bashar al-Assad appointed 18 new members to his cabinet. Their task will involve reviving the economy, generating employment and speeding up the pace of economic reform. In 2001 a new law was passed allowing the establishment of private banks in the country, albeit with fairly strict terms. It is anticipated that it will take many years to reform the state banking sector in the country but this change in policy signifies a positive shift. Foreign policy issues continue to be dominated by relations with neighbouring Israel, Syria's support for the Palestinian cause and the events of September 11.

Syria is highly dependent on the international price of oil which accounted for an estimated 70 per cent of export revenues in 2001. The forecast decline in oil prices, combined with Syria's unsettled political situation, is likely to affect the country's growth outlook. According to the EIU (as cited in www.hotelbenchmark.com), GDP growth registered 1.6 per cent in 2001, and is projected at approximately 1.5 per cent for 2002. The decline in GDP growth in 2002 is directly attributable to the expected decrease in oil prices and the slowdown in the global economy. However, growth in private consumption, improvements in the agricultural sector and an increase in oil prices should accelerate the economy in 2003 with GDP growth estimated at 3.1 per cent.

Tourism receipts in Syria represent around 7 per cent of GDP. While there is significant potential for the country to be developed as a tourist destination, there is still both a lack of awareness by potential visitors and willingness on the part of the government. However, the Syrian government has signed a three-year agreement with Lebanon for tourism co-operation, which is likely to facilitate increased visitation to the country. The tourism sector has experienced some decline due to the events of September 11, but, on the positive side, visitation to Syria from GCC countries, Lebanon, and Jordan offset the decline in international visitation. As predicted in 2003, analysts expect a recovery in terms of international tourist visitation, following improved political stability in the region, and a healthier global economy over the next few years. The development of the 297-room Damascus Four Seasons hotel has now progressed, with the completion of both the excavation and the foundations. The hotel is expected to open in 2004.

The Syrian government is increasingly committing itself to promoting tourism in the country. Joint ventures between Syrian institutions and foreign investors are likely to become a reality in the medium term. The government has started to speed up its response time for tourism project permits and to ease visa regulations. The country has good potential for tourism with excellent antiquities and approximately 120km of unexploited coastline.

United Arab Emirates

Although the oil sector will remain the main source of revenue for the United Arab Emirates (UAE), in the immediate future many emirates are still focused on diversifying the economy and will continue to seek new capital inflows;

Dubai remains at the forefront of most of the new economic initiatives. The government also plans to attract investors in technology, tourism and other service industries.

Plans were recently unveiled to transform Dubai into the financial centre of the region for both banking and capital markets. However, the unstable political environment in the region following the events of September 11 alarmed those interested in investing in the UAE and its neighbours in the short term. The decline in oil prices, combined with the global economic slowdown, resulted in a sluggish GDP growth of 2.9 per cent in 2001, compared to 5 per cent in 2000. The country's economy relies upon international demand for both the oil sector and other service sectors, such as trade and tourism.

In 2001, Dubai's crown prince, Sheikh Mohammed bin Rashed al-Maktoum, announced the development of Palm Island, a major new touristic project which is likely to cost approximately US$3 billion. Dubai has awarded the US$270 million contract to begin work on building the two islands, which are shaped like palm trees, to Van Oord ACZ of the Netherlands and Archirodon Construction of Greece. Investments of this size will ensure that the leisure sector in the UAE continues to grow.

Due to the aggressive marketing efforts made by the government, the UAE showed strong growth in visitor arrivals of 17 per cent in the first three quarters of 2001. This clearly reflects the improved reputation of the country as a leisure destination and a business hub for the Middle East. However, following the events of September 11, the UAE experienced a decline in European tourist visitation of approximately 20 per cent, which was offset by increased intra-Arab tourism during the month of December, the period of Ramadan.

Recent decline in hotel performance is attributable in part to the significant increase in hotel supply, including the opening of the design-led 156-room Hilton Creek, the 174-room Dusit hotel, the 174-room Marriott Executive Apartments, the 159-room Taj Palace hotel and the 232-room Holiday Inn Bur. As Dubai, and especially Jumeirah Beach, are experiencing substantial increases in both supply and demand, some hotel companies plan to expand into areas such as Fujairah, where the market is less mature. There are plans to develop a Rotana hotel and a 300-room Westin.

While the UAE might experience some short-term decline in hotel performance, due to the political instability in the region and additional supply, the medium- to long-term outlook for the country is very good. There have been significant touristic investments historically, which will ensure the continued improvement of the tourism sector.

Focus on Lebanon

Lebanese tourism has evolved over many centuries, with some regarding its origin as when Phoenician ships sailed the uncharted coastal Mediterranean waters. It was these Phoenician traders, an early form of business tourism, who mixed and settled with the locals in the coastal cities, trading, experiencing and exchanging different cultural values and established ways of life.

While the terms 'national culture' and 'nationality' tend (incorrectly) to be used interchangeably, the fact that Lebanon has harboured many civilizations which have succeeded one another, leads many within the country to regard themselves, in addition to being Phoenicians, as Arabs, Mediterranean and, additionally, very Lebanese. Historically, hospitality has always been a unique characteristic of the Lebanese, hence the spectacular growth in tourism during certain periods of the country's development. Having harboured the many civilizations referred to, the Lebanese are not insular, with an open society at ease with other civilizations.

Situated on the Mediterranean coastline, Lebanon is a country 250km in length and 50km wide, with snow-capped mountains including Qornet Es-Sauda and a well-established ski season. Such mountain scenery coupled with the country's rich mixture of history, culture, archaeology, natural beauty and hospitable people, all contributes to the country's ability to attract tourists throughout the year.

Turning to Lebanon's archaeological roots, the French archaeologist Maurice Dunad noted that the oldest traces of civilization at Byblos (Jbeil) go back to the Neolithic and aenolithic era. Many Lebanese historians generally accept that the 'historical' period of Lebanon dates back to the 4th millennium before Christ. This view is supported by discoveries relating to the communities who lived on the eastern coast of the Mediterranean, know as the Cana, and who are believed to be the founders of Phoenicia. In addition to the invention of and alphabet of 22 letters, the Phoenicians established a number of independent kingdoms and trading stations along the Mediterranean coast – oligarchic republics, which extended from Ruad (Arados) in the north to Askalon in the south, including Bothrys (Batroun), Byblos (Jbeil), Berytos (Beirut), Sidon (Saida), Tyre, and Segbaste (Caesarea).

Tourism economics

Tourism is an essential component of the Lebanese economy and has grown in significance since the ending of the country's internal conflicts in 1989.

Taking a historical perspective, Lebanon's economic peak performance period (between the early 1950s and the first few years of the 1970s) saw expansion mainly based in the service sectors of finance, commerce and tourism. During that period these services, represented almost two-thirds of GNP, with tourism alone contributing 14–16 per cent in 1974.

While future tourism activities in Lebanon may vary from these historical trends, analysing past demand, origin and behaviour will provide a better projection for the future direction of the tourism sector in Lebanon. Studies show that before 1974 tourism in Lebanon concentrated on three main categories of visitors: Arab summer visitors; business visitors; and other overseas visitors. Within the Lebanese tourism and hospitality industry, the consensus of opinion is that Arab visitors tend to spend more than other tourists during their stay. The majority of these Arab tourists prefer to visit Lebanon for long periods ranging from five to eight weeks during the summer, seeking cooler temperatures in the mountains' summer resort areas and also the sophisticated beach and night life. Further, they stay longer than any other category of visitor, with most European visitors tending to spend one or two weeks in three- and four-star hotels and visiting historical places. Business travellers reside, on average, one and a half weeks, are engaged in business activities and primarily stay at international five-star hotels. The future for Lebanese tourism will continue to revolve around these three market segments.

According to the official census of Lebanon in 1974, the country's population was approximately 3.5 million. During this period, Lebanon's 'golden age', the country attracted more that half its population in tourists annually with an average of over 2 million tourists visiting the country each year. Tourism increased by 15 per cent from 1972 to 1973 and subsequently by 37 per cent or 700,000 additional tourists, in the following year reaching a total of 2.6 million.

In recent years, positive trends have been detected in the country's economy with inflation not exceeding 5 per cent in 1998 – substantially different to the 130 per cent level of 1992. In September 1997, the lifting of a US ban on nationals travelling to Lebanon has made way for a significant new corporate, leisure and conference market. Tourist arrivals increased by 18 per cent in 1998 to 659,000, with positive signs of further growth in the years to come. This growth will only come from upgrading the Lebanese tourism infrastructure thus attracting more tourists back to the country.

To summarize, the change in European attitudes towards choosing destinations and tourism activities, the expected regional peace in the Middle East and Lebanon's successful tourism history should all help put the country back on the world tourism map.

Hotel industry overview: Lebanon

As the rubble from 15 years of warfare is cleared, the restoration and redevelopment of central Beirut has become the focus of national activity and pride. The intensive rebuilding of the city's once dominant hospitality industry is an important building block in this effort. Prior to the outbreak of war in the mid-1970s, Beirut had the best-developed hotel market in the Middle East. The city's appeal to leisure travellers was supported by the natural beauty of the Mediterranean and the surrounding mountains, a world-class urban environment, its resorts and a multicultural social base. To the Arab world, Beirut represented a window to the West, containing many of the benefits of a European-style environment located in a lush Arab country. To the Westerner, the opposite was the attraction – a truly Arab city, yet one with a comfortable French and European identity. This dichotomy appealed to the business world as well. Before the war, Beirut housed the regional headquarters of virtually every Western company doing business in the Middle East, particularly banks and financial concerns.

The combination of leisure activity and a strong transient commercial environment supported a large hotel market. In 1975, Beirut contained 101 hotels with 6500 rooms, including several world-class properties such as the St George, the Phoenicia and the Al Bustan. By 1983, there were just 54 hotels with 3500 rooms. In the early 1990s, due to the combined effects of war and the consequent out-migration of businesses and people, the inventory stood at 30 hotels with approximately 2500 rooms, with many former properties levelled or severely damaged.

The cessation of hostilities and relative calm that pervades the city has set the stage for an extraordinary level of restoration which continues to this day. Prime Minister Raffiq al Hariri set a number of programmes in motion, not the least of which is Solidere, a private company whose mission is to rebuild the Beirut Central District (BCD). The BCD, which measures 111 acres, was the locale of some of the war's heaviest fighting and destruction. Solidere was initially funded by a US$900 million sale of shares to the public, and is the co-ordinating force behind what is considered the largest urban renewal project in the world. Currently underway is the daunting task of rubble removal, site/infrastructure preparation and landfill. Central to the BCD is a loosely defined hotel district, which contains restorations of the St George, the Holiday Inn, the Phoenicia and the Beirut Hilton, along with one or two newly built properties.

Outside of the BCD, especially to the south, hotel development activity is furious, including the 306-room Meridien on the beachfront, a 400-room hotel/marina proposed for a waterfront site near the American University, and a 174-room Marriott near to the airport. Other important development activity includes the restoration of the Bristol Hotel and additions to the Commodore, the Carlton and the Riviera. The world famous Casino du Liban, located north of the city, has also been the focus of rehabilitation efforts.

What is capturing the attention of Lebanese and international hoteliers is a tourist and visitation market which is under-served by the existing hotel supply, both in size and quality. Due to the war, the level of hotel development activity that has occurred over the past two decades in every major city of the Middle East passed Beirut by. The current market is characterized by high occupancy and opportunistic pricing, against an inventory of hotel stock that is over 20 years old in some locations. Many hoteliers have compared the recent situation in Beirut to the early stages of other post-war (and post-Cold War) hospitality markets such as Warsaw, Moscow, Prague and Ho Chi Minh City.

The Beirut market contains approximately 3500 hotel rooms, a return to the inventory of 1983, but well below that of historical levels. Hope remains high in Lebanon for a return to its former status. Growth in GDP has ranged from 5 per cent to 10 per cent over the past three years, and as the general Middle East peace process continues, and Lebanese repatriation contributes to the country's economic and social stabilization, Beirut has taken on the characteristics of a major regional city.

Due to the general exodus of the 1970s and 1980s, however, the city's international commercial base may never return to the levels reached prior to the war. Nevertheless, the newly awakened hotel industry in Beirut will play a central role in whichever direction the country heads.

The civil war in Lebanon destroyed a growing economy as well as a vibrant capital city in Beirut – once called the 'Paris of the Mediterranean'. Following the cessation of hostilities, a major redevelopment programme was initiated, and the Lebanese economy is largely driven by this programme and the associated infrastructure and development projects now under way.

The exact extent and volume of future hotel investment in Beirut is difficult to predict, as many hotel companies consider a presence in Beirut of strategic importance. International operators are actively seeking renewed representation in the city, spurred on by the potential of the city to recover its position as a leading regional centre.

Beirut's hotel district, which is centred around the Corniche, is expected to slowly shift towards the BCD, where the majority of upscale tourist and commercial developments are taking place. Until hoteliers have established a presence in the country's capital, it is unlikely that additional international-standard developments will occur elsewhere in Lebanon, such as Tripoli or north Lebanon.

Independent forecasts demonstrate confidence in the Lebanese economy, with GDP growth expected to remain at 3 per cent without any negative impact on inflation. The anticipated regional peace process will undoubtedly encourage further inward investment and enhance the attractiveness of the area as a whole to both the international investment community and the tourist market.

Prospects for growth in Lebanon

Beirut is witnessing significant growth in commercial development projects including, most notably, local real estate giant Solidere's redevelopment of the BCD. Major international organizations and companies are returning to the city and this has spurred hotel construction, leading to an increase in available rooms.

Although the redevelopment of Beirut is far from complete, the city has already seen substantial change, and observers believe that Beirut is set to become a leading destination once again. Confidence in Beirut's future is manifest in the improvement in hotel performance. Occupancy levels in Beirut already exceed many other Middle East markets, growing modestly in the period 1998–2001, while average room rates grew in excess of inflation.

Market outlook

The growth in arrivals is impressive, considering that Beirut is still undergoing significant rehabilitation and is not yet near achieving its full commercial and touristic potential. Since the growth in supply is still moderate, hotel performances have not been affected.

Arrivals from Arab countries and Europe are dominant sources of demand. The majority of Europeans originate from France, Germany, UK and Italy, while Jordan and Saudi Arabia are the most important inbound markets from the Arab world. A large number of overseas arrivals are Lebanese expatriates.

Hoteliers in Beirut are already preparing for the flood of new supply. Boutique hotels, such as the Albergo, are catering to upmarket European tourists, while others, such as the Palm Beach and Royal Plaza, are targeting the upmarket Arab segments.

The new supply – just over 6000 rooms – is now in place, and exert a significant amount of pressure on average room occupancies and average rates.

Beirut is already perceived as an expensive destination, and the group market, which is almost non-existent here, may well be the market upon which Beirut's hoteliers rely to fill rooms in the future.

Future trends: tourism 2020

International tourist arrivals grew at an average annual rate of 8.6 per cent between 1990 and 1995, increasing the Middle East's share of world-wide arrivals from 2.0 per cent to 2.4 per cent.

The *Tourism 2020 Vision* study (WTO, 1998) forecasts a continued global rate of growth in international tourist arrivals in the countries of the Middle East at significantly above average, with an average annual rise between 1995 and 2020 of 6.7 per cent. By 2020, the volume of international tourist arrivals in the Middle East will reach almost 69 million, five times the level recorded in 1995.

The intra-regional versus long-haul split of arrivals in 1995 was 42 per cent to 58 per cent. Although intra-regional tourism will continue to record solid rates of expansion (of 6.1 per cent per annum between 1995 and 2020), the growth from all long-haul markets (except Africa) will be higher (at over 7 per cent per annum). As a consequence, the intra-regional versus long-haul ratio of arrivals in the Middle East will change to 37 per cent to 63 per cent by 2020. The Middle East's share of global tourist arrivals will rise from 2.4 per cent in 1995 to 4.4 per cent by 2020.

The growth rate of regional arrivals to the Middle East shows a certain degree of uniformity over the period 1995–2020. International tourist arrivals from both Europe and South Asia will grow at 7.4 per cent per annum over the period, and arrivals from East Asia and the Pacific and the Americas will grow at 7.1 per cent per annum.

Looked at from a different perspective, the 22 countries of the Mediterranean coastline recorded an aggregate volume of 167 million arrivals in 1995, with an average annual growth since 1990 at 2.0 per cent far below the global average of 4.3 per cent. The *Tourism 2020 Vision* (WTO, 1998) study forecasts a continued decline in the Mediterranean countries' share of global tourism, with an average annual rise between 1995 and 2020 of 3.0 per cent. By 2020, the volume of international tourist arrivals in Mediterranean countries will total 346 million, representing a decline in global market share from 30 per cent in 1995 to 22 per cent in 2020.

The strongest rate of growth among Mediterranean countries over the period 1995–2020 is likely to be achieved by those countries in the rapid growth phase of their development (e.g. Egypt), and those seeking to rebuild their tourism sectors from recent disruptions (e.g. the new countries of the former Yugoslavia, Lebanon and, in the mid- to long-term, Libya). The European coastal tourist will increasingly travel to resorts outside the European Mediterranean, with the Mediterranean countries of North Africa and the Middle East benefiting from this trend given their stability. The 'mature' tourism destinations of the European Mediterranean will need to continuously seek product development and market differentiation to avoid the spread of a 'tired' image in generating markets.

For the 22 countries either in or with coastlines bordering the Indian Ocean, the aggregate volume of tourist arrivals recorded in 1995 was 39 million, with an average annual growth of 7.4 per cent having been achieved since 1990. *The Tourism 2020 Vision* (WTO,1998) study forecasts a sustained above-average rate of expansion in tourism to the Indian Ocean countries, with an average annual rise of 6.4 per cent between 1995 and 2020. By 2020, the volume of international tourist arrivals in Indian Ocean countries will total 179 million, representing a growth in global market share from 6.9 per cent in 1995 to 11.5 per cent in 2020.

The world in 2020 will be characterized by the penetration of technology into all aspects of life. It will become possible to live one's life without exposure to other people, with automated service the norm, and full access to, and exchange of, information on everything possible from one's home. In consequence, people will crave human contact; and tourism will be a principal means through which they seek to achieve this.

By 2020, the *Tourism 2020 Vision* study forecasts that there will be close to 1.6 billion international tourist arrivals world-wide. These tourists will spend over US$2 trillion. These figures represent sustained average annual rates of growth of 4.1 per cent and 6.7 per cent respectively – far above the maximum probable expansion of 3 per cent per annum in the world's wealth. Despite these huge figures, it is important to recognize that international tourism still has much potential to exploit. If the international tourist arrivals figures are adjusted to numbers of active international tourists (through the application of factors taking account of tourists visiting more than one country per trip, and multiple trip-taking), the proportion of the world's population engaged in international tourism is calculated at just 3.5 per cent. If a further filter is applied to eliminate those people who, through age, illness/infirmity or lack of financial resources, are unable to undertake international travel, this level of penetration of the 'real' potential population in international tourism in 2020 can be seen to be 7 per cent – indicating an industry truly still in its infancy.

While the *Tourism 2020 Vision* study focuses exclusively on international tourism, domestic tourism remains many times more important both in activity and financial terms. Over the 25 years of the forecast, most industrialized countries will come close to their ceilings for domestic tourism in respect of the proportion of their populations engaging in it and the incidence of their participation. The main growth in domestic tourism will be in the developing countries of Asia, Latin America, the Middle East and Africa where the proportion of the population actively participating in domestic tourism will increase strongly. It seems highly likely that the 10:1 and 3:1 or 4:1 ratios between domestic and international tourism, for activity and spending respectively, will be maintained over the forecast period.

The top ten tourist-receiving countries will see a major change, with China (currently not in the top ten) becoming the leading destination by 2020. Whilst Hong Kong (SAR, Special Administrative Region) is part of China, for statistical purposes it tends to be treated separately, and will also become one of the main destinations by 2020. Also entering the top ten will be the Russian Federation, while the fast-growth Asian destinations of Thailand and Singapore, along with South Africa, will move rapidly up the league table, albeit not reaching the top ten. The corresponding top ten generating countries will also see a major impact from China, expected to enter ranked fourth. The Russian Federation will also become a major outbound tourism country.

References

Knowles, T., Felzenstein, C., Garces, A. (2003) Country Reports, No. 1, Central and South America, Mintel International Group, London.
Travel and Tourism Analyst No 4 (2002), Mintel International Group Ltd, London.
World Tourism Organization (1998) Tourism 2020 Vision, Madrid, WTO.

Key Internet sites

http://www.hotelbenchmark.com
http://www.iata.org
http://www.ilo.org/
http://www. sernatur.cl
http://www.world-tourism.org/
http://www.wttc.org/
http://www.green-travel.com
http://www.worldbank.org
http://www.ecotourism.org
http://www.pata.org
http://www.app.stb.com.sg
http://www.jata-net.or.jp

Index

Lightning Source UK Ltd.
Milton Keynes UK
UKHW03f1146040418
320464UK00005B/274/P